Rediscovering Public Law and Public Administration in Comparative Policy Analysis: a Tribute to Peter Knoepfel

Edited by

Stéphane Nahrath & Frédéric Varone

Rediscovering Public Law and Public Administration in Comparative Policy Analysis: a Tribute to Peter Knoepfel

With the contributions of

Benninghoff Martin, Braun Dietmar, Bressers Hans, Clivaz Christophe, Dente Bruno, Emery Yves, Epiney Astrid, Flückiger Alexandre, Font Nuria, Gerber Jean-David, Giauque David, Hill Michael, Horber-Papazian Katia, Kriesi Hanspeter, Larrue Corinne, Linder Wolf, Leresche Jean-Philippe, Nahrath Stéphane, Nicol Lee Ann, Olgiati Mirta, Ritz Adrian, Savary Jérôme, Subirats Joan, Varone Frédéric, Warin Philippe, Weidner Helmut.

PRESSES POLYTECHNIQUES
ET UNIVERSITAIRES ROMANDES

Haupt

Cet ouvrage est une co-édition des Presses polytechniques
et universitaires romandes (www.ppur.org) et de Haupt Verlag
(www.haupt.ch)

Egalement paru dans la même collection:

Contributions à l'action publique/Beiträge zum öffentlichen Handeln
Ouvrage coordonné par/Herausgeben von
Jean-Loup Chappelet

Les nouveaux défis de l'Etat social/Neue Herausforderungen für den Sozialstaat
Ouvrage coordonné par/Herausgeben von
Bonoli Giuliano, Fabio Bertozzi

Réformes de politiques institutionnelles et action publique/ Reformen institutioneller Politiken und Staatshandeln
Ouvrage coordonné par/Herausgeben von
Peter Knoepfel

Photographies de couverture: pipes du haut: © Sergej Razvodovskij & Gator,
www.fotolia.com

Les Presses polytechniques et universitaires romandes sont une fondation scientifique dont le but est principalement la diffusion des travaux de l'Ecole polytechnique fédérale de Lausanne et d'autres universités francophones.
Le catalogue général peut être obtenu par courrier aux:
Presses polytechniques et universitaires romandes, EPFL-Centre Midi,
CP 119, CH-1015 Lausanne, par E-mail à ppur@epfl.ch, par téléphone
au (0)21 693 41 40 ou encore par fax au (0)21 693 40 27.

www.ppur.org

Première édition

ISBN 978-2-88074-843-2

ISBN 978-3-258-07529-7

Imprimé en Italie

Table of Contents

INTRODUCTION

Peter Knoepfel's Legacy to Policy Analysis

STÉPHANE NAHRATH & FRÉDÉRIC VARONE

This book was conceived in homage to our colleague and friend Peter Knoepfel who celebrates his 60th birthday this year. At this respectable age, it would not be unreasonable for him to be heading towards a state of fulfilled wisdom, serenely distancing himself from (supposedly) new academic debates and the demands of professional life, and making – covertly impatient – plans for a well-earned retirement project.

However, if we take a deliberately selective perspective and consider only Peter Knoepfel's academic career, taking the defence of his doctoral thesis in 1976 as a symbolic point of reference, we are forced to admit that he is, in fact, getting younger. It is the acknowledgment of this dominant aspect of Peter Knoepfel's personality that underpins the initial idea for and the fulfilment of this project.

Nevertheless, it was never our intention to evaluate Peter Knoepfel's research retrospectively or to rationalize it *ex post*. Instead, our aim is to put it into context with a view to identifying the innovative axes of research that Peter Knoepfel, his colleagues and other policy scholars will explore in the years to come.

Thus, the main objective of this introduction is to present five thematic fields that permeate Peter Knoepfel's work and concern: the law as an action resource and corpus of institutional rules; the administration as a central actor of public action; multi-level governance; the issue of sustainable development; and the epistemological and methodological challenges posed by policy analysis.

We would like to begin this introduction with a brief account of the main milestones in Peter Knoepfel's intellectual development, his institutional responsibilities and his political involvement. To do this we adopt a chronological approach that enables us to avoid any cognitive dissonance with the sequential division of the policy cycle which is so dear to him.

Intellectual and academic development

Peter Knoepfel's initial academic education at the University of Berne was in the law, both private and public. He completed his university studies in 1976 with a doctoral thesis on the question of the democratization of land-use planning as implemented under the first Swiss Federal Act on Land-use Planning (Knoepfel, 1977). Ironically, this law never came into force as it was rejected in a referendum a few years after Knoepfel's defence of his thesis, i.e. as a result of a process that corresponds to a form of democratic expression *par excellence*. While, from a normative perspective, the main recommendations of this thesis were rendered null and void even before it was published, from a conceptual and theoretical perspective, this study remained a central and fundamental text for the remainder of Peter Knoepfel's academic career as it already carried the seed of both the famous "basic triangle" of policy actors, the idea of the significance of federal (sectoral) plans and the theory relating to the determining role of property rights in land-use planning processes.[1] This interest in property rights regimes was not purely academic in nature as Peter Knoepfel was also Secretary of the *Société suisse pour un nouveau droit foncier / Schweizerische Gesellschaft für ein neues Bodenrecht* (Swiss Association for New Land Law) from 1972 to 1977, an association that campaigned from a social justice rather than spatial planning perspective for the socialization of property income and greater social equity in relation to access to land and housing.

In addition to this preoccupation with the structuring effects of property rights on social relations and conflicts, which would be reactivated three decades later in the context of research developed with his colleagues in the field of institutional resource regimes (e.g. Nahrath, 2003; Gerber, 2006; Savary, 2008), Peter Knoepfel also assumed a number of trade-union and political roles. Between 1969 and 1970 he was Secretary of *UNES* (Union of Students in Switzerland). This position would prove to be a turning point in his career path, both in political and academic terms. Having been elected as a representative of the liberal group of the student movement, he emerged one year later and - inspired by intensive reading of Karl Marx's "*Kapital*" – was transformed into a militant socialist who did not hold back in his involvement in the anti-consumer, i.e. anti-capitalist, struggle prompted by the movement of May '68. His involvement in the *UNES* was focused on three issues: i.e. the opposition to the new Act on the Swiss Federal Institutes of Technology, the students' demands in relation to the co-management of university institutes

[1] As proof of the permanent place assumed by the issue of property rights in Peter Knoepfel's work, we may mention the fact that while we were compiling this introduction, Peter Knoepfel and Stéphane Nahrath were in the process of writing the final report for a large research study entitled "Land property and sustainable land-use planning. The political and legal strategies of large collective land owners in Switzerland and their effects on the sustainability of land use", which was financed by the Swiss National Science Foundation (SNSF, Division I, grant no 100012-107833), Pro Natura, armasuisse, the Swiss Federal Statistical Office (OFS) and the Federal Office for Spatial Development (ARE).

and the establishment of grant systems that would enable students to be truly financially independent of their parents. A member of the Bernese section of the *Swiss Socialist Party* from 1972, he also became involved as a volunteer in further education for workers (*Arbeiterbildungsausschuss*, i.e. Committee for Workers' Education) and contributed to the establishment of trade-union literature.

In 1976 Peter Knoepfel left Berne with his wife Katrin and their first daughter to take up a postdoctoral position at the *Social Science Research Center Berlin* (WZB). He had been awarded a one-year scholarship by the German Academic Exchange Service (DAAD). His initial scientific objective at this point centred on the study of the implications of policy implementation processes for public law (Knoepfel, 1979). He very quickly realized, however, that the research on policy implementation processes ("*Implementationsforschung*") was only in its early stages and that this project, which was essentially developed by political scientists, was more interesting and showed greater potential than the approach he had initially adopted in terms of public law. Thus, he joined the WZB research group led by Renate Mayntz, Fritz Scharpf and Helmut Wollmann, and it was within this group that he came to participate in the establishment of a new research field: environmental policy analysis. The famous SO_2 project[2] enabled him to develop several conceptual and methodological tools in collaboration with Helmut Weidner (Knoepfel & Weidner, 1980), e.g. the political-administrative programme (PAP) and the political-administrative arrangements (PAA), for the empirical analysis of public policies, which constituted a completely innovative research object at the time. It was also at this point that he discovered American policy analysis as a result of a number of exchanges with American scholars (for example P. Sabatier & H. Jenkins-Smith), and gained his first experience in third-level teaching: he was visiting professor at the University of Kassel and lecturer at the Free University Berlin. It was also in the context of the SO_2 project that Peter Knoepfel became acquainted with Bruno Dente (Milano), Hans Bressers (Twente), Michael Hill (Bristol), Kenneth Hanf (Barcelona), Corinne Larrue (Tours) and Martin Jänicke (Berlin). His collaboration with some of these researchers would result in the establishment of a leading European research network (which was completed by the subsequent arrival on the scene of Joan Subirats (Barcelona)), the longevity of which has been absolutely remarkable; this network remains active today.[3] A number of young researchers would later join this centre of excellence to train and, in turn, embark on prominent academic careers (Nuria Font in Barcelona, Frédéric Varone in Louvain, Emmanuel Reynard in Lausanne, Stefan Kuks in Twente, and Ingrid Kissling-Naef in Zurich). This period of five and a half years at the WZB (he returned to Switzerland in 1982) coincided with three fundamental turning points in the early career of Peter Knoepfel: i.e. the shift from legal analysis to political-

[2] Comparative analysis of the implementation of policies to counteract atmospheric pollution (stationary sources) in five European countries, financed by the Deutsche Forschungsgemeinschaft (DFG) and VW Foundation (total funding: DM 500,000).

[3] The table of contents of this book bears witness to the enduring nature of this European research network.

science analysis, from land-use policies to environmental protection policies, and from national studies to large-scale international comparative studies (clean-air research).

Contacted in 1982 by Raimund Germann, who was in the process of establishing the *Institut de hautes études en administration publique* (IDHEAP; Swiss Graduate School of Public Administration) in Lausanne, Peter Knoepfel decided to return to Switzerland having been won over by the prospective challenge posed by the development of this new institute. Thanks to his successful collaboration with his colleagues Raimund Germann, Wolf Linder, Dieter Freiburghaus and others, he succeeded in establishing the IDHEAP as a centre of Swiss expertise on all questions associated with the administrative sciences and public sector reforms. Peter Knoepfel has trained a significant number of federal and cantonal officials in policy analysis. From a scientific perspective, this period of the foundation of the IDHEAP (1983–1990) coincided with the development of the comparative policy analysis framework and its application to the implementation of the different sectoral (environmental) policies at federal, cantonal and municipal levels. This work was carried out in collaboration with Willi Zimmermann, Daniela Baroni, Rita Imhof, Martin Descloux, Pierre Moor and, again, the members of the *Swiss Commission for Environmental Monitoring*, of which Peter Knoepfel was President. During this period, Peter Knoepfel completed several research projects on the relationships between agriculture and environment (soil and water protection)[4] which gave rise to numerous publications (e.g. Knoepfel & Zimmermann, 1987; Zimmermann & Knoepfel, 1987; Knoepfel, 1990). He also carried out research on clean-air policy (Weidner & Knoepfel, 1984; Knoepfel & Weidner, 1986; Dente et al., 1984; Grant et al., 1999).

The 1990s were a decade characterized by both scientific and institutional consolidation for Peter Knoepfel. During this period he refined his policy analysis approach by conceptualizing, in particular, the action resources at the disposal of policy actors and the influence of institutional rules on the substantive content of non-environmental policies (agriculture, road traffic, military, tourism, land-use planning, energy etc.). He also developed his first studies in the direction of institutional policy analysis, in particular, through

[4] Environment and agriculture: comparative analysis of legislation in the areas of agriculture, the rural environment and food products, IDHEAP research study (1984–87) (with C. Larrue); environnement and agriculture: analysis of the implementation of programmes targeting the protection of soil and water in the area of agricultural practices: policy implementation in the cantons of Berne, Lucerne and Appenzell Rhodes Ext., SNSF research study co-financed by the station fédérale de recherches agronomiques (Federal Agricultural Research Station) in Berne-Liebefeld, the Federal Office for the Environment and the cantons involved (1985-88) (with W. Zimmermann, P. Fässler and M. Descloux; projet carried out in collaboration with the Social Science Research Center Berlin and other institutes in France, Great Britain and the Netherlands); environnement et agriculture: analysis of programming processes at the federal level in Switzerland, SNSF mandate (1984-87) (with W. Zimmermann and D. Freiburghaus).

several research studies on executive federalism.[5] In the specific area of environmental and spatial policies, he supervised the doctoral theses of Serge Terribilini, Sonja Wälti and Christophe Clivaz and provided support as a mentor or co-supervisor to those of Ingrid Kissling-Naef, Alexandre Flückiger, Peter Glauser, Patrizia Baroni and Emmanuel Reynard. He also co-supervised the postdoctoral theses (habilitation) of Corinne Larrue and Helmut Weidner. This was also the period that saw the completion of the first research studies on the environmental public administrative bodies in Switzerland (i.e. the Federal Office for the Environment, the Environmental Office of the canton of St. Gallen). Moreover, in the context of the emerging debate on New Public Management, Peter Knoepfel developed a critical analysis framework that heralded a number of aporia which have since been largely verified. At the institutional level, he made his mark in two ways. First, he assumed the role of *Director of the IDHEAP from 1994 to 2002*. The main outstanding achievements of his period as Director include: the creation of new chairs (public economics, management of network industries), the establishment of a doctorate in public administration (in collaboration with the University of Lausanne), the reorganization of the curriculum and the development of research, etc. Under his directorship, the IDHEAP underwent considerable expansion in budgetary (from CHF 3 million to CHF 7 million), demographical (students and collaborators) and spatial terms (annexe one rue de la Mouline). Second, he was *President of the Swiss Political Science Association from 1997 to 1999* and, in this capacity, carried on the process of internationalization of the association (e.g. 'Drei Länder Treffen' with German and Austrian colleagues) and assumed the enormous task of the publication of the different successive editions of the 'Handbook of Swiss Politics'. In addition, he completed several important commissions on the reform of administrative structures, for example the transformation of the Federal Office for the Environment, Forests and Landscape (carried out with Willi Zimmermann),[6] and on the evaluation of action programmes, e.g. in the areas of energy policy,[7] nature conservation and land-use management (Knoepfel et al., 1996).

In a return to the political intuitions and scientific questions that lay at the heart of his doctoral thesis, Peter Knoepfel has shifted the focus of his research once again over the past decade (late 1990s to the present day). At a time when the majority of policy-makers think that the question has been settled since the fall of the Berlin Wall, he has rediscovered the central role of the institution of (private) property in the design and implementation of

[5] Executive federalism in the context of spatially related policies: factors that stabilize/destabilize the relations between the centre and the periphery, study commissioned by the SNSF and the European Commission (UE DG XII) (with K. Horber-Papazian, M. Benninghoff, S. Terribilini and S. Wälti).

[6] Evaluation of the Federal Office for the Environment, Forests and Landscape, study commissioned by the Management Commission of the Swiss National Council (1990 - 91) (with W. Zimmermann, E. Matafora and G. Sailer).

[7] Case studies on the topic of "energy and environment" commissioned by the Federal Personnel Office, the Federal Office for the Environment, Forests and Landscape and the Federal Office of Energy (1993 - 1995).

sustainable development strategy. In response to this, he developed the Institutional Resource Regime (IRR) framework. The latter would be suitable for application to both *natural* resources (soil, forest, water, air and landscape) (Knoepfel et al., 2001; 2003), thanks to several SNSF[8] and European[9] projects, and to *manmade* resources, thanks to other research projects devoted to topics such as the "national memory",[10] housing stocks,[11] and to complex configurations of resources such as the inter-resource-based regulation of forests and water (Alpeau project),[12] the "rural soil" (SYSTERRA-international project[13]), the climate system,[14] heritage resources (in the course of development by Stéphane Boisseaux). Again, Peter Knoepfel's impressive capacity for updating theoretical approaches in the area of policy analysis motivated several young researchers to complete their doctoral theses under his supervision: Stéphane Nahrath on land-use policy (Nahrath, 2003), Jean-David Gerber on landscape management (Gerber, 2006), Jérôme Savary on the management of traffic areas (Savary, 2008), Lee A. Nicol on the sustainable management of housing stocks (Nicol & Knoepfel, 2008), Mirta Olgiati on the management of resource information, Johann Dupuis on the climate system, Johan Imesch on rural soil and Guillaume de Buren on governance of the ecological services of forests. Other theses dealing with manmade resources, for which Peter Knoepfel is acting as co-supervisor, are also currently under way, i.e. those of Patrick Csikos on the impacts of liberalization policies on the infrastructure of network industries (civil aviation and railways) and Christian Bréthaut on governance of water networks in tourist areas.

The extensive number of researchers and teachers trained by Peter Knoepfel and the professional contacts he has maintained with them throughout their careers testify to his exceptional qualities as a teacher and his concern as a researcher to sustain policy analysis in Switzerland while

---

[8] Institutional regime for the management of natural resources, SNSF research study (September 1999-September 2002) (with I. Kissling-Naef and F. Varone); institutional regimes of the resource landscape, study commissioned by the SNFS (Div. 1 and PNR 48) (February 2002-August 2005) (with R. Rodewald).

[9] International comparison of the institutional regime for the resource "water" (Euwareness project), commissioned by the European Union – Federal Office for Education and Science (December 1999-February 2002) (with C. Mauch and E. Reynard); The Landscape as a Resource: cooperative Franco-Swiss research project, financed by the French Ministère de l'équipement, carried out in collaboration with J.-D. Gerber (December 2006-late 2008).

[10] "La construction d'une politique fédérale institutionnelle de la mémoire" (The developement of an institutional federal memory policy), research financed by the SNSF, Div. I, the Swiss National Library, and the Federal Archives (2003-2009).

[11] "Institutional Regimes for Sustainable Collective Housing Stocks" Research financed by the SNSF, PNR 54, Div.4. with N. Kohler, U. Hassler, C. Ribas, J. Subirats and L. A. Nicol (June 2005–June 2008).

[12] "Projet Alpeau" research financed by the Interreg IV A Program (France and Switzerland) (2007-2013).

[13] "Nouvelle Ruralité/New Rurality" research financed by the French National Research Agency (Agence nationale de la recherche), ANR-08-STRA-09 (2009-2011).

[14] "La gestion durable du système climatique" (Sustainable management of the climate system) research financed by the SNSF, Div. I (100012_124599/1) (2009-2012).

developing it and (re-)integrating it, for example, into concepts borrowed from the law, institutional economics and the administrative sciences. Peter Knoepfel's impressive legacy to policy analysis is obvious to all of those who have collaborated with him. We are all indebted to him for our own academic careers and would like to take this opportunity to express our gratitude to him.

His influence obviously extends beyond the privileged circle which formed, or forms, his research teams and benefited from his astute advice and guidance on a daily basis. We cannot conclude this brief biographical summary without highlighting three additional points. First, Peter Knoepfel is a talented teacher who has spared no effort in his involvement in a significant number of university institutions both in Switzerland (i.e. IDHEAP, University of Lausanne, Swiss Federal Institutes of Technology Lausanne and Zurich) and abroad (University of Kassel, Free University Berlin, Universitat Autonoma Barcelona, IEP Grenoble, Oniati Conference Center etc.). To this is added, of course, the further training courses on which he lavished his time and talents in the generally comfortable surroundings of the Swiss federal and cantonal administrations and the more arduous ones of their counterparts in Ukraine (Kiev) and Kosovo, and soon, perhaps, also in Vietnam. Second, his publishing record is prolific and sustained. He has authored and co-authored almost 60 books along with 200 scientific articles and chapters in books. Apart from this impressive scientific production, which would be enough to satisfy most people, Peter Knoepfel also played a sometimes unrewarding but nonetheless important role as an academic editor keen on promoting the work of his students, doctoral students and colleagues. He manages, for example, the "*Oekologie & Gesellschaft*" ("Ecology & Society") series at Ruegger and successive editions of the 'Handbook of Swiss Politics' (Klöti et al., 2007). Finally, Peter Knoepfel disseminates the results of his research among policy-makers be it through participation in current debates at the national level (for example on New Public Management) or by assuming electoral mandates at the local level (e.g. the Municipal Council of Crissier, in the canton of Vaud, which provides an inexhaustible source of illustration and inspiration for his teaching).

Structure and contents of the book

Given the originality and variety of Peter Knoepfel's work, it would be foolish to aspire to providing an account of it in its entirety and complexity. Thus we will now present the contents of this book on the basis of five areas studied by Peter Knoepfel without, however, making any claim to covering all of his research axes exhaustively.

Law as policy resource and institutional rule

The *first section* of this book concentrates on the *law* as one of the *action resources* that policy actors mobilize to assert their interests and values and as the formal basis of several *institutional rules* that frame their individual behaviours and interactions.

Having freed himself from his initial education as a jurist, Peter Knoepfel does not consider the law from a strictly positivist or essentialist perspective. On the contrary, he re-reads legal norms from the perspective of the concrete use made of them by policy actors (Knoepfel et al., 2001). Thus, he adopts a broad perspective on the law. The corpus he considers incorporates public law (i.e. the Constitution, federal acts and decrees, governmental ordinances etc.), which legitimizes the sectoral interventions of the Welfare State; private law (i.e. the Civil Code), which guarantees the property rights of actors; administrative law, which establishes the procedural rules that frame the internal functioning and decision-making of the public administration (i.e. legality, proportionality, fair and non-discriminatory treatment etc.); and jurisprudence (i.e. the judgments of the cantonal and federal courts), which clarifies the interpretation of general and abstract norms and settles the disputes between norms that operate at different levels.

The strategic use of these different legal resources by policy actors does not lead, however, to endless legal relativism and complete unpredictability in the course of public policies; this would, of course, run counter to the principle of legal security or that of the Rule of law (*Etat de droit*). In fact, the further one advances in the policy cycle (agenda setting, formulation, implementation and evaluation), the clearer the rules of the game become. They have tended to rigidify as the range of legal norms – potentially invoked by the policy actors – has gradually been exploited. The legal rules-in-use gradually restrict, however, the potential scope as the substantive content of the policy concretizes.

According to Peter Knoepfel, the law cannot be considered as fossilized and external to the policy actors either. In effect, the latter activate or, conversely, consciously decide not to activate a given legal rule – just as they modify the legal corpus by clarifying the rules of the game inherent to each policy. To this end they negotiate institutional rules among themselves which are specific to a policy, for example the emblematic right of recourse granted to certain NGOs at the national level in Switzerland in matters concerning environmental policy.

Again, certain actors, including public ones, engage in processes of exchange of the resource "law", which strengthens their position, for other resources (for example, time, money or consensus) that they lack to enable the successful implementation of a public policy. From this point of view, the resource "law" always proves to be relational in nature as legal norms are only of value (in the context of a policy) to the extent that the actors are equally dependent on them. In short, the policy analyst endeavours to understand how the policy actors create scope for manoeuvre and affirm their power thanks to the (non-)mobilization of the law in the course of the policy-making process.

Thus, law emerges as an omnipresent force in public policy but in plural forms that have to be decoded conceptually and empirically. The four first contributions in this book embark on such a (re-)examination of the influence of the law on the conduct of public action from complementary analytical perspectives. In his brilliant essay, *Bruno Dente* reminds us of the fundamental distinction, in the continental European tradition at least, between *jus* (*droit, Recht, diritto, derecho*) and *lex* (*lois, Gesetze, legge, ley*). He then identifies various uses of the law – that encompass both *jus* and *lex* – in policy processes and provides us with several examples of how legal resources can be constructed and used for the purpose of changing policy outcomes. Finally, he explains why the concept of resources, in general, and legal resources, in particular, is so central to a "reformist" policy approach. The attempt to discover a conceptual framework that is not only suitable for exploring the complexities of policy-making in theoretical terms, but can also help the policy actors with the actual decision-making and implementation processes, naturally involves a focus on the role of the law. While it is obvious that the law is crucial for public policies in the real world, it is often far from being sufficient to solve all the problems that arise in the context of policies. Thus, it is the specific mix of macro, meso and micro-considerations – or the specific balance of "high theory" and "usable knowledge" in relation to policy-making – that gives the conceptualization of the law as a policy resource the central role it deserves in policy analysis.

Alexandre Flückiger's chapter analyses the impacts of "*soft law*" on the conception and steering of public policies. He sheds new light on one specific aspect of the policy tools implemented by the State with a view to changing the behaviour of target groups. As a matter of fact, policy instruments that are non-compulsory (from a strict legal point of view) but *de facto* compelling (from a political standpoint) are being introduced increasingly into various policy designs. Such non-binding but highly influential and even coercive tools include, for example, recommendations (e.g. the Bologna declaration on higher education), information and persuasion activities (e.g. organ donation campaigns) or gentlemen's agreements (e.g. bank regulation), and charters and incentives (e.g. prizes and awards in the cultural domain). The author demonstrates convincingly that when implementing such policy instruments the State appeals to a greater or lesser extent to the emotions of the target groups (e.g. fear, shame, joy, disgust, empathy, etc.) and tends to manipulate them in some cases. Of course, the ethical basis of such manipulation techniques is highly debatable *per se*. Furthermore, the increasing use of "soft law" in policy-making is problematic insofar as these policy instruments are not systematically subject to the principles of the Rule of law (e.g. legality, action in the public interest, proportionality, prohibition of arbitrary action, etc.). All in all, the strategic use of persuasive policy instruments by public actors to modify social behaviour should be legitimized democratically, even if their formal nature is non-legal *stricto sensu*.

The following two chapters of the book focus on the impacts of referenda and popular initiatives on public policies in Switzerland. These two *direct-democracy instruments* represent general institutional rules (of the policy game) as they are guaranteed by the Federal Constitution and are at the disposal of all actors involved in any public policy. *Wolf Linder* stresses that, with the notable exception of in-depth case studies (some of which were conducted by Peter Knoepfel and his colleagues, for the most part in the environmental sector), the topic of the impacts of direct democracy on public policy has tended to be a concern of political economy. Thus, his chapter presents an innovative historical perspective by documenting the use of the mandatory and optional referendum as well as the popular initiative in time series from 1875 to 2004. The author analyses the development and levels of success and failure of direct democracy challenges statistically, and their prevalence in the context of all federal policy projects decided on by the Swiss federal chambers. He follows this with a discussion of the permanent extension of the people's right to have their say in important policy issues, and how the risk of defeat in a referendum has prompted the political elites to cooperate with each other and develop power-sharing mechanisms. He concludes that, contrary to expectations, the emergence of the (regulatory) Welfare State after WWII did not result in the increased mobilization of the people against the federal authorities. Furthermore, the people's power of veto has not increased; indeed, Swiss citizens now follow the lead of their elite in various policy sectors more than was previously the case. Finally, Wolf Linder also demonstrates that it is not possible to draw a causal link between the polarization of citizens (according to the classical Swiss divides, i.e. Catholics vs. Protestants, the centre vs. the periphery, urban vs. rural areas and capital vs. labour) and the success or the failure of federal policies.

In his chapter, *Hanspeter Kriesi* analyses in detail, and from both an analytical-empirical and a normative standpoint, the role of the political elite during direct-democratic campaigns on specific policy issues. The starting point of his contribution is the so called "muzzle initiative" which was massively rejected by the Swiss electorate in June 2008. The aim of this initiative was to prevent members of the government and senior officials of the federal administration from intervening in the public debate during political campaigns. It specifically aimed to prohibit them from appearing in the media and participating in public events associated with a popular vote. Based on the referendum against the asylum law (2006), the referendum against the corporate tax law (2008) and the naturalization initiative (2008), the author shows, first, that the heads of the federal departments responsible for these policies (Ch. Blocher, H-R. Merz and E. Widmer-Schlumpf) regularly intervened in the public debate. Furthermore, their interventions benefited from a particular response in the media. He then argues that it is not desirable that the government and its representatives abstain from participating in the process of the formation of public opinion in a direct-democracy campaign. Either the policy proposals to be voted on are sponsored by the government and the parliamentary majority (in the case of a referendum), or the government and the parliamentary majority adopts a clear position with respect to the proposals and may have formulated a counter-proposal (in the case of an initiative). Thus the government will be held accountable by the electorate for the public policies it developed in the legislature at the subsequent elections. From a normative standpoint, it would, therefore, be highly inappropriate if the government did not defend its point of view during the direct-democratic campaigns.

Public administration as policy actor

The *second section* of this book focuses on *the public administration* as a key actor involved in all policy-making processes. From the very outset of his career, Peter Knoepfel devoted sustained attention to the analysis of political-administrative arrangements (PAA) for the implementation of public policies. In particular he developed operational dimensions for the empirical characterization of the configuration of public and private actors interacting within a PAA: i.e. the number and types of actors, the degree of both horizontal coordination (i.e. between ministries and administrative departments) and vertical coordination (between levels of power in a federalist polity), the degree of politicization, degree of openness of the PAA towards social actors (e.g. target groups and end beneficiaries of the public policy) and, last but not least, the homogeneity versus heterogeneity of the context defined by other public policies (Knoepfel et al., 2001). In relation to this last point, Peter Knoepfel has stressed the huge difficulties to be overcome in achieving proactive *intra*-policy coordination (e.g. between various environmental policies) and, furthermore, in enhancing *inter*-policy coordination (e.g. between agricultural policy and environmental policies) (see Knoepfel, 1995a).

Both the *governance* and *New Public Management (NPM)* debates presented new inputs and ideas in response to the classical question as to how best to organize a PAA in respect of policy implementation, monitoring and evaluation. The proponents of the governance approach have argued that enlarged policy networks with a less dominant role in public administration are more effective, while supporters of the NPM approach suggest that the introduction of market-based instruments, such as performance contracts and indicators, will improve the steering and controlling of individual administrative agencies. In a nutshell, both of these academic approaches (and their normative implications for politics and policy-making) fundamentally questioned the role of public administration, the superiority of hierarchy as a coordination mechanism and the basic principles of administrative law. Peter Knoepfel was not indifferent to these arguments. On the contrary, he entered the debate by critically discussing the (presumed) added value of a more polycentric organization of the PAA and of new managerial tools for controlling administrative organizations.

Indeed, in a recent article on the challenges of public administration in the 21st century, which echoes the two aforementioned debates, he presents several theories on the "Rupture of the State" ("*L'éclatement de l'état*", Knoepfel, 2003). In this article, he confirms an exponential increase in the types of organization with a formal public service mission. As a matter of fact, it is possible to observe the emergence of independent (regulatory) agencies, semi-privatized bodies, administrative bodies with performance contracts and global budgets etc. This has led to a veritable "atomization" of the public administration which is relinquishing its unitary structure and its traditional mode of functioning, which is akin to the Weberian ideal-type. More than the diversity of the new organizational forms, it is above all the "autonomization" vis à-vis the political power enjoyed by the recently created entities that Peter Knoepfel rightly highlights. This double movement in the transformation of public administrations (i.e. atomization and autonomization) translates ultimately into an inevitable fragmentation of State action. Each policy tends therefore to develop its own network and frame of reference. According to Peter Knoepfel, the outcome here is "policy egoism", a phenomenon that has the desirable effect of strengthening the force of the resource *consensus* within a policy process but, at the same time, further exacerbates the problems of *intra-policy and inter-policy coordination* which only a strong administration appears capable of promoting precisely, because it is on the interface between several actors.

The four chapters in the second part of the book largely confirm Peter Knoepfel's findings on the basis of very different theoretical frameworks and empirical fields. First, *Helmut Weidner* analyses the overall national capacities for environmental protection and sustainable development on the basis of a cross-national study. He shows that successful policies in these areas depend primarily on a well-resourced and committed public administration. Although the forms of interaction between the main actor groups in these areas have changed over time (usually from hierarchical to cooperative and multi-stakeholder relationships), a strong public agency and the spectre of possible state intervention to ensure sustainable development function as a check to keep policy in line, and constitute a basic precondition for the design and enforcement of policies in the public interest. Briefly stated, "top-down" governance proves to be more important than "governance without government" in areas characterized by conflicting interests on a massive scale. The progress made in the direction of sustainability and the remaining deficits also indicate that the "inter-sectoral integration" of different policies still represents the most challenging issue. The author also notes that environmental and political-administrative reforms are mutually supportive. Democratic structures and institutions constitute a crucial condition for effective environmental policies. Although many countries have been able to achieve environmental gains from new technologies, policies and forms of stakeholder cooperation, even the most advanced need to increase environmental policy and management capacities significantly to meet the continuing challenge of sustainable development. The big challenge for public administrations will be to accept both their own and other capacity increases as a necessary strategic institutional task.

In a similar vein, *Hans Bressers* also concludes that the public administration must take the lead in relation to the multi-actor and multi-level complexities of collaborative governance. The author's empirical study focuses on almost 60 environmental agreements negotiated between the public administration and private industrial firms and on the new paradigm of integrated water management (called "space for rivers") in the Netherlands. He proposes a model for the analysis of the cooperative interaction between policy actors in a networked context. The motives, cognitions and resources of the actors involved are the key factors that explain their relative position and the course and results of the policy-making processes. Thus, Hans Bressers carries out an in-depth analysis of the mutual resource dependencies among actors and how the dependency of some actors on other actors' resources shapes the balance of power. He also stresses that "boundary spanning" (i.e. inter-policy coordination) across various policies implies a very high level of complexity and that the public administration must be able to cope with such complexity. Finally, he identifies various mechanisms of mutual adjustment between actors involved in the inter-policy network. The intensity of network relationships grows as actors together build up a collective resource: i.e. trust.

As *Michael Hill* demonstrates in the following chapter, this resource "confidence" may also be interpreted as a key element that explains the implementation game and the policy outputs. He analyses the complex relationships between political authorities (as principal) and street-level bureaucrats (as agents, SLB) from a resource perspective. Crucial for the key decisions that are taken in the implementation process are institutional arrangements requiring the exercise of discretion, reflecting the power of target groups, the dilemmas of policy agenda setters and programmers, and the professional expertise of SLB. A negotiated implementation process is always a product of the resources possessed by the parties to a policy process. One has thus to focus on the interaction between discretion granted by political authorities and discretion asserted by SLB, making the legitimisation of implementation autonomy a critical issue. Michael Hill concludes that low-trust situations are particularly damaging to the quality of the implementation work done by SLB. If, on the contrary, policy-makers delegate very large discretionary powers to SLB, then new issues related to the accountability of SLB and the legitimacy of the implemented public policy inevitably arise. One particular question, which was also explicitly addressed by Peter Knoepfel (2003), concerns the relative weight of the (primary) legitimacy stemming from the democratic policy formulation and of the (secondary) legitimacy derived from the professional accountability of SLB.

The final chapter of the second section of this book assesses how NPM reforms in Switzerland impact on the management of the public administration in a narrow sense and on substantive public policies in a wider sense. Peter Knoepfel has always been interested in the necessarily complex relations between substantive policies (which attempt to resolve a collective problem), on the one hand, and institutional policies (which aim to alter the internal functioning of the administration), on the other. His productive debates with his late lamented colleague Raimund Germann at the IDHEAP, his warnings on the introduction of NPM in Switzerland (Knoepfel, 1995b; 1996) and, again, the editing of a recent publication on institutional policies (Knoepfel, 2009) bear witness to this. In their article, *Yves Emery, David Giauque and Adrian Ritz* analyse 12 NPM-like reforms in Switzerland from both a policy cycle and a managerial perspective. They conclude, unsurprisingly, that performance indicators are generally neglected at the outcomes level (as predicted by Peter Knoepfel 15 years ago). The definition of policy goals logically related to the collective problem to be solved takes place; however, virtually none of them are then evaluated using corresponding indicators. Thus, within most NPM steering systems, the causal links between the outputs produced by implementing agencies and the policy outcomes achieved are mainly based on plausibility. Such an over-simplification does not capture the inherent complexity of contemporary policy-making, a phenomenon that was also recognized by traditional policy analysts and by the advocates of networked governance.

Federalism and multi-level governance

The *third section* of this book analyses the evolution of the power relationships between various levels of government which jointly participate in decision-making processes and co-produce policy outputs and outcomes. The challenges of such multi-level governance are addressed in two interrelated ways in the next three chapters: first, from the perspective of the Europeanization of Swiss law and policies and second, from that of the transformation of domestic federalist arrangements.

Peter Knoepfel was himself aware of the challenges posed by vertical coordination within PAAs. In his textbook on policy analysis, he argues that a PAA must be analysed on the basis of the degree of co-operation between the political-administrative levels; for example, the European, federal, cantonal/regional and local authority levels. Federalism in Switzerland has three main characteristics: i.e. the co-existence of three formally different levels, with the lower levels enjoying a significant degree of autonomy in accordance with the principle of subsidiarity; executive federalism as the dominant mode of implementation of federal policies by the cantons and local authorities; and the frequent quest for consensus between the different levels. In short, although considerable differences may be observed between different policies, the Swiss system may nevertheless be described as one of "co-operative federalism". Thus, when analysing a PAA, it is a question of identifying the degree of effective co-ordination between the authorities and services on the various levels of the state system. A PAA will be qualified as intertwined or overlapping if the central state and regional bodies share not only legislative and regulatory, but also implementation competencies. Conversely, a PAA is defined as compartmentalized if the infra-national public bodies have extensive autonomy during policy programming and/or implementation. In the latter case, the regional and local actors may adapt the policy to their own requirements without any need for concern in relation to preliminary or concomitant decisions by actors at higher levels. Research carried out by Peter Knoepfel and his colleagues on policy implementation in Switzerland demonstrates the capacity of certain local actors to appropriate federal policies or use them for ends entirely different to those initially targeted by the national legislator (Knoepfel et al., 2001).

To demonstrate the influence of European policies on domestic policies, Peter Knoepfel has conducted several comparative research projects assessing the impacts of EU directives on the formulation, implementation and effects of national environmental policies. Three representative examples may be mentioned here. First, the *Euwarness* project (coordinated by Hans Bressers) analysed how the EU Water Framework Directive has been translated into national laws and implemented in six countries (Belgium, France, Italy, the Netherlands, Spain and Switzerland) which have different property rights systems. Second, the *subsidiarity* project (coordinated by Corinne Larrue) studied the institutional conditions in four countries (France, Italy Spain and

Switzerland) that allow the effective protection of natural areas, regardless of the national or regional economic issues at stake in these areas. Generally speaking, this research invalidates the "subsidiarity = decentralization = better protection of the environment" equation. The success of the decision-making processes relies far more on the ability of the actors who promote environmental protection to mobilize several levels of government at the same time, on the presence of an intermediary actor capable of fostering the collaboration of local and national levels, and on a balanced distribution of action resources between actors. In conclusion the authors state that in order to succeed in nature conservation policy, it is important to establish a winning coalition that brings together not only local political and social actors, but also the national ministry or independent agencies in charge of environmental protection, and, if possible, international actors working in the field of nature conservation (Larrue & Knoepfel, 1998). Finally, Peter Knoepfel and Katharina Holzinger addressed the question of whether the flexibility of the *Europeam Union*'s environmental policy as part of eastern enlargement is desirable or even unavoidable (Holzinger & Knoepfel, 2000).

The first chapter of this section of the book analyses the impacts of EU legislation on Swiss policies. In a referendum on 6 December 1992, more commonly known as "Black Sunday", the citizens of Switzerland contradicted their government's position and rejected the proposal to join the European Economic Area (EEA) based on the classical four "EC freedoms" (goods, capital, services and people). As a result, Switzerland has found itself at a disadvantage in terms of access to the European internal market as compared to its European Free Trade Association (EFTA) partners. Since taking up membership of either the EEA or the European Union (EU) has proven unviable due to domestic opposition, from early 1993 the government pursued a strategy consisting of the completion of bilateral agreements (so-called "direct Europeanization") with the aim of countering the country's economic isolation. This strategy has been simultaneously complemented by several cases of "autonomous adaptation" of the Swiss legal order and policies to European standards (so-called "indirect Europeanization"). *Astrid Epiney* analyses the various forms of Europeanization of Swiss law from a legal viewpoint and with a special emphasis on environmental policy issues. She concludes her chapter by questioning the relative advantages of the bilateral path in comparison with full accession to the EU. It would appear quite obvious that the broader the scope of current and future bilateral agreements, the more difficult it will be for Switzerland to find a consensus with an enlarged European Union.

The next chapter also focuses on the Europeanization of Swiss politics and policy. *Martin Benninghoff and Jean-Philippe Leresche* present the consequences of the decision taken by the European ministers of education in Bologna in 1999 for the configuration of actors involved in Swiss higher education policy. Their case study documents the way a political institution (i.e. federalism) is restructured through a specific policy-making process (i.e. the Bologna Declaration). The authors argue that this international agreement, which is based on non-binding "soft law", led to major changes in the Swiss governance structure and power relationships between policy actors. More specifically, it modifies the modes of coordination between the federal authorities, the cantonal governments and the higher education institutions. As a matter of fact, in this instance the Confederation entered into an international undertaking in an area of competence that was historically the domain of the cantons. This has led to an increasing centralization of the Confederation and, at the same time, to better inter-cantonal coordination and greater cooperation between the universities. This reform was possible because the Bologna negotiations constituted an international arena where actors, mainly representing the federal government, were able to circumvent domestic coalitions (e.g. no discussion about the signing of the Bologna Declaration within the Swiss Parliament). Furthermore, these actors were also able to use the decisions issuing from an international arena as a resource for the introduction of new rules in their own domestic system which benefits from both European legitimacy and the possibility of shifting the blame for the reform to the Brussels bureaucracy. This kind of "policy rescaling" process is, of course, also observable in other internationalized policy sectors.

The redistribution of policy competences and resources across various levels of power is also at work within federalist political systems. Thus, *Dietmar Braun* proposes a theoretical analysis of such phenomena by looking at the evolution of the three centralized federations of Austria, Germany and Australia, with Switzerland as a contrasting case of decentralized federation. He argues that centralized federations face two major problems in policy-making processes: the overawing of the central state, on the one hand, and free-riding by decentralized entities, on the other. This situation could lead to a "predatory federalism" that induces a gradual monopolization of policy-making prerogatives by the central state and, as a result, a downgrading of decentralized bodies to mere implementing agents. The author concludes that, under specific institutional conditions related to co-decision-making rules (i.e. absence of formal veto powers of the second Chamber), the combination of functional federalism (i.e. division of policy formulation and implementation tasks between different levels of power) and territorial federalism (i.e. decentralized entities not based on cultural divisions) is conducive to predatory tendencies on the part of the central state.

Sustainable resources management

The *fourth section* of the book bears witness to a significant moment in Peter Knoepfel's intellectual and scientific – and to a certain extent also political – trajectory as an analyst of public policy in general and environmental policy in particular. What is involved here is the "resource-related turning point" which he initiated in the late 1990s; this would lead, in turn, to the development of the *institutional resource regime (IRR)* framework (Knoepfel et al., 2001b; 2003; Knoepfel et al., 2007; Gerber et al., 2009), which is viewed as a combination of property rights theory, institutional economics and policy analysis. This resource-related turning point has its origins in a critical analysis of both the theoretical and empirical limits of the action models of contemporary environmental policies against the background of the increase in the heuristic power of sustainable development. Peter Knoepfel very quickly adopted the conviction that the debate surrounding sustainability is concerned primarily with the question of the management of systems of resources of all kinds, i.e. not only biophysical resources (i.e. water, air, soil, forest, biomass etc.), but also cultural or "immaterial" (landscape, information) and manmade (housing stocks, network infrastructures, roads, etc.) resources. In effect, as Peter Knoepfel sees it, only the sustainable management of (global) systems of resources is likely to guarantee a sustainable supply of common-pool goods and services, the *sine qua non* for development that is both economically viable and socially equitable.

This resource-related turning point also corresponded to the – both theoretical and empirical (and one could also say political) – rediscovery by Peter Knoepfel of the potential offered by binding tools with a redistributive aim such as (global and individual) quotas and other binding mechanisms, which alone are capable of balancing and quantifying, i.e. also *limiting* and *redistributing*, the property and use rights of different user groups based on the quantities of units of the resources effectively available within, or reproducible by, a given resource system (see, for example, Knoepfel, 2002). Thus, Peter Knoepfel was one of the first policy analysts to propose the *inversion* of the dominant action logic of spatial and environmental policies. He suggests substituting the approach based on establishing how to enable the continuation of consumption at the same levels (economic and social "sustainability") while reducing (proportionally or absolutely) pollutant emissions and/or the other effects on the environment ,with a new approach that is more restrictive and probably the only approach that is actually compatible with the requirements of sustainable development in the broader and complete sense of the term. This new approach is based on an alternative action logic that consists in proportioning or making the different use rights to be authorized or attributed dependent on the number of resource units effectively available in the long term (be it in the form of stock or products). As a political scientist, Peter Knoepfel is obviously well-placed to quantify the problem posed by the political conditions associated with the emergence of such an inversion of the dominant logic of the organization and management of relations between human societies and their environment and the scale of the resulting social, economic and political implications.

For Peter Knoepfel there is little doubt that a change in the course of the development trajectories of our societies towards greater sustainability will not, ultimately, be able to avoid the return of certain quota-based logics and the use of quota-like instruments inspired by the "war economy". This is probably why this resource-based turning point also corresponds to a return to – and, at the same time, strengthening of – his political convictions, which were established during his studies (late 1960s and early 1970s) and the period in which he wrote his doctoral thesis and had remained fundamentally socialist and in certain respects (neo-)Marxist. It is as though Peter Knoepfel's work of the past ten years largely consists of a return to the old questions and old intellectual positions (for example the "old debates" on landed property), the importance and significance of which he and we have been rediscovering.

In their contribution to the book, *Nuria Font and Joan Subirats* testify to this resource-related turning point in the work of Peter Knoepfel and demonstrate it on the basis of the findings of two research projects in which he was involved in recent years: i.e. "European Water Regimes and the Notion of a Sustainable Status (Euwarness)" and "Institutional Regimes for Sustainable Collective Housing Stocks". The authors show, in particular, the relevance of the application of the IRR framework and highlight the analytical added-value it provides in terms of understanding the main challenges and institutional conditions involved in the sustainable management of resources as varied and different as, in the cases in question, water and housing stocks. In doing this they demonstrate clearly, as does Gerber et al.'s contribution (see below), the applicability of the IRR framework to both natural and manmade resources. On this occasion, the two authors insist not only on the innovative character of this analytical framework but also on the strong explanatory potential of the comparative process involving different types of resources initiated by Peter Knoepfel: "In his approach, Peter Knoepfel tries to go beyond the specificity of sectoral policies and analytically compares, for example, natural habitats, clean air, housing or the cultural heritage. This comparison, which is bold from an analytical standpoint, unquestionably harbours great potential. What are the common patterns in institutional regimes for natural and manmade resources? What, for example, do water resources or the housing stock have to do with each other? In both cases, they are unique resources that generate different goods and services and are used by multiple users. (...) The presence of multiple users vying for a single resource and threatening its reproductive capacity and economic, environmental and social cohesion is the cornerstone of Peter Knoepfel's analytical framework. Identifying common patterns of functioning in the institutional regimes of natural and artificial resources might be a risky analytical challenge, but is also undoubtedly a promising one. The analytical framework of institutional regimes has been applied in numerous studies on the water regime, forest, air, landscape and housing stocks in several European countries. These studies have contributed to a clearer picture of under what conditions institutional regimes are shifted towards more integrative and sustainable management models". In this regard, the authors clearly demonstrate the full importance of achieving a real coordination of the different policies that directly or indirectly affect the management of a particular resource through their role in the attribution of rights of access and use to the different goods and services provided by the resource in question: "If housing stocks are to be an element of a sustainable built environment, they must not only develop sustainably themselves, but their goods and services must be able to be used sustainably by other stakeholders within the system. This means that other stakeholders, practices and policies that are often not considered part of this policy should be included in the scenario of housing policy". Furthermore the authors suggest the extent to which the IRR approach also involves a rupture with the dominant sectoral logic in policy analysis. Finally, their summary of the case studies carried out on the management of two different housing stocks in the suburbs of Barcelona presents an interesting contribution to the discussion of the relationships between formal and informal regulations in that it demonstrates clearly how informal arrangements between the owners and end users of the resource that develop contrary to the formal rules of the IRR framework will hamper its effective implementation and this, in turn, will contribute to the weakening of the capacity of the IRR to guarantee the sustainable development of the stocks of the resource in question.

In their contribution, *Jean-David Gerber, Lee A. Nicol, Mirta Olgiati and Jerôme Savary*, all current or former PhD students of Peter Knoepfel, focus their attention on the contribution of the application of the IRR framework to the analysis of manmade resources such as housing stocks, landscape, public roads and information. Through the systematic application of the analytical dimensions of the resource concept (i.e. stock, yield, reproducibility, scarcity, rivalry, use conflict and use regulation), they derive several important lessons for anyone who wishes to consider the concept of resources from a comparative perspective. Their contribution also highlights the importance of the not only strictly material but also social and legal structure of all manmade resources. Thus, they show that these resources are constructed not only in the strict sense of the term by "material producers" but also through an intensive process of formalization of the property and use rights that play a far from negligible role in the very definition of the resource. The resources "information" and "landscape" are particularly illustrative in this regard. According to the authors, another distinctive characteristic of the majority of manmade resources is the fact that they are resources that could be described as "composite", a fact that has implications for both the conditions of their reproducibility and the regulation of their uses: "In three of the four examples presented (with the exception of roads), we observe that artificial resources are the result of a superposition of fundamental and secondary resources. This signifies that an important part of their regulation is made in an indirect manner. This characteristic is a distinctive one of artificial resources in contrast to natural resources, explaining therefore their higher degree of complexity". However, what the analyses developed by the authors in their respective thesis also shows, confirming one of the intuitions to which Peter Knoepfel holds the key, is that not only are the uses of these resources increasing in number and intensity on a far greater scale than is generally imagined but, also, that the uses that may be defined as "secondary" or "peripheral", for example the non-residential uses of housing stocks, often occupy the central place in the structure of the use rivalries and need to be taken in hand within the institutional regime with a view to managing the resource in question sustainably.

Overall, the two chapters by *Font and Subirats* and *Gerber et al.* demonstrate exemplarily that the regulation capacity of an IRR depends not only on the extensive and coherent regulation of the main direct uses of the resource but also, and in some cases essentially, on making these rules governing the direct or "central" uses consistent with the regulations for indirect or (apparently) "secondary" uses. The main message here is that only the coordinated regulation of *all* of the different stakeholders (owners, appropriators, end users), including the most indirect and apparently "peripheral" of these, will enable the establishment of a regulatory regime that will result in the sustainable management of the resource system. One of the main findings of these studies consists, therefore, in showing by analogy with the network analyses demonstrating the "strength of weak ties" (Granovetter, 1983), that a veritable "weight of indirect and peripheral uses" exists within IRRs.

In his chapter, *Christophe Clivaz* tackles a different aspect of Peter Knoepfel's contribution to the debates surrounding sustainable development which concerns the challenges associated with the establishment of systems of sustainability indicators (SSI) at the different institutional levels, i.e. varying from international and national to local. Based on the example of Switzerland, the author attempts to answer the following two questions which had previously been investigated by Peter Knoepfel (see, for example, Knoepfel, 2005): (1) How do the SSIs influence the power relations between actors?; (2) Why and how does such a system become a policy tool that is normative in scope? Based on various empirical surveys carried out in the context of research projects analysing different processes for the development and implementation of SSIs at federal, cantonal and, above all, local level, the author confirms the main reflections, hypotheses and theories defended by Peter Knoepfel on this matter with the help of empirical evidence. He stresses that the establishment of such SSIs contributes to the reinforcement of the power position of the administrative bodies responsible for issues relating to sustainable development (generally new units with a transversal vocation created *ex nihilo* with the sectoral administration) as a result of the concentration of information flows, from which they benefit as the managers of these SSIs. The author also shows how the development and implementation of SSIs goes back to an entire series of rivalries between institutional levels (Confederation versus cities), between public administrations, experts and civil society actors or, again, between general experts and specialists. However, he also notes that the establishment of SSIs, at the local level in particular, sometimes presents an opportunity for extending the circle of actors involved in problem-definition and decision-making processes. Far from being purely technical tools, SSIs constitute fundamentally political phenomena in reality, particularly in view of their multidimensionality; in addition to their normative potential, SSIs contribute to the (re-)definition of policy problems and objectives, they are clearly also a policy tool and they are also mobilized as an evaluative element.

Epistemology and methodology of comparative policy analysis

The *fifth and final part* of this book tackles the question of Peter Knoepfel's epistemological and methodological position, in particular from the perspective of comparative policy analysis. This question is not easy to document and discuss in that, in effect, very few explicit indications in this regard can be found in his writings. Peter Knoepfel appears to take a certain pleasure in practising epistemological and methodological deflation. This is not to say, however, that these preoccupations are entirely absent from his work; on the contrary. In effect, all those who have had the good fortune to work with him have been able to discover gradually the existence of an entire series of – for the most part implicit – epistemological and methodological principles that structure and organize his position and style of work in an enduring fashion. Peter Knoepfel is, without doubt, a fervent empiricist who is not fascinated by "big theories". However, behind this apparent lack of interest in the major theoretical debates taking place in the international journals (in which he, nonetheless, published widely in the 1980s) lie two certainties which, paradoxically, are not devoid of theoretical ambition: first, the conviction that the systematic and open-minded observation of empirical reality often teaches us far more than the majority of the great theoretical debates and, second, that the development of a "conceptual imagination" based on these in-depth empirical observations – we are very close to "grounded theory" here – are more powerful vectors of the production of new and original knowledge of the social world than the infinite duplication of research protocols aimed at systematically testing the same hypotheses from the "classical" worlds of the established theoretical literature. As we can see, Peter Knoepfel is not a *lector* but a creator and conceptual inventor, close to the figure of the *auctor* in the sense employed by Pierre Bourdieu. It is the combination of this extremely fertile "political-scientific imagination" and his extensive academic experience based on the highly robust theoretical foundations laid with Renate Mayntz and Fritz Scharpf at the Social Science Research Center in Berlin in the 1970s and 1980s that forged this "seeker's instinct", and has enabled him not only to take his place among the most productive researchers working in Swiss political science but also to remain at the forefront of innovation in the field. The two contributions in this final section of the book each testify in their own way to this particular and original position.

The aim of *Corinne Larrue and Katia Horber-Papazian's* contribution is to clarify the importance and distinctive nature of the comparative process in the work of Peter Knoepfel. To do this, they examine the role of this methodological approach in three of the four stages of the policy cycle as conceptualized by Peter Knoepfel: i.e. policy programming, policy implementation and policy evaluation. It emerges from this examination that "The prism of implementation orients the comparative analysis of public policy programmes. It is the capacity to frame implementation that is central in the analysis of public policy programmes and therefore implicitly constitutes the comparative structure. The public policy programmes and their production process are not compared in themselves but in relation to what they tell us about the capacity to frame the implementation processes". Thus the two authors also demonstrate that the purpose of comparison in Peter Knoepfel's work is less to produce knowledge about the similarities and differences between sectoral policies and/or countries than to enable the development and strengthening of the robustness of the conceptual framework while recording in the most empirically concrete way possible the dependent and independent variables that are constitutive of his analytical framework. They suggest in this regard that a comparison that is directed at the research of not only similarities but also differences, and even the incommensurable, could also make a beneficial contribution to the development of the analytical framework. It also emerges from this that the preferred scale for comparison is not the nation-state but a more restricted area, i.e. regional or local, within or between different countries which make it possible to demonstrate that the variations in implementation processes may sometimes be more significant between the regions in one and the same country than between regions located in different countries. The authors insist on the need for the establishment of an international network of researchers of maximum stability and endurance to enable the completion of major comparative studies: the composition of the contributors to this book in homage to Peter Knoepfel testifies, in part, to the success of this process. Finally, the authors also present a number of critical reflections on the limits of the comparative process developed by Peter Knoepfel, in particular the contribution of his analytical framework to the evaluation of public policies. In relation to this point they suggest that the process should not be confined solely to the evaluative process at the end of the policy cycle but, instead, that its varying presence should be acknowledged in all stages of the cycle.

In his excellent contribution *Philippe Warin* presents an extremely detailed and relevant analysis of Peter Knoepfel's epistemological position. This analysis is based on an attentive reading of the latter's work and on several years collaboration with him on a joint seminar staged at the Institut d'Etudes Politiques de Grenoble. The author associates this position with a form of *pragmatic constructivism*, characterized by an approach that is both *systemic* (each stage of a public policy refers not only to a specific equilibrium between the actors but, to a certain extent, is the result of the decisions and activities of the preceding stage) and *non positivist* (policies are the result of explicable processes of construction based on a particular number of variables, of which the configurations are contingent) in terms of the analysis of public policies. However, the strength of Philippe Warin's contribution lies in the demonstration of this dual dimension in Peter Knoepfel's epistemological position: i.e. it is at once clearly constructivist – the definition of public problems, the causal stories and intervention models are obviously social constructs – and at the same time pragmatic – material (nature of the problems, resources at the disposal of the actors) and institutional (possessional and procedural institutional rules) conditions exist that structure, demarcate and limit the process of social construction of the constitutive elements of public policies. The author also shows that when Peter Knoepfel works on the definition of these explanatory variables (actors, resources, institutions) of the substantive content of policies, he remains once again pragmatic as it involves an eventual sociological theory of action: "The pragmatism of the approach is measured, therefore, in terms of the deliberately *a minima* treatment reserved for the actors' personal variables (interests, motivations, intentions, beliefs). These exist and influence the actors' behaviours but they are excluded from the analysis because they are not independent of the actors. Pragmatism here resembles a form of *realism*. The analyst retains only those statements which enable him or her to relate any consideration of the actors and their rationale empirically to the reciprocal conditioning between context (set of resources and rules) and action (interactions between decision and activities). In other words, apart from the observation of this mutual conditioning, nothing can be said about the actors' action from the scientific point of view". In the final part of his contribution, Philippe Warin takes advantage of this reflective exercise, with a certain elegance, by putting his own scientific position into perspective, which he proposes labelling as "pragmatic of democracy": "For all of these reasons, the constructivist pragmatism underpinning Peter Knoepfel's approach is clearly distinguished from policy analysis as *'pragmatic of democracy'*, as it appears from the cognitivist perspective (Giraud & Warin, 2008). (...) In other words, these two perspectives do not have the same scientific goal. In the one, policy analysis serves reflection on politics and democracy. In the other, it aims to understand how policies are made – and that is the underlying intention of the approach developed by and around Peter Knoepfel".

Transverse topics

A transverse reading of the different contributions collected as part of this reflection on the work of Peter Knoepfel allows us to draw a number of general conclusions. We have decided to focus our attention here on *four conclusions* which appear to us to maintain a particular link with the main theses and scientific contributions formulated by Peter Knoepfel throughout his career. In keeping with the spirit of this IDHEAP books collection, these reflective conclusions should be conceived as possible research channels for the future rather than purely retrospective assessment.

The Rule of law

The first conclusion that may be drawn from the reading of several of the contributions in this volume concerns *the relationship between the Rule of law* and what legal scholars call *soft law.* While the Rule of law constitutes a legal and political principle and, at the same time, an absolutely central scientific topic in Peter Knoepfel's conceptual system and while also confirming the central role of the principle of the Rule of law, some chapters of this book show, however, that soft law, or arrangements and systems of rules whose success and the force of their effects depend paradoxically on their rather informal nature and the fact that they have little or no legally binding force, play an increasingly important role in national and, above all, international regulations. The example of the very structuring effects of the Bologna Declaration, a corpus of non-legally-binding agreements, on the entire systems of higher education in different European countries constitutes a particularly convincing illustration of this phenomenon as clearly demonstrated by Martin Benninghoff and Jean-Philippe Leresche. Everything appears to unfold, in effect, as though the classical legal mechanisms of the Rule of law (i.e. Max Weber's legal-rational domination type) were not always sufficient to underpin the legitimacy of public regulations. This is the case, in particular, when public policies concern new transnational or supranational issues and areas; the latter often necessitate, in effect, the development of new forms and procedures of legitimation, which, as demonstrated by Alexandre Flückiger, are based on other, in particular, emotional motivations, such as fear, shame, joy, surprise, empathy etc., motivations which enable the explanation of our tendency to obey the rules of soft law. These observations invite us therefore to question as Bruno Dente does the role of law – in the double sense of *lex* and *jus* – in policy making processes, while asking ourselves, for example, about the extent to which the emergence of regulations on the mode of soft law refers – or not – in certain societal sectors to a deeper shift in the direction not only of a *soft lex*, but equally and more fundamentally in the direction of a *soft jus* with all of the implications this can have for the principle of the Rule of law and for the (re-)definition of the resource "law" in Peter Knoepfel's conceptual system. In effect, one of the central questions that arise is whether, and if yes, under what conditions, it is legitimate to derogate to certain principles of the Rule of law so as to increase the effectiveness of public action; whether, therefore, it is sometimes desirable to bank on the secondary legitimation of policies (while testifying to their positive effects) rather than on their primary legitimacy (through the definition and respect of legal rules). This question merits debate to the extent that several empirically observed exchanges of the resource "law" for other resources (money, time and consensus, in particular) and the recourse to soft law, in particular in the course of domestic policy reforms which are initiated by (informal) international norms, are taking place case by case, sector by sector with no theoretical basis or general normative reflection. There can be no doubt that these are questions that Peter Knoepfel's indefatigable "desire for conceptualization" will not fail to explore.

Substantive and institutional dimensions of public policy

A second conclusion that appears to emerge from this transverse reading, which has links to the first, concerns the relationships – also central within Peter Knoepfel's conceptualization – between *the institutional and substantive elements of policies.* Hence, a number of contributions, such as those by Wolf Linder, Helmut Weidner, Astrid Epiney, Martin Benninghoff and Jean-Philippe Leresche and, to a certain extent, those by Hanspeter Kriesi, Dietmar Braun and Yves Emery, David Giauque and Adrian Ritz, show how, irrespective of whether they are rooted in public or private law, constitutional law, federal public or cantonal law, administrative law or private law, the (changes in) institutional rules have significant effects on the substantive content of public policies in the tradition of Peter Knoepfel's work. However, what Astrid Epiney's contribution on the different forms of relationships between European and Swiss law demonstrates equally well is that what is involved here is not only the structuring effects of European law on Swiss law but also, as clearly demonstrated by the structure of bilateral agreements, the role of the more specifically *sectoral* regulations in the actual establishment of these agreements, which remain fundamentally sectoral in their logic. This example enables us to see how Swiss federal policies have a determining effect on EU-Swiss politics. However, it also enables us to observe a counter effect of EU-Swiss politics on the substantive content of policies in the form of an increase in the relations of interdependence between (the contents of) federal sectoral policies, to the extent that the perpetuation of bilateral agreements (and hence the stabilization of the substantive content of certain policies) depends on the modification of the substantive content of other federal policies (cf., for example, the extension of the policy of free movement of persons to Rumania and Bulgaria so as to save all of the other sectoral agreements in Bilateral Package I). Here too, there is no doubt that these new conclusions concerning the relations between the institutional rules and substantive contents of policies combined with the challenges of multi-level governance, will provide material for new conceptual and theoretical reflections that will enable the refinement of the policy analysis framework developed by Peter Knoepfel and his colleagues over a period of 20 years. In conclusion, the fundamental question raised here, which Peter Knoepfel correctly identified (Knoepfel 2009), does not solely concern intra-policy and inter-policy coordination, factors that are complicated in themselves but have already been thoroughly analysed by policy scholars (see, for example, the contributions of Helmut Weidner and Hans Bressers in this book); instead, it concerns much more the complex links between polity, politics and policies. Thus the question arises as to how these institutional reforms will impact on the political game and the (substantive and institutional) content of various public policies. The exploration of this question is a priority even if it means abandoning the famous formula "policy determines politics" proposed by the forerunners of policy analysis, in particular Theodore Lowi.

The power of policy actors

The third conclusion to be drawn consists, in reality, in a question, to which it is not easy to provide a very clear response, as is sometimes suggested between the lines in the contributions of Hans Bressers, Bruno Dente, Michael Hill, Dietmar Braun and Christophe Clivaz: i.e. "*What conception does Peter Knoepfel have of power?*" An inital response consists in noting the predominance of a relational conception of power in his public policy approach. This relational conception is illustrated perfectly by the very figure of the famous "basic actor triangle" and the relationships of interdependence between the political-administrative actors, the target groups and the beneficiary groups (not to speak of the third-party actors), who exchange resources in contexts characterized by both collaboration and confrontation in order to defend their collective or individual interests, values and beliefs. The development of the concept of "policy resources" is totally in keeping, therefore, with this relational interpretation of power. A second response consists in noting the absence of an *a priori* global theoretical conception of power (or, moreover, the conditions of cooperation). In effect, Peter Knoepfel's work does not contain a predetermined conception of the structure of power (or domination) in a given political space but, conversely, the predominance of a pragmatic and empirical conception of power. The latter is based on the analysis of redistribution of conflicts from case to case, whereby the "case" corresponds to the area of the actors who are relevant to given (sectoral) policy. This pragmatic and empirical conception is manifest in the (axiological presumption of the) capacity of actors (target or beneficiary groups, political-administrative actors or third-party groups) to develop strategies – the famous "direct and indirect games" – for all stages in the policy cycle. These strategies enable them to try to (re)position themselves so that they can influence, to a greater or lesser extent, or actually reverse, the hypotheses that underlie the action logic of the policy and, as a result, structure the policy's actor configuration at a given moment in time. This non-deterministic conception of the power relations between the actors is illustrated in one of Peter Knoepfel's favourite messages presented in the context of his teaching and which consists in noting the extent to which the "actors never let go" (throughout a policy cycle). Finally, we may well ask whether one of the keys to understanding Peter Knoepfel's conception of power is not provided by Philippe Warin when he notes the difference that exists between the objectives and explanatory ambitions of Peter Knoepfel's pragmatic constructivism and axiomatic neutrality and other epistemological postures such as, for example the "pragmatic of democracy", in which Warin recognizes his own position and to whose development he recently contributed with our colleague and friend Olivier Giraud (Giraud & Warin, 2008). Philippe Warin is probably also right when he refers this difference back to the academic and institutional conditions of Peter Knoepfel's intellectual development: "In the final analysis, the constructivist pragmatism which I see as characterizing the public policy analysis proposed by Peter Knoepfel can probably be explained by his idea of his profession as a university lecturer, researcher, expert and, at the heart of all that, teacher and adviser. The axiomatic neutrality characterizing his approach corresponds to his main objective of equipping analysts, scientists and practitioners with a framework for understanding situations. His scientific contribution lies in the fact of making possible an ethnography of public policies. By being wary of the analyst who has only 'stories to tell', Peter Knoepfel reminds us in a way of an international figure in anthropology, Claude Levi-Strauss, who started his famous popularized book Tristes tropiques ([1955] 1985) with the following incipit: 'I hate journeys and explorers'. Let us therefore dare to compare pragmatic constructivism at the service of a logical reasoning in policy analysis to Lévi-Strauss's break with the travel novel genre, with the aim of establishing an intellectual experience of another kind, that of structural logic. The more fundamental question raised by this third observation is whether this axiological neutrality in relation to power relations does not ultimately overlook the more structural relations of domination in a way that approaches that of democratic pluralism. And is such a position not in contradiction to Peter Knoepfel's political convictions as a citizen and activist. Finally, is this not also paradoxically in contradiction to certain postulates of the IRR analytical framework which insist specifically on the structural inequalities of power between actors generated by the unequal distribution of property and use rights to natural and/or manmade resources?

Time and history

The fourth and final conclusion which we have chosen to focus on concerns Peter Knoepfel's relationship with *temporality and historicity*. It is important to note that he is one of the few (Swiss) political scientists, along with Wolf Linder of course, who has systematically considered that taking into account of *temporal dynamics* in the long term (i.e. in the political-science sense of the term, i.e. a duration of around a century) constitutes an indispensable position and powerful tool for understanding contemporary policy processes. A particularly successful illustration of this both epistemological and theoretical position can be found in the studies that implement the IRR analytical framework, and which is testified to here by the contributions of Nuria Font and Joan Subirats, on the one hand, and Jean-David Gerber, Lee A. Nicol, Mirta Olgiati and Jérôme Savary, on the other. In these studies, the recourse to long-term historical analysis with the help of the "historical screening" method, for example, is explained by the fact that both the regulated elements (for example, systems of biophysical or manmade resources) and regulatory elements constitutive of these regimes, i.e. primarily the property rights, are tools which are based empirically in a long-term temporality. This recourse to the explanatory use of temporality can also be found, however, in the method for the sequentialization of case studies used as far back as the 1980s and 1990s when Peter Knoepfel was working more specifically on environmental policies and policy comparisons (cf. contribution of Corinne Larrue and Katia Horber-Papazian in this book). In these studies, the comparative strategy was not solely spatial or intersectoral but also temporal (comparison of action logics underlying public policies over time). However, as is the case with the issue of power, the relationship maintained by Peter Knoepfel with the discipline of history, in general, and the question of temporality and historicity, in particular, remains voluntarily characterized by pragmatism. The question concerning the division of cycles or rhythms of temporality is answered on an empirical basis. As opposed to this, in most cases, the criteria used to apportion the sequences or stages within the case studies are defined very clearly and carefully on the basis of the analytical categories employed. In short, Peter Knoepfel essentially considers temporality and diachronous analysis as a methodology rather than an end in themselves. This position is, of course, entirely laudable, particularly in view of the short term view generally adopted in the majority of policy analyses. Nonetheless, in our view, it would gain something if it were accompanied by more extensive reflection on the actual concepts of temporality and historicity themselves. A promising reflective perspective here would consist in a more systematic exploration of the implications for policy analysis of the findings in relation to the existence of variable temporalities both in the different corpuses of institutional rules (property rights enshrined in long-term provisions and policies that change every ten years) and the dynamics of the actor configurations (stable configurations in the long term, varying coalitions in the short term), problems defined in the agenda-setting phase (recurring and long-term problems versus sporadic and short term problems), or, again, action logics developed to resolve them. More concretely, the challenge of such an exploration would consist in reflecting on the theoretical and methodological implications of the integration of variables rooted in different temporal scales into one and the same theoretical framework.

This book would not have been possible without the generous participation of the many authors, whose contributions we have summarized very briefly here and whose outstanding work we invite you to read in full. We would like to thank them most sincerely for their contributions which reflect equally their scientific interest in Peter Knoepfel's work, their former collaboration with him and their friendship with him. In addition we would like to thank Professor Jean-Loup Chappelet, Director of the IDHEAP, for his indispensable support in the publication of this book and, last but not least, Christine Eden of the Institute University Kurt Bösch (IUKB) who was responsible for the layout and processing of the manuscript.

References

Dente, B., Knoepfel, P., Lewanski, R., Mannozzi, S., & Tozzi, S. (1984). *Analisi di una politica regolativa: politica contro l'inquinamento atmosferico.* Roma: Ufficiana.

Gerber, J.-D. (2006). *Structures de gestion des rivalités d'usage du paysage. Une analyse comparée de trois cas alpines.* Zürich, Chur : Rüegger Verlag.

Gerber, J.-D., Knoepfel, P. Nahrath, S., & Varone, F. (2009). Institutional Resource Regimes: Towards sustainability through the combination of property-rights theory and policy analysis, *Ecological Economics*, 68 (3): 798-809.

Giraud, O., & Warin, P. (dir.) (2008). *Politiques publiques et démocratie.* Paris: La Découverte.

Granovetter, M. (1983). The strength of weak ties: a network theory revisited, *Sociological Theory.* volume 1, pp.201-233.

Grant, W., Perl, A., & Knoepfel, P. (éds) (1999). *The Politics of Improving Urban Air Quality.* Cheltenham UK, Northampton USA: Edward Elgar.

Holzinger, K., & Knoepfel, P. (eds) (2000). *Environmental policy in a European Union of variable geometry? The challenges of the next enlargement,* Basel/Genf/München: Helbing & Lichtenhahn.

Klöti, U. Knoepfel, P., Kriesi, H., Linder, W., Papadopoulos, Y., & Sciarini, P. (Eds.) (2007). *Handbook of Swiss Politics,* Zürich: NZZ Verlag.

Knoepfel, P. (1977). *Demokratisierung der Raumplanung: grundsätzliche Aspekte und Modell für die Organisation der kommunalen Nutzungsplanung unter besonderer Berücksichtigung der schweizerischen Verhältnisse,* Berlin: Duncker & Humbolt.

Knoepfel, P. (1979). *Öffentliches Recht und Vollzugsforschung, Beiträge der sog. Implementationsforschung zur staats- und verwaltungsrechtlichen Parlamentsdiskussion.* Berne: Haupt (Reihe Staat und Politik, Band 24).

Knoepfel, P., & Weidner, H. (1980). *Handbuch der SO_2-Luftreinhaltepolitik. Trends, rechtliche Regelungen und Verwaltungssysteme in den EG-Staaten und in der Schweiz.* Band 1: *Problembeschreibung und vergleichende Analyse*; Band 2: *Vergleichende Länderanalysen.* Berlin: Erich Schmidt-Verlag.

Knoepfel, P., & Weidner, H. (1986). *Luftreinhaltung (stationäre Quellen) im internationalen Vergleich.* Berlin: Sigma (6 Bände).

Knoepfel, P., & Zimmermann, W. (1987). *Oekologisierung von Landwirtschaft. Fünf Geschichten und eine Analyse.* Aarau, Frankfurt am Main, Salzburg: Sauerländer.

Knoepfel, P. (Ed.) (1990). *Landwirtschaftliche ökologische Beratung - Ein Modell für die allgemeine Umweltberatung?,* im Auftrag der Schweizerischen Arbeitsgemeinschaft für Umweltforschung (SAGUF). Bâle: Helbing & Lichtenhahn (série Ecologie & Société, vol. 4).

Knoepfel, P. (1995a). New institutional arrangements for a new generation of environmental policy instruments: intra- and interpolicy coordination. In B. Dente (Ed). *Environmental policy in search of new instruments.* Kluwer: Dordrecht, Boston, London, pp.197-233.

Knoepfel, P. (1995b). Le New Public Management: est-ce la panacée? *Swiss Political Science Review,* 1 (1):133-148.

Knoepfel, P. (1996). Plädoyer für ein tatsächlich wirkungsorientiertes Public Management, *Swiss Political Science Review,* 2 (1):151-164.

Knoepfel, P., Achermann D. & Zimmermann Willy (1996). *Neue Instrumente einer nachhaltigen Bodenpolitik. Bilanzstudie Bodenpolitik 1990-1995.* Cahiers de l'IDHEAP, n°162, Chavannes-près-Renens, Novembre 1996.

Knoepfel, P., Kissling-Näf, I., & Varone, F. (Eds.) (2001). En collaboration avec K. Bisang, C. Mauch, S. Nahrath, E. Reynard, & A. Thorens. *Institutionelle Regime für natürliche Ressourcen : Boden, Wasser und Wald im Vergleich / Régimes institutionnels de ressources naturelles: analyse comparée du sol, de l'eau et de la forêt.* Basel, Genf, München: Helbing & Lichtenhahn.

Knoepfel, P., Larrue, C., & Varone, F. (2001). *Analyse et pilotage des politiques publiques.* Bâle: Helbing & Lichtenhahn (série Analyse des politiques publiques / Politikanalyse no 2).

Knoepfel, P. (Ed.) (2002). *Begrenzen um mehr zu erreichen. Kontingente als Instrumente der Umwelt- und Raumordnungspolitik / Limiter mieux pour obtenir plus. Les contingentements - instruments de la politique de l'environnement et de l'organisation du territoire.* Bern: EPA/OFPER.

Knoepfel, P., Kissling-Näf, I., & Varone, F. (Eds) (2003). *Institutionelle Regime natürlicher Ressourcen in Aktion / Régimes institutionnels de ressources naturelles en action.* Genève/Bâle/Munich : Helbing & Lichtenhahn

Knoepfel, P. (2003). L'éclatement de l'état: Acht Thesen zur Abdankung der einheitlichen, allgemeinen Staatsverwaltung, in: Schweizer, Rainer J und Claude Jeanrennaud, Stephan Kux, Beat Sitter-Liver (Hrsg). *Verwaltung im 21. Jahrhundert. Herausforderungen, Probleme, Lösungswege.* Freiburg: Universitätsverlag Freiburg.

Knoepfel, P. (2005). "Quand les indicateurs deviennent la norme – trois variations sur un thème avec finale sine brio" in Bovay Benoît, Nguyen Minh Son (éd.), *Mélanges Pierre Moor,* Berne: Staempfli, pp. 115-128.

Knoepfel, P. (Ed.) (2009). *Réformes de politiques institutionnelles de gestion des ressources de l'action publique - Reformen institutioneller Politiken zur Ressourcensteuerung öffentlichen Handels,* Contributions à l'action publique 3, Lausanne, PPUR/Haupt. A Paraître.

Knoepfel, P., Nahrath, S., & Varone, F. (2007). Institutional Regimes for Natural Resources: An Innovative Theoretical Framework for Sustainability. In P. Knoepfel (Ed), *Environmental Policy Analyses. Learning form the Past for the Future.* Berlin: Springer, pp. 455-506.

Larrue, C., & Knoepfel, P. (1998). *Environmental protection, principle of subsidiarity and spatial-related policies* . Tours: Cahier n° ENVA-CT96-0238.

Lévy Strauss C. ([1955] 1985). *Tristes Tropiques.* Paris: Plon ,Terres humaines.

Nahrath, S. (2003). *La mise en place du régime institutionnel de l'aménagement du territoire en Suisse entre 1960 et 1990.* Lausanne, IDHEAP-Université de Lausanne, Thèse de doctorat.

Nicol L. A., & Knoepfel, P. (2008). Institutional Regimes for Sustainable Collective Housing Stocks. *Swiss Political Science Review,* 14 (1):157-180

Savary, J. (2008). *Politiques publiques et Mobilité urbaine. Analyse de processus conflictuels dans quatre villes suisses.* Zürich: Ruegger Verlag.

Weidner, H., & Knoepfel, P. (Eds) (1984). *Luftreinhaltepolitik in städtischen Ballungsräumen, ein internationaler Vergleich.* Frankfurt a.M., New York: Campus.

Zimmermann, W., & Knoepfel, P. (1987). *Landwirtschaft und Umwelt im politischen Alltag. Drei Fälle für die Schule.* Im Auftrag des Bundesamtes für Forstwesen, des Bundesamtes für Umweltschutz, des Bundesamtes für Raumplanung und des Bundesamtes für Landwirtschaft. Berne: EDMZ; Bundesamt für Umweltschutz.

Part I

Law as Policy Resource and Institutional Rule

CHAPTER 1

The Law as a Policy Resource: Some Scattered Thoughts

BRUNO DENTE

The point of departure

In this short contribution I will try to show the importance, both in Peter Knoepfel's thinking, and in the theory of public policy analysis of the use of the law as a policy resource. In doing so, I will also try to clarify some of my own assumptions and hypotheses on this subject. In fact I share with Peter not only the same intellectual background – I too have a legal training – but I actually "discovered" public policy as a field of scientific inquiry when I met Peter for the first time, at the Grenoble ECPR workshop on Implementation chaired by Renate Mayntz in 1978.

This common history, reinforced by collaboration in at least 6 or 7 different research exercises, mostly, but not solely, in the field of environmental policy, allows me, I hope, a certain amount of freedom in interpreting Peter Knoepfel's work, possibly forcing some concepts in order to achieve a better understanding of the difficult relationship between the law (and more in general the institutions) and policy. I will try to link my understanding of the originality of Peter Knoepfel's approach to some different elements of his scientific programme, and namely the fact of being rooted into the European continental tradition of civil law, the central role that empirical research has represented in the large amount of work done by him in the last 30 years, and finally the "reformist" approach that has been the actual *fil rouge* of his scientific career.

Necessarily, therefore, this contribution will be more a "think piece" than a "proper" scientific paper. It is tentative, it is rough and it is certainly not well balanced. I am probably too old to be still able to write an article *comme il faut* (actually, I was never very good at it) but I hope that this contribution will be of some use to Peter's many friends and students (and to Peter himself, of course) in order to stimulate them to think more deeply of the theoretical underpinnings and implications of his approach. The lack of the usual academic niceties (for instance a proper bibliography) symbolizes the unorthodox nature of this short paper.

The point of departure of the analysis is quite simple. Peter Knoepfel's successful textbook (Knoepfel et al. 2001) is, to my knowledge the only one introduction to public policy analysis devoting a substantial amount of space to the discussion of the many different resources that are used in the policy process. And it is the only one, again, to my knowledge, which presents the law as a policy resource.

This lack of interest of mainstream policy scholars towards the concept of resource is rather surprising. After all it is common experience that in any given policy game there are actors that are more able to influence other actors' behaviours – they are more "powerful" – and that this differential is explained by the fact that they are able to use some "goods" that have a certain value for the other participants (my own definition of resource). This of course depends on the fact that the definition of power we share is relational: the actor A has power on the actor B if he is able to influence his behaviour, i.e. if we are able to explain the behaviour of B only if we know the behaviour of A. And in order to alter the "natural" behaviour of an actor the use of some resource that is valued by the latter is needed: it is rather unlikely, for instance, for a small group of people and scattered in different constituencies to influence the behaviour of a politician by the promise of electoral consensus, but of course this changes immediately if the said group has access to the media and is able to guarantee some sort of public recognition. All this is standard political analysis and it is well known. It is therefore difficult to understand the reasons for this lack of interest. May be there is the fear of being pigeonholed in the "naïve pluralism" category, even if, at least since the Lindblom of *Politics and Markets*, it is very clear that the fact that policy games are ultimately decided by the interplay of resources does not mean that all the actors are necessarily at the same level, some of them having structural advantages.

I suspect that the scarce interest of mainstream policy analysts toward the concept of resource derives from the fact that they are simply not very interested in actually solving "real world" policy problems, but more in defining "models" and "middle range theories" able to classify some specific recurring configurations and therefore present some simplified version of the policy process with an eye to the generalisation more than to the actual understanding of what happens in the field. But I will come back to this point at the end of my contribution when I will speak of the levels of analysis.

For the time being the fact that there is no real interest in the concept of resource means that the law, and more in general the norms, are treated by many policy analysts as something that is at least partly outside the reach of the actors. In other words according to the dominant schools of thought, the law defines the roles of the actors, constrains their behaviour, limits their possibility to enter the decisional arena, and so on. Sociologists like March and Olsen or Powell and Di Maggio, but also other more structurally oriented scholars like Peter Hall, tend to consider the law as something that is outside the policy field, a part of the environment, that might grant structural advantages to some of the participants, but that it is not really "acted upon" by concrete actors. Even the authors that share a "contractualist" and finally functionalist approach to institution building – think of Elinor Ostrom – in fact downplay the role of the actors in the use of the law (rules in use), and of the institutional setting: maybe at the beginning the legal rules were established in order to secure cooperation, but in any given moment they are outside the possibility of the actors to use them in a differentiated way.

Jus versus lex

Here there is in my opinion the first point of originality I referred to above. We non English policy analysts often lament the fact that in our national languages there is not the possibility to easily distinguish between politics and policy (and polity, for that matter), thus *de facto* claiming a sort of structural superiority to our American and English colleagues. Maybe the reverse is true when we talk, even from a political science point of view, of the law. Actually I contend that all the above mentioned conceptualisations of the so called neo-institutionalism are in fact the result of a typically Anglo-Saxon approach to the study and the notion of the law. The point is that, as Peter Knoepfel knows very well, being deeply rooted in the European continental tradition of civil law, there is a very fundamental distinction to be drawn between *jus* and *lex* that is very difficult to capture in English, while it is absolutely clear in all the other languages (*droit/loi*, *Recht/Gesetz*, *diritto/legge*, *derecho/ley*, etc.). The distinction is clear enough and I can remember very well my teachers at the Law Faculty trying to instil it in our minds. The *lex*, not only in modern constitutional States, is basically a decision taken by a legitimate authority (the Senate in ancient Rome, the King in the absolutist State, nowadays the Parliament) through which the behaviours of individuals, public or private organisations are constrained (or more precisely there is the promise of punishment to those individuals, public or private organisations that do not adapt their behaviour to the prescription of the law itself). The *jus* on the contrary is not only the whole of the existing laws, but it is also a *corpus* containing the principles according to which the *lex* has to be interpreted. In other words, and from a political science point of view, while the political power can, and indeed does, modify the *lex*, it cannot, at least in the short run, change the *jus*. But we have to go further: it is common experience that the *lex* passed by Parliament will be interpreted by the courts, the administration and the citizens on the basis of the principles of the *jus*, sometimes even disregarding the "real" intentions of the legislator. It is important to note that the distinction goes much further than the distinction between constitutional norms and ordinary laws, as also the Constitution, is part of the *corpus juris*, and will be interpreted by the Constitutional Courts, where they exist, in the light of principles and criteria that are not necessarily written in a *lex*, but that nevertheless exist and are very important (e.g. *pacta sunt servanda*).

This distinction is very relevant for policy analysis. For instance all Peter Knoepfel's theorisation about the concept of "institutional regime" that was actually at the basis of our research on water regimes in Europe (Euwarness), basically combining policies with property rights regimes, can be also read in terms of the distinction between *jus* and *lex*. In fact the same *lex* that establishes a new policy can try to alter the distribution of property rights, but, in doing so, it has to accept and recognize the principles of *jus*. This is the reason why property rights regimes tend to be more stable than policies. And, as we have tried to show in the Euwareness research, in order to design policies that are effective in bringing about sustainable consumption of natural resources it is necessary to take into account the actual distribution of property rights, i.e. the (legal) policy resources that some actors are able to mobilise either because the *lex* (public policies) gives them some advantage or because the *jus* (property rights regimes) recognises that they have a superior legal position.

In other words, many of the contemporary neo-institutionalist conceptualisations of the law have their origin, and their main weakness, in a confusion between *jus* and *lex*. What they seem to be missing is the fact that only the former is somewhat structural and, in any given policy making process, can be considered as a part of the environment. On the contrary the latter is very much a resource that can be used selectively by the actors that own it, and its use will be defined ultimately by the interests and the goals of the individual actor.

The many uses of law in policy making

We can now go back to the main stream of this contribution, i.e. the importance of the law (from now on, of the *lex*) in public policy making.

As already said, it is its conceptualisation as a policy resource that makes all the difference, because the resources have to be used by the individual actors.

Because policy resources are fundamentally relational, the first obvious implication is that, if nobody is actually willing to use it, the mere existence of a legal rule does not make any impact in the policy process. For instance a corrupted official can sell his or her legal "power" (for instance the authority to issue a permit) to the highest bidder; the fact that this behaviour is illegal is a mere academic point if nobody wants or can raise the problem of a gap between the legal prescription and the reality. Even discarding this example as too extreme, one can think of the numerous instances in which an actor or an interested party refrains from going to court against illegal behaviour, and that the court will certainly redress, on a simple calculation of the costs associated with the judicial procedure (in terms of money, time and stress) compared to the benefits of having his or her right actually recognized.

But an actor can also avoid using his or her legal resources on the basis of another type of calculation, i.e. the fear that said resources are not sufficient to overcome the resources that other actors, e.g. his or her opponents, can actually mobilise. For instance if a policy entrepreneur needs the active cooperation of other actors in the policy implementation phase in order to achieve his or her main goals, to use fully the legal powers in the decision phase in order to force a specific policy design is a very bad strategy, as it will generate, in the best scenario, only a reluctant and partial cooperation in the subsequent phase. In other words, in may cases the resource "consensus" is more important than the resource "law" and this should alter the strategy of an actor.

Another implication of conceptualising the law as a resource is that this emphasizes a truth well known to all lawyers, namely that the law is not necessarily a set of inflexible rules constraining everybody's behaviour. A public authority, for example, can use its own discretionary powers (usually recognized by the *jus*, even when they are not explicitly mentioned in the *lex*) in order to achieve better results at the cost of some delay in compliance by the target groups. In the first instance in which I had the opportunity to work with Peter (the big WZB research on the implementation of air pollution control policy) we found many instances in which the deadline for the enforcement of the regulations was postponed in order to allow the polluters to change radically the production process instead of simply complying with the emission or immission standards through the adoption of some end-of-pipe solution. Here again we find ourselves, as in the previous example, in a situation in which one resource can substitute another: in this case it is the resource "time" that can substitute and complement the law.

But this flexibility of the law operates also in a different direction. For instance in very decentralised political systems (think of Switzerland and even of the European Union), the interplay between the confederation and its constituent political units can and indeed does generate a situation in which there is at the same time a strong emphasis on the legality of the process, and a differentiated enforcement of the same rules.

This latter example, i.e. the importance of what nowadays we call "multilevel governance", clarifies another point in which the difference between Peter Knoepfel's approach and the more naive neo-institutionalist theorisations is striking. The main point is a realistic understanding of the simple fact that what is often called "the State", is far from being a monolithic structure, but is composed of several different components, all with some degree of legitimacy, but with different, and sometimes conflicting, missions and points of view. This implies that these different components interact in the policy game all using, among others, the legal resources they possess.

This is the reason why inter-policy cooperation, so important in the environmental policy field, is also so difficult to achieve, and Peter Knoepfel, by trying to design institutional arrangements able to bring it about, actually designed ways of altering the distribution of legal and non legal resources to the different actors.

But this line of reasoning goes further than that. The point is that different parts of the State are in charge of different and potentially conflicting interests and values, using to this end the resources granted to them by Parliament (money and legal rights, mainly), and that this division of powers operates not only in the horizontal (i.e. functional) dimension but also in the vertical (i.e. territorial) one. Therefore the opposition of a specific region (or Canton, or Land or Commune) to the initiative of a different part of the State (e.g. a national department) can be triggered not only by the fact that the substantive goals are not shared, or the actual solution designed is not considered satisfactory, but also because the balance of power between centre and periphery is altered in an unacceptable way. This was very apparent in the research exercise we did together (under the direction of Peter Knoepfel and Corinne Larrue) on the topic of the relation between environmental protection and the subsidiary principle, and this shifts the attention to the very fundamental distinction between actors' goals and objectives related to the content of the problem and goals and objectives related to the policy process, i.e. to the relationship with other actors. This distinction, that in my opinion represents one of the most distinctive contribution of the political science tradition to the theory and practice of public policy analysis, is very often linked exactly to the different distribution of legal resources in a policy system.

Passing to another point there is no need to recall that legal resources are not the only ones that the actors, be it individuals, public or private organisations, can mobilise. Knowledge and information, money, political support and others are also very important and, as we already mentioned, they can substitute for the lack of a proper legal basis.

The level of information and knowledge (that is: the availability of the basic data relevant for a policy problem, and the ability to offer theories and models able to organise them, and finally make sense of them) can ensure the relevance of an actor in the policy process, even if he or she lacks any other type of resources in a relevant amount. Why so? Because many if not most of contemporary policy problems not only show an high level of complexity, in the sense that they have many different aspects interacting with each other, but also high level of uncertainty, in the sense that we lack definite evidence, or at least a shared knowledge, about what works in really solving them. This is a reason why the role of experts in policy making is nowadays so important and why they are able to actually make a difference in pushing governments and administration in the right (and lamentably also in the wrong) direction. This increases the responsibility of policy analysts, the social and political science scholars trying to make sense of the ways in which policies are formulated and implemented, and this is a challenge that we have to accept if, as I will try to show in the last section of this paper, we actually want to be able to come out with "usable knowledge".

But, going back to the problem of which is the specific place of the law among policy resources, one cannot forget that the reverse is also true. Not only can other types of resources substitute for the lack of a proper legal basis, but the law can and indeed does decrease drastically the importance of other resources. We came across this point in the discussion of the so called precautionary principle, a simple legal statement according to which the lack of definite scientific evidence about the adverse effects of some human activity does not represent a sufficient reason for preventing the regulation of said behaviour. This actually means that all the negative evidence (e.g. research showing weak or no correlation between the activity and the adverse effect) all of a sudden, and because of the ability of some policy actor to claim the applicability of the precautionary principle, loses any weight in the policy game. In the environmental field, where the level of uncertainty on the long term consequences of human behaviours is invariably very high, this simple legal statement can, and indeed does, make a lot of difference. Suffice to think of highly controversial policies as the prevention of electro-magnetic pollution, the regulation of genetically modified organisms or genetically engineered organisms, the whole issue of climate change and its relation with greenhouse gas emissions.

We could certainly find other instances in which the legal resources are able to modify policy games. A good research programme could actually be to try and collect systematically real world instances in which the law is used by policy actors in order to influence the outcome of policy processes in non orthodox ways. And of course we have to remember that policy actors are very often in a position to change the law, and that this can happen in a strategic way.

A good example of this use is represented by the case in which a "superior" norm is created in order to constrain the legislator behaviour. Think of the willingness that national governments sometimes show to push very stringent legislation at the international level, in order to overcome domestic difficulties. The Maastricht and the Kyoto Treaties are good, even if not necessary successful, examples of this practice. The imposition of external constraints is used in trying to bypass the blockages of national policy making where powerful interest groups are able to influence national Parliaments through the mobilisation of strong political support. As I already said this tactic sometimes fails, but is still another example of how legal resources can be built and used in order to change the outcomes of the policy processes.

Focus on empirical research

All these examples of the different uses of legal resources have something in common: they were all "discovered" in the course of empirical research. And this is the second important element of Peter Knoepfel's research programme that I want to mention here: the fact that he has devoted an enormous amount of time to the detailed reconstruction of what actually happens *sur le terrain*. This, it has to be said, should be the central interest of any student of policy, but, unfortunately, is not so.

It is therefore worth remembering that the right attitude in scientific inquiry is one that considers the theories and models relevant in so far as they are able to provide a better understanding of what happens in the real world and not vice-versa, one in which the scholar goes looking only for problems and empirical situations able to prove the value of some conceptual construct. Maybe I am becoming a grumpy old man, but, when I read the work of some young or old scholar "demonstrating" through sophisticated and complex models some obvious truth, I cannot avoid a moment of deep irritation.

The right attitude, well exemplified by Peter Knoepfel's vast body of empirical research, is the continuous attempt to adapt the tools of policy analysis to the complexity of the real world in order to come out with some novel interpretation, some fine tuning of said tools, etc. And of course this approach, stemming from the natural curiosity of the true scholar, is actually much more fun than the opposite, and today so popular, one.

But what is more important is that this approach is the real reason, in my opinion, why some scholars, like Peter Knoepfel and, I should add, myself, put so much emphasis on the concept of resource and of legal resource in particular, while many others barely mention them.

The point is that if you want to explain (and therefore predict) what actually happens in the real world, you definitely need to understand real actors, interplay, i.e. the complex and sometimes contradictory goals they have and the many different tools that they can use. And of course if you do not know which type and what amount of resources they are able to mobilise, you are not able to capture the imbalances of "power" and influence they have and the reasons why some of them are winners – they actually succeed in reaching their goals – and some are losers.

Furthermore, as we mentioned in passing beforehand, in the policy game almost invariably there are actors – politicians and bureaucrats – whose relation with the legal resources is rather peculiar. On the one hand they, like everybody else, are constrained in their behaviours by the existence of the law, if some other actor is in the position of using it "against" them. But, on the other hand, they are often also the actors that "make the law", in the sense that they are able to modify it in a purposive way in order to change the outcome of the policy game. Obviously in doing so they are not totally free, as they have to take into account the other resources that can be mobilised by the actors (think of political support and interest groups, for instance), but this cannot cancel the fact that they have a privileged access to the generation of legal resources that makes their role in public policy making of special importance.

But this brings about the consideration of what policy analysis is actually for and which is the right level at which the scientific inquiry should position itself.

From meso to micro: interpreting or changing the world

The final question we have to ask ourselves is actually the first one we posed at the beginning of this paper. Why very few scholars follow Peter Knoepfel's example and put a big emphasis on the issue of policy resources and legal resources in particular? Why, on the contrary, most Policy Analysis textbooks actually ignore the topic?

The two elements we mentioned beforehand - the distinction between *jus* and *lex* on the one hand, and the importance of empirical research on the other – can help us a bit in finding an answer but are not sufficient. There are several European scholars that know very well the continental legal tradition and that perform empirical research, but still are not interested in identifying policy resources, measuring them, understanding the ways in which the different types can substitute each other.

If we are looking for a convincing answer we have to dig deeper, and we have to discuss a more fundamental point, that is the purpose of scientific inquiry in the field of public policy analysis.

My contention, in closing this paper, is that there are, by and large, two, certainly legitimate, but actually very different ways of doing this job, or, if you prefer, two different reasons why one scholar should spend his time studying public policy.

The first alternative is possibly the one that dominates in international scientific journals. According to this school of thought the purpose of public policy analysis is not different from the purpose of Comparative Politics. The aim is to develop "middle range theories", à la Merton, trying to find regularities and conclusions that are generalizable in law-like statements, using the comparative method. The idea is to develop second order concepts able to make sense, through a simplification of the complexity of the real world, of the outcomes of the policy processes by correlating them to some independent variable. The effect seems to be often to provide reasonable explanations of the most apparent phenomena by "giving a name" to them. Economists when they study public policies and institutions offer the more striking examples of this approach. Two examples: the relationship between proportional representation in electoral rules and public budget deficits, or between the degree of formal independence of central banks and the rate of inflation. But also a lot of political scientists, political sociologists and public management students use the same approach: they try explicitly, or – mostly in the case of public management scholars – implicitly, to find causal links more or less valid in general. Following the imperative that sinners should not throw the first stone, we have to confess that most of us – including the small group of people that has been working with Peter in the last 30 years – have been sooner or later using this mental frame, i.e. adopting the comparative method and some form of correlational analysis. And, as I have already said, this is a perfectly legitimate approach and sometimes it is actually able to succeed, in the sense of providing some interesting conclusions that apply to a plurality of policy situations. For instance, I strongly believe that, as a rule of thumb, one should expect that, in order to solve a complex policy problem, it is necessary for the policy making process to show the same level of complexity, at least in the sense that the number and diversity of actors involved should reflect the type of interests affected by the problem and/or by the solution [the First (and Only) Dente Law of Policy Making].

The problem however is that, as we know all too well, to obtain generalizable, non obvious and non tautological findings is very hard indeed. One of the reasons is that in social and political science the intervention of the researcher is not neutral. It is a rather extreme application of what the physicists call the "observer effect", i.e. the changes that the act of observation will make on the phenomenon being observed. As a matter of fact if a public policy researcher is able to come out with new and interesting concepts, it is more than likely that this will alter the behaviours of the real actors, as this knowledge will be, sooner rather than later, transferred to them.

But also discounting this consideration, a more down to earth observation is that even the First Dente Law has exceptions and applies, as we say, only *ceteris paribus*. But the point is that a *ceteris paribus* world does not exist, or more precisely that each real world situation is, at the end of the day, different. This is the main reason why in the trade-off between spending a lot of time in trying to reach some general truths or laws, and being able to explain convincingly a specific situation some of us, and Peter Knoepfel is certainly among them, chose the latter alternative. This is the second approach to public policy analysis.

The research strategy becomes therefore very different: we look for the basic elements of the policy game (the actors, the resources, the stake, the patterns of interaction, etc.) and we try to figure out which specific configuration of these elements provides a convincing explanation of what happened in the individual case. The interesting thing about this strategy, and a big part of its appeal, is that of course it can be used also in the design phase of a policy, in the sense that, if we have enough information about the policy field, we can try to design the policy configuration maximising the chances of success of the policy itself, both in the sense of decisional success (i.e. the ability to actually adopt a non incremental transformation of public programmes) and in the sense of substantial success (i.e. the ability to contribute to the "solution" of the policy problem).

In any case, both for retrospective or prospective purposes, this approach has some specific characteristics. In the first place it is deeply rooted in the theory of policy making and implementation, as we need to look for the basic elements – the atomic and sub-atomic particles – composing our reality. But, on the other hand, it is also strongly based on the reconstruction of the real world, if it maintains its promise of reaching conclusions able to point out the real reasons for success or failure in solving a specific problem. In other words, no *ceteris paribus* clause here.

Obviously we have a price to pay. And the price is quite high, namely the virtual impossibility to generalize our conclusions to a whole class of policy problems and/or policy configurations. For instance, we don't know, in general, if the fact that a policy network shows a high level of density (in the sense that all the actors are actually connected with each other) is in itself a good thing in order to increase the probabilities of success. In some cases this configuration, which can obviously be spontaneous or artificially created, has actually been able to enhance the level of trust between the actors, bringing about a smoother development of the process, a cross-fertilization, etc. In other cases however we have to register the emergence of non-negotiable conflicts bringing about a blockage or a breaking down of the policy process. These totally different outcomes can occur for a myriad of different reasons: the nature of the stake of the game, the type of goals pursued by the actors, the intensity of their preferences, mistakes in the strategic approach to negotiation, etc.

The fact of knowing that the density of the network can make a difference, even if we do not know in which direction, however, is far from useless. At the very least it provides another concept for the toolbox of the policy analyst, adds another item to the mental checklist that we all use, and therefore increases the probability that in a future situation we will be able to come out with something interesting and useful to say.

Doest it means that policy analysis, as Wildavsky suggested many years ago, is more art and craft than science? Maybe, even if I do not find anything particularly scientific in stating the obvious with sophisticated methodologies, as we too often find in many scientific journals.

What I do know, however, is that this approach is able to keep its promise if the real purpose of scientific inquiry is to provide tools for having better policies, solving real world problems, actually changing in some micro situation the world for the better. Instead of proclaiming more or less pompously "laws" that maybe, and just maybe, apply to different situations, I very much prefer to say something that is very likely to work in one, and may be in one only, specific circumstance. And I am fairly confident that Peter shares the same sentiment.

The reference to Marx's 11th Thesis on Feuerbach in the title of this section is to point out the main purpose of this approach. And I strongly believe that the quest for real world relevance not only justifies, but actually requires, the fact of giving a lot of attention to the basic elements of the policy game, among which the resources, and the legal resources in particular, play a major role basically because their distribution can be altered by the actors themselves. Because these, in other words, are some of the things we can easily manipulate in order to reach our goals.

Conclusions and perspectives

In closing this piece and in accordance with the scattered nature of my thoughts I want to point out three very different implications, or corollaries, of what we have been saying until now.

The first is that the main difference between the two approaches I have discussed here is about the problem of which is the "right" level of analysis. By and large the "comparative politics approach to policy analysis" believes that the right level is the meso one. One should be looking for middle range theories, for statements that situate themselves somewhere mid-way between the empirical reality and the general theory. The alternative approach – an actor based policy analysis – is strongly situated at the micro level, in the sense that one wants to produce statements that are totally valid for the specific situation investigated, and, exactly for this reason, interact strongly with the macro level, that is the basic elements of the policy making and implementation theory. This has also important consequences for the methods to be used. If the first school of thought is somewhat condemned to use the comparative method, we have much more freedom in choosing the right techniques for our investigations, ranging from narrative approaches to case studies to the use of experimental methods.

The second point is that I am not sure that those using the actors based approach are definitely a minority, even if this is what one can derive from a quick scan of the international political science journals. The point is that the vast majority of analyses are not only done in domestic policy fields in national languages, but are done by individuals that are not academic researchers (the ones that write and read scientific journals). Sometimes these analyses are not even written down but are discussed in more or less open meetings in which the interested parties gather in order to find solutions to real problems. I suspect that their approach is more similar to our than sometimes we think, and that, as a matter of fact, the whole process is very different indeed from what the followers of the "comparative politics approach to policy analysis" assume is actually happening. Actually this is more than a suspicion, as I have participated myself in such meetings and I have found that our conceptual tools, if they are not used in a scholastic way, can actually be useful in order to help the understanding and the development of this process and can easily be grasped by the real policy makers. In other words the real problem is not if the actor based approach is dominant in the scientific community, but if it is dominant in the policy making community…

This brings me to the third point, i.e. the fact that the job description of a political scientist, and any other scientist, for that matter, includes teaching. And the product of this teaching cannot be solely the production of other researchers. This of course is one part of the outcome but only a part and possibly not the biggest. We actually teach, and in Peter Knoepfel's case this has been a choice made many years ago, to people that are likely to become, and sometimes already are, policy actors. This is what makes teaching interesting; as some of these people have already a knowledge of how the game is played that can be compared with what we have elaborated in our books and articles. And even if they are young students, the purpose of teaching policy is actually to improve their chances to be able to influence, when they will enter the real world, the policy processes in which they will find themselves involved. When I was hired by the Politecnico di Milano in the Planning Department, someone explained to me that the dominant philosophy of the university was that the teachers should actually try to involve themselves in real projects - building houses and bridges, designing machinery, etc. – basically because no one trusts an engineering or architectural professor that has never been active in realising some real projects. From time to time I wonder what, apart from the use of sophisticated conceptual tools, some of our more mainstream colleagues are actually able to teach to their students.

Summing up, and going back to the main argument of this short paper, in my opinion the attention devoted to resources, and to the use of law, in Peter Knoepfel's scientific programme, is a consequence and a reflection of his reformist approach. The idea that providing conceptual frameworks, analytic tools, evidence and insights able to ease the solution of real world problems is not only the "right" thing to do by a socially responsible scholar, but it is also much more fun than the alternative.

CHAPTER 2

Why Do We Obey Soft Law?

ALEXANDRE FLÜCKIGER

Introduction[1]

Compliance with law

"*What explains this singular habit of respecting laws, which only a few 'abnormal' people obey only when compelled to do so?*"[2] Can this habit be explained by coercive sanctions? The fear they instil, or the threats they represent? The guilt and shame they evoke? In short, do we respect laws because of the emotions they stir within us?

This is certainly part of the answer, though not the entire answer. The authority of law stems not from coercion alone. Explanations vary depending on the point of view: neuroscientists cite the activation of cerebral zones specific to compliance with norms,[3] psychologists the emotions, sociologists social norms, ethicists the sense of values, theologians morality, economists efficiency, psychiatrists the superego, and so on.

Compliance with soft law

If compliance with hard law is not easy to explain, compliance with soft law is even more complex. It is astonishing-to a legal mind at least-that certain non-binding instruments, such as recommendations, declarations, information and persuasion activities, gentlemen's agreements, charters and other incentive instruments, compel respect. The rules of soft law may, in practice, be respected regardless of whether or not they are of a legal nature. The rate of compliance does vary, as it does widely with binding instruments: "In some instances, compliance with non-binding norms and instruments is extremely good and probably would not have been better if the norms were contained in

---

[1] This text is the short version of an article published in the *Revue européenne des sciences sociales*, 2009, 144, p. 73ss entitled "Pourquoi respectons-nous la soft law? Le rôle des émotions et des techniques de manipulation."

[2] [Trans.] Gaudemet, J., in Papaux, Alain, *Essai philosophique sur la qualification juridique : de la subsomption à l'abduction : l'exemple du droit international privé*, Brussels [etc.] 2003, p. 215.

[3] Spitzer, M. et al., "The neural signature of social norm compliance," *Neuron* 2007, 56, p. 185ss. In neuro-marketing (relationship between sales and cerebral zones), see Lee, N./ Broderick, A.J./ Chamberlain, L., "What is 'neuromarketing'? A discussion and agenda for future research," *International journal of psychophysiology* 2007, 63, p. 199ss.

a binding text."[4] The Joint Declaration of the European Ministers of Education convened in Bologna on June 19, 1999 (Bologna Declaration), a non-binding instrument, is an example of the potentially powerful effects of soft law. This text was followed and implemented much more effectively and quickly in universities than the rule imposing a fine on pedestrians who use a bicycle path when a sidewalk is available. This is a remarkable phenomenon for a jurist: rules of law, though compulsory, are sometimes less respected than rules of soft law, although clearly rules of hard law are often more effective than rules of soft law taken in isolation,[5] and soft law is by far not always as effective. The most marked effect certainly results from a combination of rules of law, their enforcement and soft law instruments. Neither a compulsory nature nor a penalty alone is a determining factor in the analysis of compliance with rules.

The need to legitimize the State's non-normative action

Since a non-compulsory rule may be enough to change individuals' behaviour, the State has made a habit of using such rules in addition to, or instead of, conventional legal instruments. This circumvents the burdensome legal processes that apply to rules of law and contributes to strengthen the State's hold. The phenomenon is not a new one. There are traces of it, for example, in Michel Foucault's concept of governmentality.[6] However, its originality resides in jurists' awareness of the power of these "weak" instruments, with the legal system conveniently brandishing their non-legal nature as an excuse to avoid addressing the legality or constitutionality of such instruments. The challenge, then, is to convince the State to develop appropriate legitimation mechanisms. Constitutional law did so in the past by democratizing law and subjecting it to requirements of precision and the control of constitutionality, while administrative law did so by requiring procedural guarantees for the adoption of administrative decisions or certain plans.

With this end in mind, we will explore how soft law exerts its influence. We will detail these mechanisms from a psychological perspective. The role of emotions in persuasion techniques as well as manipulation techniques that affect individuals' behaviour without their knowledge will then be examined.

The role of emotions in persuasion techniques

The concept of emotion is not easily defined. Still today, many references are made to the six basic emotions identified by Paul Ekman: anger, fear,

---

[4] Shelton, Dinah, "Soft Law," Handbook of International Law, Routledge Press, 2008, ch. 4.

[5] See, for example, studies showing that the existence of an obligation to wear seatbelts results in a far greater change in behaviour than a simple recommendation (Killias, Martin, Précis de criminologie, 2nd Ed., Berne 2001, p. 453ss).

[6] See Flückiger, Alexandre, "Régulation, dérégulation, autorégulation: l'émergence des actes étatiques non obligatoires," Revue de droit suisse II, 2004, p. 170ss.

disgust, joy, sadness and surprise.[7] Research in the field has only made the concept more complex by distinguishing emotions from other affects such as feelings, passions or moods by categorizing and broadening them to such an extent that it is impossible to find a unanimously recognized definition today.[8]

Emotion and reason: Two readings of the same reality

Emotion is not opposed to rationality, but interwoven closely with it. Far from interfering, emotion helps us make rational decisions in situations of uncertainty, for example.[9] Emotion can also be described as rational.[10] It follows, therefore, that it is more appropriate to imagine different ways of reading the same reality: while it is reasonable to drive on the right side of continental roads, an emotional reading of the issue might focus on the fear of an accident (not to mention a fine). The rational choice theory might lead someone to prefer a solution that involves deliberately breaking the law, if this is less costly in terms of both money and image, as studies in law and economics have theorized.[11] On the other hand, an emotional reading would show that desire for wealth, greed or fear of impoverishment would weigh more than pride and honour in compliance with law or the embarrassment that guilt stemming from a violation might evoke. The opposition between reason and emotion is in fact used for persuasive purposes in all decision-making processes, whether legal, political, economic or other: an individual who calls another to reason is actually trying to show him that his decision may be based on other emotions that could prevail or that certain emotions can be appeased.

As such, the intention is not to oppose reason and emotion, but to probe the emotional variable in the mechanisms at work with observation of rules. Although this perspective is restrictive, it opportunely completes more conventional political, sociological and economic analyses.

---

[7] Ekman, Paul, "An Argument for Basic Emotions," Cognition and Emotion, 1992, 6, 169ss; Ekman, Paul, Emotions in the Human Face, Cambridge 1982.

[8] See Deonna, Julien/ Teroni, Fabrice, Qu'est-ce qu'une émotion? Paris 2008.

[9] Elster 1999 [note 17], p. 283ss; Damasio, Antonio, L'erreur de Descartes: la raison des émotions, Paris 1999 (new ed. 2008); Scherer, Klaus, „Zur Rationalität der Emotionen," in Rössner, H. (Ed.), Der ganze Mensch, p.181ss, Munich 1986.

[10] Bandes, Susan, The Passion of Law, New York, 2000, p. 10; Elster 1999, p. 284ss.

[11] See in particular the economic analysis of criminality according to which the offender is supposed to act "rationally" when committing a reprehensible act by comparing the benefit of that act to its cost (amount of the criminal penalty, monetary equivalent of a sentence depriving him of freedom): Becker, G.S., "Crime and Punishment: An Economic Approach," Journal of Political Economy 1968, p. 1ss; Garoupa, Nuno, "The Theory of Optimal Law Enforcement," *Journal of Economic Surveys* 1997, 11, p. 267ss; Polinsky, Mitchell/ Shavell, Steven, "The Economic Theory of Public Enforcement of Law" *Journal of Economic Literature, American Economic Association* 2000, 38, p. 45ss. For a behavioural approach to the economic analysis of law, see Sunstein, Cass, *Behavioral law and economics*, Cambridge [etc.] 2000.

Emotion at the service of compliance with hard and soft law

To improve compliance with soft law, the State can use various persuasion techniques by appealing more or less strongly to emotions. This approach is not original, to the extent that the role of emotions can be shown easily in the application of conventional law: criminal law, in its primitive punitive aspect (confinement, exclusion, impoverishment, humiliation, suffering and death), is designed to inspire fear,[12] anxiety and terror in the public, as well as evoke shame, embarrassment or guilt among those found guilty, and assuage the anger, rage and desire for vengeance felt by victims in order to impose compliance with the rule of law. The justiciable obey law because of an emotional tie, which for some involves fear of punishment or the resulting shame,[13] and for others, positive emotions such as respect for or commitment to the public good.[14] Fear of punishment, however, is far from the only explanatory factor.

In the context of soft law, research on compliance with social norms[15] and persuasion techniques[16] are of great interest. Observance of non-binding rules cannot be explained solely by the rational choice theory, but is attributable essentially to emotional mechanisms, particularly anticipation of shame, guilt or embarrassment in the event of violation as well as pride in compliance,[17] with shame being evoked by others' disgust or scorn.[18]

The emotional reading is but one possible reading of rule compliance mechanisms. Although it has a high potential to explain changes in attitude, consideration must be given to other levers that a purely emotional approach only partially explains. That is why, in the second part, we will examine manipulation techniques that prompt individuals to unwittingly change their behaviour. Some research also gives less importance to the effect of emotion (in this case, fear of punishment) in compliance with law. According to this

---

[12] Lange, Bettina, "The Emotional Dimension in Legal Regulation," Journal of Law and Society, March 2002, p. 197ss, 209.

[13] Miller, William, "Fear, Weak Legs, and Running Away: A Soldier's Story," in Bandes, Susan (Ed.), The Passion of Law, New York, 2000, p. 242.

[14] Deigh, John, "Emotion and the Authority of Law," in Bandes, Susan (Ed.), The Passion of Law, New York, 2000, p. 285ss.

[15] Posner, Eric, Law and Social Norms, Cambridge Mass 2000; Posner, Eric (Ed.), Social Norms, Nonlegal Sanctions, and the Law, Cheltenham, Northampton 2007; O'Donnell, Patrick, "Social Norms & Law: An Introduction," Theory & Science 2007, vol. 9/2.

[16] Petty, R./ DeSteno, D./ Rucker, D., "The role of affect in attitude change," Forgas, Joseph (Ed.), Handbook of affect and social cognition, Mahwah 2001, p. 212ss; Petty, Richard/ Gleicher, Faith/ Baker, Sara, "Multiple roles of affect in persuasion," Forgas, Joseph (Ed.), Affect and Judgment, London 1991, p. 181ss.

[17] Elster, Jon, Alchemies of the Mind: Rationality and the Emotions, Cambridge 1999, p. 145ss. In Gagné's view (Gagné, Learry, "Non-rational compliance with social norms: sincere and hypocritical," Social Science Information 2007, 46, p. 445ss), based on the work of Pierre Bourdieu, non-rational compliance is more acceptable to the group than sincere compliance.

[18] Elster 1999 [note 17], p. 149.

work, law is observed when individuals believe in its legitimacy[19]-defined procedurally[20]-by complying spontaneously with it.[21] Moral, ethical and justice-related explanations find in this type of work a welcome foundation: I personally don't kill other humans, not because I fear the criminal penalty, but from a personal conviction of the correctness, fairness and legitimacy of that rule. Hence, there is no point in the legislator escalating implementation mechanisms to distil fear, instead of making the legal system more worthy of respect by improving its legitimacy.[22]

The emotional motives for obeying soft law

The non-compulsory effect of soft law

Because soft law is not a legal norm, it has no binding effect. Its effect is rather to modify the behaviour of the targeted groups without legally requiring them to do so. Yet, it retains its normative nature, since the norm is not necessarily imperative. In fact, normativity must not be confused with imperativity: "*The normative is a genus with two main species: the imperative and the appreciative.*"[23] The behaviour of soft law's targeted audience is left to their own *appreciation.*[24] As such, the normative nature of soft law is appreciative rather than imperative. It arises not from "*Sollen*" (must be), but "*Sollten*" (should be).[25]

Obedience of authority

The first effect stems from the ascendancy or prestige of the author's figure and the emotions thus evoked (diffuse fear, desire to please or need for recognition, admiration). A recommendation from a public authority has more weight than the same advice from an unknown person or an obscure association. This is the case, for example, with recommendations by the Competition Commission[26] or the *Surveillant des prix*, which "at least has a certain moral weight."[27]

A bet is made on the author's influence when authorities deliberately adopt an exemplary behaviour as part of public policy (sorting waste, renovating

---

[19] Tyler, Tom, Why People Obey the Law, Princeton 2006 (2nd Ed.).

[20] Tyler 2006 [note 19], p. 272.

[21] Killias, Martin, *Précis de criminologie*, 2nd Ed., Berne 2001, p. 457s et 467ss for whom fear of police officers is less important overall than most people's spontaneous compliance with law.

[22] Tyler 2006 [note 19], 4e from cover.

[23] [Trans.] Lalande, André, *Vocabulaire technique et critique de la philosophie*, Paris 1993 (1st Ed. 1926), under the entry for "normatif." See also Amselek 1991, p. 143.

[24] Flückiger 2004 [note 6], p. 230.

[25] Flückiger 2004 [note 6], p. 190.

[26] Tercier, Pierre, *ad* art. 45 LCart, ch. 45, p. 948 and Martenet, Vincent, *ad* art. 8 LMI, ch. 8, p. 1392, in Tercier, P.; Bovet, C. (Ed.), *Droit de la concurrence: loi sur les cartels, loi sur la surveillance des prix, loi sur le marché intérieur, loi sur les entraves techniques au commerce: commentaire*, Geneva, etc. 2002.

[27] [Trans.] Bonvin, Jacques, *ad* art. 14 LSPr, ch. 40, p. 1172, in Tercier, P.; Bovet, C. 2002 [cites earlier note].

public buildings for energy efficiency), giving individuals a model to follow and accustoming them in the hope of sweeping them along. Citizens perceive the State's publicity of its new behaviour as a real recommendation to adopt the same attitude.[28]

Research in social psychology on obedience shows the importance of the weight individuals give to a figure of authority,[29] regardless of whether there is a mandatory legal relationship.[30] Credible sources are more convincing. For example, experts have proven to be influential within the framework of anti-smoking campaigns.[31]

Some non-binding instruments are adopted, drafted and formulated *like* binding instruments, resulting in a bluff effect on the intended audience.[32] Here, obedience is the product of a transfer, as it were, where secret hopes are invested in the normative power of the written word[33] or where the solemnity of the adoption procedure is impressive, as with some non-binding international declarations[34] like the Rio Declaration (environment) or the Bologna Declaration (education).

In other cases, respect for authority is strategic. It may arise from the need to foster a climate of trust by maintaining harmonious relations with the administration, a determining factor in non-binding arrangements (or gentlemen's agreements).[35] The fear of a deterioration in relations leads to compliance with non-binding instruments. This motive is particularly strong in public international law, where the necessity of maintaining good relations among States means that violating a purely political commitment may result in a range of retaliatory measures.[36]

---

[28] Flückiger 2004 [note 6], p. 201s.

[29] Girandola, Fabien, "La source," in Girandola, Psychologie de la persuasion et de l'engagement, Besançon 2003, p. 17ss.

[30] Milgram's experiment where subjects were pushed to obey inhumane orders must be understood from the perspective of hard law, to the extent that the experimentor gave them direct orders (Milgram, Stanley, "Behavioral Study of Obedience," Journal of Abnormal and Social Psychology 67, 1963, p. 371ss).

[31] Falomir Pichastor, Juan Manuel/ Mugny, Gabriel, Société contre fumeur: une analyse psychosociale de l'influence des experts, Grenoble, 2004.

[32] Flückiger 2004 [note 6], p. 247.

[33] Tschannen, Pierre, Der Richtplan und die Abstimmung raumwirksamer Aufgabe, Berne, let. e, p. 325.

[34] Nguyen Quoc Dinh/ Daillier, Patrick/ Pellet, Alain, Public International Law, 7th Ed. Paris 2002, ch. 247, p. 378.

[35] Kautz, Steffen, Absprachen im Verwaltungsrecht: Zulässigkeit, Grenzen und Folgen, Berlin 2002, p. 80s; Müller-Graf, Thomas, Entrechtlichung durch Informalisierung? ein Beitrag zur Handlungsformen- und zur Rechtsverhältnislehre im Verwaltungsrecht, Bâle, etc. 2001, p. 173s.

[36] Virally, Michel, "La distinction entre textes internationaux de portée juridique et textes internationaux dépourvus de portée juridique (à l'exception des textes émanant des organisations internationales): rapport provisoire," Annuaire de l'Institut de droit international, vol. 60, tome I, Paris 1983, p. 231s.

This effect is so wide-ranging that the legislator itself sometimes feels bound by soft law, at least politically. In public international law, "*recommendations can be highly restrictive from a political standpoint. They are an undeniable means of political pressure.*"[37] There is also a similar psychological basis for the model law and model treaty technique, in which a higher authority proposes to follow a model law to standardize a practice in areas where it may not be competent.[38]

Fear

Fear and anxiety are powerful vectors of obedience. A State has only to wield them in soft law instruments to strongly encourage the target audience to modify its behaviour. While it is generally true that the greater the fear, the more persuasive the message, psychologists and criminologists in particular have attempted to show the limitations of this approach.[39]

Fear can be related to other negative emotions that strengthen its impact, such as disgust, aversion, indignation, anger or sadness. For example, fear of global warming's effects can lead to sadness or anger, while in anti-smoking campaigns, fear of disease can be accentuated by revolting images.[40] These other negative emotions alone can certainly influence behaviour: I refrain from spitting because I feel disgust when I see spittle on the ground, not necessarily because I fear disapproving looks or other social penalties. In other words, my own aversion to behaviours that offend my sensitivities and sense of justice and fairness keep me from adopting them.

This is the case with many information campaigns in the area of public health: the fear of death, disease, decline or shame in AIDS prevention; fear of the shortage of organs in campaigns to promote organ donation; fear of cancer in anti-smoking campaigns; fear of endangering the health of the elderly, the sick and babies in information campaigns during heat waves; fear of dying forests and global warming in environmental protection campaigns;[41] fear of accidents in awareness campaigns for road safety or occupational safety;

---

[37] [Trans.] Nguyen 2002 [note 34], ch. 247, p. 378. See along the same lines Virally, Michel, "La distinction entre textes internationaux de portée juridique et textes internationaux dépourvus de portée juridique (à l'exception des textes émanant des organisations internationales): rapport provisoire," *Annuaire de l'Institut de droit international*, vol. 60, tome I, Paris 1983, p. 233, for whom purely political commitments are sometimes more restrictive than legal commitments.

[38] See Flückiger 2004 [note 6], p. 200s.

[39] Petty et al. 2001 [note 16], p. 217ss; Leventhal, H., "Findings and theory in the study of fear communications," Berkowitz, L. (Ed.), *Advances in experimental social psychology*, vol. 5., 1970, p. 120ss. See also the thesis of Tyler 2006 [note 19] and Killias 2001 [note 21].

[40] See the reproduction of authorized images in schedule 1 of the order of the Département fédéral de l'intérieur concerning combined warnings on tobacco products (RS 817.064).

[41] Some philosophers have inferred from it an "heuristic method" (see the heuristics of fear according to Hans Jonas, *Le principe responsabilité: une éthique pour la civilisation technologique*, Paris 2003 [transl.] [1979]).

fear of disease in prevention campaigns against obesity; fear of the enemy revealing its ferocity in military propaganda,[42] etc.

In fact, these primal fears are not the only emotions that prompt individuals to follow the behaviours advocated by such campaigns. Reality is not as clear-cut. Effectiveness must be understood in combination with other tools, including legal instruments. The effect of anti-smoking or anti-drinking information campaigns is thus reinforced with special taxes on cigarette packets and strong alcohol.[43] Parallel motivations sometimes meet, as with the rate of protected sexual intercourse, a part of which can be attributed directly to AIDS prevention campaigns while another part may stem from competing motives such as a desire to assuage the fear of unwanted pregnancy, other sexually transmitted diseases, or a criminal penalty.

The images used in such campaigns indisputably enhance their emotional impact, as illustrated with anti-smoking and road accident prevention campaigns. Nevertheless, the influence of images in a propaganda context is controversial today.[44]

Finally, more generally, an individual may feel pressure to change from the social group to which he belongs, if he fears conflict with the group. Social psychologists call this attitude *conformity*.[45]

Regret is also at play in obedience mechanisms, especially the anticipated *fear* of *regret* or *remorse* that may arise from behaviour contrary to a recommendation. Economists have even proposed a "theory of regret,"[46] according to which the fear of regret (e.g., for an investor to miss a future increase or sustain a later loss) leads to irrational decisions. Other examples of regret or remorse include that felt after failing to wear a condom for risky sexual intercourse or an earlier failure to sign one's organ donor card when awaiting a transplant.

Legal mechanisms of using fear in soft law instruments

The legal order may provide for legal mechanisms intended to strengthen observance of soft law rules. This does not mean they become legally binding.

---

[42] Géré, François, *La guerre psychologique*, Paris, 1997.

[43] See, for example, l'effect of the alcopop tax on consumption of these beverages (*Feuille fédérale* 2003 1984).

[44] For the origin of theories on the effectiveness of such images, see Tchakhotine, S., *Le viol des foules par la propagande politique*, 1939, new ed., Paris, 1992; Ellul, Jacques, *Propagandes*, Paris, 1990. *Contra:* Gervereau, L., *Histoire du visuel au XXe siècle*, Paris, 2003.

[45] Asch, S. E., "Effects of group pressure upon the modification and distortion of judgment," H. Guetzkow (Ed.) *Groups, leadership and men.* Pittsburgh 1951; Doise, W., Deschamps, J.-C. and Mugny, G., *Psychologie sociale expérimentale*, 2nd Ed., Paris, A. Colin, 1991, chapter 7. On the role of conformity in compliance with soft law in finance, see Roth, Monika, *Soft law: Ordnungsvisionen in flux: eine Standortbestimmung mit Fokus auf compliancerelevante Fragestellungen*, Berne 2006, p. 89.

[46] Loomes, Graham/ Sugden, Robert, "Regret Theory: An Alternative Theory of Rational Choice Under Uncertainty," *The Economic Journal*, vol. 92, no 368, 1982, p. 805ss.

Yet the psychological mechanisms the law evokes can be similar to those of binding instruments. There is a fine line between legal sanctions and the "pressures" that encourage non-mandatory behaviours.[47]

This is the case of the financial pressure behind *incentive taxes.* These involve non-mandatory recommendations, as well as payment of a sum of money. They consist of dual components, imperative and non-imperative. The advocated behaviour is not compulsory, but simply recommended. However, the intended audience may perceive this instrument as a financial penalty very similar to regular legal penalties: individuals who fail to sort their waste must pay a tax.[48] The difference is that in the recommendational variant, the payment of a tax does not have the same symbolic scope as in the legal variant where a fine is imposed. Fear of impoverishment or a desire to not waste money, generated in both hypotheses, are doubled in the second variant of anxiety that is specific to the commencement of a criminal trial symbolically related to feelings of shame and guilt. In practice, however, the difference tends to fade each time small sums are at stake, to the extent that the legal process is then simplified. The penalty is then perceived as "*just a tax*"![49]

The pressure may also be regulatory, decisional or jurisdictional in nature. The targeted audience will obey from fear that the authorities will carry out the threat to adopt regulations, render a decision or institute proceedings. The greater the credibility of executing the threat imminently, the greater the effect.

At one end of the spectrum, this pressure may be very diffuse, political in nature, like non-binding, informal arrangements intended to avoid a *regulatory act.* Examples include the gentlemen's agreements[50] used by the Banque nationale as of the 1930s[51] or the industry-wide agreements[52] used in environmental law since the 1970s.[53] At the opposite end of the spectrum, the pressure may be "juridicised", while remaining a fact, when there is a *Damocles' law.* This type of law institutionalises the part of the agreement binding the State to individuals by legally guaranteeing that the public body will not adopt state regulations in a given area in return for the "voluntary" adoption of autonomous private regulations.[54] Although individuals are not legally obligated to adopt a self-regulated solution, in reality, their behaviour is dictated by fear that the State will enact less favourable regulations. There are

---

47 Timsit, Gérard, "Sur l'engendrement du droit," *Revue de droit public* 1988, p. 49.

48 Flückiger 2004 [note6], p. 249s.

49 Hart, H.L.A., *Le concept de droit,* Brussels 1976, p. 58.

50 Poltier, Etienne, "Les gentlemen's agreements à participation publique," *Revue de droit suisse* I 1987, p. 395.

51 Zufferey, Jean-Baptiste, *La réglementation des systèmes sur les marchés financiers secondaires: contribution dogmatique et comparative à l'élaboration d'un droit suisse des marchés financiers,* Fribourg 1994, p. 318.

52 Pfenninger, Hanspeter, *Rechtliche Aspekte des informellen Verwaltungshandelns,* Fribourg, 1996, p. 25.

53 Examples in Flückiger 2004 [note6], p. 213s.

54 Flückiger, Alexandre, "La loi Damoclès," in *Mélanges en l'honneur de Pierre Moor: théorie du droit, droit administratif, organisation du territoire,* Berne 2005, p. 233ss.

examples of this in environmental law, energy law, film law, and consumer law.[55]

Fear of *a trial* is also an instrument that encourages parties not only to reach a non-binding arrangement, but also to respect it.[56] Effectiveness is greater when the chances of success are high and the feared proceedings are long and costly. The effectiveness of the right of recourse of environmental protection organisations is based on this psychological mechanism. The effectiveness of this right does not depend on its actual use, which is extremely infrequent, but on the concrete threat of the right in the eyes of manufacturers, due to its judicious and successful use.[57]

When a court finds, or may find, that a given public or private recommendation is applied in determining the limits of negligence or carelessness, the fear of *liability for unlawful acts*, or even lawful acts, is a powerful factor in encouraging an individual or an authority to respect a non-binding instrument. Yet the intended audience remains free to choose another behaviour and will only be affected *a posteriori*, that is, if damage occurs.[58]

Shame

Evoking shame and guilt is commonplace in criminal law. Similarly, soft law has the greatest effect in relation to the *fear* of experiencing these emotions. Because damage to a company's reputation may cost it dearly, the corporate image and an impeccable reputation must be maintained to avoid shame, embarrassment or humiliation.[59] The private economy can achieve this through soft law instruments, like the *Swiss Code of Best Practice for Corporate Governance*[60] or the many codes of ethics and good conduct adopted by certain professions (lawyers, physicians, journalists, etc.), including the public administration.[61]

So-called *naming and shaming* processes, which consist of publicly denouncing individuals, organisations or States in order to provoke

---

[55] Flückiger 2005 [previous note], p. 233ss; Flückiger 2004 [note 6], p. 216.

[56] Müller-Graf, Thomas, *Entrechtlichung durch Informalisierung?: ein Beitrag zur Handlungsformen- und zur Rechtsverhältnislehre im Verwaltungsrecht*, Bâle, etc. 2001, p. 174.

[57] Flückiger, Alexandre/Morand, Charles-Albert/Tanquerel, Thierry, *Evaluation du droit de recours des organisations de protection de l'environnement*, Berne, 2000, p. 85ss.

[58] Flückiger 2004 [note 6], p. 254. Sur la responsabilité de l'Etat pour ses activités non décisionnelles, see Schwarzenbach, Hans Rudolf, *Staatshaftung bei verfügungsfreiem Verwaltungshandeln: mit praktischer Anleitung zum Vermeiden/Vermindern dieser wachsenden Risiken (Riskmanagement)*, Berne 2006.

[59] Roth, Monika, *Soft law: Ordnungsvisionen in flux: eine Standortbestimmung mit Fokus auf compliancerelevante Fragestellungen*, Berne 2006, p. 103ss.

[60] Adopted March 25, 2002, by the apex organisation economiesuisse, setting a line of conduct and formulating recommendations. Regarding codes of conducts for multinationals, see Roth, Monika, *Soft law: Ordnungsvisionen in flux: eine Standortbestimmung mit Fokus auf compliance relevante Fragestellungen*, Berne 2006, p. 13ss.

[61] Schindler, Benjamin, "Ethikförderung in der Verwaltung: Modetrend oder Notwendigkeit?," *Schweizerisches Zentralblatt für Staats- und Verwaltungsrecht* 2003, p. 61ss.

indignation, anger, rage or disgust, play on these same motives.[62] The effect of such processes for individuals can be far more painful than recourse to binding legal instruments, as the example of warnings against hazardous products shows: the necessary advertising is clearly more detrimental to the manufacturer than a simple notice of prohibited distribution, since the manufacturer's image is tarnished.[63] Their effectiveness is questioned, especially as regards government stakeholders, as illustrated by the implementation of the open method of coordination in European law (non-compulsory method of coordinating public policy).[64]

Information campaigns that play on the fear of deadly disease or accidents often provoke shame or guilt in their targeted audience, as do organ donation promotions that make non-donors feel guilty for not wanting to save the lives of others.

Joy

Joy and other resulting positive emotions like pride, self-esteem, desire and pleasure are emotions that can change the behaviour of individuals without forcing them to do so.

This is the intent of all redistributive economic instruments that play on the pleasure of winning money and the desire for profit. Thus, when a recommendation is supported by state *funding*, the economic incentive strengthens the recommendation's appreciative nature commensurate with the sum at stake.

By awarding prizes and distinctions to reward exemplary attitude (see, for example, the order on the Prix du cinéma suisse),[65] authorities are indirectly recommending the adoption of a specific behaviour. This kind of

---

[62] Stein, Jana von, "'Naming and Shaming" in the United Nations Commission on Human Rights: When and How Does it Matter?" *Paper presented at the annual meeting of the International Studies Association 48th Annual Convention* (published on www.allacademic.com/meta/p179882_index.html). The same process is used to implement the open method of coordination (OMC) in European law (Collignon, Stefan et al., "La Stratégie de Lisbonne et la méthode ouverte de coordination: 12 recommandations pour une stratégie à plusieurs niveaux plus efficace," *Policy paper* no 12, 2006, p. 10 [www.notre-europe.eu – rubrique travaux]).

[63] Kautz, Steffen, *Absprachen im Verwaltungsrecht: Zulässigkeit, Grenzen und Folgen*, Berlin 2002, p. 86, with ref. cit. to German doctrine. See also *ibidem*, p. 156 et 281s; Tschannen, Pierre, "Amtliche Warnungen und Empfehlungen," *Revue de droit suisse* II 1999, p. 432; Nützi, Patrick, *Rechtsfragen verhaltenslenkender staatlicher Information: Strukturen, Zulässigkeit, Haftung: illustriert an den Beispielen AIDS und Listeriose*, Berne 1995, p. 181ss

[64] Implementation of the open method of coordination in European law is based on a peer pressure system that [Trans.] *"has not functioned correctly, partly due to the fact that members do not wish to 'name and shame' their peers. Stakeholders are not very motivated to engage in this type of process: the various members fear they will make enemies and reap the negative consequences in other political areas where they show little progress."* (Collignon 2006 [note 62], p. 10).

[65] RS 443.116.

recommendation plays on the recipient's joy, pride, pleasure, and even the desire, envy or jealousy that such an award may arouse in others.

Information campaigns may also aim to excite feelings of joy and happiness: the pleasure of eating healthily to counter obesity; the joy of watching a young athlete with a heart transplant promote organ donation; the magic of a stroll in the shaded woods to prevent the death of forests.

Finally, we can revisit the phenomenon of social conformity discussed in the section on fear. Conformity motivated by complacency—in which an individual who fears conflict with the group prefers the pleasure of peace—must be distinguished from conformity motivated by identification. The latter is based not on fear but on joy, pride or desire for recognition when the individual conforms in order to establish his or her place in the group and maintain positive relations with it in the hope of eventually obtaining prestige and visibility.[66]

Finally, it should be noted that pleasure is an ambiguous emotion in this context, since it is often a factor opposed to the implementation of soft law rules. The individual is constantly required to balance the fears raised by an anti-smoking or AIDS prevention campaign with the pleasure of smoking or lovemaking without a condom.

Surprise

Soft law presents an interesting characteristic in this regard in comparison with hard law, in that the former often has an experimental function to test a potential future rule of law.[67] This allows the State to study the reaction of the intended audience and either withdraw the tested measures or make them permanent, depending on the observed impact. Soft law thus accustoms citizens, or gradually acclimatizes them, to a new regime by avoiding any surprise on the day it evolves into hard law (smoking is first discouraged, then prohibited in public places; helmets and seatbelts are first encouraged, then imposed; etc.). We find a variant of this process when non-imperative planning progressively creates accomplished facts that become increasingly difficult to counter over time.[68] Certain manipulation techniques, like the door-in-the-face technique or deceit, knowingly make use of the surprise effect.

---

[66] Baggio, Stéphanie, *Psychologie sociale,* Brussels 2006, p. 22; Doise, W., Deschamps, J.-C. and Mugny, G., *Psychologie sociale expérimentale,* 2nd Ed., Paris, A. Colin, 1991, chapter 7.

[67] See Abi-Saab, Georges, "Cours général de droit international public," *Recueil des cours de l'Académie de droit international,* t. 207, 1997, p. 207, 210. There is a similar phenomenon in hard law: legislative experimentation (Flückiger, Alexandre, "Voter, élire et signer par Internet: le droit expérimental à l'épreuve de la sécurité," in Journées 2002 d'informatique juridique, Berne 2003, p. 107ss [ref. cit.]). In German law, see Maass, Volker, *Experimentierklauseln für die Verwaltung und ihre verfassungsrechtlichen Grenzen: zugleich ein Beitrag zu § 7a BerlHG,* Berlin 2001).

[68] Regarding such effects in planning, see Flückiger, Alexandre, *Le régime juridique des plans: l'exemple du plan de gestion des déchets,* Berne, 1996, p. 117ss (ref. cit.).

Soft law creates a gradual habituation that foils any subsequent surprise and any potential rejection that may result from surprises.

Empathy

Empathy is the psychological mechanism through which an individual understands another's feelings and emotions, without feeling them himself.[69] More specifically, it is the ability to feel emotions in general rather an emotion per se.

Without doubt, empathy is indispensable to the success of non-legal dispute resolution processes like mediation.[70] It is also at play, with compassion, sympathy or pity, in the use of biographic stories that facilitate emotional expression by stirring the reader, thereby encouraging him to act in a specific way. This technique is currently used in promotion campaigns for organ donations in which the testimonies of transplant recipients add a human, palpable aspect to the suffering of those awaiting organs, giving an emotional face to the shortage of organ donors.[71] In terms of the relationship between medical staff and the donor's family, the rate of consent is higher when doctors show empathy and lower when they behave coldly.[72]

Manipulation techniques

Instead of creating public awareness with emotional arguments that modify behaviour without the rule of law, social psychologists have shown that certain techniques are effective in manipulating individuals without their knowledge and in making them choose to act in ways they otherwise would not.

These techniques include commitment theories, strategic use of cognitive dissonance, and context effects (contrast and compromise).

Commitment theories

Commitment theories show an efficacy, some say, that is potentially greater than awareness and information strategies.[73]

---

69 Davis, M. H., "Empathy," Stets, J. E./ Turner, J. H. (Ed.), *Handbook of the Sociology of Emotions*, New York 2006, p. 443ss; Deonna, Julien, "The Structure of Empathy," *Journal of Moral Philosophy* 4.1, April 2007.

70 Guy-Ecabert, Christine, *Procédure administrative et médiation: inscription d'un modèle procédural dans un contexte en mutation*, Zurich etc. 2002, p. 255.

71 Hammer, Raphaël, "Le traitement médiatique de la pénurie et du don d'organes: variations discursives et normatives dans la presse francophone suisse," contribution to a collective work (Thiel, M.-J., Ed.), Presses Universitaires de Strasbourg (not yet published).

72 See the study by Annemarie Kesselring, cited in "L'art de parler du don d'organes avec les proches," *Fonds National suisse - Horizons*, June 2005, p. 19s.

73 See the compared effectiveness of awareness, persuasion and commitment strategies in AIDS prevention as concerns condom use (Joule, Robert-Vincent;

Such practices do not make direct use of individual emotions, but condition emotions at the unconscious level, particularly through deceit, deception and surprise. Contrary to hard law but like soft law, the subject is placed in a situation that gives him a feeling of free choice. This perception of freedom is a determining factor in the success of manipulation techniques. The individual *must* believe he is making a free, informed decision without being influenced, despite behaving differently than he would have without the unseen manipulation. Commitment theories are the basis for such processes.[74] The principle is that the subject's conduct is determined by one or more earlier behaviours that are elicited without his knowledge. Subjects become caught up in the process, one that is increasingly difficult to halt as time advances.[75] Several methods can be used:

- The foot-in-the-door technique, which consists of making an initial trivial request before the main request. The trivial request involves little cost and is not necessarily related to the main request (for example, asking the time); the subject is then asked to perform the desired action, which he likely would have refused had it not been preceded by the initial request.[76]
- The door-in-the-face technique, which on the contrary consists of making an initial excessive, though not abusive, request before the main request in order to obtain less; in fact, the "less" is exactly what the requestor wants. The effect of calming surprise gives the subject an illusion of gain that makes him statistically more likely to consent.[77]
- Priming, which consists of getting an individual to agree to an action, the true cost of which is initially concealed and revealed fully only at a later time.[78]
- Deception, a variant of priming, in which the requestor asks the subject to perform an attractive behaviour the requestor knows to be impossible, then informs him of that fact and proposes an alternative that is more costly and that the requestor initially had in mind.[79]

In order to achieve the desired effect, the individual must believe himself to be free. Empirical research in social psychology has shown that explicitly telling someone they are free to choose significantly increases the rate of a proposal's acceptance. The "sense of freedom" thus becomes an elegant manipulation technique in itself.[80] Soft law is based on exactly this type of reaction because it is defined as not legally *mandatory*. Equally relevant is the concept of *psychological reactance*, in which individuals, who believe their

---

Beauvois, Jean-Léon, *La soumission librement consentie: comment amener les gens à faire librement ce qu'ils doivent faire?* 5th Ed., Paris 2006, p. 137ss).

[74] C.A. Kiesler, *The Psychology of Commitment*, New York, 1971

[75] Baggio, Stéphanie, *Psychologie sociale*, Brussels 2006, p. 28.

[76] Joule, Robert-Vincent; Beauvois, Jean-Léon, *Petit traité de manipulation à l'usage des honnêtes gens*, Grenoble 2002, p. 97ss.

[77] Joule/Beauvois 2002 [note 76], p. 117ss

[78] Joule/Beauvois 2002 [note 76], p. 53ss.

[79] Joule/Beauvois 2002 [note 76], p. 68ss.

[80] Joule/Beauvois 2002 [note 76], p. 160.

behavioural freedom is being diminished, manage to resist attempts at persuasion.[81]

These techniques tend to be used to support information and persuasion campaigns. They have been tested successfully in the area of energy efficiency in encouraging people to turn lights off when no longer needed and to turn down heating instead of opening windows when they are hot,[82] as well as in the area of occupational health and safety to encourage workers to wear hearing protectors in noisy environments, [83] in the area of AIDS prevention to encourage use of condoms[84] and undergo testing,[85] and to promote organ donation.[86]

The ethics of authorities using such techniques is highly debatable, particularly those techniques based on deceit and deception, since they may be contrary to the constitutional principles of good faith and proportionality.

Strategic use of cognitive dissonance (effect of the duty to state reasons)

According to the cognitive dissonance theory, an individual feels uncomfortable when faced with contradictory "cognitions," where cognition refers to a person's knowledge of self, behaviour and environment.[87] This state of unpleasant tension motivates the individual to reduce dissonance in order to achieve cognitive balance (or consonance).

Some methods of reducing cognitive dissonance have been used strategically to modify individuals' behaviour. This is the case when a person is asked to *explain* a solution he does not support, in which case he tempers his final position in an effort to harmonize his behaviour with his ideas.[88]

Context effects (contrast and compromise effects)

Context effects (contrast and compromise effects) introduce biases into the decision-making process. These effects have been used in marketing since its inception[89] and have been tested recently in the legal decision process.[90]

---

[81] Baggio [note 66], p. 66ss.

[82] Joule/Beauvois 2006 [note 73], p. 95ss.

[83] Joule/Beauvois 2006 [note 73], p. 110ss.

[84] Joule/Beauvois 2006 [note 73], p. 127ss.

[85] Joule/Beauvois 2006 [note 73], p. 142ss.

[86] Eyssartier, Chloé, Du don de sang au don d'organes: une recherche appliquée, Université d'Aix-Marseille (http://slhs.univ-fcomte.fr / rech/psycho /colloque/social/resumes.htm#e).

[87] Festinger, Léon, A Theory of Cognitive Dissonance, Evanston [etc.] 1957, p. 9.

[88] Baggio [note 66], p. 62ss.

[89] Huber, J./ Payne, J.W./ Puto, C., "Adding asymmetrically dominated alternatives: Violations of regularity and the similarity hypothesis," *Journal of Consumer Research*, 1982, 9, p. 90ss; Simonson, "Choice Based on Reason: The Case of Attraction and Compromise Effects," *Journal of Consumer Research*, 1989, 16, p. 158ss.

[90] Schweizer, Mark, „Kontrast- und Kompromisseffekt im Recht am Beispiel der lebenslänglichen Verwahrung," *ZStrR* 4/2005, p. 438ss; Kelman, M./ Rottenstreich, Y./

With the *contrast effect*, the same option is assessed more positively in the presence of similar, less favourable alternatives than in the absence of such choices.[91] This effect exists optically with the Ebbinghaus Illusion: a circle of the same diameter is perceived as being smaller when surrounded by larger circles.

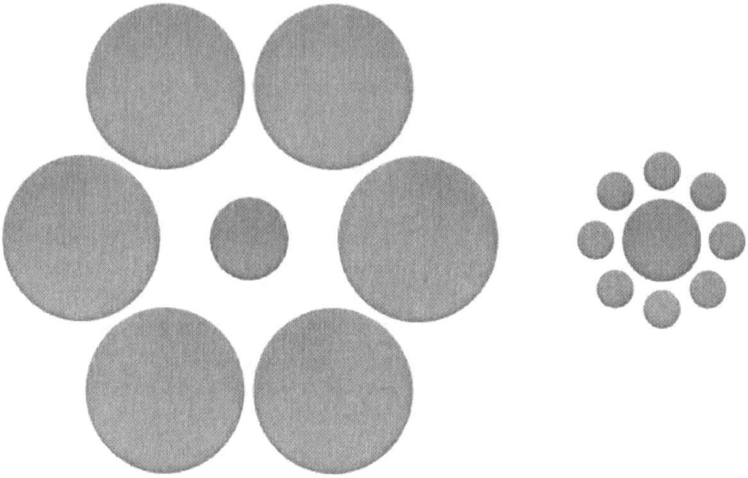

The *compromise effect* results from the observation that the same option is assessed more favourably when seen as the middle solution in a group of alternatives than when presented as an extreme.[92]

A first American experiment showed that, based on the same established facts, the probability of being found guilty of murder rose from 38% to 55% when capital murder is among the choice of offences.[93] This compromise effect means that the accused risks receiving a higher sentence when the law provides for capital murder, even if he is not found guilty of that offence.[94] The experiment was repeated with similar results with 230 civil and criminal judges in the cantons of Bâle, Berne and Graubünden. Their rulings based on the same established facts were compared depending on whether life imprisonment was among the available criminal penalties.[95] Introducing an extreme option among the range of potential solutions increases the proportion in favour of the median solution.[96]

Tversky, A., "Context-dependence in legal decision making," in Sunstein, Cass, *Behavioral Law and Economics*, Cambridge [etc.] 2000, p. 61ss;

91 Kelman et al. 2000 [note 90], p. 61.

92 Kelman et al. 2000 [note 90], p. 61; Simonson 1989 [note 89].

93 Kelman et al. 2000 [note 90], p. 67.

94 Schweizer 2005 [note 90], ch. V, lit. A.

95 Schweizer 2005 [note 90], ch. VI.

96 Schweizer 2005 [note 90], ch. VI, lit. C.

These conclusions can be transposed to the area of soft law. This type of reaction is counted on with Switzerland's new organ donor card, which offers three options:[97] authorization for removal of all organs, non-authorization and, as the intermediate alternative, selective donation with boxes to check for various organs (heart, lungs, liver, kidneys, small intestine, pancreas, cornea, skin and other tissues and cells). Although not confirmed by a study, one can reasonably hypothesize that the presence of an intermediate option will be considered more favourably.

Conclusion

States have long been aware that conventional legal instruments are occasionally ineffective in piloting public policy. Soft power[98] is rediscovered, thematised and used with sometimes startling effectiveness, particularly in synergy with conventional legal means. Soft law has an even greater impact because its persuasive strategies involve skilful use of emotions, and even manipulation techniques.

The question is this: To what degree can authorities use emotions to increase the rate of compliance with soft law instruments, knowing that, in a constitutional state, they are less democratically legitimate than legislative and regulatory means? As such, the State cannot employ just any manipulation method to develop transplant medicine. However, as we see in road safety communication campaigns, it can certainly bank on the heuristics of fear by showing an hypothetical catastrophe leading to an accident, in order to make it more probable in the eyes of the targeted audience.[99]

Soft law's effects, as measured by the emotions they evoke, show that non-legally binding instruments can compel obedience. An absence of legal effects in the conventional sense would therefore not exempt them from the adoption of an adapted legitimation and control system, like that which has applied to the rules of hard law in constitutional states for a long time. Consequently, soft law instruments should be subject—relatively speaking and based on their effects, including emotional effects—to the material principles of the constitutional state,[100] such as legality, action in the public interest, good faith and proportionality, the requirement of fair and non-discriminatory treatment, the prohibition of arbitrary action, as well as formal rules like the definition of specially adapted procedural guarantees like recourse to mediation or, in certain cases, legal processes.[101] Public consultation and participation mechanisms should also be developed when adopting soft law rules, like citizen forums and consensus conferences, so as to establish a true "administrative

---

97 See www.swisstransplant.ch

98 Nye, Joseph, *Bound to Lead: The Changing Nature of American Power*, New York 1990.

99 Joule/Beauvois 2006 [note 73], p. 202.

100 In detail on this proposal, see Flückiger 2004 [note 6], p. 262ss.

101 Flückiger 2004 [note 6], p. 270ss.

democracy."[102] Greater legitimacy for such instruments would make them more effective, as research in social psychology has shown.[103]

This conclusion in no way detracts from the legitimacy of soft law's use of emotions, or even certain non-problematic, well targeted manipulation techniques. It simply requests a legal framework suited to the specificities of non-binding state instruments in order to avoid circumventing the principles of a constitutional state. Otherwise, soft law's very effectiveness would simply be challenged, given the importance and scope of its emotional effects.

102 Flückiger 2004 [note 6], p. 275ss

103 See the work of Tyler 2006 [note 19] regarding compliance with law, but whose conclusions may be transposed to soft law in our opinion.

CHAPTER 3

The Impact of Direct Democracy on Public Policies: a Historical Perspective

WOLF LINDER

Introduction

Political scientists analysing direct democracy have been preoccupied with the citizens' political behaviour, their motivation for participation, their values and interests, the shaping of the voters preferences in the campaigns by political parties and other factors that determine the outcomes of the direct participation process. Thus, the mainstream of direct democracy research is, theoretically and methodologically, much in line with the research on electoral behaviour. Less attention, however, has been paid to the impacts of citizen's direct participation on public policies. This question is relevant for two reasons. First, in the course of the development of the Swiss polity from 1848 to our days, the institutions of direct democracy have been gradually opened to new categories of parliamentary decisions, and thresholds of launching referenda became lower. Thus, one might expect that more and more decisions of parliament have to be ratified by the people before they can be enacted. Indeed, in the end of the 19th century, we find hardly more than one popular vote per year, while today, the people have almost ten opportunities to say their "Yes" or "No" to constitutional amendments or laws. Second, we observe a tremendous secular change of federal policies. In the 19th century, the competencies of the Federation were limited to an almost "minimal state", and the fathers of the Swiss constitution intended that federal policies should be implemented by the cantons. Until World War II, federal competencies were extended only slowly. This changed completely in the second half of the 20th century, when federal responsibilities were extended or developed in all fields-economic, social, infrastructural, and environmental regulations and policies as well. From a "minimal state", the Swiss Federation has become a modernized interventionist State like others. Yet, despite this development, direct democracy is used as ever and still is functioning.

These secular trends—the continuous opening of parliamentary decisions to direct participation of the people, and the growing importance of federal policies—give raise to several questions which are addressed in this article:

- How did the relationship between direct democracy and federal policies evolve over time? Did the opening of direct participation lead to a higher

impact of direct democracy, in which proportionally more and more policies are the subject of referenda challenges?
- Did the chances of political authorities for getting approval of their policies grow or diminish with the development of the modern regulatory state?
- Did the development of power-sharing mechanisms or the evolution of the classical cleavages have a persistent effect on the success of federal authorities in realizing their policies in the popular vote, and how can we explain stability and change in the success of the federal authorities to get majorities for their policies?

Before I try to answer these questions, I briefly present the function of direct democracy devices, and their impact on the evolution of public policies in the light of political science literature.

The function of direct democracy devices in the political process

From the rich literature of political science (Trechsel, 2006; Kriesi, 2005; Hug & Papadopoulos, 2004; Linder, 2005, 2006), we can sum up some findings and theoretical insights that explain not only the function of direct democracy devices, but also their indirect influence in the pre-parliamentary and parliamentary decision-making.

First, the referendum is an instrument of the opposition, and the success of the opposition is a formal veto, a negative decision, which means that a public policy proposed by the government and the parliament is not taking place. Second, if the people (and the Cantons) approve a project, it is mainly a constitutional amendment or a formal law, which leaves many things open with regard to the implementation. On the federal level, the referendum is open mainly to decisions on an abstract level and less to the process of implementation. This marks an important difference from direct democracy in the cantons and the communes, where people can vote on concrete projects like the construction of roads or other infrastructural projects[1]. Third, the referendum, analytically, is a veto point in the sense of Hug and Tsebelis (2002), which means that the political process is characterized by a status-quo bias: it restricts the political elite's aspirations for innovation and leads to solutions close to the status quo ante. Fourth, the veto points of direct democracy have led to the institutionalisation of political power sharing. Reducing the risks of direct democracy was a strong incentive for co-operation

[1] The difference is relative because the popular initiative opens ways to concrete issues. Formally limited to constitutional amendments, the popular initiative is in practice open to concrete decisions, for instance on the protection of natural sites, on a work-free national holiday, or on speed limits on national highways. Moreover, the referendum on international treaties can apply to concrete decisions like membership of the UN.

of the political parties in an over-sized coalition and has led to the Swiss "concordance". Together with the veto point of federalism, this incentive was so strong that government and parliamentary factions have maintained the "grand coalition" for almost 50 years without any common political program amongst the four ruling political parties. Fifth, the development of the "pre-parliamentary arena", giving vested interests a forum for bargaining and compromise, has become an important element of the political process. It contributes to pareto-optimal decisions in which theoretically no actor capable of launching a referendum is hurt in his status-quo interests. Under these conditions, the referendum is partially converted from a people's right to a group-right. Indeed, 93 percent of all laws pass without a referendum. Sixth, while the referendum has a braking effect on political decisions, the popular initiative has the opposite function: it can stimulate reform. Nevertheless its direct success is rare. Only about ten percent of the people's propositions for constitution amendments are accepted.

General impacts of direct democracy on public policies

From the functions mentioned above, literature proposes some general impacts on the outcomes of policies which are attributed to the referendum and the popular initiative:

- The constitutional referendum has had a braking effect on centralization. As any new competency of the federation, according to article 3 of the Constitution, has to pass the high hurdle of the double majority of the people and the cantons, direct democracy slowed down the development of federal public policies. The cantons, eager to defend their autonomy, use their own competencies to the fullest before federal solutions become feasible. Therefore, federal policies are often limited to financial grants or a general framework while implementation rests within the hands of the Cantons. Direct democracy has led to a bottom-up development of federal policies and the preference for subsidiarity let successfully realize.
- These general observations are best illustrated with the example of fiscal policies. For a long time, direct income tax was the privilege of the Cantons, and a federal income tax could be introduced only on a temporary base when, in the years before World War II, federal authorities urgently needed resources for military defence. The Swiss federal government may be one of the few that is not allowed to collect income taxes from its inhabitants on a permanent basis. As for consumer taxes, a traditional prerogative of the central government, we observe them to be lower than in EU countries.
- Comparative analysis shows that in many respects, the entire Swiss public sector is relatively slim, consuming less of the national revenue than in other OECD countries but performing well in the quality of public services and in market regulation. As the "braking effect" of the referendum functions at all federal levels, these characteristics are often attributed to the ef-

fect of direct democracy. Economists, particularly, have become enthusiasts of direct democracy as a device for a liberal but effective state: liberal because state consumption is low, effective because public goods correspond to the people's preferences and because in their view, direct democracy makes "people happier" (Frey & Stutzer, 2000, Kirchgässner et al., 1999).

- While the long term braking effect of the referendum is well known, the mobilising effects of the popular initiative are much more diverse for several reasons. As a first point, the popular initiative can have main intentions other than direct influence on federal policies. Political parties, for instance, use the popular initiative for electoral success, while grass-root movements try to mobilize new tendencies or changes of political awareness. For the latter, the 1989 initiative on the abolition of the Swiss army is a good example. Their protagonists were fully aware that their proposition would not find a majority in the popular vote but successful intended, to overcome the political taboo of Swiss armed neutrality. Secondly, as already mentioned, about 90 percent of all initiatives do not get the double majority of the people and the Cantons. In the best case, then, they have an indirect success if the parliament later takes up some of their ideas in subsequent legislation. The impact of accepted popular initiatives varies to a great deal. While some of them - such as the introduction of the proportional voting system (1918), gender equality (1981) or Swiss membership in the UN (2002) - belong to the most important political decisions and were directly implemented, others had more difficulties. The protection of natural moor sites (1987), for instance, was hardly implemented, which fits into the larger pattern of implementation gaps in land-use and environmental policies, as shown by Knoepfel et al. (1996). Thus, contrary to the referendum, the effect of the popular initiative on federal policies is rare, punctual, diverse or even uncertain.

Relations between direct democracy and federal policies: a long-term perspective

As shown in section 2, direct democracy is not an isolated device but closely linked with other elements of the decision-making process, notably parliamentary and executive power sharing and federalism. Thus, one should be prudent in "explaining" the outcomes of public policies by the single effect of direct participation. The objective of this study, therefore, is more modest: In an explorative way, it looks for the long-term relations between direct democracy and public policy. In this perspective, federal policies and direct democracy have two things in common: evolution and growth. As for the institutional development of direct democracy, we notice a steady extension of the people's rights. In 1848, the Federal Constitution allowed only for constitutional amendments. The system was extended in 1874 with the introduction of the optional referendum for laws (1874), with the popular initiative (1891) and the referendum for international treaties (1921). In 1977, six years after the introduction of women's suffrage, the number of signatures required for the optional referendum was raised from 30 to 50,000, and for the popular initiative from 50 to 100,000 in order to compensate for the doubled electorate. The same year brought a first extension of direct democracy in foreign policy, and in 2003, a second reform opened the optional referendum for all substantial international treaties. Finally, in the same reform of 2003, the use of the popular initiative was extended, but in an unhappy way. The procedure is too complicated, has never been used and will probably be abolished one day.

As to federal policies, one could distinguish, in a rather approximate way, two entirely different periods (Linder, 1983).

In the first period, the seventy years from 1875 to the end of World War II, which I define as "Period I", the Federation remains almost restricted to a minimal state. National consensus is difficult, and so was the extension of the few competencies of 1848, which were the army, postal services, and money. The nationalisation of railroads is controversial in the last decades of the 19th century, as well as the creation of a national bank. The unification of civil law succeeds before World War I, and the federal penal law is introduced in 1938. In economic policy, activities of the federation are almost restricted to farmers who succeed in getting protection through subsidies, trade regulations and tolls. Social policy is limited to some regulations on the labour market and health insurance, while a general pension regime is not implemented.

The second period after World War II, "Period II", is entirely different. It is characterized by a permanent extension of federal policies in almost all fields. Social policy starts in 1947 with the pension scheme, then with social insurance for unemployment and invalidity, and public health. Economic growth requires the continuous modernization of national infrastructure (roads, electricity, air traffic, public transport and communication), regional policies, and a high commitment of the federation to the university system and to their research. Market regulation and other economic policy, traditionally protecting particular industries like agriculture and watches, undergoes two periods of liberalization, the first in the 1950s, the second in the globalization process starting in the1990s. Immigration (20 percent of the residents in Switzerland are of foreign origin), land use planning, or environmental policies have become important fields of regulation, while the proportion of national defence in the federal budget is declining.

The proposed distinction between "Period I and II" fits well into the picture of a historical sequence of different "institutional resource regimes" drawn by Peter Knoepfel et al (2001): In a first phase, land use or the protection of natural resources like forests and water was limited to regulations of private property, mainly on the base of the code of civil law. After World War II, in a second phase, we see a continuous development of sectoral policies, based on public law and with national programs to be implemented at the different federal levels.

The secular trends of direct democracy and federal policy development lead me to two hypotheses. The first: With the opening of more categories of parliamentary decisions to direct participation, the impact of referenda on public policy is increasing. The second: With the modernisation of the state, the veto effect of the referendum becomes stronger.

The theoretical reasoning for the hypotheses is simple. Access to the optional referendum has not only been widened but "technical" hurdles to collect the necessary signatures became lower. With the lapse of time, the percentage of voters required to call the referendum becomes lower as the population grows. More important: With the modernization of the State, public policies become more complex, cost more, and have re-distributional effects with more groups of net-winners and –losers. Tax resistance may increase, the result of the vote becomes less predictable. For these and further reasons, getting majorities in popular votations, becomes more difficult.

In the following, I test these hypotheses with data of 13 decades from 1875-2005. They include the number of Constitutional Amendments and of Laws passed by the Federal Chambers, which are taken as indicators for the long-term development of federal policies. The comparison between all legislative projects and those challenged by the optional referendum can be taken as an indicator of the impact of direct democracy on regulatory policies. In addition, I compare direct democracy success and failure of the federal authorities for all decades. Popular initiatives, despite their high absolute number, are not taken into account because their success, with only about 10 percent, is low and their impact on policies uncertain.

As every new competency of the Federation needs a Constitutional base, the number of constitutional or obligatory referenda is a valid indicator for the development of federal competencies, while the number of laws proposed by parliament indicates the extent of regulatory policies. Columns (1) and (4) of Table 1 give prove of an entirely different central state before and after World War II. In the first seven decades of the Federation (Period I), the number of constitutional amendment is lower than ten, the number of parliamentary bills does not exceed one hundred per decade, and the low level of state regulation is rather constant. This contrasts sharply with Period II after World War II.

In the decade of 1945-1954, the number of constitutional amendments as well as of parliamentary laws triples, and we see a constant growth of parliament's law production since then. Is this a sign of a centralisation of the Swiss federal system or of a late development for the regulatory state? A direct comparison between the Federation and the Canton of Vaud 1947-82 indicates that cantonal regulatory activities even exceed the growth of federal legislation (Linder, 1985). Moreover, the proportion of personnel, fiscal revenue and expenses between the communes, the cantons and the federation is rather constant for the last 60 years. I would therefore reject the centralisation hypothesis and, instead think of a general growth of the interventionist and regulatory state at all federal levels.

Decade	Proposed Constitutional Amendments (Subject to Obligatory Referendum)			Proposed Laws (Subject to Optional Referendum)				
	Number of Amendments (= Number of Votes)	Amendments Accepted by the people and the Cantons	Percent Accepted	Number of all Laws proposed	Number of referenda Challenges	Percent of all laws	Laws Accepted by the people	Percent accepted
	(1)	(2)	(3)	(4)	(5)	(6)	(7)	(8)
Period I								
1875-1884	3	1	33	83	12	15	2	17
1885-1894	6	5	87	80	6	8	3	50
1895-1904	9	6	67	64	8	13	3	38
1905-1914	3	3	100	53	3	6	3	100
1915-1924	8	7	86	72	5	7	1	20
1925-1934	9	7	78	88	8	9	2	25
1935-1944	4	3	75	60	5	8	3	60
Total Period I	42	32	76.1	500	47	9.4	17	36.1
Period II								
1945-1954	12	7	58	186	13	7	4	31
1955-1964	21	16	76	208	8	4	5	63
1965-1974	26	20	77	242	7	3	3	43
1975-1984	36	26	72	278	18	6	11	61
1985-1994	21	16	76	349	31	9	21	68
1995-2004	21	15	71	486	30	6	18	60
Total Period II	137	100	72.9	1749	107	6.1	62	57.9

Table 1 Development of constitutional and regulatory referenda, success and failure of the Federal Authorities, and regulatory activities of the Parliament 1875-2004.

Let us consider now the first hypothesis, claiming growing impact of direct democracy over time. Constitutional amendments are always a co-decision of parliament, the cantons and the people. Thus, their growing number after World War II alone cannot be taken as a valid indicator for a higher impact of direct democracy. Some constitutional lawyers insist, however, that political practice has become more severe in the requirement for a constitutional base for new competencies of the Federation. This practice may partly be the cause of the growing number of constitutional amendments. In this sense, one could speak of a greater influence of the people (and the cantons) on constitutional policies in Period II. The hypothesis is not confirmed, however, on the level of regulatory policies. The number of laws decided by parliament, as already mentioned, is constantly low in Period I but after World War II illustrates steady growth of federal regulations and policies. (Column (4)). The number of the optional referenda remains relatively low up to 1974 and then grows in the last three decades (Column (5)). The decisive indicator for the impact of the people now is the proportion of laws decided by the parliament and the referenda challenges leading to a popular vote. As we see from Column (6), the proportion of referenda challenges of all bills of parliament is decreasing in the long run (column (6)): Less than 7 percent of all laws are challenged by a vote in the second period after World War II, while from 1875 to 1944, more than 9 percent of the parliamentary bills were attacked by optional referenda. The result is against theoretical expectations. The weapon of the optional referendum has never again regained the force it had in the first decades after its introduction, when a fierce opposition of the Conservatives successfully challenged the policy of the majority Radicals.

For our second hypothesis, lower success of the authorities with growing regulation, we notice no substantial change for constitutional policies between Period I and II: 76 percent of all constitutional amendments are accepted before World War II, 73 percent in the time after. For regulatory policies in optional referenda, though, we find a rising acceptance of parliamentary law. In period II, 62 of the 107 projects, corresponding to 58 percent of all referenda campaigns, end with a victory of the government coalition, while before World War II, the authorities were successful only in 17 of the 47 referenda, which corresponds to a rate of 36 percent. Period II begins with a decade of strong opposition, indicating that the modernisation of the State had a difficult start. After that, Period II is characterised by high stability: we observe a stable acceptance of about 75 percent for the many new competencies of the central state, and in four of five decades, the people accept more than 60 percent of the parliaments' regulatory policies. This is astonishing, the more as Period II can be characterised by many ups and downs of the economy, by fundamental changes between an "interventionist" and a "neo-liberal" strand, the rise of two of the four classical cleavages (urban against rural, and capital against labour), and by the development of two new cleavages as well (traditional closure against modernist openness, and materialist against post-materialist values) (Hug & Sciarini, 2002; Linder et al., 2008).

As a result, we partly reject both hypotheses: The modernisation of the federal state, which started after 1945, was accompanied by a considerable growth of the numbers of referenda. But contrary to theoretical expectations, modernisation and the development of the regulatory state did not mobilize the people more against the federal authorities: compared with the first period of the "small state" before World War II, the proportion of laws going to a vote is lower. However, as the parliament links the development of new policies more often with constitutional amendments, the people and the cantons have more chances of direct participation in the basic development of constitutional policies. Second, and most important: the people's veto power does not grow stronger. Today, the people follow their elites more than in earlier times.

Explaining stability and change

The long-term stability of direct democracy- in terms of the stable or even diminishing proportion of regulatory policies challenged by referenda, and of the rising success of the federal authorities in the popular vote- is in all an astonishing fact. Neither societal change, economic development nor the modernisation of the state nor the opening of the rules for direct participation[2] have had a sustainable impact on the dialogue between the people and the political elite.

Yet, in the medium term, we observe considerable differences of success in optional referenda: In the four decades 1875-84, 1915-24, 1925-34, 1945-54 oppositions have been very strong, where the authorities were defeated by the people in at least two cases out of three. This contrasts with "normal" decades, in which the opposition has less than a 50 percent chance to win. While success in a single votation depends on the issues, on the coalition of the political parties and the campaign (Hug & Papadopoulos, 2004; Kriesi, 2005) and probably on the economic conjuncture (Schneider et al., 1981), we can ask if institutional changes or long term political changes have had an influence on the oscillating success of federal policies.

This leads us first to the question of an eventual impact of the mechanisms of political power sharing. According to Lijphart (1999), power sharing leads to political integration, and for Swiss politics, the reduction of referenda risks has been one of the strongest motives for power sharing. The first and the last steps in the development of power sharing seem to be particularly important ones. First, in the late 19th century, with the participation of a Conservative in the Federal Council, the majority politics of the ruling Radicals came to an end. Last, the "magic formula", practiced since 1959, brought comprehensive power sharing in the Swiss government amongst the four historical parties through proportional representation according to their voting power. Thus, we could expect that at least these two steps of political integration would have had a positive impact on the acceptance of federal policies.

At first glance, our data are in line with the hypothesis. In the decades after the integration of the Catholics, the success rate of federal policies proposed by the parliament is drastically growing in popular votes. To a less degree, we can observe the same effect after the full integration of the Socialists after 1959. And, in both cases, these political forces were integrated after a period of high opposition in popular votes against federal policies, which may have promoted ideas of co-optation and of integration. But, in the light of historical in-depth studies, things seem to be more complicated. As shown by Bolliger and Zürcher (2004), the integration of the political elite was appreciated only by a part of the Catholic people, and in the years after, a number of projects continued to be defeated in popular votes because of the Conservatives. Similarly, socialists continued to challenge federal policies after 1959 almost as much as before their proportional representation in the Federal Council. Finally, the integration effect of full power sharing is fading away. While in the first decade of the "magic formula", the four governmental

[2] The irrelevance of the change of rules is less of an enigma: The opening of referenda against international treaties, introduced in 1921, extended in 1977 and 2003, was institutionally important but the cases of foreign policy referenda are rare. One can also exclude influences from the introduction of women's suffrage (1971) because the number of signatures required to hand in referenda or popular initiatives was raised from 30,000 to 50,000 (optional referenda) and from 50,000 to 100,000 (initiatives) in 1977, thus practically compensating for the increase in the electorate.

parties unanimously defended four of five projects of the Federal Chambers, at least one partner of the governmental coalition makes opposition in four of five cases (Linder et al., 2008). This has to do with the fact that the Peoples Party, besides the Socialists, has been using the opposition role more and more. Thus, sustainability of political integration through governmental co-optation is all but certain. But why, then, has acceptance of federal policies by the people in the last three decades remained high and stable?

For possible answers, one can look at the development of the classical political cleavages as proposed by Lipset and Rokkan (1967). As Zürcher (2006), Bolliger (2007) and Linder et al. (2008) have shown in their longitudinal studies, these cleavages play an important role for direct democracy. One or more of them are articulated in most voting campaigns. Political parties opposed to the project mobilise their clientele along one side of the cleavage, while the protagonists try to overcome the basic conflict line and stress a common interest. To a certain degree, success of a policy depends on a successful integration of opposed interests in the cleavages, while mobilisation of basic conflicts diminishes the chances of the project. While the political parties' decision for support or "casewise opposition" depends on the specific conditions of the votation, the citizen's awareness for political cleavages changes considerably in their long term-development. For instance, political polarization between Catholics and Protestants was high in times of the "Kulturkampf" at the end of the 19th century, but since then, the religious cleavage has cooled off. Under these circumstances, one can expect that lower polarisation in this cleavage increases the chances of success for a federal project touching a religious issue in the popular vote, and vice versa. A similar trade-off between polarisation and chances of success can be proposed for all cleavages and their respective issues at the vote. The following figures illustrate the polarization of citizens in popular votes from 1874-2006, as well as the success of opposition in the votations for which the corresponding cleavage was relevant.

We do not yet have complete in-depth analyses of the relation between cleavages and the success of federal policies in the popular vote. Nonetheless, we can make some first observations. First, the polarization of the people - measured in all votations from 1874-2006 - has different historical peaks for each of the four cleavages. Federal policies never had to face times of political crises in which more than two cleavages were at the peak. This may have helped political stability. Under the assumption that high polarization lowers the chances of success of federal policies, one can relate cleavage and referenda data at least with one important development of Period I, namely the decline of the religious cleavage in the first three decades after 1874. This was the aftermath of the "Kulturkampf" during which the Catholic Conservatives fought against the laic and centralist majority of the Radicals with great success.

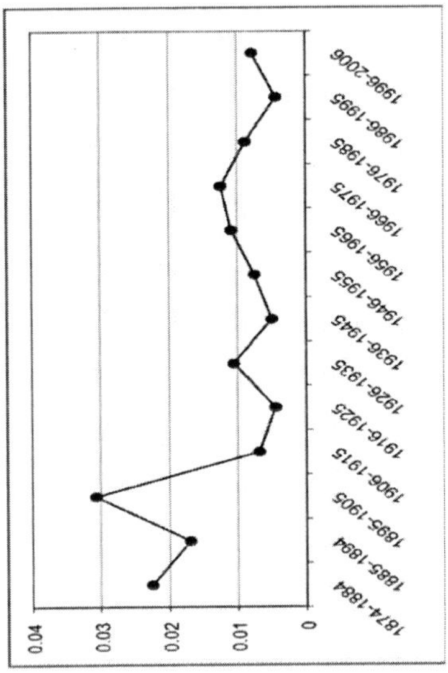

Fig. 1a: Cleavage Catholics vs. Protestants: Polarization (b-coefficients)

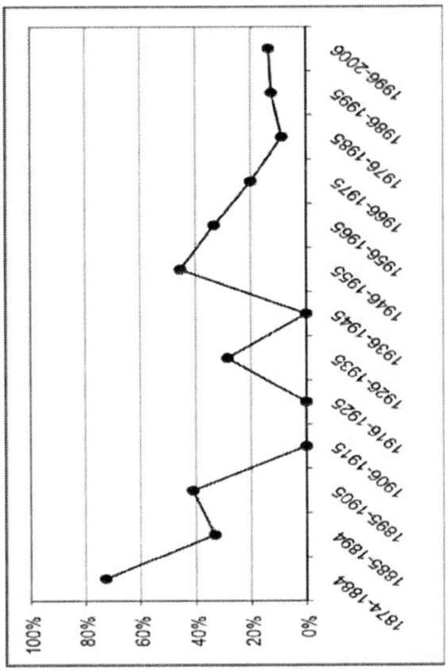

Fig. 1b: Share of rejected projects in which the religious cleavage was Significant

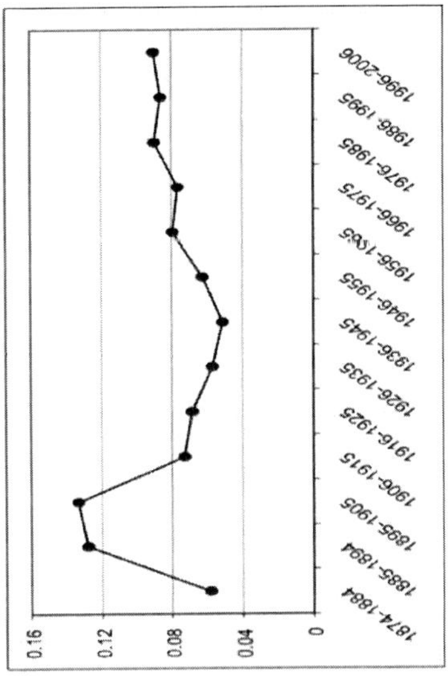

Fig. 2a: Center vs periphery (German /French: Polarization (b-coefficients)

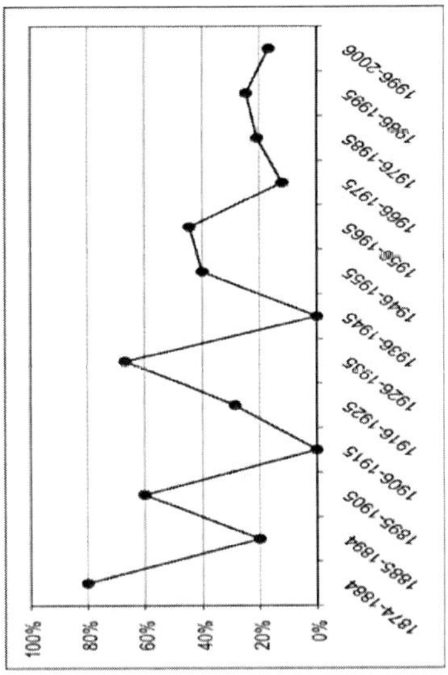

Fig. 2b: Share of rejected projects in which German/French cleavage was significant

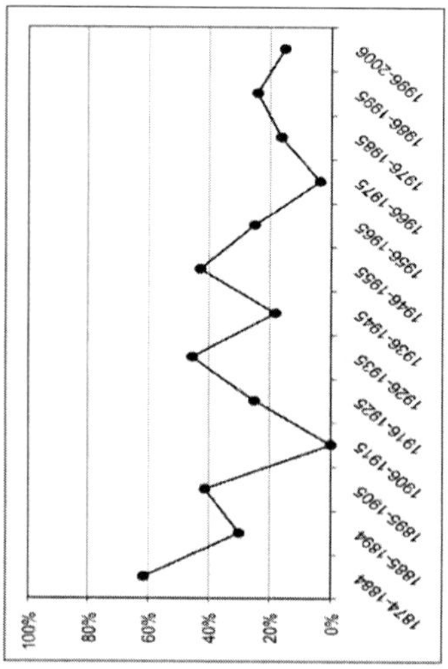

Fig. 3a: Urban against rural: Polarization (b-coefficients)

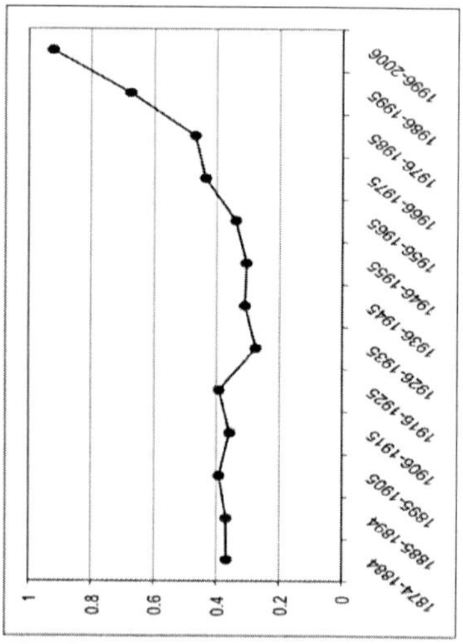

Fig. 3b: Share of rejected projects in which the urban/rural cleavage was significant

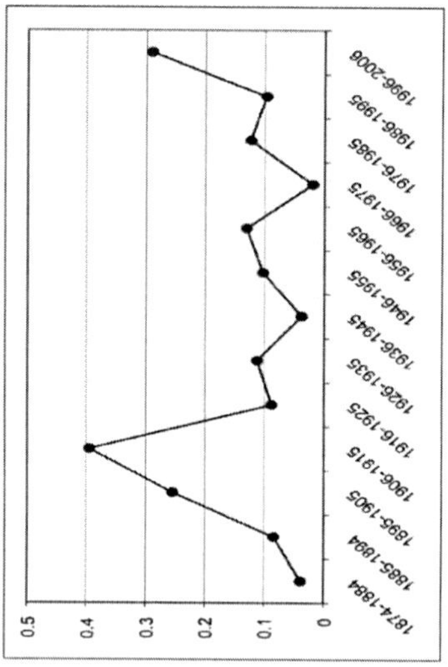

Fig 4a: Capital against labour Polarization (b-coefficients)

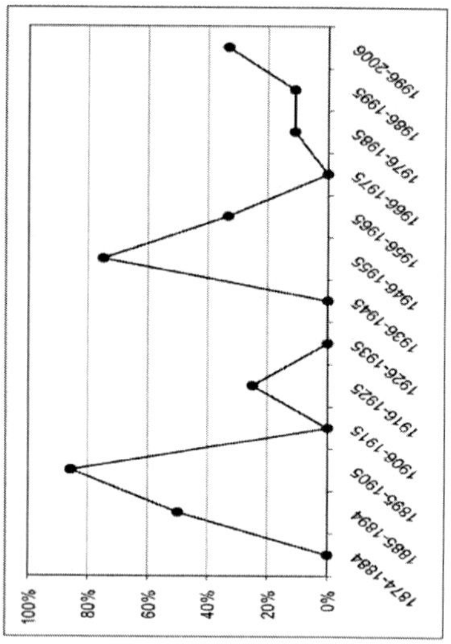

Fig. 4b: Share of rejected projects in which capital against labour was significant

Sources and data of Fig. 1a-4a are taken from Linder et al. (2008). Polarization for each of the four cleavages was measured on the voting behaviour of subcantonal units (Bezirke) with different social structures. The method of multivariate regression analysis allowed for simultaneous estimations of the impact of socio-structural characteristics (religion, language, urban/rural, capital/labour) of the subnational units on the vote. Polarizations were calculated for every of the 511 federal votations from 1874-2006. Success rates (Fig. 1b-4b have been calculated for this study. For details on methods and data see: Bolliger (2007) und Zürcher (2006).

The co-optation of the Conservatives into the formerly "mono-colour" Federal Council not only calmed the religious cleavage (Fig. 1a and 1b) but let chances of votations on federal policies rise. However, relations between cleavage development and direct democracy success are less clear for the following decades. Fading opposition in linguistic issues (Fig. 2b) tells of a long-term success of political integration of the linguistic minorities but its "ups and downs" are not congruent with the curve of polarisation (Fig. 2a). In the first half of the 20th century, the Socialists, completely excluded from power until 1943, became the main opposition power and fully opened the capital-labour conflict. Yet, for period I, cleavage polarization and opposition success in class issues do not go hand in hand. Congruence can be observed in period II only: The political integration of Social-Democrats in 1959 was followed by a significant decline of the capital-labour cleavage and success of economic policies, while the last decade is characterized by a significant increase of economic polarization and a higher rate of failure of federal policies (Fig. 4a and b). Finally, a high divergence is found in the urban-rural-cleavage (Fig. 3a and 3b). Neither peaks of opposition success nor the long term fading of the opposition forces can be found in the measured polarization of the cleavage. Between the two World Wars, Radicals, Conservatives, and later the Peoples' Party formed a large bourgeois coalition. The latter was often divided, however, in questions of economic intervention opposing rural and urban interests. As expected, success of opposition is high but polarization of the citizen in the cleavage is low in this period. Most surprising: the spectacular growth of polarization of the last decades between urban and rural does not show up in a similar success of oppositions. At the state of our research, therefore, we cannot establish a direct relation between citizen's polarisation and success or failure of federal policies.

What are alternative explanations? First, it is possible that the political parties' dealing with the cleavages (mobilising conflicts or attenuating them in the voting campaigns) is not only interrelated with the people's perception of the basic conflict lines but also more important for success. Second, pre-parliamentary bargaining procedures, which offer opportunities for finding pareto-optimal solutions, were developed only after World War II. As Neidhart (1970) has shown on many referendum cases, these bargaining procedures are decisive for the preparation of winning policies. Their absence or existence can explain low levels and changing rates of success in Period I, as well as high and stable levels of success in Period II. This suggests that the institutionalisation of the pre-parliamentary arena has more important and sustainable effects than power sharing between the political parties. Third, pressure from the outside may have integrating effects that help to get political majorities also in popular votes. This was the case in the years before World War II, when the political and economic crisis was overcome in face of the threats of the Hitler Regime, and in the last 20 years when globalisation put Switzerland under politico-economic pressure for liberalisation and privatisation. Fourth, Schwarz and Linder (2006) have shown that in the parliamentary arena, power sharing and compromise, despite growing political polarisation, still work well. If compromise is achieved among three political parties in changing coalitions from issue to issue, the referendum risk is low.

This indicates, fifth and last, that pertinent answers on the impact of direct democracy on public policies must take into account the politics of the political elite. Yet, parliament and direct democracy are different political arenas and follow different logics. This could mean that long term relations between public policies and direct democracy are contingent, that is, not more predictable than history.

References

Bolliger, C. (2007). *Konkordanz und Konfliktlinien in der Schweiz. Parteienkooperation, Konfliktdimensionen und gesellschaftliche Polarisierungen bei den eidgenössischen Volksabstimmungen von 1945 bis 2003.* Berner Studien zur Politikwissenschaft. Bern: Haupt.

Bolliger, C. & Zürcher, R. (2004). Deblockierung durch Kooptation? Eine Fallstudie zur Aufnahme der Katholisch-Konservativen in die schweizerische Landesregierung 1891. Schweizerische Zeitschrift für Politikwissenschaft 10 (4):59-92.

Frey, B. & Stutzer, A. (2000). Happyness, Economy and Institutions. Economic Journal 110, no.466 : 918-38

Hug, S. & Sciarini, P. (2002). Changements de valeurs et nouveaux clivages politiques en Suisse. Paris: L'Harmattan.

Hug, S. & Tsebelis, G. (2002). Veto players and referendums around the world. Journal of Theoretical Politics 14(4): 465-515.

Hug, S. & Papadopoulos, Y. (2004). Résultats des votations fédérales et prises de position des partis politiques et des groupes d'intérêt (SIDOS - 6841). Genf, Lausanne: Université de Genève, Université de Lausanne.

Kirchgässner, G.,. Feld, L.P. & Savioz, M. (1999). Die direkte Demokratie. Modern, erfolgeich, entwicklungs- und exportfähig. Basel : Helbing und Lichtenhahn.

Knoepfel, P., Achermann, D. & Zimmermann, W. (1996). Bilanzstudie Bodenpolitik 1990 bis 1995, Cahier de l'IDHEAP 162/1996.

Knoepfel, P., Kissling-Näf, I. & Varone, F. (Hrsg.) (2001). Institutionelle Regime für natürliche Ressourcen: Boden, Wasser und Wald im Vergleich, Basel / Genf / München: Helbing & Lichtenhahn.

Kriesi, Hanspeter. 2005. Direct Democratic Choice. The Swiss Experience. Lanham: Lexington Books.

Linder, Wolf. 1983. Entwicklung, Strukturen und Funktionen des Wirtschafts- und Sozialstaats in der Schweiz. In: Handbuch Politisches System der Schweiz. Band 1: Grundlagen, herausgegeben von A. Riklin. Bern, Stuttgart: Haupt. 255-381.

Linder, W. (1985). Überrollt uns eine Gesetzesflut? Eine empirische Untersuchung über die quantitative Entwicklung des schweizerischen Rechts. Schweizerisches Zentralblatt für Staats- und Gemeindeverwaltung 86 (10):417-444.

Linder, Wolf. 2005. Schweizerische Demokratie. Institutionen - Prozesse - Perspektiven. Bern, Stuttgart, Wien: Haupt.

Linder, Wolf. 2006. Direkte Demokratie, in: Handbuch der Schweizer Politik, Zürich: NZZ-Verlag. 103-124.

Linder, W., Zürcher, R. & Bolliger, C. (2008). Gespaltene Schweiz- geeinte Schweiz. Gesellschaftliche Spaltungen und Konkordanz bei den Volksabstimmungen seit 1874. Baden: Hier+Jetzt.

Lijphart, A. (1999). Patterns of democracy: Government forms and performance in thirty-six countries. Hew Haven: Yale University Press.

Lipset, S.M. & Rokkan, S. (1967). Party Systems and Voter Alignments: Cross National Perspectives. New York: Free Press.

Neidhart, L. (1970). Plebiszit und pluralitäre Demokratie : eine Analyse der Funktion des schweizerischen Gesetzesreferendums. Bern: Francke.

Schneider, F., Pommerehne, W. & Frey, B.S. (1981). Politico-Economic Interdependence in a Direct Democracy: The Case of Switzerland, in: Douglas A. Hibbs (ed.): Contemporary Political Economy, Amsterdam: North Holland.

Schwarz, D. & Linder, W. (2006). Mehrheits- und Koalitionsbildung im schweizerischen Nationalrat 1996-2005 , Studie im Auftrag der Parlamentsdienste der schweizerischen Bundesversammlung, Bern: Institut für Politikwissenschaft, Universität Bern.

Trechsel, A. (2006). Volksabstimmungen, in: Handbuch der Schweizer Politik, Zürich: NZZ-Verlag. 459-488.

Zürcher, R. (2006). Konkordanz und Konfliktlinien in der Schweiz. Eine Überprüfung der Konkordanztheorie aufgrund qualitativer und quantitativer Analysen der eidgenössischen Volksabstimmungen von 1848 bis 1947. Berner Studien zur Politikwissenschaft. Bern: Haupt.

CHAPTER 4

The Role of the Federal Government in Direct-Democratic Campaigns

HANSPETER KRIESI

Introduction

On June 1, 2008, three out of four Swiss voters and all the Cantons rejected the so called "muzzle"-initiative, which wanted to prevent members of government and high officials of the federal administration from intervening in the public debate during direct-democratic campaigns. In particular, the initiative wanted to prevent them from appearing in the media and from participating in public events linked to the direct-democratic vote. The initiative, which had been launched by a committee composed of members of the radical right, had been triggered by a series of votes on foreign affairs in the more recent past. Given its ignominious defeat, the initiative will be quickly forgotten. But it touched on a sensitive aspect of Swiss political culture – popular sovereignty and its relationship with the new forms of political communication, which is why it is worth taking a closer look at the points it raised. I shall, first, introduce a series of theoretical considerations, then present some empirical illustrations, and, finally, discuss two key questions linked to this debate.

The Swiss version of direct-democracy

There are different versions of direct-democracy. One variant is the populist, unmediated form of direct-democracy, which best corresponds to the practice in the member states of the U.S.. When the populist and progressive reformers of the late 19th century introduced direct democratic procedures in the U.S., they did so above all to restrict the power of political parties and their political machines, which were in control of the state parliaments at the time (Cronin, 1989: 50-57; Smith & Tolbert, 2001: 740, 2004: 112ff.; Bowler & Donovan, 2006). In the U.S., the popular initiative, still today, is primarily used by social movements and interest groups to circumvent the state parliaments controlled by the parties. This is possible, because the popular initiatives are submitted to the popular vote without the intervention of the state governments and their parliaments. The polar opposite to the populist version of direct-democracy is what I would call its plebiscitary version, the one we know from the French Fifth Republic, where the ability to propose a referendum constitutes one of the key legislative prerogatives of the President. De Gaulle has effectively used this prerogative to increase his power and prestige[1]. The key characteristic of the plebiscitary version of direct-democracy is that it constitutes an instrument in the hands of the governing elites, which keep it under complete control.

The Swiss variety of direct democracy is located somewhere in between these two extremes. On the one hand, it has always been much more organized and more tightly controlled by the political elites than the populist version of the United States. Both government and Parliament have an important role to play in the preparation of the proposals submitted to the voters. In contrast to the practice in the U.S., the government and the parliament discuss the text of the initiative before it is submitted to the popular vote. They provide it with a voting recommendation that almost always recommends its rejection, and sometimes they formulate a direct or indirect counter-proposal. In the case of the referendum, the proposal submitted to the popular vote originates in governmental legislation in the first place. In addition, the public debate among the elites during direct democratic campaigns provides the key cues for the voters' choices. On the other hand, the elites cannot call a vote on an ad hoc basis as in the plebiscitary version of direct democracy. The vote is either constitutionally required (as in the case of a compulsory referendum), or demanded by a group of at least 50,000 (in the case of an optional) or 100,000 (in the case of an initiative) citizens. Moreover, the political elites do not exercise full control over the voting process. The Swiss direct democratic procedures imply risk of governmental defeat, for reasons that, contrary to what is suggested by their sceptical critics, have very little to do with questions of citizen competence, but most often quite a lot with questions of preexisting political preferences on the part of the voters and the outcome of the political struggle between majority and opposition. The Swiss version of direct-democracy is not at all a ritual exercise of "democratic gymnastics" (Papadopoulos, 1991, 1995: 441).

For the populists from the new Swiss radical right, who distrust the government and the parliamentary majority, the government's control over the direct-democratic process has gone too far, especially in the cases where they lost the vote. In fact, they are convinced that the "people" (in the singular, because the "people" is, to them, a homogenous unit) is on their side. From their point of view, the only reason why they lose some popular votes – as they do, above all in the domain of foreign affairs, which is of greatest concern to them – is that the government succeeds in manipulating the popular will. From the point of view of its initiators, the purpose of the "muzzle" initiative was to stop the government from manipulating the people's will. Unsurprisingly, the

---

[1] Ironically, as is noted by Roper (2002: 257), the French president cannot unilaterally propose a referendum, but needs the support of a majority of Parliament in order to do so. If the parliamentary majority concurs with the presidential majority, this is, however, not an issue. Only under cohabitation does this pose a problem. Moreover, from our present point of view, under all circumstances, the referendum in France remains a unilateral instrument in the hands of the governing elites.

initiative was not only supported by the groups in which it originated, but also by the Swiss People's Party (SVP/UDC), the Swiss version of the new populist right, which had become the largest Swiss party by the 2007 federal elections, leaving all other competitors far behind.

The Swiss version of government campaigning

Direct-democratic campaigns take place in an institutional and issue-specific context. Political institutions define the rules of the game of the direct-democratic process and as such they are, as Sniderman (2000: 69) points out, the "organizers of political choices". They organize the choices not only for actors leading the campaign, but also for the voters. They do so by imposing constraints and opportunities on the communication strategies of the campaigning actors, which, at the same time, prestructure the fundamental options available to the voters. It is very important to keep in mind that, in direct-democratic votes just as in elections, "citizens are presented with an organized set, or menu, of choices" (Sniderman & Bullock, 2004: 338). The format of the choice is given and so are the alternatives on the menu from which the citizens can choose.

Given the institutional framework of Swiss direct-democratic campaigns, the authorities largely control the voting agenda, they have an advantageous position with respect to the framing of the issue and they even have some leeway in the interpretation of the vote's outcome. With respect to the agenda, the authorities set the time-table for the votes. As Knoepfel et al. (2006: 86f.) have pointed out, time/timing is a very important resource in policy-making in general. With regard to the initiatives in particular, the authorities currently have the possibility to delay a vote for more than three years, if they do not present a counter-proposal, and for more than four years, if they formulate an explicit counter-proposal. Compared to California, where an initiative has to be voted within at most 619 days from its submission, these delays are very long. They may serve to take the steam out of a proposal (Delley, 1978: 102ff.), and there are several examples where they have, indeed, served precisely this purpose. The initiative for the encouragement of public transport is a case in point. Launched by the Alliance of Independents (LdU/AdI) in 1984 and submitted to the authorities in 1986, it only came up for the vote in 1991. By this time, its objectives had already been partially attained as a result of the adoption of "Rail 2000" in 1987, and, with the rejection of a "coordinated transport policy" in 1988, the overall direction of the "global conception of Swiss transport policy", which it had initially wanted to influence, had already been considerably clarified.

The agenda-setting capacity of the elites has another very important, but often overlooked, aspect; the number of times the Swiss vote is a function of the number of proposals that are queuing up for submission to the vote. There are up to four voting dates per year and the federal government sets the agenda in such a way that the proposals to be submitted to the voters are spread throughout the year. Very important issues, such as the EES Treaty or the new

Constitution are presented individually, with no other projects on a given date. Less important issues are often grouped together. The average number of proposals submitted per voting occasion at the federal level is about three. The modal value is two and in only one, notorious, instance the number of projects submitted exceeded six. It is true that the federal proposals are not the only ones to be voted on a given date: there usually are additional cantonal and local projects submitted to the vote together with the federal proposals. Nevertheless, the total number of proposals to be voted on a given date is far more limited than the set that is usually submitted to a Californian voter. This means that the campaign and the voters' attention are usually concentrated on a limited number of specific issues, which facilitates the debate not only for the government, but also for all possible participants. In fact, direct-democratic campaigns constitute the key occasions for issue-specific public debates in Switzerland, as has been shown by two detailed case studies, one on abortion and one on the Swiss relations with the EU (Höglinger, 2008, Tresch, 2008). The case studies also show that the parties' standing in the media is reinforced during a direct-democratic campaign, and that, by providing them with access to a public audience which far exceeds their usual reach, these campaigns constitute "windows of opportunity" for weak political actors more generally.

With respect to *information*, the government also enjoys some important advantages. Since the early 1970s, a member of the federal government has had the opportunity to address the citizens on radio and tv during prime time in order to present the official point of view on the submitted proposals – initiatives or referenda alike. In addition, since 1978, the government and Parliament present their point of view in a ballot pamphlet which is sent to each citizen. This is in sharp contrast to the populist Californian case, where the authorities have to adopt a neutral position with regard to an initiative (von Arx 2002: 204). The pamphlet also presents the challengers' point of view, but the government's position is always presented first and in more detail. However, as in the U.S., the Swiss government does not have the right to spend public funds on a publicity campaign (von Arx, 2002: 207)[2]. Since the late 1980s, members of the government have also accepted to participate in tv-debates on the issues up for a direct-democratic vote, and since 1993, when Otto Stich, then Minister of Finance, participated for the first time in Arena – the most important of these tv-debates on Swiss German television – members of government have also regularly been present in this most important public forum. Finally, the members of government are increasingly participating in the campaigns by holding speeches related to the issues at stake in the upcoming direct-democratic votes, and by giving interviews to the media, where they expose the government's point of view.

More generally, against the background of a changing media environment, and of the introduction of new methods of political campaigning, the information task of the government has been greatly extended in the more recent past. In line with these changes, the idea that the governmental

---

[2] In one exceptional case, the vote on the European Economic Space (EES), the government has spent 6 million francs for a publicity campaign in favour of the ratification of the treaty (see Goetschel, 1994).

department responsible for the issue at stake should be able, and even obliged, to actively engage in public relations in favour of its position during the campaign has imposed itself. This is expressed in the revision of the law concerning the organization of the federal government and administration (1997)[3], and in the more recent revision of the law concerning political rights (2007)[4].

While the agenda-setting and advisory roles of the government in the context of direct-democratic campaigns have become unquestioned elements of the Swiss institutional practices, it is this more recent increasing involvement of the government and the administration in the campaign activities, which has met with resistance and has motivated the challenge by the initiative. The government rejected the initiative outright considering it to impose much too constraining conditions on its political communication activities. But, in broad circles of the Swiss political elite, the challengers' critique of the increasing presence of the government in the campaigns nevertheless struck a responsive chord. These sympathetic reactions can only be understood, when we take into account the informal, traditional consensus on the government's role in direct-democratic campaigns. According to this traditional conception, which is reflected in the respective jurisprudence of the Federal Court[5], the authorities of the state are expected to exercise their campaigning role with a certain restraint. While entitled to provide the voters with a balanced diet of information, the authorities should, according to the traditional view, leave the opinion formation in the general public primarily to civil society, the social and political forces of the country. While the dominant doctrine of the Swiss Constitutional lawyers deduces from Art 34 alinea 2 of the Constitution that the authorities have the right, or even the obligation, to inform and communicate with the citizen public[6], there is a strong sense that this obligation should not give rise to outright propaganda on the part of the government.

In fact, the widespread uneasiness among the political elite with the increasing role of the government in the campaigns has induced the National Council – against the explicit intention of the government (and originally also against the position of the Council of States) – to formulate an indirect counter-proposal to the initiative. This counter-proposal consisted in a modification of the law on political rights and stipulated that, in the event of the initiative's rejection in the popular vote, this law would be modified by adding formal rules for the information activities of the government and the federal administration during campaigns. According to these rules, the information of the federal government must be "continuous", "factual", "transparent" and "proportionate". And the government may not adopt a

[3] SR 172.010

[4] SR 161.1

[5] BGE 130 I 290, S. 295-304; BGE 119 Ia 271, S. 275.

[6] 05.054 Botschaft über die Volksinitiative "Volkssouveränität statt Behördenpropaganda" vom 29. Juni 2005, BBl 2005 4384ff.

recommendation that differs from that of Parliament[7]. As the ballot pamphlet maintained, the formal specification of these rules implies that the government may not engage in voting propaganda[8]. Where to draw the line between information and propaganda is, of course, very difficult and lies in the eyes of the beholder. But this is not the point here. The point I would like to stress here is that, to some extent, the parliamentary majority seems to have shared the challengers' view that the government should not use its position to influence the voters' choices.

The system of concordance

These restrictions on the government's role in direct-democratic campaigns are closely linked to the Swiss system of government, which is unique in that it differs from all the other classic versions of representative government – be they parliamentary, presidential or semi-presidential systems. The Swiss directorial system has several particularities (see Kriesi & Trechsel, 2008), but the one most directly linked to our present discussion is that, according to the (entirely informal) principle of *concordance*, the most important political parties have been co-opted into government and remain in the executive on a permanent basis. While such "oversized cabinets" or "grand coalitions" containing one or more "unnecessary parties" (Lijphart, 1984: 60) exist elsewhere, the Swiss case represents its most radical and – simultaneously – most stable form. From 1959 to 2007, the partisan composition of the Federal Council has remained identical. Only after the federal elections of 2007, has there been some change in this respect.

As a consequence of the system of concordance and its heterogeneous partisan composition, the Swiss government has governed without any real legislative programme, has followed a rather technocratic approach – tending to administer rather than govern the country, and its members have been constrained to adopt a rather non-partisan attitude in their public discourse. This system of government has allowed for the issue-specific opposition by one or more of the governing parties, and, as a matter of fact, as long as the opposition varied from one issue to the other, the possibility to deviate from the governing majority on a case by case basis served as a safety valve for the system's stability (Linder, 1987: 216).

As a result of the "variable geometry" of alliances between the four coalition partners, the coalitions that confront each other in direct-democratic campaigns typically include the government and the parliamentary majority on

---

[7] Such a difference has, to my knowledge, only occurred once in the past, with respect to the modified Labour law, which was submitted to the voters in December 1996, In that case, the government did not support the law adopted by Parliament, but did not oppose it either.

[8] Schweizerische Eidgenossenschaft. Volksabstimmung vom 1. Juni 2008. Erläuterungen des Bundesrates, p. 22.

the one side, and one of the government parties – most often the Social-democrats (in about half of the cases in the more recent past) or the Swiss People's Party (in roughly a quarter of the cases in the more recent past) – on the other side. In other words, the direct-democratic campaigns are typically fought by a centre-right governmental coalition against the united Left (including the Social-democrats), or by a centre-left governmental coalition against the populist right. In the event of a governing party challenging the government in a direct-democratic vote, the principle of *collegiality*, which constitutes an integral part of the principle of concordance, forces the members of government, whose party challenges the government on a given issue, to remain loyal to the government and to defend its position against their own party. Traditionally, with few exceptions, the members of government have been loyal to the principle of collegiality, which has contributed to the low-key approach of the government in direct-democratic campaigns and served to stabilize the system.

A number of developments have undermined both the system of collegiality and the system of concordance since the 1990s. Leaving aside the factors linked to the pressure exercised by the increasing internationalization of policy-making and the concomitant overload and inefficiency of this system of government, I would like to focus here on the domestic factors linked to the increasing polarization and mediatization of Swiss politics.

The increasing polarization is a result of the rise of the Swiss People's Party and its populist mobilization against the "political class". While the left has always had a double role of being at the same time in government and part of the opposition, the systematic opposition (in public discourse, if less in actual legislative behaviour) by the new populist right has introduced a considerable repolarization of Swiss politics, which contrasts with the contrary development in other West European countries. The Swiss People's Party wholeheartedly embraced the methods of media-centred modern campaigning, which include professionalization and personalization of campaigns, permanent and negative campaigning (Swanson & Mancini, 1996). This party has set new standards in terms of permanent campaigning, professionalism, and negative campaigning. After the election of its polarizing leader (Christoph Blocher) to the Federal Council in 2003, the traditional homogenizing mechanisms have repeatedly broken down, which eventually led to his ousting from the government after the following federal elections in 2007, and to the explicit adoption of the opposition's role by his party.

Mediatization, i.e. the increasing role of the media for politics in established democracies, reinforces the polarizing tendencies and contributes to the difficulties of the system of concordance. In this context, the media's strategy of personalization is of particular importance. By highlighting the role of personalities, the media enhance the focus on party leaders and chief executives. Everywhere, this trend undermines the organizational structure of political parties because the growing significance of media personalities and public images empowers individual political figures at the expense of the parties' authority. Today, the political leader directly addresses the public and directly reacts to changing public opinions. Accordingly, Fishkin (1991: 46) observes "the spread of the plebiscitary model of leadership and representation". In parliamentary democracies, the spread of this model of leadership implies the declining importance of parties, what Mair (2002) has, somewhat exaggeratedly, called the rise of a "partyless democracy", and a growing *"de-parlementarization"* (Mény & Surel, 2000: 111) or *"presidentialization"* (Poguntke & Webb, 2005) of politics. In the peculiar Swiss system, however, the spread of this model takes on a meaning of its own – it undermines both the system of concordance, and the traditional low key approach of the government in direct-democratic campaigning.

It undermines the system of concordance for two reasons: first, because, instead of attributing responsibility to the governmental college, it tends to attribute responsibility to the individual ministers who head the departments in charge of the issues at stake; and second, because it renders public what the system of concordance has traditionally hidden from the public's view – the dissensions within the government, and the contrasting personal views of the different members of government. Thus, the whole country knew about the important differences within the Federal Council concerning European integration at the time of the crucially important vote on the EES Treaty (1992). And since the leader of the SVP had become a member of government in 2003, the media were revealing, on an almost daily basis, the increasingly frosty climate within the college. Personalization undermines the government's low key approach and leads to plebiscitary tendencies in direct-democratic campaigning, because it attributes responsibility to individual members of government (and no longer to the college), because it forces the individual members of the government to defend the government's position publicly, but also because it provides the members of the executive with greater opportunities to influence the outcome of direct-democratic campaigns. In a mediatized polity, the prominence (i.e. the generalized capacity to get access to the media), and prestige (i.e. the generalized capacity to get public support) of the members of government is greatly enhanced[9]. Under these conditions, members of government who have "charismatic communication skills", i.e. "demonstrated skills, performance, and talent in the political communication arena" (Wolfsfeld & Sheafer, 2006: 338) are very likely to find access, resonance and support in the media and in the citizen public.

An empirical illustration

I would like to illustrate these theoretical observations by some pertinent aspects of one recent case of a direct-democratic campaign – the referendum against the asylum law (September 2006), and some complementary information from two other recent cases – the referendums against the corporate tax law II (February 2008) and the naturalization initiative (June 2008). The government's campaigns were led by different members in each one of these three cases. The campaign for the asylum law fell under the

[9] For a discussion of the concepts of prominence and prestige, see Neidhardt (1994, 1995).

responsibility of the Minister of Justice, the leader of the populist right, Christoph Blocher. The government's campaign for the corporation tax was led by the Minister of Finance, Hans-Rudolf Merz, and its campaign against the SVP's naturalization initiative was in the hands of Blocher's successor in the Ministry of Justice, Evelyne Widmer-Schlumpf. All three of them heavily engaged in the campaign, not only by presenting their point of view at the government's official press conference, and in the official statements on radio and tv, but also by making public speeches at various occasions (general assemblies of interest associations, universities, festivities for the national holiday), and by granting interviews to the press and the electronic media. *Table 1* presents a (probably incomplete) overview of these activities in the three cases.

In the case of the asylum law, it is possible to present a more detailed analysis of the impact of the government and the federal administration in the course of the campaign. In a project of the NCCR-democracy[10], we have identified all the organizations who have participated in this campaign – either in support of the new asylum law, or opposing it. Overall, we have found no less than 47 organizations (political parties, ad hoc campaign committees, churches, public and economic interest groups, and the federal government and administration), who in one way or another actively participated in the campaign. Only two actors representing the federal government and the administration – the Federal Ministry of Justice and Police (EJPD), and the Federal Office of Migration (BFM), who are responsible for the Swiss immigration policy – belong to the key actors in the campaign. But these two actors were very influential, as can be seen from *Table 2*, which not only lists the types of actors involved, but also their average influence. An organization's influence during the campaign was operationalized by a reputational measure[11]. As it turns out, the SVP was estimated to have been the most influential organization in this campaign (with a score of 77). Interestingly, however, the two actors mobilizing in the name of the federal executive were very influential as well: the Federal Ministry of Justice and Police (EJPD) was considered to have been the second most important actor (with a score of 58), and the Federal Office of Migration (BFM) sixth most important actor (with a score of 46), right after the two major coordinating committees (BK and K2N) and the major humanitarian organization (SFH) leading the opposition to the

[10] Vgl. http://www.nccr-democracy.uzh.ch/nccr

[11] This reputational measure is based on a set of questions referring to the list of all organizations involved (Kriesi et al., 2006). In personal interviews, the representatives of the 47 organizations were first asked to name all organizations on the list containing the names of these 47 organizations, which, from their point of view, had been particularly influential during the campaign. Next, they were asked to name the three most influential organizations, and, finally, the most influential one. For each actor, the summary indicator presented in Table 2 counts the number of times he was mentioned by the other respondents in reaction to these questions: mentions as 'most influential' are coded as '3', mentions among the 'three most influential' as '2', and mentions as 'influential' as '1'. The values of the indicator range from 0, for an organization that has never been mentioned as influential, to 141 for an organization that would have been considered to be the most influential actor by all 47 respondents.

proposed law. On average, no other category of actors was considered as influential as the two organizations representing the government. Note that Christoph Blocher, the leader of the most influential organization – the SVP – was at the same time the member of government in charge of the Ministry of Justice – the second most influential organization.

Activity	Asylum (Sept. 2006) Blocher	Corporation Tax (Febr.2008) Merz	Naturalization initiative (June 2008) Widmer-Schlumpf
Public speeches	5	3	4*
Interviews, oped	14	20	15
Arena	yes	yes	yes

*Including three speeches by top officials of the Department
Source: ongoing research by Regula Hänggli

Table 1 Activities of Department heads responsible for the proposal during the campaign.

Actor type	Frequency		Influence	
	Abs	%	Mean	s.d.
Government, fed. administration	2	4.3	*51.5*	9.2
Ad hoc committees	5	10.6	*39.2*	12.0
Big 5 parties	5	10.6	*31.4*	26.7
Churches+	5	10.6	12.6	9.5
Citizens' interest groups	12	25.5	11.8	12.4
Other parties	11	23.4	4.1	2.5
Economic interest groups	7	14.9	3.0	3.4
Total	47	100%	15.4	18.1

Source: Kriesi et al. 2008.

Table 2 Distribution of actor types and their influence, in the Asylum law campaign.

Under contemporary conditions, the campaigners' goal is to get their arguments into the media, and under such conditions, influence means the capacity to get access to and resonance in the media. For the case of the asylum law, we have made an attempt to assess the capacity of the organizations of the pro- and the contra-camp to get access to the media[12]. We have also attempted to assess the capacity of key personalities to obtain media access and resonance. In this campaign, each one of the two sides primarily relied on two arguments of their own, and attacked the same two arguments of the other side (see Hänggli & Kriesi, forthcoming). The pro-side mainly argued with the abuse of the existing law by foreigners who were not politically persecuted and who did not have any claim to asylum in Switzerland, and with the inefficiency of the existing law. Both arguments were intended to justify the tough measures introduced by the modified law. The contra-side mainly argued that these modifications violated human dignity and human rights, that they endangered religious norms, and that they were contrary to the Swiss humanitarian tradition. In addition, it argued that the provisions of the new law undermined the rule of law, and that they violated international law.

For the assessment of the impact of individual personalities in this particular case, we chose Christoph Blocher, the key personality on the government's side, and, on the challengers' side, the socialist Ruth Dreifuss, a highly respected, now retired former member of government. *Table 3* presents the average number of arguments mentioned in the media as a function of the media input (on press conferences, in press releases etc.) by these two protagonists on the previous day – whether alone or in combination with their respective organizations. As can be seen from this table, the input by either of these two personalities not only greatly increased the reporting of the key arguments of their own camp, but also the reporting of the respective counter-arguments. Either leader is most successful with the most important argument of his / her own side.

These brief empirical illustrations suggest that the federal government is, indeed, a major force in direct-democratic campaigns, and that individual personalities who have the required charisma and communication skills can make a big impact on the agenda-building in the media during direct-democratic campaigns.

---

12 For this analysis, we rely on a content analysis of *all* the campaign material produced by the previously mentioned 47 political actors for communication with the media – input for earned media coverage ('media input': press releases, speeches from media conferences or public statements), as well as on a content analysis of the media's news reporting ('media output'). This material was coded with the same codebook on a daily basis for the three months prior to the vote. For the media's news reporting, we selected the 13 most important papers in the Swiss German part of the country, and the 5 most important ones in the French-speaking part. In addition, we also analyzed the most important news and political information programmes of the public television stations in the two parts of the country. In each document – press release, newspaper article, TV news programme etc. – we coded *all* the arguments provided by/reported for each one of the relevant actors (organizations or their individual representatives) in our study.

	Abuse	Efficacy	Human trad	Rule of law	Others
Pro					
Blocher + Organization	**10.7**	**7.7**	**8.8**	**2.0**	**8**
Blocher	**6.5**	**4.6**	**4.1**	**2.2**	**6**
Organization	**4.5**	**1.5**	**1.4**	**0.0**	**4.8**
Without input	**0.9**	**0.6**	**0.7**	**0.4**	**1**
Contra					
Dreifuss	**5.3**	**3.9**	**13.5**	**3.0**	**8.5**
Organization	**4.5**	**1.9**	**7.7**	**2.3**	**4.9**
Without input	**2.0**	**0.9**	**3.6**	**1.2**	**3.6**

Table 3 Arguments in the media, as a function of input by two key protagonists on either side (Christoph Blocher and Ruth Dreifuss): average number of arguments per day, asylum law campaign.

Discussion

Now, two related questions remain for discussion: a) is this tendency towards a reinforced presence of the federal government during direct-democratic campaigns bad for direct-democracy – as suggested by the challengers who had launched the initiative, and as implicitly also suggested by the majority of Parliament who introduced the guiding principles for the government's political communication, and b) does it imply the coming end of the Swiss system of government?

With respect to the first question, it is interesting to observe that the apparent uneasiness of the political elites with the increasing role of the government in direct-democratic campaigns is not shared by the public. In the VOX-survey for the federal vote on June 1, 2008 (Engeli et al., 2008: 36f.), a two-thirds majority of the respondents rejected the idea that the Federal government exerted too much influence on public opinion formation. And overwhelming majorities of the respondents (of 85 percent and more) agreed that the government has to be able to defend its point of view and to react to new arguments/events introduced during the campaign, that the voters have a right to be informed about the government's position on the issues at stake, and that the government must have the possibility to react to false and misleading considerations concerning the texts submitted to the voters. Even two-thirds and more of the supporters of the initiative subscribed to these points, too.

This suggests that the voters have understood what often seems to be less than clear to the members of the Swiss political elites: a government's task is to govern. In the context of the system's direct-democratic opening, this means that the government is, indeed, expected to defend its position on the propositions submitted to the vote. These propositions are either directly sponsored by the government and the parliamentary majority (in the case of referendums), or the government and the parliamentary majority have adopted a clear position with respect to them (in the case of initiatives), always cast in a voting recommendation, and sometimes in the form of direct or indirect counter-proposals, too. In other words, the government is always a key party in the direct-democratic choice. It has to assume the responsibility for its proposals, and it ought to be held accountable for its recommendations, should they turn out to have been less than adequate.

There should, of course, be a clear division of labour between the government and the federal administration, a division of labour which is not always as clear as it should be in a country, where the government is often content to administer (Couchepin, 1987: 71), and where the top of the administration has increasingly assumed political tasks. The Swiss system of government serves to diffuse the responsibilities not only among the members of the governing college, but also between the college and the administration. It is the government's task to publicly defend its proposals, and not the task of its top officials.

Contrary to the populists' vision of the people, the voters do not speak with one voice. Their preferences are inarticulate, imprecise, and contradictory, which opens up a manoeuvring space for the government providing it with autonomy, discretion, and independent judgement. And the differential mobilizing capacity of voters with different types of preferences implies that the government is likely to be more attentive and more responsive to certain types of preferences than to others. These implications are central for a vision of representative *and* direct democracy, which focuses on the *political supply* by the elected and non-elected representatives (the political elites). From the point of view of this vision, the citizens' vote appears as a reaction of the voters to the terms proposed by the elites. Manin (1995: 290) has formulated this vision very pointedly by positing that, in politics, there is no demand which is independent of supply. For this supply-side vision, political communication and information processing by decision-making representatives and voters become crucial for the democratic process. On the one hand, this vision recognizes that ensuring accountability requires that the voters are provided with the information enabling them to evaluate the responsiveness of their representatives who, in their name, make political decisions, and allowing them to impose their sanctions on representatives who do not prove to be responsive. On the other hand, this vision also recognizes that the relevant information is to a considerable extent controlled by the very politicians who are held to be accountable by the voters. In other words, according to this vision, political actors can be principals as well as agents, and agenda-setting, priming and framing by the political strategists become key elements of opinion formation and democratic choice.

Once we adopt a supply-side perspective and allow for the possibility that the public's preferences are not exogenously given, but actively shaped by the politicians' agenda-setting, priming and framing, the crucial question becomes how they use these instruments of communication in the direct-democratic campaign. Do they use them to resort to "crafted talk" (Jacobs and Shapiro 2000), or "plebiscitary reason", as Chambers (2004) has called the strategies of manipulation, pandering, and image-maintaining? Or do they use these instruments in a more deliberative sense, which facilitates public discussion, and allows for their being held in check by a public that is capable of assessing the validity of their talk? I would like to suggest that, in the final analysis, the degree to which the public debate is led in terms of plebiscitary or deliberative reason depends less on personal character of the leaders involved, or demand-side factors (characterizing the voters) than on the *competitiveness* of the political process. Competitiveness in this context is not only a question of party competition. A viable civil society consisting of, on the one hand, multiple interest associations and social movement organizations articulating a large spectrum of different interests and points of view, and, on the other hand, of a myriad of informal, heterogeneously composed discussion groups, serves as an additional mechanism to hold in check "plebiscitary reasoning" and to facilitate deliberative public discussion.

The independence, resourcefulness and plurality of the news media also provide guarantees that the public sphere remains open for a rational and critical debate. To the extent that political elites are engaged in competition with each other and the news media provide a forum for all the actors involved, plebiscitary rhetoric risks to be exposed by the political adversaries and countered by an alternative set of appeals to the public. As Sniderman and Theriault (2004: 158) point out, "in a properly democratic polity opposing camps campaign on behalf of competing ways of understanding what is at issue". And they suggest that the clash of political arguments, "far from overwhelming or perplexing or blinding the political judgements of ordinary citizens, may be a condition of the possibility of their exercising it."

This chain of arguments implies that the best way to counter a possible preponderance of the government, and of its proper camp in the direct-democratic campaign is not to prevent it from defending its position, but to guarantee that the competition of ideas is not suppressed by the preponderance of any actor during the campaign – be it the government or some actor from civil society. Surprisingly, this question has not been the object of a serious public debate in Switzerland so far.

Finally, does the increasing involvement of the government in direct-democratic campaigns imply the end of the Swiss system of government? As we have seen, the indirect counter-proposal to the "muzzle" initiative tried to provide clear guidelines for the future political communication of the members of government. But these rules will hardly be able to settle the issue. In September 2008, just three months after the rejection of the initiative and the concomittant adoption of these new rules, Moritz Leuenberger, the Minister at the time responsible for environmental policy, participated in an event of the ecological associations, who prepared the campaign against the initiative seeking to restrict their right to legal appeal for large construction projects, which was to be submitted to the voters three months later, at the end of November 2008.

This initiative had been launched by the Liberal Party – a member of the governing coalition, but was rejected by the government and a majority of Parliament. In other words, by joining the ecological associations in their preparation of the campaign against the initiative, the Minister did nothing else but defend the government's position. He did this, however, before the official campaign had been launched, and before the voters had received the ballot pamphlet. For the Liberal Party, this was an "intolerable" act for a member of government[13], and the commentator of the NZZ considered this behaviour as "objectionable"[14]. By joining the event organized by the ecologists' campaign, the Minister had obviously shown a lack of restraint, but had he violated the criteria of continuity, transparency, factuality and proportionality? Proportionality seems to be the most critical one here, but what can it mean in the present context? Does it mean that a minister should take into account that a party in the governing coalition does not agree with the government's official position and with the majority of Parliament? And how should he or she go about doing this?

It seems to me that, inimical to the clear attribution of responsibility, to transparency, and accountability to voters, the Swiss system of government is hard to reconcile with the new world of mediatized and polarized politics, which is at the roots of the increasing presence of the government in direct-democratic campaigns. To plead for personal restraint appears to be rather vain in a time when political success crucially depends on a presence in the media, and where permanent campaigning has become the order of the day. The personalization of politics by the media attributes responsibility to individual ministers and expects them to defend their proposed legislation publicly. The lukewarm or half-hearted defence of the government's policies by ministers who are forced by the principle of collegiality to defend positions that they do not really share, is no longer tolerable in a world of mediatized politics. It undermines the credibility of the government, and its legitimacy. Mediatization implies an intensification of political communication with the voting public, and, in combination with the trend towards polarization, it implies a politicization of this communication, too.

These are less than propitious developments for the unmodified survival of the Swiss system of government - a system inherited from the 19th century, and, it should be stressed once again, unique in the world. Hopefully, these developments might lead to "policy learning", and eventually result in institutional reform. However, the obstacles to policy learning in the domain of institutional reform are quite formidable. As Peter Knoepfel and Ingrid Kissling-Näf (1998) have suggested on the basis of their comparative interpretation of no less than 28 case studies of Swiss policy-learning processes, the key ingredient for policy learning is an expansion of the scope

[13] NZZ, Internationale Ausgabe, Nr. 207, Freitag, 5. September 2008, p. 33.
[14] NZZ, Internationale Ausgabe, Nr. 208, Samstag/Sonntag, 6./7. September, p. 34.

of consensus, i.e. the development of a shared understanding - not necessarily at the level of the core beliefs, but (in Sabatier's terms) at the levels of the policy core and the secondary aspects. Now, the widespread uneasiness among the political elite with the increasing role of the government in campaigns does not augur well for an expansion of the scope of consensus in the case of the reform of the Swiss system of government. According to Knoepfel and Kissling-Näf, the learning process also needs to be launched by individual leadership – a strong personality committed to the reform process, who takes the initiative to "shake up" the policy network by assembling the key players around a table. But, in the case of the institutional reform of government, there is no committed leadership in sight. Finally, according to their analysis, the potential for subsequent learning depends on the availability of formalised arrangements for the production and dissemination of knowledge in the policy network. If the relevant knowledge remains in the hands of a few specialists, it will be difficult to develop a shared understanding. This condition may be easier to fulfil than the other two. The knowledge is there, it is in the public domain, and, maybe, this Festschrift will contribute to its dissemination, although the channel is not very formalized.

References

Arx, von N. (2002). *Ähnlich, aber anders. Die Volksinitiative in Kalifornien und in der Schweiz.* Basel: Helbing und Lichtenhahn.

Bowler, S., & Donovan, T. (1998). *Demanding choices. Opinion, voting, and direct democracy.* Ann Arbor: The University of Michigan Press.

Chambers, S. (2004). Behind Closed Doors: Publicity, Secrecy, and the Quality of Deliberation. *The Journal of Political Philosophy* 12, 4: 389-410.

Couchepin, F. (1987). Coordination des actes d'un Gouvernement collégial, *Pouvoir* 43, 65-72.

Cronin, T.E. (1989). *Direct democracy: the politics of initiative, referendum and recall.* Cambridge University Press.

Delley, J.-D. (1978). *L'initiative populaire en Suisse - Mythe et réalité de la démocratie directe.* Lausanne: L'Age d'Homme.

Engeli, I., Lloren, A., & Nai, A. (2008). Analyse des votations fédérales du 1er juin 2008. *VOX* du 1er juin, gfs.Berne.

Fishkin, J.S. (1991). *Democracy and Deliberation. New Directions for Democratic Reform.* New Haven: Yale University Press.

Goetschel, L. (1994). *Zwischen Effizienz und Akzeptanz. Die Information der Schweizer Behörden im Hinblick auf die Volksabstimmung über den ewr-Vertrag vom 6. Dezember 1992.* Bern: Haupt.

Hänggli, R., & Kriesi, H. (forthcoming). *Political framing strategies and their impact on media framing in a Swiss direct-democratic campaign. Political Communication.*

Höglinger, D. (2008). Verschafft die direkte Demokratie den Benachteiligten mehr Gehör? Der Einfluss institutioneller Rahmenbedingungen auf die mediale Präsentz politischer Akteure, *Swiss Political Science Review* 14, 2: 207-43.

Jacobs, L.R., & Shapiro, R.Y. (2000). *Politicians Don't Pander. Political Manipulation and the Loss of Democratic Responsiveness.* Chicago: The University of Chicago Press.

Knoepfel, P., Larrue, C., & Varone, F. (2006). *Analyse et pilotage des politiques publiques.* Chur : Rüegger.

Knoepfel, P., & Kissling-Näf, I. (1998). Social Learning in Policy Networks. *Policy and Politics* 26, 3: 343-365.

Kriesi, H., & Trechsel, A. (2008). *The politics of Switzerland. Continuity and Change in a Consensus Democracy.* Cambridge University Press.

Kriesi, H., Bernhard, L., & Hänggli, R. (2008). *Coalition formation in direct-democratic campaigns: a case study of the vote on the Swiss asylum law.* NCCR-Democracy 21, Working paper N° 12.

Kriesi, H., Adam, S., & Jochum, M. (2006). Comparative analysis of policy networks in Western Europe. *Journal of European Public Policy* 13, 3: 341-361.

Lijphart, A. (1984). *Democracies. Patterns of Majoritarian and Consensus Government in Twenty-One Countries.* New Haven: Yale University Press.

Linder, W. (1987). *La décision politique en Suisse Genèse et mise en oeuvre de la législation.* Lausanne: réalités sociales.

Mair, P. (2002). *Populist democracy vs Party Democracy.* pp. 81-98. In Y. Mény & Y. Surel (Eds). Democracies and the Populist Challenge. Basingstoke: Palgrave.

Manin, B. (1995). *Principes du gouvernement représentatif.* Paris: Calman-Lévy.

Mény, Y., & Surel, Y. (2000). *Par le peuple, pour le peuple. Le populisme et les démocraties.* Paris: Fayard.

Neidhardt, F. (1994). Öffentlichkeit, öffentliche Meinung, soziale Bewegungen". pp. 7-41. In F. Neidhardt (Ed.). Öffentlichkeit, öffentliche Meinung, soziale Bewegungen. *Kölner Zeitschrift* Sonderheft 34. Opladen: Westdeutscher Verlag.

Neidhardt, F. (1995). Prominenz und Prestige. Steuerungsprobleme massenmedialer Öffentlichkeit". pp. 233-245. In *Berlin-Brandenburgische Akademie der Wissenschaften.* Jahrbuch 1994. Berlin. Akademie Verlag.

Papadopoulos, Y. (1991). *La Suisse: un "Sonderfall" pour la théorie politique?* Travaux de science politique N° 2, Université de Lausanne, Institut de science politique.

Papadopoulos, Y. (1995). Analysis of functions and dysfunctions of direct democracy : top-down and bottom-up perspectives. *Politics and Society,* 23, 4, 421-448.

Poguntke, T., & Webb, P. (eds.) (2005). *The Presidentialization of Politics: A Comparative Study of Modern Democracies.* Oxford University Press.

Roper, S.D. (2002). Are all semi-presidential regimes the same? A comparison of Premier-Presidential Regimes. *Comparative Politics* 34, 3: 253-72.

Smith, D.A., & Tolbert, C.J. (2001). The Initiative to Party: Partisanship and Ballot Initiatives in California. *Party Politics* 7, 6: 781-99.

Sniderman, P.A. (2000). Taking Sides: A Fixed Choice theory of Political Reasoning, pp. 67-84. In A. Lupia, M.D. McCubbins & S.P. Popkin (Eds), *Elements of Reason: Cognition, Choice, and the Bounds of Rationality.* Cambridge University Press.

Sniderman, P.A., & Bullock, J. (2004). A Consistency Theory of Public Opinion and Political Choice: The Hypothesis of Menu Dependence, pp. 337-57 in W.E. Saris & P.M. Sniderman (Eds), *Studies in Public Opinion. Attitudes, Nonattitudes, Measurement Error, and Change.* Princeton University Press.

Sniderman, P.M., & Theriault, S.M. (2004). The Structure of Political Argument and the Logic of Issue Framing, pp. 133–65. In W.E. Saris & P.M. Sniderman (Eds), *Studies in Public Opinion: Attitudes, Nonattitudes, Measurement Error and Change.* Princeton University Press,

Swanson, D.L., & Mancini, P. (1996). Patterns of Modern Electoral Campaigning and Their Consequences. 247-276. In D.L. Swanson & P. Mancini (Eds.), *Politics, Media and Modern Democracy: An International Study of Innovations in Electoral Campaigning and Their Consequences.* London: Praeger.

Tresch, A. (2008). *Öffentlichkeit und Sprachenvielfalt. Medienvermittelt Kommunikation zur Europapolitik in der Deutsch- und Westschweiz.* Baden-Baden: nomos.

Wolfsfeld, G., & Sheafer, T. (2006). Competing Actors and the Construction of Political News: The Contest over Waves in Israel. *Political Communication* 23: 333-354.

Part II

Public Administration as Policy Actor

CHAPTER 5

Administrative Capacity Building for Sustainable Development

HELMUT WEIDNER

Introduction

The late 1960s saw the beginning of an intense debate on the societal consequences of environmental disruption and resource depletion. A considerable number of social scientists took the view that the existing politico-administrative systems were unable to prevent the emergence of ecological crises (Helfrich, 1971; Roos, 1971). Japan was even thought to be committing "ecological hara-kiri" (Tsuru and Weidner, 1989). However, at the same time some advanced industrial countries (e.g., USA, Japan, Great Britain, Sweden) established basic environmental institutions (agencies, laws) which later on stimulated other countries to follow these "pioneers". International organizations also took up the subject of the environment. In 1969, NATO established the Committee on the Challenges of Modern Society, and in 1970 the OECD set up a panel for environmental issues. In 1972, the first United Nations Conference on the Environment was held in Stockholm, the second in Rio de Janeiro (1992) and the third-focusing on sustainable developing-World Summit took place in Johannesburg in 2002. These summits were decisive for capacity building in developing countries.

Forms of response to environmental challenges changed over time. The prevailing approach shifted from pollution dilution and pollution control (reaction and cure, dilution/end-of-pipe treatment), to pollution prevention (precaution, sophisticated end-of-pipe treatment/integrative environmental technology), towards ecological modernization (emphasizing structural ecological transformation of the economy and society), and since the late 1980s, to the vision of sustainable development (a holistic and integrative societal development approach emphasizing the needs of developing countries).[1] Paradigmatic change and partly impressive reductions in pollution load in various environmental areas occurred.

[1] This heuristic identification of distinct succeeding phases does not mean that the phases and approaches are clearly delimited nor that the process need necessarily have been a steady, linear one without downturns. With respect to the concept or vision of

The ecological modernization paradigm (Jänicke, 2000; also Mol and Sonnenfeld, 2000) offered industrial countries a broad, accepted basis for coexistence between environmental and economic interests, since it appeared to be able to generate win-win solutions. The concept of sustainable development (see Knoepfel, Nahrath and Varone, 2007, especially pp. 455-465), in turn, was quite attractive for developing countries because of its balanced view of ecological, social and economic interests.[2] These two related but in important aspects differing concepts (see Langhelle, 2000) obviously had a positive effect on environmental capacity building in the North but also in the South. It is also plausible that by this time in the wake of globalization the anticipated strong erosion of environmental achievements and weakening of environmental standards-trends which would result in a veritable "race to the bottom" and creation of "pollution havens" in developing and newly industrialized countries-did not take place (see Holzinger, Jörgens & Knill, 2007). The worldwide spread of institutions and arrangements for effective environmental protection, and the rapidity of their diffusion (see Jänicke, 1992; Jänicke & Weidner, 1995) were decisive for preventing such backlashes.

If globalization is in fact weakening national environmental policies, then environmental capacity-building should be slowing down or reversing, and countries strongly integrated in world markets would likely not be front-runners in environmental policy. The 30-country study reported in section 3 of this chapter suggests that environmental policy has not yet become a "globalization loser." Indeed, diffusion of innovations in environmental policy has accelerated in the last decade. In developing countries, too, environmental policy capacities have expanded strongly. And what is also highly important: environmental policy is being globalized in political response to challenges of economic globalization.

In most countries (and major firms) environmental policy is guided much more strongly by the standards and practices of environmental front-runners than by those of latecomers. However, the cross-national study came to the conclusion that even in environmental pioneer countries considerable additional environmental capacity still is needed to enable the transformation of conventional environmental policy towards sustainable development. Before this result is discussed with a focus on politico-administrative capacities a short description of the capacity building approach is given.

---

sustainable development this article follows the definition and conceptualization by the so-called Brundtland Commission (cf. WCED, 1987).

[2] Sustainable Development, in general, became an important trademark in all spheres of society. Both international organizations, supranational institutions like the European Union, and many nation states, municipalities, companies, and associations with widely ranging areas of responsibility and interests have chosen sustainable development as a guiding principle for their activities. Some national governments (notably Sweden) are beginning to orient their overall policy on this principle or vision.

The capacity building approach

According to the OECD Task Force on Capacity Development, "[...] capacity in environment relates to the abilities of a society to identify environmental problems and solve them, capacity development in environment relates to the 'process' by which those abilities are developed" (OECD, 1994, p. 9; see also Ohiorhenuan & Wunker, 1995).

Using a combination of actor and system-oriented approaches, *the development of environmental capacity may thus be defined as a multi-factorial process determined by:*

1) usually conflicting organized actor groups, their resources, their ability to form alliances, and their ability to cooperate in identifying and seizing (or even creating) situational opportunities;
2) cultural, political and economic (structural) conditions, the environmental situation, and public awareness; and
3) the nature of the problem to be resolved (as partly constituted by these factors); how easy it is to solve-which usually depends on the kind of interests and the clout of the polluters involved, the systemic nature of the problem, whether it is conventional or latent/ creeping, etc.

Capacity building is not necessarily a steady, linear process: systems with low learning potential may fail to accumulate capacities for solving environmental problems, and even high capacities can decline. Furthermore, as this approach is concerned primarily with building and expanding capacities for environmental protection, the focus is on environmental proponents, whereas target groups (polluters) are in principle seen as restrictive factors-without excluding possible changes for the better.

In more analytical terms, *capacities for environmental policy and management are constituted by:*

1) the strength, competence and configuration of governmental and organized non-governmental proponents of environmental protection; and
2) a. cognitive-informational,
   b. political-institutional, and
   c. economic-technological framework conditions.

The utilization of existing capacities depends on:

3) the strategy, will and skill of proponents and
4) their situative opportunities.

This has to be related to:

5) the kind of problem: its urgency, its complexity, and the power resources and options of target groups, their allies and supporters (Jänicke, 1997, p. 8).

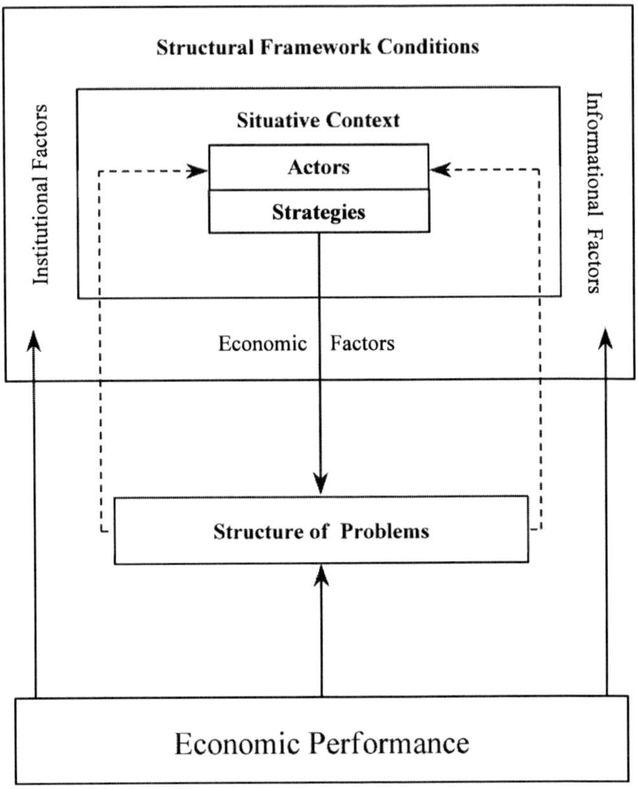

Source: Jänicke, 1997

Figure 1 Capacity Building: Model of Policy Explanation.

A country with a high capacity for environmental policy and management would have, for example: (1) many well-organized environmental player groups with well-established cooperative inter-organizational relations; (2a) comprehensive and accessible monitoring and reporting systems, a high degree of environmental awareness among political elites, the general public and the mass media as well as the capability to interpret the information in a politically strategic way; (2b) comprehensive and effective regulations, instruments and well-resourced institutions as well as a high degree of intra- and interpolicy co-operation; (2c) a flourishing, innovative environmental business sector and a modern industrial structure; (3) committed and strategically skilled actor groups; (4) high-pollution industries shaken by environmental scandals and highly visible progressive environmental initiatives by international organizations; (5) highly visible damage for which feasible solutions are available and a target group striving for a "greener image." If these ideal conditions were met, along with a sound level of social welfare, good economic prospects and a pro-innovation culture with a high esteem for post-material values, environmental success would, so to say, be inevitable.

This core definition of capacity building,[3] together with some basic assumptions about the interaction of the central categories (see Weale, 1992; Majone, 1989; Vogel, 1986; Hajer, 1995), provides a useful analytical framework for examining the importance, development and interplay of environmental capacities. It was used by the author and M. Jänicke in a cross-national study of environmental capacity building in 30 countries (see Jänicke & Weidner, 1997; Weidner & Jänicke, 2002).[4] The capacity building approach was used by all authors (usually environmental policy experts) of individual country studies; Peter Knoepfel, for instance, contributed as author of two country studies (Switzerland and Morocco). The countries examined are very diverse, including highly advanced front-runners, transitional economies, and newly industrializing and developing countries. Developed countries are over-represented: results and interpretation are biased correspondingly.

Results of the cross-national study

Results from the 30-country cross-national study highlight promising domestic approaches to environmental protection as well as potentially threatening tendencies. This article focuses on four sets of findings especially relevant to the dynamics of ecological modernization[5]: the institutionalization of environmental policy; the diffusion of environmental innovation; the interrelation between democracy and environmental capacity-building; and the effects of globalization on environmental policy and capacity.

Institutionalization of environmental policy

Environmental issues have established their place on national political agendas, so that today, for example, it would be hard for actors to follow a strategy of deliberate ignorance or suppression of environmental concerns such as occurred in Japan in the 1950s and early 1960s. As a result, key public

[3] See Jänicke (1997) for a comprehensive description.

[4] In Stage I, countries studied (with their investigators) were: Chile (Eduardo Silva), China (Yu-shi Mao), Denmark (Mikael Skou Andersen), Germany (Martin Jänicke/Helmut Weidner), Great Britain (Albert Weale), Japan (Hidefumi Imura), the Netherlands (Hans Th. Bressers/ Loret A. Plettenburg), Nigeria (Fatai Kayode Salau), Russia (Ivan Potravny/Ulrich Weißenburger), South Korea (Young Suck Nam), Sweden (Lennart Lundqvist), Switzerland (Peter Knoepfel), and the USA (Richard Andrews).

Countries studied in Stage II were: Australia (Elim Papadakis), Austria (Marina Fischer-Kowalski/ Christof Amann), Brazil (Kathryn Hochstetler), Bulgaria (Susan Baker), Canada (Robert Paehlke), Costa Rica (Eduardo Silva), Czech Republic (Adam Fagin), France (Corinne Larrue), Hungary (Joanne Caddy/ Anna Vari), India (Arun Agrawal), Italy (Bruno Dente/ Rudolf Lewanski), Mexico (Stephen P. Mumme), Morocco (Peter Knoepfel/ Marie Fauconnet), New Zealand (Ton Bührs), Poland (Magnus Andersson), Taiwan (Tan Shui-Yan), and Vietnam (Le Thac Can).

[5] See Jänicke, 2000; Mol & Sonnenfeld, 2000.

and private players react to new challenges by institutional adaptation. In the countries studied, such adaptation occurred in two broad waves, in the 1970s and 1990s. In addition, there were important changes over the course of these decades in which countries provided global leadership in environmental policy and management.

In Western democratic countries, the first moves towards institutionalizing environmental issues as a policy area were taken in the late 1960s (for details see Weidner & Jänicke, 2000, pp. 418f.). Incentives were usually domestic (for example in the USA, Britain, Japan, and Sweden), but sometimes came from elsewhere (as in Germany, Austria, Italy). Actions by international organizations (especially the UN Conference on the Human Environment in Stockholm 1972) set off the first broad global wave of institutionalization of environmental capacity, in the early 1970s; this encompassed countries of the former Soviet bloc, too.

With few exceptions, developing countries experienced significant institutionalization only in the aftermath of the Brundtland Commission and 1992 Rio Conference. These events triggered a second global wave of institutionalization of environmental capacity. Industrialized countries such as Great Britain, Sweden and Japan adopted new, foundational environmental legislation and reorganized environmental governance systems. Later, international aid organizations and multilateral environmental agreements boosted expansion of environmental capacity and reorganization of existing institutions in developing and transitional countries. The European Union (EU) also strongly influenced some transitional countries. In contrast to the early 1970s, it can be said that in the 1990s major quantitative and qualitative progress in governmental institutionalization was remarkably rapid and far-reaching throughout the world.

Furthermore, in the 1990s environmental institutions expanded considerably at various levels and in various areas of the politico-administrative system especially in the developed countries, but also in "latecomer states." Typically, parliamentary or cabinet committees and councils, or specialized ("mirror") units in other ministries (transport, industry, agriculture, etc.) were established, occasionally in the hope of checking the growing influence of environmental interests (e.g., Japan, Germany, France). Such institutions became increasingly important in interpolicy cooperation (see Knoepfel's influential article on inter- and intrapolicy coordination published as early as 1995; reprinted in Knoepfel 2007, pp. 131ff.), and were helpful in establishing strong administrative links between environmental and other policy areas, such as transport, land use planning, and agriculture (Denmark, Switzerland, the Netherlands, Britain, etc.). The inherent dynamics of institution-building should therefore not be underestimated, fuelled by administrative self-interest and the desire to expand functional scope and powers as well as the positive impact of cross-jurisdictional networking on policy learning. Such developments have hampered governmental attempts to reduce environmental capacities through rapid hierarchical action, as in Japan, Chile, Poland, and elsewhere.

In the developed countries, capacity building has continued apace since the 1970s in almost all areas of society, in the shape of organizational-institutional differentiation or integration. Be it in science, culture, politics, economics, or in civil society, all relevant organizations have created institutions specializing in environmental matters, or have expanded competencies in existing structures through training and education. This is also the case in research institutions, the Churches, the trade unions, the media, in business-including in medium-sized firms, and in broader social networks. In civil society, the institutionalization of environmental interests has been particularly marked. The number of NGOs in some countries almost defies listing. Sometimes NGOs have larger memberships than traditional interest groups such as trade unions or political parties (as in the Netherlands or Switzerland; for the latter see, Knoepfel, 1997).

Thus, the environmental movement in many countries has been subject to institutionalization for some time (Kriesi et al., 1995). Green parties have been founded. In Western Europe, the USA and elsewhere, a wide-ranging ecological commercial sector has emerged, including consulting firms, research facilities and service companies (for Switzerland, see Knoepfel, 1996, reprint 2007, pp. 331ss.). Such businesses' affinity for the environmental movement and NGOs has helped stimulate environmental organizations' interest in and enhance their capability for the cooperation with polluting industries. In Germany, for instance, (as in the Netherlands, Denmark, Switzerland, and Austria) all major environmental organizations are engaged in cooperative projects with business and government. Such projects have addressed a wide array of issues, from the development of environmental standards, to product environmental lifecycle analysis. Over the past decade, NGOs and even some of their most serious foes such as the chemical industry increasingly have sought to solve problems together.

Although the institutionalization of environmental interests in civil society is still weak in developing countries, there is already a clear trend in this direction, encouraged by international organizations and the sustainable development paradigm. Costa Rica, for example, has become a leader among developing countries in experimenting with partnership projects for biodiversity protection; and in Vietnam, almost all relevant elements of the country's environmental policy are the result of close collaboration between public institutions and transnational governmental and nongovernmental environmental organizations.

The development of environment-related organizations and networks has been supported and stimulated by politico-legal institutionalization in the form of laws and regulations. Environmental legislation has created new markets, areas of activity, and demands to which private businesses have reacted through specialization. Changes in fiscal or electoral law have promoted the emergence and stabilization of NGOs and green parties (Germany, Australia, New Zealand, etc.). The expansion of participatory, informational and other procedural arrangements, or the creation of new pluralistic institutions (such as governmental advisory councils, local Agenda 21 (see Lafferty & Eckerburg, 1998) processes, round tables or other forms of consensus-oriented bodies) has encouraged the emergence of sometimes highly specialized organizations in science and society (e.g., for environmental conflict resolution: USA, Canada, Germany, Austria, Switzerland). Overall, this has fostered the capacity and need for cooperation among different interest groups. This has led in turn to the establishment of new institutions like national round tables for the development of environmental long-term strategies (Canada, Great Britain, etc.), national councils for sustainable development (Switzerland, USA, Germany, etc.), and corporatist environmental standard-setting bodies (Austria, Germany, Denmark, Netherlands, France, etc.) (for Switzerland, see Knoepfel, 1995).

This broad advance of institutionalization is particularly pronounced at the international level, where there are now more than 200 multilateral environmental agreements and a large number of bodies and other facilities where environmental interest groups have a seat and a say (Vig & Axelrod, 1999). Some new environmental institutions have been created and many existing institutions have assumed environmental responsibilities as part of their broader missions (Werksman, 1996). Although the actual impact of Agenda 21 on national policy is still weak, it has strongly stimulated the discourse on economic growth and environmental preservation, thus encouraging new institutions and regulations in many countries. The International Council for Local Environmental Initiatives (ICLEI) has contributed decisively to the global spread of Agenda 21 activities and to the emergence of a global network of environmentally progressive local communities. In addition to international environmental network building and institutionalization, there are more and more regional and cross-national forms, for example those focusing on environmental capacity building in the transitional economies of the Baltic Sea. The spread of "epistemic communities" (Haas, 1992) should also be mentioned.

There are innumerable variants of formal and informal institutionalization, from local to global levels. Since the end of the 1980s, organizations from the transitional and developing countries have been increasingly involved. This is particularly important when politico-administrative institutions and NGOs in these countries have reduced capacities, mainly owing to economic crises. This was the case in transitional countries a few years after the shift toward democracy. The reason for the sometimes substantial cutbacks in capacity-in personnel and financial resources-was that opponents of the incumbent communist regimes often "took shelter" in ecological organizations. For many different categories of player, ecological criticism of the system created a provisional, common basis for action, in the sense of a lowest common political denominator. With the change in system, the various interests went their own ways (Poland, Czech Republic, Bulgaria, Hungary, Russia). International organizations strongly encouraged environmental capacity-building in these countries, including in the NGO sector, with positive results. Pressure from the EU also checked reduction of environmental capacity in the transitional countries: those wishing to accede to the EU are required to attain certain levels of environmental institutionalization (see Baker & Jehlicka, 1998; Holzinger & Knoepfel 2000).

In the 1970s, environmental institution building was initiated and strongly influenced by countries like the United States and Sweden. Japan, after a severe ecological crisis, became a short-term pioneer in pollution control during this period, as well: Japanese flue-gas purification technology, the compensation system linked to an SO^2 charge, and voluntary environmental agreements stimulated progress in Japanese environmental policy overseas as well as at home (see Tsuru & Weidner, 1989). In the 1980s, Germany quite unexpectedly became a leader in environmental policy and a major exporter of pollution control technology. Much of this impetus was lost in the 1990s, following German re-unification and the most severe economic recession since WWII. However, capacities were reduced only in peripheral areas of environmental policy. Germany has remained a progressive player in most areas of international environmental policy (Weidner, 1997).

For many industrialized and practically all developing countries, the incentive for and models of environmental institution building continue to come from the pioneering advanced industrial countries and-increasingly-from international organizations (especially UNEP, EU, OECD). Despite a number of much discussed and sometimes imitated instruments (emission trading, least-cost planning in the energy sector, etc.), the United States has not been among the front-runners for the past decade, largely because of its restrictive global environmental policy (Paarlberg, 1999) and weak environmental performance. The lead has been taken by countries like Denmark (for a certain period of time), the Netherlands, and Sweden. This has been achieved by far-reaching institutional reorganization in various policy areas to steer integrative environmental policy towards ecological modernization and sustainable development (see Andersen & Liefferink, 1997; Hanf & Jansen, 1998).

The Netherlands and Sweden are particularly interesting. In many countries, central elements of Dutch and Swedish environmental policy strategy, such as flexible, cooperative governance, strategic long-term planning, the ecological footprint concept, eco-taxes, and stakeholder orientation, have triggered intensive discussion within the environmental movement and political and scientific circles. Such measures have been emulated in Germany, Austria, Switzerland, Hungary, and Japan. The EU's Fifth Environmental Programme (1993-2000) was strongly influenced by the Dutch National Environmental Policy Plan of 1989 (Liefferink, 1997). In the realm of climate change policy and related energy policy (renewables, efficiency, etc.), Germany's policies and instruments are at present strongly influencing not only the EU and its member countries but also other international organizations and countries all over the world (see Weidner & Mez 2008). Global processes of capacity-building thus demonstrably depend on national innovation.

Legal and governmental institution building is a basic precondition for effective public policy. It institutionalizes vested interests in the politico-administrative system as well as responsibilities and accountability, and increases the opportunity for civil society players to exert influence (Weaver & Rockman, 1993). Of course, the actual contribution of this institutionalization to environmental capacity depends on additional factors such as resources, competencies, kinds of embeddedness, etc.

In the 30 countries studied, there is a broad range of quality of environmental institutions. Trends indicate an overall rise in environmental capacity:

1) acceleration of general institutionalization and its spread to almost all countries in the world (see World Bank, 2000; UNEP, 1999);
2) expansion of existing capacities (resources, specialized staff, regulations, etc.) and only seldom a massive reduction; marked fluctuations in developing countries are seen, however;
3) increase in power and functions of environmental institutions in countries where initial institutionalization had tended to be formal or symbolic in nature;
4) modernization (reorganization, renewal) of institutions, especially since the late 1980s, with the aim of greater efficiency, often in association with new public management strategies and in reaction to international developments and agreements (e.g., Agenda 21, sustainable development, national environmental planning);
5) "ecologicalization" of many institutions and organizations in various societal systems (and scientific disciplines) in the developed countries, this is slowly progressing in developing nations, too (e.g., India, Costa Rica, Vietnam);
6) further increase in capacities generated by existing environmental institutions themselves, through various and partly innovative means, e.g., network formation (e.g., International Association of National Environmental Expert Councils) and informal practices (e.g., voluntary environmental cooperation).

In all 30 countries studied, institutional environmental capacities are greater now than in the 1970s, sometimes substantially so. The increase has been particularly marked since the globalization debate reached a peak in the 1990s. Nevertheless, there are still major capacity deficits in advanced countries that are a serious hindrance to "ecological modernization" and especially to sustainable development. There are, for instance, weaknesses in sub-national implementation, and environmental monitoring and reporting systems are deficient. There are particular inadequacies in interpolicy cooperation ("integrative environmental policy") and in the capacity for legal and political intervention against powerful polluters (e.g., standing to sue, strict liability, joint and several liability). Shifting structural asymmetries in the societal parallelogram of power in favor of environmental proponents is, of course, a matter of general democratization and goes far beyond the sphere of environmental policy (see Lafferty & Meadowcroft 1996).

Diffusion of environmental innovation

The primary aims of environmental innovation are to reduce consumption of natural resources and improve environmental quality, and to maintain those reductions and improvements over the long term; it should also improve the ratio between technology costs and benefits. In light of today's environmental challenges and policy deficiencies (see UNEP, 1999), development and diffusion of innovation must be seen as key components of successful environmental policy. Many consider ecological modernization to be, in essence, innovation policy (Wallace, 1995; Jänicke, 2000).

Today, technological innovations spread far more rapidly than in the 1970s and the 1980s, when even highly developed industrial countries with serious pollution problems needed a decade or more to adopt certain abatement technologies. This is the case, for example, with flue gas scrubbers, catalytic devices for cars, and wastewater purification systems. These technologies were best practice in the United States and Japan long before being introduced in other countries. Even transitional and developing countries now adopt new environmental technologies relatively quickly, at least in new facilities. International aid in environmental technology has certainly contributed. In several countries studied, innovation in environmental technology has become a dynamic sector of the economy, sometimes with a considerable impact on industry and employment in general. The United States, Germany, and Japan are the three largest exporters of environmental products, and further growth is expected owing to the great backlog of demand in many other countries.

In technical and especially organizational-institutional innovation, the United States was long considered *the* front runner in environmental policy (but not in climate change policy!). The innovations introduced in the United States include NEPA, EPA, TSCA, CERCAL (or Superfund), various economic instruments, alternative dispute resolution procedures (ADR), eco-sponsoring, investment funds based on ethical-ecological criteria as well as innovative abatement technologies such as catalytic devices. In one form or another, almost all have been adopted in many other countries, and have helped boost environmental capacities and environmental proponents. For example, Environmental Impact Assessment has become a basic instrument in many countries in promoting environmental interests in public and private land use. Strict liability rules have strengthened the legal hand of those affected by pollution. The Freedom of Information Act has ensured greater clarity, and ADR have brought productive conflict resolution and broken deadlocks in multi-stakeholder negotiations (Napier, 1998).

In contrast, the United States has very seldom explicitly adopted and implemented ideas from elsewhere. Where it has done so, the result has generally been below par, as was the case with the eco-label system (EPA, 1998). Emission trading has become a core element of the Kyoto Protocol for climate protection in the United States, leading to the worldwide spread of the concept. However, until recently the United States did not use the instrument to reduce greenhouse gas emissions.

For some years now, the Nordic countries and the Netherlands, now and again Germany and Britain have made major contributions to environmental policy innovation and its diffusion. The most important have been the precautionary approach, green ministers, consumer access to renewable energy,[6] closed-loop material cycles, comprehensive production and product responsibility ("from the cradle to the grave"), eco-labeling, eco-auditing schemes (e.g., the Eco-audit and Management Scheme [EMAS], and ISO 14001), resource stream management, separate waste management systems and the "Green Dot System" for packaging waste, voluntary environmental agreements, green public procurement policy, environmental accounting, eco-taxes, and Local Agenda 21 initiatives.

Some policy innovations have spread worldwide with particular rapidity, including comprehensive national environmental action plans (NEAPs), sustainability strategies, environmental labeling,[7] and voluntary agreements (World Bank, 2000). There were isolated NEAPs in the late 1980s (in the Netherlands, Britain, Canada, Denmark, etc.). With the 1992 Rio Conference and adoption of Agenda 21, diffusion has been fast throughout the world-in Western industrialized countries, Eastern Europe, and in developing countries (Jänicke & Jörgens, 2000). International organizations have done much to promote rapid diffusion (OECD, UN institutions, EU, World Bank).

NEAPs are increasingly contributing to capacity building. Just how important certain capacities are in other environment-related areas often becomes apparent in the process of long-term national environmental planning. This is the case with cooperative capabilities and cognitive-informational factors (e.g., monitoring, cross-sectoral coordination, evaluating complicated problem complexes). Sweden, for example, has adopted a particularly ambitious national environmental plan ("The Future Environment-Our Common Responsibility") with the aim of making the country sustainable within about 25 years (Lundqvist, 2000).

There are many reasons why environmental innovations have been spreading more rapidly throughout the world:

1) Environmental policy has become internationalized. International regimes and institutions have become more important (UNEP, CSD, World Bank, OECD, IUCN, etc.), actively monitoring and reporting innovations and fostering their diffusion (e.g., World Bank, 2000; OECD, 1999; UNEP, 1999).
2) "Governance by diffusion" has developed at all levels of government (local to national). Increasingly, outstanding approaches to solving environmental problems are imported from front-runner countries to enhance local action and problem-solving capacities (Kern, Jörgens & Jänicke, 2000). This underlines the key role of pioneer countries in the diffusion of environmental innovation. Innovations spread conspicuously among non-governmental players, especially in the environmental movement (protest forms, resource mobilization) and in science (theories, approaches, research organization). Diffusion of environmental innovation

---

[6] "Eco-power supply-on-demand," as it is referred to in Europe, provides customers with the option of choosing electricity from renewable energy resources (excluding nuclear energy). This is more expensive than the regularly-supplied electricity (which includes nuclear-generated power).

[7] For a systematic overview and discussion, see Kern, et al., 2000.

has also accelerated in the business sector, especially in eco-auditing, product chain environmental management strategies, stakeholder cooperation, eco-risk insurance, and voluntary agreement-based negotiations with parties affected by pollution.

All in all, a process of global environmental policy learning is being firmly established (Rose, 1993). Along with growing business interest in innovation for a global market, and an expanding transnational network of environmental NGOs, this mitigates against a massive "race to the bottom" in environmental standards and the spread of "pollution havens."

Democracy and capacity-building

Development of democratic institutions and rules is a key precondition for building environmental capacity, gaining support of environmental proponents, and creating an opportunity structure to publicly address environmental problems (Lafferty & Meadowcroft, 1996). Democratic institutions and rules are essential when the preferences and problem-solving concepts of players are at variance with the norms and problem perceptions of the political and economic elites, as is often the case with progressive environmental movements.

The great importance of democratic structures for effective environmental policy is evident in many of the countries studied, especially where liberal-pluralistic democratic institutions are non-existent or weak. In eastern European countries and Latin American dictatorships, significant capacity building and environmental effects occurred only after a change in political system. In South Korea and Taiwan, general democratization processes have very markedly enhanced the opportunity structure for environmental interests and-compared with the long time it took to develop an environmental policy in Western democratic countries-have led to the relatively rapid establishment of a solid capacity basis. This has permitted at least an effective conventional (end-of-pipe) environmental policy, and has fostered first, tentative moves toward ecological modernization. In South Korea NGOs and environmental campaigning have increased since democratization started in 1987 (see also Japan Environmental Council, 2000). In Taiwan, the environmental arena also profited from government efforts to achieve an image of responsive democracy. The Taiwanese government needs international support, especially in the conflict with mainland China. In China and Vietnam, political liberalization, essentially the consequence of a new economic policy, has promoted the building of institutional and technical capacities in the environmental field. They are still too weak to counter the negative ecological impact of a dynamic industrial growth policy.

In all the eastern European countries under study (Poland, Hungary, Czech Republic, Bulgaria, Russia), environmental conflicts and environmental proponents have helped change the political system. Environmental organizations often provided the only platform for openly criticizing shortcomings in the political system and the statist economy. The system could thus be subjected to political criticism under an ecological guise.

Although environmental capacity-building elements, proponents, and supporting factors in transitional and developing countries are similar to those in developed countries, their mode of action, interaction, and contextual relations can be very different with very different results. For example, although the professionalization of environmental organizations achieved with foreign support engenders the necessary cognitive-informational capacities, it can help isolate such organizations from socio-political processes, or reduce their social credibility (as in Bulgaria, Czech Republic, and also in Brazil, as militant conflicts between environmental groups and the landless movement demonstrate). This shows that strategies for strengthening environmental policy must take historical political culture into account. This is particularly important in countries with little experience of democratic institutions, where historical experience has produced a deep-rooted mistrust of politico-administrative institutions and of mobilization for "public goods", where civil society is passive, and the old politico-administrative mechanisms of rule and ruling elites still loom large (e.g., in Morocco, Nigeria and sometimes increasingly so in Russia and Bulgaria).

Despite the problems for environmental policy capacity building associated with democratization processes in newly industrializing and transitional countries, it is evident that democratization and strong democratic structures and procedures are the *sine qua non* for an environmental policy that goes beyond pollution control toward achieving ecological modernization. Country studies show this to be equally true for the advanced industrial countries.[8] There are innumerable cases in point: Italy's partly Mafia-controlled politics; the closed neo-corporatist arrangements in Austrian or German policy decision-making; the opaque policy decision-making processes in Japan; the exclusion or even marginalization of environmental actor groups from program formulation and decision making, long the case in Germany; limited access to the courts for environmental interest groups in many developing countries-and in developed countries; a legal dogmatism with a strong bias in favor of polluters' interests; the strong and institutionalized influence of economic interests in politics, administration, and the public media; and systemic political bias engendering inequity and the systematic violation of the principles of environmental justice.

Democratization has proved a basic condition for effective capacity building, and has significantly improved the opportunity structure for environmental proponents throughout the world by increasing the participatory, integrative, and cognitive-informational capacities of political systems. Democratization might therefore be considered a "meta-capacity" for environmental capacity building.

Much remains to be done. For instance, Amnesty International (Schneider 2000) has reported on the massive repression suffered by environmentally committed individuals or NGOs in Russia, Mexico, Brazil, India and other countries. However, many developed countries still have to democratize political structures that exempt polluters from the need to learn and adopt

[8] For a different opinion, see Saretzki, 2007.

sustainable procedures. The problem is particularly acute in sectors like transport, energy, construction and agriculture, where environmental interests confront almost closed policy networks, which have been strong enough nearly everywhere to obstruct preventive environmental measures that go beyond end-of-pipe treatment.

Although support from Western countries and international organizations has been decisive for environmental capacity building in newly industrializing and transitional countries, the transfer of Western instruments and innovations is not unproblematic. The studies have shown that the same instruments and procedures almost inevitably have a different effect than in established, liberal-pluralistic democracies. This is particularly true for instruments designed to promote active public commitment and responsible participation, or those that presuppose functioning legal and administrative systems. Far too little account has been taken of these aspects in promoting environmental policy capacity building, especially by the EU in negotiating the accession of eastern European countries (see Carius et al., 2000; Holzinger and Knoepfel, 2000). As the transfer of adoptable technologies to developing countries has been on the agenda for many years, foreign organizations should pay greater attention in their assistance policies to the political-cultural compatibility of democratic institutions. Policy learning and the corresponding capacity building is, therefore, also demanded of Western countries, and especially of international organizations.

Globalization and environmental capacities

Economic globalization's positive effects on environmental policy have received significantly less attention than its negative consequences (Weidner and Jänicke, 2001). The strong increase in environmental activities by a wide range of actor groups, the establishment of global environmental actor networks and "global environmental governance" by international institutions indicate the emergence of a global environmental policy in which the central players are non-governmental actors.

Studies on global governance (e.g., Young, 1997) as well as our research findings do not support the thesis that national governments would wither away or lose power as a result of globalization, with a consequent decline in environmental standards. National governments continue to play an important role in coping with environmental problems. National governments have many sources of power-they systematically enable and frame forms of global governance, network-building, etc. or use more traditional power resources.

Governments in Western industrial countries often have very high national budgets and corresponding public purchasing power, giving them the wherewithal to integrate environmental objectives in the manufacturing and consumer sectors. Even without higher national budgets, their scope for ecological policy formation is considerable, for example by reallocating environmentally unsound (or even "perverse") subsidies in favor of ecological modes of production. The new EU agricultural policy has likewise taken this course.

Furthermore, some countries-and especially those strongly involved in international market processes, like the Netherlands, Denmark, Sweden, and Switzerland-have demonstrated their ability to initiate and implement progressive environmental concepts even at the height of globalization and often under unfavorable domestic economic conditions. These "pioneer countries" thus contribute to the learning process in global environmental policy. Although globalization is often used as an excuse for environmental policy deficiencies, the arguments have a rather weak empirical basis. Shortcomings in national environmental policy are often the main cause (Jänicke and Weidner, 1997).

Moreover, the overwhelming majority of empirical studies on the economic effects of globalization on environmental policy (cf. Rugman and Verbeke, 2000) produce no evidence for a race to the bottom in environmental standards or for "pollution havens". And there is no correlation between progressive environmental policy and economic decline (see Sturm et al., 2000). In contrast, tough regulations usually stimulate innovation, making firms generally fitter and more competitive (Wallace, 1995; see also Ashford 2002).

In sum, for the 30 countries studied, positive forms of globalization predominated with respect to environmental policy. This finding may not be generalizable however, since most were advanced industrial societies. Other studies, especially those concerned not only theoretically with the globalization phenomenon, reach a more differentiated result on the consequences of globalization (e.g., Spaargaren, Mol and Buttel, 2000; Mol and Sonnenfeld, 2000; Angel and Rock, 2000; UNEP, 1999).

Discussion

This article has presented findings of a study covering 30 countries that used the environmental capacity building approach and addressed a number of factors central to the ecological modernization and sustainable development of national societies. Among other things, these results show that a remarkable institutionalization of environmental competencies has taken place worldwide. Taking into account the time that far-reaching institutional and social change usually requires, this process has been astonishingly rapid in both breadth and depth. As had been the case in the industrial countries, much institutionalization in developing countries is still strongly formal or symbolic in nature. But experience in the industrialized world has shown that this is an important first step in the substantive development of institutions.

In one regard the industrial countries-which include all "environmental pioneers"-can be described as latecomers, namely in the social aspects of environmental policy as a holistic concept. In developing countries, economic and social issues have always played a central role in this field, whereas many industrial countries have limited their attention more strongly to environmental problems in the sense of an eco-centric approach. They began to pay greater attention to social and economic aspects at home and abroad only with the advent of the sustainable development vision. Ecological modernization and, still more so, sustainable development appear to be producing worldwide convergence in conceptual approaches to, or the "framing" of, the ecology issue and global challenges.

In the case of democracy, the cross-national analysis of 30 countries shows that democratic structures and procedures in all areas of society and not only in the political system are key preconditions for effective environmental policy. This is particularly true of an environmental policy guided by the concepts of ecological modernization or sustainable development. It requires strong capacities for conflict resolution, innovation, integration, and strategy building.

Overall, the cross-national study shows that a radically dichotomizing discussion about environmental policy structures, institutions, instruments, concepts, or strategies-pitching economic instruments against regulatory-interventionist policy, conflict against cooperation, economic growth against a steady-state economy-cannot do justice to the complexity of the environmental policy context and its dynamics. One thing at least is clear. A broad base of elements is needed, and they need to be intelligently linked.

Paradoxically, capacity for sustainable development could, at first sight, also be strengthened by abolishing capacities, namely such capacities which might be called "bad" or "negative capacities."[9] This term refers to material and immaterial (cognitive, networking, strategic, etc.) capacities existing within the politico-administrative realm and which have proven to be restrictive and counterproductive for achieving sustainable development, e.g., environmentally adverse subsidy schemes, old-fashioned networks made up of public bodies and powerful but pollution-prone economic sectors, governance structures and procedures favoring one-dimensional, technocratic and time-consuming decision-making. However, just as countries have path-dependent weaknesses in sustainable environmental policy making, they also have path-dependent strengths (e.g., the capability of achieving multi-stakeholder consensus in the public interest), which should be preserved and developed. The overarching goal of a modern environmental policy should therefore be to raise the level of environmental policy performance and not "mechanically" to streamline policy approaches and reduce administrative capacities. A promising development in this direction can be seen in the increasing number and types of multi-stakeholder cooperation initiated, stimulated or promoted by governmental actors. Even at the international level NGOs, governments, and the scientific community increasingly have combined forces in negotiating (Lipschutz, 1996). Sometimes, governments have enlisted the aid of NGOs to lobby on behalf of mutually agreed positions in other countries or in international organizations. Not only the German government-even under a conservative coalition-has given NGOs financial and other assistance in preparing international negotiations. Emphasis on the evidently positive effects of networking and coalition building among civil, economic, and state actors to pave the way for sustainable development policies is not to be confused with calls for undermining or even abolishing hierarchically regulating and acting

[9] For the general concept of „negative capacities," see Keller, Lowi & Gendlin, 2000.

governments. All case studies revealed the decisive role strong governments have in paving the way to ecological modernization and sustainable development (Jänicke, 2007).

A country's capacity to identify and solve environmental problems depends not only on the abilities of government and private proponents. They act within a national context, which provides systemic opportunities and restrictions. From various case studies of developing countries we learn that the elementary precondition for environmental policy-making and management is a minimum of political and economic stability. Another systemic precondition of policy success is the internal integration of relevant environmental activities of the government. This is a difficult and time-consuming task. Intersectoral integration of different policies is even more complicated (see Knoepfel 1995/2007). The integration of environmental and transport policy, for instance, does not seem to be functioning anywhere. The same can be said of energy policy in many countries, although, with the growing relevance of climate policy, energy and climate policy become rather closely interlocked at least in the "pioneer countries."[10] Other political areas where the integration of environmental policy is still problematic are usually agriculture and construction.

The available knowledge about problems or options, and the capacity to learn and to apply that learning to environmental policy processes is another important systemic resource of environmental policy and management. For a long time global policy-learning in this field was heavily dependent on the scientific capacity and experience of the United States. Only later on did countries such as Germany, Great Britain, Netherlands, Sweden, and Switzerland develop a broad scientific infrastructure to provide independent environmental expertise of a standing which could not be challenged by industrial opponents. The rise of global environmental "epistemic communities" and global research networks, such as the Intergovernmental Panel of Climate Change (IPCC), provides opportunities also for smaller countries to participate in top-level research and/or to profit from state-of-the-art research results. In a certain respect, these countries could compensate for lacking research capacities through networking capacities.

The conceptual framework presented in the second chapter stressed the character of the environmental problem to be solved as one of the main factors influencing policy outcomes and capacity needs. Models of environmental policy-making have often ignored this category. Our case studies, however, give valuable indications of the importance of this factor. It is no coincidence that certain problems have not undergone significant improvement in many countries. Thus, although capacities for environmental policy and management have continued to expand remarkably over the past decade, particularly from the institutional point of view, the global ecological challenges (especially in climate change) and certain national and regional

[10] Inter- and intra-policy coordination is still a vast and almost untapped reservoir of possible improvements to increase the administrative capacities for sustainable development policies (see Knoepfel 1995/2007).

problems (such as decreasing biodiversity, soil pollution, depletion of water resources, deforestation, growing traffic emissions, urban sprawl) have increased. The explanation for these developments could be in the structure of the problem, in terms of its visibility and urgency, the availability of a standard technological solution and the societal importance and composition of the relevant target groups (Jänicke, 2000).

Conclusion

From the main findings of the cross-national study the following conclusions can be drawn:

- There has been a remarkable increase in capacities for environmental policy and management in the last 25 years which could not have been anticipated at the outset. The rapid development of specialized policy institutions, including even a (cautious) penetration of other policy fields, seems to be without precedence in the history of the modern state. The most important characteristic of this development is nevertheless "societal" capacity building beyond government institutions.
- With innovations such as new forms of participation, information rights, self-regulation, networking or cooperative planning, the ecological question has contributed to the general process of political modernization. In more advanced countries, such as Denmark, Sweden, the Netherlands, Switzerland, Japan or Germany, it has also become a motor of economic modernization and innovation.
- This development can be described as a process of global environmental policy learning. We can thus see from our case studies that the process of globalization not only leads to greater ecological stress world-wide. It also significantly enlarges domestic capacities for environmental protection in most countries.
- The communicative mechanisms of this global learning process seem to be bilateral imitation at first, then diffusion through international institutions-especially the UN system, later also the OECD-and finally learning within a broad international network of environmental government institutions and non-governmental organizations, the media, research institutions, and "green business" organizations.
- Throughout the countries included in the study, a global environmental policy convergence can be observed, irrespective of national differences in, e.g., policy style. The patterns of environmental policy have become similar even under extremely varying domestic conditions. Even the change of the dominant environmental policy paradigm-from end-of-pipe treatment and government command-and-control to softer instruments and more sustainable approaches-takes place on a global scale.
- Thus it is not so much the general policy pattern but the problems, capacities, and outcomes of environmental policy and management which differ

significantly in global terms. In some parts of the world, the new "standard" environmental policy institutions and laws were only introduced on paper, and have no effective basis within government or society. The main problem lies in the field of implementation, which points to the enormous importance of implementation studies in environmental policy research.[11]

- Although many less developed countries have suffered a general deterioration in the environmental situation and high pollution levels-especially in urban areas-globalization has not been the main cause. It lies in the aggregation of long-standing structural problems such as poverty and population growth, and in economic growth according to old patterns (UNEP, 1999). This may explain why environmental capacities *and* ecological problems can paradoxically increase concurrently.
- Economically advanced countries have often achieved impressive environmental improvements in a wide range of areas (UNEP, 1999; see also Jahn, 1998; Scruggs, 2003). But they are usually restricted to specific pollutants and to problems that are highly visible and amenable to technical solution without the need for structural changes in economic procedures. In most average countries, especially highly developed ones, certain problems have increased rather than abated. This has been the case with traffic emissions, waste production, soil contamination, and extensive land use. Even environmental front runners display major shortcomings if, from the perspective of concepts like ecological modernization and sustainable development, evaluation takes account of general resource consumption, biodiversity, and inter- and intra-generational environmental equity and equality. In most advanced countries, too, existing environmental capacities have usually sufficed for more or less standard solutions based mainly on technological progress. Greater capacities are clearly needed to develop effective strategies against environmentally harmful land use patterns and materials flow management, and for soil and climate protection.

All of the above point to persisting structural limits to policy and management striving at sustainable development, even in environmentally most advanced countries. While in some areas the problems can be ascribed to unused or underused capacities (capacities may exist but lie idle owing to actors' lack of will and skill), the problems mentioned indicate an overload of

---

[11] In the late 1970s implementation research in the field of environmental policy boomed. The results of this line of research contributed strongly to the progress made in theory-building for environmental policy research; see, e.g. (for Germany) Mayntz 1980, 1983. Peter Knoepfel and I enjoyed the privilege of being members of the Implementation Research Group directed by Renate Mayntz and Fritz W. Scharpf. Unfortunately, with the rise of the governance paradigm comprehensive and empirical implementation studies—encompassing norm-setting, program formulation, implementation, and evaluation (see Knoepfel & Weidner, 1982; Knoepfel & Weidner, 1985)—were rarely undertaken. However, it seems as if recently there is a growing awareness of the limitations and deficits of governance studies when they fail to stringently include capacities and outcomes/impacts in policy analyses – scientific progress for some, déjà vu for others...

existing capacities and a need to develop new capacities suitable for handling economic and politico-societal conflicts of interest and power. Interpolicy coordination (Knoepfel, 1995) could be an important step towards this goal.

References

Andersen, M.S. & Liefferink, D. (Eds.) (1997). *European environmental policy: the pioneers.* Manchester University Press.

Angel, D. & Rock, M. (Eds.) (2000). *Asia's clean revolution: Industry, growth and the environment.* Sheffield: Greenleaf Publishing.

Ashford, N. A. (2002). Government and Environmental Innovation in Europe and North America. In *American Behavioral Scientist,* 45(9), 1417-1434.

Baker, S. & Jehlicka, P. (Eds.) (1998). Dilemmas of transition: The environment, democracy and economic reform in East Central Europe. *Environmental Politics* (special issue), 7(1).

Carius, A., von Homeyer, I., Bär. S., & Kraemer, R.A. (2000). *Die umweltpolitische Dimension der Osterweiterung der Europäischen Union.* Stuttgart: Metzler-Poeschel.

EPA (1998). *Environmental labeling issues, policies and practices world wide.* (EPA-742-R-98-009). Washington DC: Office of Prevention, Pesticides, and Toxic Substances.

Haas, P.M. (1992). Introduction: Epistemic communities and international policy coordination. *International Organization,* 46, 1-36.

Hanf, K. & Jansen, A.-I. (Eds.) (1998). *Governance and environment in Western Europe.* Essex: Longman.

Hajer, M.A.J. (1995). *The Politics of environmental discourse: Ecological modernisation and the policy process.* Oxford: Clarendon.

Helfrich, H.W. (Ed.) (1971). *Agenda for survival.* New Haven: Yale University Press.

Holzinger, K., Jörgens, H. & Knill, C. (Eds.) (2007). Transfer, Diffusion und Konvergenz von Politiken, *Politische Vierteljahresschrift,* Sonderheft 38. Wiesbaden: VS Verlag für Sozialwissenschaften.

Holzinger, K. & Knoepfel, P. (2000). *Environmental policy in a European Union of variable geometry?* Basel: Helbing & Lichtenhahn.

Jänicke, M. (1992). Conditions for environmental policy success: an international comparison. *The Environmentalist* 12(1), 47-58.

Jänicke, M. (1997). The political system's capacity for environmental policy. In M. Jänicke & H. Weidner (Eds.), *National environmental policies. A comparative study of capacity-building.* Berlin, Heidelberg etc.: Springer, 1-14.

Jänicke, M. (2000). Ökologische Modernisierung als Innovation und Diffusion in Politik *und Technik. FFU-report 00-01.* Berlin: Freie Universität Berlin.

Jänicke, M. (2007). Umweltstaat. In K. Jacob, F. Biermann, P.-O. Busch & P. H. Feindt (Eds.), Politik und Umwelt. *Politische Vierteljahresschrift,* Sonderheft 39. Wiesbaden: VS Verlag für Sozialwissenschaften, 342-359.

Jänicke, M. & Jörgens, H. (Eds.) (2000). *Umweltplanung im internationalen Vergleich. Strategien der Nachhaltigkeit.* Berlin, Heidelberg, New York: Springer.

Jänicke, M. & Weidner, H. (Eds.) (1995). *Successful environmental policy. A critical evaluation of 24 cases.* Berlin: Edition Sigma.

Jänicke, M. & Weidner, H. (Eds.) (1997). *National environmental policies. A comparative study of capacity-building (13 countries).* Berlin, Heidelberg, New York: Springer.

Jahn, D. (1998). Environmental performance and policy regimes: Explaining variations in 18 OECD-countries. *Policy Sciences,* 31, 107-131.

Japan Environmental Council (Ed.) (2000). *The state of the environment in Asia 1999/2000.* Tokyo: Springer.

Keller, W. W., Lowi, Th. J. & Gendlin, G. (2000). Negative capital and the wealth of nations. In *International Studies Perspectives,* 1, 75-87.

Kern, K., Jörgens, H., & Jänicke, M. (2000). Die Diffusion umweltpolitischer Innovationen. Ein Beitrag zur Globalisierung von Umweltpolitik. *Zeitschrift für Umweltpolitik und Umweltrecht,* 23(4), 507-546.

Knoepfel, P. (Ed.) (1995). *Lösung von Umweltkonflikten durch Verhandlungen.* Basel: Helbing & Lichtenhahn.

Knoepfel, P. (1995/2007). New Institutional Arrangements for a New Generation of Environmental Policy Instruments: Intra- and Interpolicy Cooperation. In P. Knoepfel (Ed.), *Environmental Policy Analyses. Learning from the Past for the Future – 25 Years of Research.* Berlin, Heidelberg, New York: Springer, 131-175 (reprint from 1995).

Knoepfel, P. (1996/2007). Ecobusiness and the State-Analysis and Scenarios. In P. Knoepfel (Ed.), *Environmental Policy Analyses. Learning from the Past for the Future – 25 Years of Research.* Berlin, Heidelberg, New York: Springer, 331-363 (reprint from 1996).

Knoepfel, P. (1997). Switzerland. In M. Jänicke & H. Weidner (Eds.), *National Environmental Policies. A Comparative Study of Capacity-Building.* Berlin, Heidelberg, New York: Springer, 175-197.

Knoepfel, P. (Ed.) (2007). *Environmental Policy Analyses. Learning from the Past for the Future – 25 Years of Research.* Berlin, Heidelberg, New York: Springer.

Knoepfel, P., Nahrath, S. & Varone, F. (2007). Institutional Regimes for Natural Resources: An Innovative Theoretical Framework for Sustainability. In P. Knoepfel (Ed.), *Environmental Policy Analyses. Learning from the Past for the Future – 25 Years of Research* Berlin, Heidelberg, New York: Springer, 455-506.

Knoepfel, P. & Weidner, H. (1982). Formulation and Implementation of Air Quality Control Programmes: Patterns of interest consideration. *Policy and Politics* 10(1), 85-109.

Knoepfel, P. & Weidner, H. (1985). *Luftreinhaltepolitik (stationäre Quellen) im internationalen Vergleich.* 6 volumes. Berlin: edition sigma.

Kriesi, H., Koopmans, R., Dyvendak, J.W., & Giugni, M.G. (1995). *New social movements in Western Europe. A comparative analysis.* Minneapolis: University of Minnesota Press.

Lafferty, W.M. & Eckerberg, K. (Eds.) (1998). *From the Earth Summit to Local Agenda 21. Working towards sustainable development.* London: Earthscan.

Lafferty, W.M. & Meadowcroft, J. (1996). *Democracy and the environment. Problems and prospects.* Cheltenham, Brookfield: Edward Elgar.

Langhelle, O. (2000). Why Ecological Modernisation and Sustainable Development should not be Conflated. *Journal of Environmental Policy & Planning* 2 (4): 303-322.
Liefferink, D. (1997). The Netherlands: A net exporter of environmental policy concepts. In M.S. Andersen & D. Liefferink (Eds.), *European environmental policy: the pioneers.* Manchester: Manchester University Press, 210-250.
Lipschutz, R. (1996). *Global civil society and global environmental governance.* Albany: State University of New York Press.
Lundqvist, L.J. (2000). Capacity-building or social construction? Explaining Sweden's shift toward ecological modernisation. *Geoforum* 31, 21-32.
Majone, G. (1989). *Evidence, argument and persuasion in the policy process.* New Haven, London: Yale University Press.
Mayntz, R. (Ed.) (1980). *Implementation politischer Programme. Empirische Implementationsforschung.* Königstein/Taunus: Hain.
Mayntz, R. (Ed.) (1983). *Implementation politischer Programme II.* Opladen: Westdeutscher Verlag.
Mol, A.P.J. & Sonnenfeld, D.A. (Eds.) (2000). *Ecological modernisation around the world. Perspectives and critical debates.* London, Portland/OR: Frank Cass.
Napier, C. (Ed.) (1998). *Environmental conflict resolution.* London: Cameron May.
OECD (1994). *Capacity development in environment.* Paris: OECD.
OECD (1999). *Voluntary approaches for environmental policy. An assessment.* Paris. OECD.
Ohiorhenuan, J.F.E. & Wunker, S.M. (1995). *Capacity building requirements for global environmental protection.* Global Environment Facility Working Paper No. 12. Washington DC: World Bank.
Paarlberg, R.L. (1999). Lapsed leadership: US international environmental policy since Rio. In N.J. Vig & R.S. Axelrod (Eds.), *The global environment. Institutions, law and policy.* Washington DC: CQ Press, 236-255.
Roos, L.L. (1971). *The politics of ecosuicide.* New York: Holt, Rinehart and Winston.
Rose, R. (1993). *Lesson-drawing in public policy.* Chatham, NJ: Chatham House
Rugman, A.M. & Verbeke, A. (2000). Environmental regulation and the global strategies of multinational enterprises. In A. Prakash & J.A. Hart (Eds.), *Coping with globalization.* London and New York: Routledge, 77-93.
Saretzki, T. (2007). Demokratie und Umweltpolitik: Konzeptionelle und methodologische Probleme der makroquantitativ ausgerichteten vergleichenden Umwelt- und Demokratieforschung. In K. Jacob, F. Biermann, P.-O. Busch & P. H. Feindt (Eds.), Politik und Umwelt. *Politische Vierteljahresschrift*, Sonderheft 38. Wiesbaden: VS Verlag für Sozialwissenschaften, 409-429.
Schneider, M. (2000). Verfolgte Umweltschützer. *ai-journal* 9, 6-10.
Scruggs, L. A. (2003). *Sustaining Abundance: Environmental Performance in Industrial Democracies.* Cambridge University Press.
Spaargaren, G., Mol, A.P.J., & Buttel, F.H. (Eds.) (2000). *Environment and global modernity.* London, Thousand Oaks/CA, New Delhi: Sage.
Sturm, A., Wackernagel, M. & Müller, K. (2000). *The winners and losers in global competition. Why eco-efficiency reinforces competitiveness. A study of 44 nations.* Chur and Zurick: Rüegger.

Tsuru, S. & Weidner, H. (Eds.) (1989). *Environmental policy in Japan.* Berlin: Edition Sigma.

UNEP (1999). Geo – 2000. *UNEP's Millennium Report on the Environment.* London: Earthscan.

Vig, N.J. & Axelrod, R.S. (Eds.) (1999). *The global environment. Institutions, law and policy.* Washington DC: CQ Press.

Vogel, D. (1986). *National styles of regulation – Environmental policy in Great Britain and the United States.* Ithaca/NY, London: Cornell University Press.

Wallace, D. (1995). *Environmental policy and industrial innovation. Strategies in Europe, the US and Japan.* London: Earthscan.

WCED (World Commission on Environment and Development) (1987). *Our Common Future.* Oxford and New York: Oxford University Press.

Weale, A. (1992). *The new politics of pollution.* Manchester, New York: Manchester University Press.

Weaver, R.K. & Rockman, B.A. (Eds.) (1993). *Do institutions matter? Government capabilities in the United States and abroad.* Washington DC: The Brookings Institution.

Weidner, H. (Ed.) (1997). *Performance and characteristics of German environmental policy. Overview and expert commentaries from 14 countries.* WZB-discussion paper FS II 97-301. Berlin: Wissenschaftszentrum Berlin für Sozialforschung.

Weidner, H. (2002). Capacity Building for Ecological Modernization: Lessons from Cross-National Research. In D. A. Sonnenfeld & A. P. J. Mol (Eds.), Globalization, Governance, and the Environment. Special Issue: *American Behavioral Scientist,* 45(9), 1340-1368.

Weidner, H. & Jänicke, M. (2001). Die umweltpolitischen Chancen der Globalisierung. In L.-M. Röller & C. Wey (Eds.), *Die soziale Marktwirtschaft in der neuen Weltwirtschaft.* Berlin: edition sigma, 293-326.

Weidner, H. & Jänicke, M. in collaboration with Jörgens, H. (Eds.) (2002). *Capacity-building in environmental policy: a comparative study of 17 countries* (National environmental policies Vol. 2). Berlin, Heidelberg, New York: Springer.

Weidner, H. & Mez, L. (2008). German Climate Change Policy: A Success Story With Some Flaws. *The Journal of Environment & Development* 17, 356-378.

Werksman, J. (Ed.) (1996). *Greening international institutions.* London: Earthscan.

World Bank (2000). *World development indicators.* Washington DC: The World Bank.

Young, O.R. (Ed.) (1997). *Global governance. Drawing insights from the environmental experience.* Cambridge, MA: MIT Press.

CHAPTER 6

From Public Administration to Policy Networks: Contextual Interaction Analysis

HANS BRESSERS

Introduction

The field of public policy and sustainability has seen the rise of community and business driven concepts that challenge the role of public administrations in the quest for sustainability. The proclaimed trend by several authors is "from government to governance" or even "governance without government". The role of community consultations as in Agenda 21 processes and of local institutions governing local natural resources has been studied with much ex ante sympathy. Business driven concepts on sustainability tumble over one another: eco-efficiency, triple bottom line, corporate social responsibility, zero-emission, super-optimizing, or even 'cradle-to-cradle', asking how business can contribute to nature and environment rather than limit the damage done. While these all fit in the fashionable view on governments as losing ground and becoming less central in society that has dominated the last 25 years, it's an open question to what extent such a retreat really occurred, especially when sustainability issues are at stake.

When concrete efforts to protect and improve environmental quality are studied another picture arises. While it is true that many efforts include the collaboration of various organizations, many of the organizations in such networks are public administrations themselves. Nevertheless the scientific challenge posed by the greater role of multiple actors in policy networks is a real one: that of achieving collaborative governance. Peter Knoepfel has recognized this quite early, stressing that not only the extent, but also the coherence of governance becomes a core issue under such conditions.

In the next section I will first deal with some theoretical issues in the analysis of networks. The following section will present some research on the environmental governance of industry. Section four does the same for projects in water management. Section five revisits theory and describes a model that can assist the analysis of interaction processes in a "networked" context.

Networks as models of analysis

Thinking in terms of policy networks belongs to the vocabulary of policy studies for at least three decades (e.g. Heclo 1978). Nevertheless the use of the concept became much more wide spread after the eighties. This period saw the rise of neo-liberalism, influencing political ideology all across the political spectrum. Public authorities came under high pressure to limit and even retreat their interventions in society. While in many countries social security arrangements were economized, it is hard to prove whether state intervention in society as such declined. What it in any case did was to open the minds of many more politicians, civil servants, journalists and even political scientists than before, to the interorganizational character of policy processes. And secondly that in such a group of relevant organizations not only public, but also private organizations could very well be important actors. While new concepts in social science often are presented as responses to real developments in society, it might be very well that they merely shed light on phenomena that have always been there, at least to some extent. So: is there really a development "from public administrations to policy networks"? Or are we just better aware of the networked character of policy processes because our mental frames of reference are more open to it?

Thinking in terms of policy networks makes us see them everywhere. It can disguise the fact that in at least some instances networking is not an inevitable course of action for modern government, but a choice (Bressers & O'Toole, 1994: 214). Policy network literature at some point even runs the risk of getting stuck in just finding them and characterizing them with the help of a myriad of classifications (Van Waarden, 1992). Much more interesting is the question of how networks relate to real actions and interactions of actors, and what thinking in terms of networks can contribute to the understanding of such interactions. When trying to link policy networks to the course and results of policy processes it is necessary to use one or more of the classifications as variables. An example is the attempt I made in earlier work to connect two aspects of the coherence of policy networks to the likelihood of a certain policy instrumentation strategy to be selected (Bressers, 1998). These aspects are interconnectedness (intensity of interaction, both within and outside the current process) and cohesion (empathy with each other's main goals by shared values and worldviews).

Thinking in terms of networks has led some to believe that the role of public administrations should shift from direct interventions to "network management", although the most careful work has been fairly clear that the idea of "management" connotes a more directive and muscular function than is likely to be possible in networked settings (see Kickert et al., 1997). Instead, "network management" involves such important but potentially multilateral tasks as facilitating exchange, identifying potential options for multi-actor agreement, and helping to craft patterns of communication as well as multilevel and multi-actor governance arrangements. Still, heavy doses of caution are in order. Any attempt to alter the structure of a network requires, itself, direct interventions by public administrations, often with "classic" instruments, albeit instruments aimed at intervention points in the system other than the ultimate targets. While such efforts clearly widen the scope for possible influence, they do not solve many of the lingering difficulties that are posed by such interventions.

Next to and following shortly upon the concept of "policy networks", the concept of 'governance' is more and more used in the field of policy studies. While its roots are again numerous, one can clearly see the link with the policy networks concept when one views the two most commonly used additives to 'governance': multi-level and multi-actor. The first refers to the fact that actors at various levels can simultaneously be relevant for concrete interactions in society. Thus in a sense it could also be viewed a network aspect, next to the more horizontal one that is meant in the multi-actor additive. In fact as a consequence of these two multiplicities also the usual elements in concepts of public policy (problem perception and goal ambitions, instruments and strategies and responsibilities and resources for implementation) get a "multiplicity". This leads to the following elaboration of the concept of "governance" as an enlargement of the concept of "public policy" (Bressers & Kuks, 2003).

Multiple levels and scales. Which levels of governance dominate the policy discussion? What is the accepted role of government at various scales? Which other organizations are influential in the governance activities on these levels? Who decides or influences such issues? How is the interaction between various levels of governance organized?

Multiple actors in the policy network. How open is the policy arena? Open to whom and where, precisely? What role do experts play? How do the various governmental and other organizations relate to each other?

A multiplicity of problem definitions and goal ambitions. What are the dominant maps of reality? What is seen as the problem and how serious is this considered to be? Where are the recognized points of intervention? What are the goal ambitions in relevant policies? Where coordination is required with other fields of policy, what are the links accepted by the actors?

Multiple instruments - possibly even belonging to more than one relevant policy strategy. Which (other) instruments belong to the relevant strategy or strategies? What are the target groups of the instruments, and what is the timing of their application? What are the characteristics of these instruments?

Multiple responsibilities and resources for implementation. Which organizations (including government organizations) are responsible for implementing the arrangements? What is the repertoire of standard reactions to challenges known to these organizations? What authority and other resources are made available to these organizations by the policy?

In uses like this, the network or governance concepts are not presented as a proclaimed new state of affairs, but as a basis for scientific variables that can be used for empirical studies. In the Euwareness project in which I had the pleasure of working with Peter Knoepfel, the governance concept outlined above was used in precisely such way. It was under Peter Knoepfel's influence that as a central dimension to turn this concept into a useable variable, the dimensions of extent/ scope and especially coherence were chosen, both within and among these elements of governance. This proved to be a very powerful explanatory factor in this project. Another addition was that next to these elements of governance, property and use rights were added, that play such an important part in institutional resource economics (Bromley, 1991; Ostrom, 1990 and 1999). Together with his collaborators Peter Knoepfel has integrated this approach with policy analysis and natural resource theory (Knoepfel, 2000) in his "institutional natural resource regime approach" (e.g. Knoepfel, Kissling-Näf & Varone, 2001 and 2003; Knoepfel, Nahrath & Varone, 2007; Gerber, Knoepfel, Nahrath & Varone, 2009). The dimensions of extent and coherence do not only refer to separate policies for specific purposes, but include the relations between multiple relevant policies and the relation with relevant property and use rights.

In the next two sections, two examples are presented of steering in a networked context that indeed did produce forms of multi-actor governance, but without the fall in importance of public administrations that many authors tend to attribute to this phenomenon.

Governance for sustainability: industry

The Dutch Target Group Policy, introduced to implement the first National Environmental Policy Plan in 1989, quickly became the central element in the current Dutch system of industrial environmental regulation. Since NEPP represented an ambitious new step, it was obvious that these targets could not be reached by conventional policy-instruments only. The publication of the aspiring NEPP coincided with a growing lack of confidence in the traditional policy approach with its emphasis on direct regulation. The combination of new ambitions with a lack of confidence in traditional approaches thus called for a new strategy and style. The new strategy would aim more specifically at eliciting private initiative and 'shared responsibility'. Instead of setting technology-forcing standards unilaterally the approach builds on close collaboration with target groups. Environmental negotiated agreements are thought to be the key instrument in this approach. Through negotiating processes and the agreements that result from these, the Dutch government has tried to improve the effectiveness of the environmental policy system.

While an extensive literature has evolved on environmental negotiated agreements and their effects, these studies are mostly essays, theory or case studies (e.g. Carraro & Lévêque, 1999; Croci, 2005; de Clercq, 2002; Mol et al., 2000; Orts & Deketelaere, 2001; Ten Brink, 2002; Jordan et al., 2003: 7) state that the literature "tends towards description and is also quite normative". The study on the Dutch system of environmental negotiated agreements that forms the basis of our analysis, enabled us to build and use a much larger database, on 59 agreements signed between - mostly - the Ministry of the Environment and private parties – usually industrial branch organisations.

With this unique basis some issues addressed in literature could be illuminated in a new empirical way.

Besides the direct effects on the environment, working with negotiated agreements can also have all sorts of side-effects that improve the initial position for a further development of environmental benefits. Given that the environmental results of negotiated agreements can be characterised as reasonably successful, but not creating radical innovations, these resource building side-effects is where the main long term advantage of negotiated agreements over other government instruments can be sought.

The possible side-effects we concentrated on were classed in three groups. The first three aspects are more 'motivational' and are extensions of each other. Both together and individually, they reduce the risk of unproductive conflicts later:

- a changing attitude of the target group in respect of environmental issues (74% positive);
- the degree to which both parties gain a greater understanding of each other's position (78% positive);
- the degree to which a negotiated agreement has led to better collaboration between the target group and government at all levels (80% positive).

The next four aspects are more 'cognitive' in nature. Learning processes can arise among both the target group and levels of government that increase the feasibility of a subsequent improvement of environmental benefits:

- the *knowledge* that accrues to achieve ambitious environmental objectives (69% positive);
- the degree to which the negotiated agreement makes possible further *policy development* by government (64% positive);
- application of further *product or process innovations*, not already included in the agreement (55% positive);
- the development of new production methods and technologies (44% positive).

Finally, we looked at the consultative process after the agreement had been concluded, which potentially increases the policy's integration. Several authors, like Peter Knoepfel (1995) and Lafferty (2002), regard policy integration as essential to a further improvement of the environmental benefits, certainly when they are placed in the context of sustainable development:

- it advances a coherent approach within the environmental policy for the industrial sector (what is called *internal integration* – 77% positive);
- it contributes to the harmonisation between projects and measures in the context of the agreement and government policy in other policy areas (which is called *external integration* – 64% positive).

The conclusion is that most of these important side-effects deal with the position vis-à-vis public administrations and that the great majority of the respondents had a positive view of these results in the case of nearly all side-effects. Improved collaboration and mutual understanding are markedly positive. Nearly 80% agree (entirely) that these improvements have actually occurred. The same holds for the improvement of coherence in environmental policy for the industrial sector. The external integration and harmonisation with other government policy, is clearly more difficult. Nevertheless, here, too, an ample majority judge it positively, in common with the other items.

Thus, research on the interaction between government and industry to achieve continuous improvements regarding environmental and energy efficiency in the Netherlands shows public administration in an active stimulating and coordinating role, which could hardly be called less central compared to the old "command from a distance and let lower authorities control" policies, of the start of environmental policies. Not so much because of a retreat of government, but more because of the scaling up of both business (globalisation) and governance (Europeanization); in the last couple of years national negotiated agreements between industries and government have become much more difficult to conclude. Some state that the business driven concept of "Corporate Social Responsibility" (CSR) has taken over the initiative in governance for sustainable development. Could this imply that public administrations have become obsolete at last?

At the Center for Clean Technology and Environmental Policy at the University of Twente (CSTM), Arno Mathis (2008) studied the relation between the so-called business driven concept of Corporate Social Responsibility (CSR) and government. An objective was to identify how different governance patterns respond to the emergence of CRS and how much they are able to influence and stimulate the private sector to take up the business management approach CSR. Some of his conclusions (Mathis, 2008: 453-4) are: "CSR as a business-driven concept has a long history which can be traced back the 19th century. CSR should not be seen as a new phenomenon, but rather as an ongoing process of defining and operationalising the relationship between business and society and its responsibilities towards it." "Public authorities have only limited capacities to influence and stimulate the private sector to become more engaged in CSR. The case studies showed that soft steering mechanisms such as self- and co-regulation did not directly lead to higher levels of CSR in the focused business sectors." However, on the other hand: "CSR engagement by companies can have a positive impact on the interaction between companies and public authorities." "Companies that engage in CSR are likely to benefit in the form of generally better contacts (more intense and better mutual understanding) and more access points to public authorities. The increased number of access points results in an increased influence capacity in the general public policy-making process. Most interesting for companies that consider becoming active in the field of CSR is the finding that CSR engagement leads to direct benefits on lower governmental layers."

In his study, Mathis also made "*social network analysis*" (for a quite accessible explanation of the methodology see Regeczi, 2008: 119-135) graphs of the centrality (closeness, betweeness, and eigenvector), information exchange structure and status of the case companies and the organisations that are relevant in their context. These network analyses clearly show that always public administrations belong to the most central organisations in the relevant networks. In terms of status the first rank is in all analyses for a government or government agency.

So, research on the centrality of companies that work on corporate social responsibility in the networks relevant to them, does not only demonstrate that an active orientation might help them in becoming more central in those networks, but also that the top-of-the-bill of those networks still consists of ministries and other public actors.

Governance for sustainability: water management

After long periods during which water management implied working against nature, to ensure 'progress' for mankind, in the last one or two decennia there has been a remarkable paradigm shift. Several European countries, including the Netherlands experienced floods and risky high waters, caused by rivers. Though further improving dikes and embankments has typically been a first response, it has also lead to a reconsideration of the basic underlying principles of water management. Instead of only containing rivers, the new paradigm seeks to make maximum use of opportunities to make nature an ally in striving to stabilize water levels and prevent floods. In the Netherlands this new paradigm is accompanied by slogans like 'space for rivers', 'living with water' and 'building with nature'. The predicted further increase of irregular rainfalls caused by climate change on the one hand, and the emphasis of the European Water Framework directive on respecting ecology and natural river basins on the other contribute to this paradigm shift in water management.

Working with rather than against nature to ensure human purposes, comes however at a price, which is especially relevant in densely populated countries like the Netherlands. It almost invariably costs a lot of space. Part of the reason behind the creating of 'unnatural' interventions in the past was precisely the 'rationalization' of the use of space. All space in the Netherlands already has one (or more) purposes. Interventions will have to deal with these purposes too. So working with nature also poses new challenges to the water projects, which become more and more multi purpose. With every new purpose that one tries to serve in a single project, not only new resources are opened (financial, legal, etc.), but also new actors, rules and requirements are to be integrated in very complex decision making processes. Some of these actors hold public governance assets, but others have also private "property and use rights" that can be crucial for the chance of success of the project (Knoepfel et al., 2000, and 2001). For example: in a project that started with the purpose of protecting houses and cattle against river floods, eventually also nature development, preserving a denominated 'precious landscape', improving agricultural infrastructure, recreation and tourism purposes, and preserving views for inhabitants, were included. All of those brought extra sources of support, but also extra complexities for the project. The necessary couplings can involve different levels and scales, different aspects or policy sectors and different time scales.

We will give another example, one in the Dutch region of Twente. In the past, interventions in the water system have in many regions disrupted the natural systems of brooks, streams and other water courses (Huitema and Kuks, 2004). With the purpose of rejoining the creeks of part of the region to the main watercourse basin system and also to enable the separation of rural (rain) water and urban (treated sewage) water a plan was developed to create a new, 13 kilometres long, watercourse. In subsequent phases to these purposes new ones were added, each of them implying enlarged boundaries of the problem domain and adding new actors, resources and procedures: safety against flooding, connecting nature areas to be part of the national nature system (this extension actually transferred the lead from the waterboard to the province and widened the projected water and flooding area from 25 to 75 meter), preventing droughts, buffering between a new regional industrial estate and municipal residential districts, rural renewal (land reallocation for improving agricultural infrastructure and socio-economic development planning), emergency water storage and – for the time being – finally, landscape, recreation and tourism.

The array of scales includes levels from the EU (e.g. Habitat, subsidies requiring recreation facilities), national (e.g. national ecological highway system, national administrative agreement on water), provincial (took over the lead because of nature development component), regional (e.g. the geographical area of the waterboard and the regional industrial estate), local (e.g. municipalities, citizens in residential districts, farmers unions) up to the level of individual farms and gardens. The array of aspects includes sectors like – next to various aspects of water management – nature policy, agricultural policy, and tourism, and has recognised interaction with industrial and urban development. The time horizons of objectives and resources (e.g. requirements for subsidies) for all these aspects are very different, creating much stress for the process. Nevertheless the project is developing reasonably well and is actually being built while the detailing of the planning is still continuing. In 2014 it should be ready.

Water projects like these are not rare anymore. With the vast array of actors of all levels and with all kinds of problem perceptions and goals, instruments at their disposal and resources, such projects seem to be characteristic examples of "governance instead of government". And they are. Yet, it is also clear that among the many actors that are involved in the continuous consultations that make up much of the decision-making process, public administrations (yes, in plural) make up most of the relevant actors, though not all of them.

What it does imply is that a certain government has to learn how to handle these kind of multi-actor processes in which it is only one of the relevant actors even thought its core purposes can only hope to be realised in such settings. Coping with such complexity requires a lot of 'boundary spanning'. Such adaptive attitude needs a strategy for the convergence of the views of the actors involved. To realise better conditions for boundary spanning in the process, various intervention points can be recognised. Note that the institutional rules creating an arena for action and the motivation and resources of actors also belong to Peter Knoepfel's toolkit for policy analysis.

Actors and arenas

New actors can enter the scene, creating other network relations. For instance "policy brokers" (Sabatier and Jenkins-Smith 1999), for which boundary spanning is core business. Or media actors that expose the issue to a wider public or NGO's. Also new arenas, meeting points with specific characteristics, can help bridge boundary judgments and wider issues.

Cognitions

As cognitions of actors are influenced through the filtering process by which observations are processed, stories, analogies, one-liners etceteras that change these reference frames can be important. Of course learning processes based on their own experiences can influence actor's cognitions.

Motivation

Own learning is also dependent on motivation; think of the concept of selective perception. Both the positive or negative direction and the saliency of motivations are important here. Sometimes motivations can also be seen as "intervention points" themselves. For instance when new and for that reason yet uncomfortable goals are in fact in correspondence with actor's interests or when it is a matter of coping with external pressures. Much boundary spanning is such a mix of discovery of corresponding interests and recognition of mutual dependency.

Resources

Such pressures are dependent on resources, which therefore become an intervention point of their own too. The position of the actor in terms of power depends on its image of strength in the network, on crucial moments confirmed – or not – by its position in mutual resource dependencies with other actors. The pressure needs not to be negative. Having enough of the resource "money" can for instance open the option to change the motivation of other actors by compensation. For influencing other actors' cognitions, relevant resources are the centrality and respect and trust the coordinating actor has in the network.

Thus, research on water management demonstrates that many projects, e.g. those that serve to adapt to the vulnerability to climate change and the European Water Framework Directive, involve complex arrays of actors, many public, and some private. But it also shows that the coordination of these networks mostly lies in the hand of the traditional responsible public authorities. Coping with such complexity requires a lot of 'boundary spanning'.

Contextual interaction theory

The challenge of achieving coherent collaborative governance requires policy analysis models that go beyond the standard network approaches that often get stuck in proclaiming that there are networks and what kind of characteristics they have, or their functional or even democratic superiority. Governance is first and foremost a set of interaction processes. It always was. What is new is that there are many simultaneous games between several actors even when one case or issue is at stake. The position of actors in these games is not only influenced by the others in the specific case, but also by the public policies and property and use rights that form a more structural context. Around these even wider, cultural, economical, technological, etc. contexts shape the setting. The last part of the paper explains this model for the analysis of collaborative governance.

There are zillions of factors conceivable that might influence the course and outputs of an interaction process. Fifteen factors, each with only two values, define nevertheless more than 30.000 different combinations of circumstances. But since interaction processes are human activities, all influences flow via the key characteristics of the actors involved. Thus, it is possible to set an inner core of factors that is far more parsimonious, at least to begin with. In Figure I include these factors (inputs and outputs of the process are not shown in this figure).

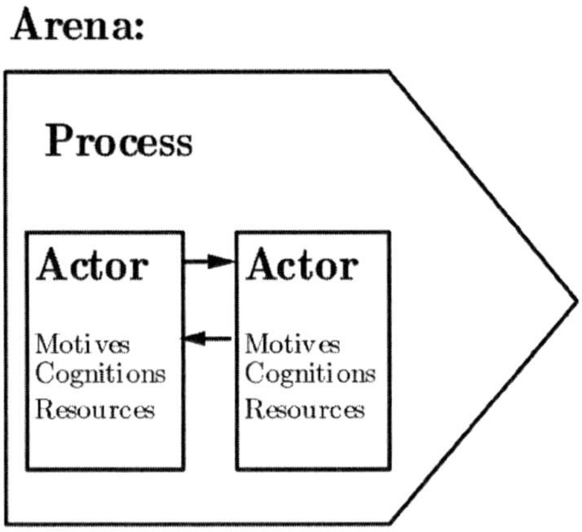

Figure 1 Process model with the actor characteristics used in Contextual Interaction Theory.

The basic assumptions of Contextual Interaction Theory are quite simple and straightforward. There is a dynamic interaction between the key actor-characteristics that drive social-interaction processes and in turn are reshaped by the process. The theory's main assumptions are:

Policy processes are actor interaction processes.

- Many factors have an influence but only because and in as far as they change relevant characteristics of the involved actors.

- A first layer of such factors is specified in the boxes of the Figure 2, including how they influence the core actor characteristics. Of course these factors can in turn be influenced by numerous other factors from within or outside the process.
- These characteristics are: their motivation, their cognitions (information held to be true) and their capacity and power (see also Bressers 2004).
- These three characteristics are influencing each other, but cannot be restricted to two or one without losing much insight.
- The characteristics of the actors shape the process, but are in turn also influenced by the course and experiences in the process and can therefore gradually change during the process.
- The characteristics of the actors are also influenced from an external context of the governance regime (a/o. institutions and more or less stable network relationships, but also property and use rights) (represented further in Figure 3).
- Around this context there is yet another more encompassing circle of political, socio-cultural, economical, technological, and problem contexts (see Figure 3). Their influence on the actor characteristics may be both direct and indirect through the governance regime.

In Figure 2, many theorems and other ideas are employed that are not elaborated upon in this text. Nevertheless many relations will be understandable. Compared to Figure 1 this figure does also show process development (change processes – in the form of the processes over time). The actor characteristics are much more elaborated here, not visualised as linked to specific actors and for presentation reasons placed outside of the process box. This also shows the mutual influences between these factors and the process itself.

The "*motivation*" box seeks the origins of motivation for behaviour, including for the positions taken in interaction processes, in first instance in own goals and values. Self-interest, like in many economic theories, plays of course a strong role here. But also more altruistic values can directly lead to genuine own goals (Gatersleben and Vlek 1998). External pressures can be also a motivating force. Like all motivational factors they could in principle also be conceptualised as belonging to one's "own" purposes. However, the likelihood is large that in practical analysis such conceptualisation will make them forgotten or underemphasised. These pressures can be based on force, but even more often will be softer influences from normative acceptance of the legitimacy of such external wishes and even by identification with the group from which such expectations come. Last but not always least as a motivational factor also the 'self-effectiveness assessment' (Bandura 1986) can play a large role. This concept points to the demotivational effect that can occur when an actor perceived its preferred behaviour as beyond its capacity. It shows part of the relation between motivation and the availability of resources, own resources or those made available by others.

The "*cognitions*" box is based on the recognition that the cognitions of actors (interpretations of reality held to be true) are not only a matter of observations and information processing capacity, though these aspects are important and with the information technology revolution are a source of quick changes. In policy sciences the so-called 'argumentative turn' (Fischer, 1995), reflects a variety of approaches that emphasise that knowledge is produced itself in mutual interactions, based on interpretations of reality of actors, that themselves are mediated by frames of reference. Some frames of reference are termed by Axelrod (1976) as "cognitive maps", by Schön (1983) as "frames", by Sabatier and Jenkins-Smith (1999) as "policy core beliefs" and "deep core beliefs". Dryzek (1997) speaks of "discourses", thereby also stressing the language dependency of understanding and the role of word, one-liners, stories and the like to guide, but also to restrict and bias understanding. While these approaches are quite different in their conceptual understanding and methodology of reconstruction, they also share some understandings: that cognitions are not just factual information, but more interpretations of reality, and that such interpretations are influenced by filters, frames and interactions with other actors. Not the whole of the theoretical approaches mentioned, but only this "common ground" is incorporated in the cognitions box of the contextual interaction theory.

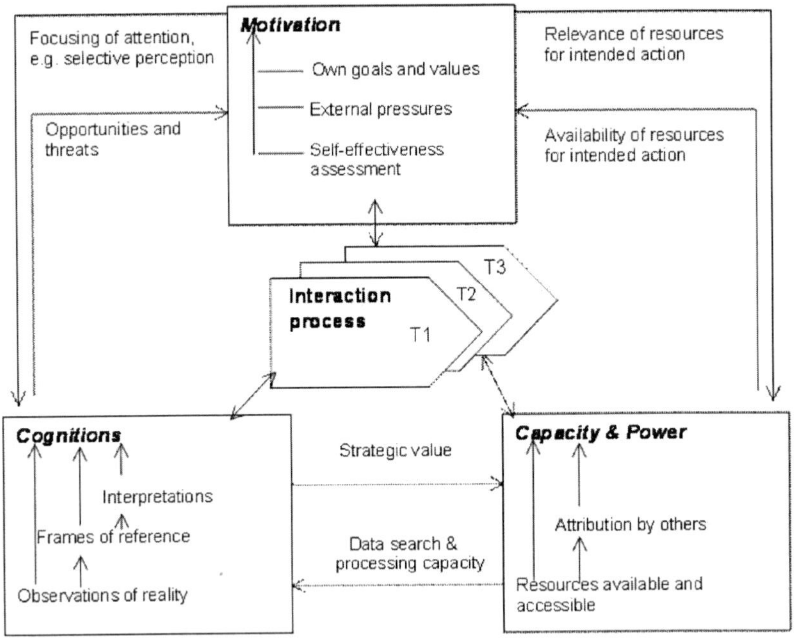

Figure 2 Dynamic interaction between the key actor-characteristics that drive social-interaction processes and in turn are reshaped by the process.

While resources as an actor characteristic are important to provide capacity to act, in the relational setting of an interaction process they are also relevant as a source of power. Therefore this box is labelled "*capacity and power*" in Figure 2. The relationship between power and resources is not always direct.

Power is in first instance largely a result of attribution to an actor by others. However when this attribution is not backed by real resources it is far from stable. The resources that are the root of these powers encompass much more than formal rules, though legal rights and other institutional rules can be an important part of it, next to resources like money, skilled people, time and consensus. Not only the resources of the actors themselves, but moreover the dependency of an actor on the resources of another actor shapes the balance of power. A classical example is the dependency of authorities on the jobs created by industry, which industry can use as a source of negotiation power. Resources not only shape power relations, but are also a prerequisite for action as such, determining the capacity to act of any actor. The resource base for action can be greatly enlarged by engaging in dependencies with other actors with relevant resources, at the expense of loss of autonomy and thus – in some cases – power. Whether a specific resource contributes to power depends on the action that is intended. Resources that seem irrelevant to get certain things done might be essential to get other things done.

There are mutual relations between the three key actor characteristics. Every change in one of the three has influences on the other two. While we typically start with mentioning motivation in this paper, many would like to start with the way reality is understood and problems and chances perceived, or whether some technical information is available (pertaining to technology, economics, social or environmental information), as a prerequisite for motivation. It must be borne in mind that the influence is mutual: without certain interests and values, available data may be overwhelming and too time consuming to process. The development of information needs some focusing of attention (creating selective perception as a bias). The actions for which an actor is motivated require resources, and the availability of those resources is bound to influence the actors' ambition, for instance because a lack of necessary resources creates a low self-effectiveness assessment (Bandura, 1986). While 'knowledge is power' may be in some contexts an exaggeration, it is certainly true that information can serve strategic purposes and hence can be used as one of the bases of power. On the other hand gathering and processing data is also an activity that needs resources. The three factors are not only shaping, but are also (re)shaped by the activities and interactions that happen in the process.

These three key factors have proven also in empirical research to have a strong explanatory power of the course and results of interaction processes. When we revisit the two example subjects of sections 3 and 4 the following results can be mentioned.

The signing of a *negotiated agreement* is normally not the end of the consultations between the parties. Often the "covenant" text is only a provisional end and rings the bell for the next round, making follow up consultations an essential part of the negotiated agreement approach. A major risk is that the negotiated agreements can become eroded under the influence of progressing negotiations and the pressure of external, often economic circumstances, meaning that ambitions are downgraded or that the industry's implementation of measures is placed far down on the agenda. In response to the point that, "The original agreements are eroded in the follow up consultations", 21% agreed (45% disagree, 26% entirely disagree, 8% don't know / not applicable). So, while this seems to cover a minority of cases, it can involve a considerable loss of environmental effectiveness. The explanation of the results of the follow up consultation should be sought in the motivation, information and power relationships of the government institutions and target groups involved. Four factors (two representing positive and negative motivation respectively) produced an equation that relates clearly ($r = .811$) to the answer to the 'erosion of agreements' question, explaining 66% of the variation in responses.

In the domain of *water policy projects*, Katharine Owens (2008) tested the hypotheses scheme for the explanation of the course and effects of implementation processes that is derived from the contextual interaction theory (Bressers 2004). These hypotheses specify for all combinations of the motivation, cognitions and power of both the implementers and target groups the expected nature of the interaction process and expected implementation outcomes. She first did three full-fletched case studies, followed by a series of no less than 48 small studies on wetlands restoration projects in two European states (Netherlands and Finland) and two US states (New Jersey and Oregon). While in two (Finnish) cases the available information proved incomplete and thus the theory not applicable, only in one (New Jersey) case the hypothesis based on the theory proved to be wrong in 'predicting' the course and results of the process.

In all three descriptions of the main variables, the role of others is part of the factors that shape the main characteristic. Yet, the multi-actor (often including actors for multiple levels) context of policy processes has additional influences on the explanation of the multi actor interaction process. Who is regarded as an "actor" is to some extend a choice by the analyst himself. They vary from individual people to coalitions of organisations. These coalitions are then complex 'corporate actors' (even regarding an organisation as an actor already requires such an assumption). The coalitions might consist of more and clearly identifiable organisations that all take actively part in the process. But it is also possible that while one or two 'representative' organisations take part in the process, these are part of larger networks of which most members do not. Actually this is not unusual. So it is important to have an open eye for these kinds of network-relation influences while estimating the value of the characteristics of the actors in the process. Basically it means that actors are playing a double game in which they are not only dealing with the issue at stake but also try to do so in such a manner that it improves their position in the network both later in the process, but also in every network that is important to them.

A first observation from a network perspective is that actors not only interact during the research period, but also before and after. They are influenced therefore by the history and predicted future of these interactions. Furthermore, actors often not only interact in the process under study but in other fields as well. Also this can influence them. Thirdly, from a network perspective one should reckon that actors not only act on their own behalf, but also are influenced by background actors in the network that do not actively intervene in the process under study, but still are important to the actors that do.

How this impacts motivation is obvious. With cognitions the impact can include the risk of 'tunnel' vision and 'group think' (against the background of shared 'cultural bias', discourses etc.). With power one should pay attention to the possible resources that an actor that is active in the process could obtain to use from background network actors (think of the possibility of environmental NGO's to mobilize ordinary citizens into action when they threaten to loose ground in negotiations).

The dynamics in the development of partnerships between actors are as well related to the three actor characteristics and the way they are influenced in the course of time. First of all there is a set of mechanisms that increase the bonds in a well-functioning partnership as time goes by as an influence from the activities and interactions that happen in the process on each of the characteristics. The first mechanism is that mutual adjustment arises from the tendency of actors to act from a set of consistent values, avoiding 'cognitive dissonance' after accepting compromises. The second mechanism is that mutual adjustment arises from the tendency of actors to use a common reference frame to interpret cognition. The third mechanism is that mutual adjustment (increased dependence of actors on each other's resources) arises from the tendency of actors to concentrate on their relative strength. Of course external change drivers can disrupt such tendencies. But these 'natural tendencies' will then provide a degree of resistance preventing disturbances, because all together they build up a collective resource: trust. Furthermore, standard operation procedures and sunk costs prevent deterioration of cohesion. The opposite might also happen. Failed attempts can disrupt motivation, let the actors perceive the possibilities in a more negative way (cognitions), and can lead to a retreat to solitary (non) action.

The multi-level and multi-actor network, institutional and other contexts are represented in contextual interaction theory as factors that influence the motivation, cognitions and resources of the actors involved (in fact they are only influential in as far as they do). When the boxes with actor characteristics are folded back in the process, there is room to visualise the further contexts as assumed in Contextual Interaction Theory. Figure 3 shows these contexts as overlapping entities. The figure can be best read from right to left, implying that each step leftwards gives a context for the previous circle, while not excluding the possibility of direct impacts of the broader contexts. The most direct context is the case context of specific circumstances and previous decisions made that form a direct input into and sometimes even the starting point of the process studied.

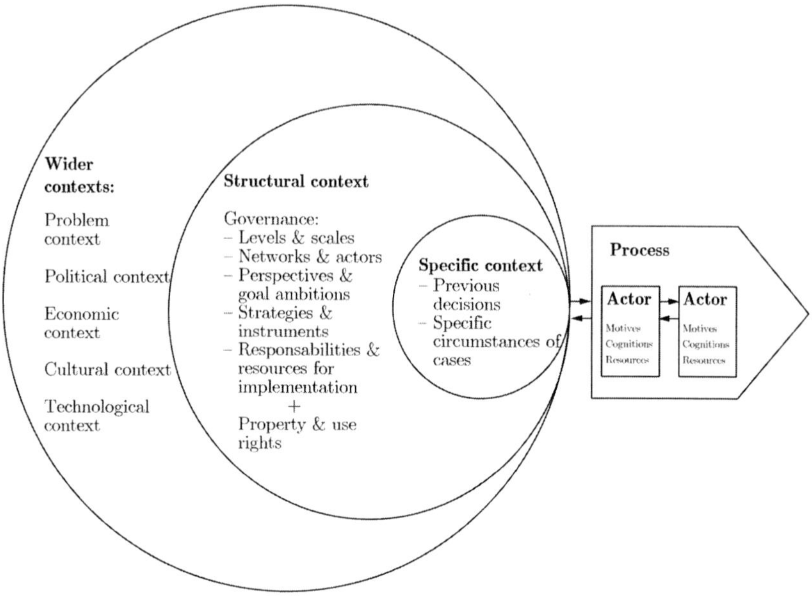

Figure 3 Layers of contextual factors for actor characteristics.

The next context that we discern is the 'structural context' (see section 2; one could also label it the "regime" context), that is not actor specific, but is more or less uniform for all actors in the process, though sometime with different implications for them. It is in this layer that the multi-level and multi-actor aspects of modern governance are to be found, but also the dominant (or competing) problem perceptions in society on the issues at stake, and the institutional setting that is provided by all relevant strategies and instruments and the responsibilities and resources for implementation. Part of these will have the form of legal rights and demands; others will have a softer basis. They can guide to some extent the motivations of the actors in the process, but also serve as a pool of resources they can try to get access to and use for their purposes. In fact, this conceptualisation of 'governance' as an extended understanding of the more narrow concept of 'public policy' (see Bressers and Kuks 2003, see also section 2 of this paper for a brief explanation), combined with the institutional aspect of private 'property and use rights' was also used in the Euwareness study, were what is called the "structural context" here, was used as the specification of the "institutional resource regime" (Bressers and Kuks, 2004: 24-29). Around the structural or regime context there are still wider contexts. While these often exert their influence more indirectly, it is also conceivable that environmental disasters or a bank crisis exert direct influence on the motivations of actors in the process. For that reason all these contexts are visualised as having direct connection with the actor characteristics.

All kinds of interaction processes can be studied this way and also the re-creation of the structural regime context (governance & property and use rights) itself. All social processes simultaneously convert specific inputs into outputs, but also are both influenced by more encompassing contexts as input and might change these to some extent at the same time. Note that in this figure there is also an arrow back from the process to its layered inputs. Processes are dealt here primarily as conversion processes, rather than 'changes of a phenomenon over time'. But this does not imply that both the inputs (context) and the nature of the process will not also change over time. On the contrary, it is likely that this change is also partially produced by the same process(es) that is/are impacted by these factors. Thus the process influences to a certain degree the contexts under which it develops.

The growth in intensity of network relationships might thus be as well a product of policy processes that anticipate such relationships, than an external given fact which policy makers just have to cope with. And even while networked relationships seem abundant in modern governance, the role of public administrations seems to be changed, not removed – except when they chose it to be that way, that is.

At the period this paper was finalised, the same public administrations that seem to have defined themselves into a quite marginal role in modern governance, shying away for a critical audience of sceptical voters, prove to be capable of mobilizing astonishing amounts of money to prevent the extreme capitalism of the past decade to fully collapse. And most people seem to love it! While the way the financial crisis is dealt with shows all the multi-level and multi-actor complexities of modern governance, it is very clear that it is public administrations who take the lead, also in the 21st century. Of course! Who else?

References

Axelrod, R. (Ed.) (1976). *Structure of decision: The cognitive maps of political elites.* Princeton: Princeton University Press.

Bandura, A. (1986). *Social foundations of thought and action: A social cognitive theory.* Englewood Cliffs, N.J.: Prentice Hall.

Bressers, H. Th. A. (1998). The choice of policy instruments in policy networks. In B. Guy Peters & F. van Nispen (Eds.). *Public policy instruments.* Cheltenham: Edward Elgar, pp. 85-105.

Bressers, H. Th. A. (2004). Implementing sustainable development: How to know what works, where, when and how. In W.M. Lafferty (Ed.). *Governance for Sustainable Development: The Challenge of Adapting Form to Function.* Cheltenham: Edward Elgar publishing, pp. 284-318.

Bressers, H., & O'Toole Jr., L.J. (1994). Networks and water policy. In H. Bressers, L.J. O'Toole, Jr. & J. Richardson, *Networks for water policy: A comparative perspective.* Special issue Environmental Politics, Vol. 3, No. 4, pp. 197-217.

Bressers, H. & Kuks, S. (2003). What does "Governance" mean? From conception to elaboration. In H.Th.A. Bressers & W.A. Rosenbaum (eds.), *Achiev-*

ing Sustainable Development: The Challenge of Governance Across Social Scales. Westport: Praeger, pp. 65-88.

Bromley, D.W. (1991). *Environment and economy: Property rights and public policy.* Oxford: Blackwell.

Carraro, C., & Lévêque, F. (Eds.) (1999). V*oluntary Approaches in Environmental Policy.* Dordrecht: Kluwer Academic.

Croci Edoardo (Ed.) (2005). *The handbook of environmental voluntary agreements: Design, implementation and evaluation issues.* Dordrecht, Berlin: Springer.

De Clercq, M. (Ed.) (2002) *Negotiated environmental agreements in Europe: Critical factors for success.* Cheltenham: Edward Elgar.

Dente, B., Fareri, P., & Ligteringen, J. (1998). A theoretical framework for case study analysis. In B. Dente, P. Fareri & J. Ligteringen (Eds.), *The waste and the backyard.* Dordrecht: Kluwer Academic Publishers, pp. 197-223.

Dryzek, J.S. (1997). *The politics of the Earth: Environmental discourses.* New York: Oxford University Press.

Fischer, F. (1995). *Evaluating Public Policy.* Chicago: Nelson Hall.

Gatersleben, B.. & Vlek, Ch. (1998). Household consumption, quality of life, and environmental impacts: A psychological perspective and empirical study. In K.J. Noorman & T.S. Uiterkamp, *Green households? Domestic consumers, environment and sustainability.* London: Earthscan, pp. 141-183.

Gerber, J.-D., Knoepfel, P., Nahrath, S., & Varone, F. (2008). Institutional Resource Regimes: Towards sustainability through the combination of property-rights theory and policy analysis. *Ecological Economics.* Article in press, 2008

Heclo, H. (1978). Issue networks and the executive establishment. In A. King (Ed.) *The new American political system.* Washington DC: American Enterprise Institute, pp. 87-124.

Huitema, D., & Kuks, S. (2004). Harbouring water in a crowded European delta. In H. Bressers & S. Kuks (Eds.) *Integrated governance and water basin management.* Dordrecht, Boston, London: Kluwer Academic Publishers, pp. 59-98.

Jordan, Wurzel, & Zito (2003). New Instruments of Environmental Governance. *Environmental Politics,* vol. 12, 1: 1-224 (special issue)

Kickert, W.J.M., Klijn, E.-H., & Koppenjan J.F.M. (Eds.) (1997). *Managing Complex Networks: Strategies for the Public Sector.* London: Sage.

Knoepfel, P. (1995). New institutional arrangements for a new generation of environmental policy instruments: Intra- and interpolicy-cooperation. In B. Dente (Ed.) *Environmental policy in search of new instruments.* Dordrecht: Kluwer, 197-233.

Knoepfel, P. (2000). *Natural resource quotas and contracts: A new institutional regime for our common resources.* Chavannes-près-Renens, Suisse: Idheap.

Knoepfel, P., Kissling-Näf, I., Varone, F. (2001). *Institutionelle regime für natürliche ressourcen.* Basel: Helbing & Lichtenhahn.

Knoepfel, P., Kissling-Näf, I., Varone, F. (Eds.). (2003). *Institutionelle Ressourcenregime in Aktion / Régimes institutionnels de ressources naturelles en action.* Basel, Genf, München: Helbing & Lichtenhahn.

Knoepfel, P., Nahrath, S., &Varone, F. (2007)., Institutional Regimes for Natural Resources: An Innovative Theoretical Framework for Sustainability. In P. Knoepfel, *Environmental Policy Analyses: Learning from the Past for the Future - 25 Years of Research.* Berlin, Springer, pp. 455-506.

Lafferty, W.M. (2002). *From environmental protection to sustainable development: Environmental policy integration as a challenge for applied science, inaugural speech CSTM.* Enschede: University of Twente.

Mathis, A. (2008). *Corporate social responsibility and public policy-making: Perspectives, instruments and consequences.* Enschede: University of Twente.

Mol, A., Lauber, V.and, & Liefferink, D. (Eds.). (2000). *The voluntary approach to environmental policy: Joint environmental policy-making in Europe.* London: Oxford University Press.

Orts, E. W., & Deketelaere, K. (Eds.). (2001). *Environmental Contracts: Comparative Approaches to Regulatory Innovation in the United States and Europe.* The Hague: Kluwer Law International.

Ostrom, E. (1990). *Governing the commons.* Cambridge: Cambridge University Press.

Ostrom, E. (1999). Institutional rational choice: An assessment of the institutional analysis and development framework. In P.A. Sabatier (Ed.), *Theories of the policy process.* Boulder: Westview, 1999, pp. 35-72.

Owens, K. A. (2008). *Understanding how actors influence policy implementation.* Enschede: University of Twente.

Regeczi, D. (2008). *Private equity; Public principle: Evaluating the legitimacy and sustainability of private-public partnerships.* Enschede: University of Twente.

Sabatier, P. A., & Jenkins-Smith, H. C. (1999). The advocacy coalition framework: an assessment. In P: A. Sabatier (Ed.), *Theories of the policy process.* Boulder: Westview Press, pp. 117-168.

Schön, D. A. (1983). *The reflective practitioner: How professionals think in action.* New York: Basic books.

Ten Brink, P. (Ed.). (2002). Voluntary Environmental Agreements: Process, Practice and Future Use. Sheffield, Greenleaf.

Van Waarden, Frans (1992), Dimensions and types of policy networks, in: European Journal of Political Research, Vol. 21, No's 1-2, pp. 29-52.

CHAPTER 7

The Roles of Street Level Bureaucrats in the Implementation Process

MICHAEL HILL

Introduction

The theory of street-level bureaucracy is set out in Lipsky's book of that title. It is further developed in work by two of his former research students, Weatherley (1979) and Prottas (1979). Lipsky says of his book:

> *I argue that the decisions of street-level bureaucrats, the routines they establish, and the devices they invent to cope with uncertainties and work pressures, effectively become the public policies they carry out. (Lipsky, 1980, p. xii)*

Lipsky's view is that this process of street-level policy making does not involve, as might be hoped, the advancement of the ideals many bring to personal service work but rather the development of practices that enable officials to cope with the pressures they face. Lipsky argues that street-level bureaucrats (SLBs) develop methods of processing people in a relatively routine and stereotyped way. They adjust their work habits to reflect lower expectations of themselves and their clients. Thus Lipsky handles one of the paradoxes of street-level work. Such workers see themselves as cogs in a system, as oppressed by the bureaucracy within which they work. Yet they often seem to the researcher, and perhaps to their clients, to have a great deal of discretionary freedom and autonomy. This is particularly true of the many publicly employed semi-professionals – people like teachers and social workers who secure a degree of that autonomy allowed to professional workers.

The aspect of Lipsky's work that many scholars have seized upon is the argument that street-level bureaucrats cannot readily be brought under the control of a superior. Lipsky argues:

> *The essence of street-level bureaucracies is that they require people to make decisions about other people. Street-level bureaucrats have discretion because the nature of service provision calls for human judgement that cannot be programmed and for which machines cannot substitute. (Lipsky, 1980, p. 161)*

In this sense Lipsky portrays the street-level bureaucrat as making policy, carrying out a political role that determines 'the allocation of particular goods and services in the society' (ibid., p. 84). Hence Lipsky is cited by many who explore issues about 'top-down control as if this was his central message. In those terms he is co-opted in support of the political Right's argument for market solutions to distribution problems, to circumvent the capacity of suppliers to control public monopoly services. In fact, however, what Lipsky says is rather different, indeed much more subtle. He speaks of the street-level bureaucrat's role as an 'alienated' one (Lipsky, 1980, p. 76), stressing such classic features of alienation as that work is only on 'segments of the product', that there is no control over outcomes or over 'raw materials' (clients' circumstances), and that there is no control over the pace of work. Lipsky also emphasises the 'problem of resources': street-level bureaucrats face uncertainty about just what personal resources are necessary for their jobs, they find that work situations and outcomes are unpredictable, and they face great pressures of inadequate time in relation to limitless needs. In a sense Lipsky is providing a new variant of the Marxist dictum: 'Man makes his own history, even though he does not do so under conditions of his own choosing' (translation of the opening of the second paragraph of Marx, 1852).

Hence the widely expressed simplified view of street level bureaucrats as people who subvert the implementation process neither does justice to Michael Lipsky's nuanced original formulation (which was about public officials finding it difficult to put ideals into practice) nor comes to terms with the complex issues of power and legitimacy involved.

This paper argues that it is crucial to understand the reasons key decisions are taken by street level bureaucrats in the implementation process, including in particular the complexity of the tasks involved, the dilemmas of policy agenda setters and programmers who might have been expected to structure decision frameworks more fully and the impact of the power of key target groups in determining institutional arrangements requiring the exercise of discretion.

The normative context for the exploration of street level roles

It is important to recognise that the feasibility of establishing an objective approach to the examination of street-level roles is affected by the strong feelings people have about these roles. I have elsewhere (Hill, 2009, chapter 13) presented Lipsky's approach in a chapter that starts with a very different concern about street-level work: Merton's (1957) analysis of bureaucrats as rigid rule followers who lose sight of the purposes of the rules, substituting means for ends. Table 1 takes its starting point from this by setting out side by side alternative negative and positive perspectives on street level bureaucrat roles.

SLB's as 'bad guys'	SLB's as 'good guys'
People who break rules	People who adapt rules to real needs
People who disobey their superiors	People who are sensitive to the needs of the public they serve
People who use whatever discretion they have to advance their own interests	People who use whatever discretion they have to advance service ideals

Table 1

To these may be added a rather more sophisticated version of that contrast, which cannot be simply dichotomised into 'good' or 'bad' alternatives, embedded in some interesting contemporary discussions of SLB roles:

- SLBs implicitly reinforce traditional moralities, with their categorisations of people as 'deserving' or 'undeserving' (this is a key theme in Maynard-Moody and Musheno's revisitation of SLB roles *Cops, Teachers, Counsellors*, 2004).
- In contrast to this is an alternative view embodied in some recent explorations of 'representative bureaucracy' highlighting predispositions of street-level staff in terms of the extent to which the way they exercise their discretion carries advantages for their clientele inasmuch as they share ethnic, gender or class identifications with them (Meier et al., 1991: 173-4, see also Pitts 2005).

Meyers and Vorsanger, in an insightful review of the subject with which this chapter has much in common, offer another set of contrasts:

> *In some studies these workers are portrayed as occupying a powerless position downstream of political and bureaucratic decisions; in others they emerge as loyal public servants who pursue the public good even when it means bending agency regulations; in still others they are described as self-interested bureaucrats whose coping mechanisms frustrate the will of elected officials (2003, p. 245).*

When looking at all these contrasts another influential analysis of public service roles comes to mind, that of Freidson when talking about professions:

> *In contrast to the negative word 'bureaucracy' we have the word 'profession'. This word is almost always positive in its connotation, and is frequently used to represent a superior alternative to bureaucracy. Unlike 'bureaucracy' which is disclaimed by every organisation concerned with its public relations, 'profession' is claimed by virtually every occupation seeking to improve its public image. When the two terms are brought together, the discussion is almost always at the expense of bureaucracy and to the advantage of profession. (Freidson, 1970, pp. 129–30)*

Now, at least partly because of the attack Freidson himself mounted against professional self-interest, I do not think that statement entirely rings true today. Nevertheless arguments continue about the extent to which it is appropriate for at least some SLB roles to be professionalized. This implies explicitly investing them with a measure of discretion. We will come back to this later.

After a version of this paper was delivered at a conference a discussant said, in effect, that of course SLBs should often be trusted to make decisions. At risk of being repetitive, the argument here is not primarily about that. In the real world of public administration and public management a great deal of effort is made to control SLB behaviour. Most of us will surely accept the desirability of at least some of this effort. But, before getting into any discussion of the circumstances in which control is or is not desirable there is a need to explore the circumstances in which such control is in fact difficult (or indeed perhaps impossible). In this sense discretion is not just something that may be given or not given, according to the judgement of legitimate 'top-down' policy makers. In the next section therefore we examine the sources of discretion.

Sources of discretion in the policy process

Officials have discretion if their behaviour is not pre-programmed by rules. Obviously they may also effectively 'take' discretion by breaking rules. That leads us naturally to two key considerations:

- While there may rarely be situations in which discretion is – in terms of its context – more or less unlimited, it is generally most appropriate to see discretion as embedded in a rule structure. In this sense discretion is what Dworkin colloquially calls the "hole in the donut": "an area left open by a surrounding belt of restriction" (1977, p. 31).
- That 'belt of restriction' may itself be complex, including rules that are hard to interpret or rules that conflict with other rules.

This leads us on to a crucial question: is the structuring of the donut a social and political product or is the residual element of discretion inevitable? In other words, would it have been logically possible for the hierarchical authority that established the rule structure to have drawn it more tightly? This is a topic that has been addressed by various administrative law theorists (see Hawkins, 1992, for a good review of this work). The following are some, certainly by no means exhaustive reasons why it may be very logically very hard to eliminate discretion:

- Where what is at issue is the application of *standards*, where the translation of standards into explicit rules is so difficult as to be practically impossible. Jowell (1973) shows how many of the considerations with which decisions must be concerned are inherently difficult to specify in rules. Legislators are concerned to prevent *dangerous* driving, for example, to ensure that food is *pure*, and that factories are *safe*. Standards may also involve questions of taste – as in respect of policies to protect historic districts or building. They may also be matters of choice between alternatives: Jowell here uses the example of picking players for a football team. This issue brings into focus a group of SLB's with rather different roles to the service delivery workers particularly highlighted in Lipsky's work, workers with responsibilities for regulatory policy. These have of course been given particular attention in Peter Knoepfel's work on pollution control.

- Where action depends upon perception of a complex situation and determination of appropriate action, often within a constrained time frame. Much of the police discretion literature upon which Lipsky draws in developing his theory addressed this sort of issue. Essentially police may be expected to be strict rule followers, who keep in touch with their superiors and formally report their actions, yet much must depend upon what they see or choose to see and what they do, for example, when they come around a corner on a dark night and encounter some form of public disorder.
- An extension of aspects of those last two points is that constraining complex activities with rules may have to involve very elaborate rule structures so that action will *de facto* involve choices about which rules to apply. Jewell's (2007) exploration of social assistance in Germany suggests that high discretion emerges principally from the difficulties staff have in navigating through complex and ever changing rules.
- A related phenomenon, also given much attention by Lipsky is the choice problem posed by too much work relative to the resources available (amongst which the SLBs own time is particularly important) forcing decisions about how to allocate them between large numbers of clients/ pupils etc. It may be objected that this source of discretion is not logically inevitable, many SLBs will draw attention to the failure of their 'masters' to make sufficient resources available, nevertheless Lipsky argues that it is often inevitable that demand will exceed supply.

In relation to that last point it must be acknowledged, that there are other ways of imposing service cut-offs through rules, or indeed through markets. In general it may be argued that the suggestion that discretion is inevitable should not be over-stated. Those determined to curtail discretion can push this a long way, particularly in this age of electronic communication, record keeping and surveillance (see Bovens & Zouridis, 2002). The question that then arises, however, is whether these efforts may be counter-productive in respect of the intended policy goals. This is the sense in which we need to consider these issues about the logical inevitability of discretion alongside the social or political phenomena that affect it.

It is possible to take as the starting point, for the consideration of this, a simple principal/ agent model, asking the question: why do principals not impose more effective restrictions upon discretionary powers? We are here, as suggested by the issues about the difficulties in curbing discretion, in the territory of Matland's (1995) notion of 'experimental implementation' in which high levels of ambiguity in terms of the means/ ends assumptions embedded in the policy make flexibility in the implementation process desirable. So in some cases we may have a principal/ agent relationship in which there is consensus on objectives but a shared recognition of a need for street-level discretion.

But that is a very simple rational and politics free way of looking at street level discretion. Matland's model recognises alternatives in which there will also be goal conflict, interacting with ambiguity. It is much more realistic to work with three assumptions about the politics of policy making:

1) That there will be conflict over the making of policy and the consequences of this will be either unresolved issues or compromises embedded in the mandates for SLBs and therefore generating and affecting their discretionary powers.
2) There is a related point to this first one, this is that it may be seen as politically expedient to leave difficult policy issues unresolved, facilitating 'blame- avoidance', the shifting of responsibility for such decisions down to SLBs.
3) That (as is now widely argued in challenges to the stages model of the policy process) there is unlikely to be any neat separation between policy making and policy implementation so that the 'games' between contending interests that started during the initial parts of the policy process will continue in ways that will impact upon the activities of SLBs (who may themselves indeed be participants in those games).

The games perspective based upon the work of Peter Knoepfel and his colleagues (2006, 2007) leads us to a perspective on the SLB role that has two characteristics:

- Firstly, the implementation process is only completed with the production of decisions and activities that directly address those affected … Thus, it is always characterised by interactions between public and private actors. These exchanges often take the form of negotiations …
- Secondly, no PAP [this is shorthand for 'political-administrative programme' that is the expression used by Knoepfel et al to characterise the structuring of implementation (MH)], even the most concrete and well developed, can replace or entirely predetermine implementation by claiming to be 'self-executing'…the legislative and regulatory norms contained in the PAP present themselves as a more or less relevant set of 'rules of the game' which distribute the positions and resources of the different actors involved in the 'implementation game' (expression coined by Bardach, 1977). Even if these rules are clearly established, the game itself always remains to be played (Knoepfel et al, 2007, p. 189-90).

In following this perspective on the discretion of SLBs the next sections examine separately:

- The issues about political- administrative programmes
- The issues about the continued interplay of actors.
- The extent to which SLBs may themselves be significant actors

Political-administrative programmes (PAPs)

Knoepfel's (1997) approach to the analysis of the importance of PAPs for the implementation process goes back to his work with Weidner on air pollution control policies (1982, 1983). Essentially this involves seeing the PAP as a set of concentric circles. In these case studies, at the core lies concrete policy objectives (air quality standards), these are surrounded, moving outwards, by evaluative elements (ways of measuring pollution) and operational elements (systems to secure control over polluting behaviour). Then there is an outer shell consisting of political-administrative arrangements (administrative systems and resources – including finance) and procedural elements embedding control activities in the wider national political and legal framework.

Whitmore (1984) uses Knoepfel and Weidner's approach to analyse a very different policy issue, the prevention of child abuse. For him the core is the problem of child abuse but it is located in a disputed specific paradigm (a 'behaviour change/ social control' one as opposed to one in which social inequalities are addressed, p. 247) bringing a measure of conflict to the very heart of policy implementation. Moving outwards his other 'rings' have much in common with Knoepfel and Weidner's except that he also emphasises another explicitly complex area 'inter-organisational resource dependencies (p. 251-5).

Taken together these two usages of the notion that any policy implementation activity is embedded in a complex PAP structure highlight the potential multiple sources of SLB discretion. Interestingly a recent examination of the policy area Whitmore explored provides an example of dissensus lying close to the core of the policy. Murray (2006) explores the roles of social workers in Scotland who have, in collusion with their clients, refrained from implementing certain procedures. But this was done in a context of shared assumptive worlds between the social workers and their first-level managers. Murray offers this as a challenge to two of what she calls legacies of Lipsky (I would call them simplifications of Lipsky) that SLB non-implementation is in opposition to their managers and that clients are passive. What this seems to me to offer is reinforcement of the need to put SLB action in its complex context. But it is also pertinent to bear in mind Whitmore's stress that there may be contestation of the core concerns of a policy system.

Complexity arising from the outer 'core' of PAPs is highlighted in various ways in Knoepfel's work in respect of the fact that issues about administrative arrangements inevitably impinge on the political issues about inter-governmental relationships and organisational autonomies, whilst procedural elements remind us of the ways in which issues about rules and rule interpretations are embedded in national legal systems and legal cultures (Knoepfel, 1997). This is particularly evident in Knoepfel and Weidner's work on systems of air pollution control in Europe where they write of 'institutionalised public participation' varying between countries and opening the decision system more in some countries than others (Knoepfel and Weidner 1983, p. 206-10).

The continued interplay of actors

It is implicit in the now generally accepted view of the policy process that rejects the idea that it is rigidly staged, that the politics that prevailed during the generation of policy will continue into the implementation stage:

> *Since definitions of specific policies tend to emerge from any initial policy-making process complex, ambiguous and perhaps carrying riders likely to have a significant impact on action, it must follow that they are subject to further transformation as they are translated into action. But furthermore the forces that created ambiguity and complexity during the initial phase are likely to continue to have an impact. Conflicts which probably started early in the life of a policy continue. Furthermore new interests, which were not able to participate in those early stages, may also become involved (Barrett and Hill, 1984, P. 226).*

In relation to the roles of SLBs a great deal is likely to depend upon the extent to which their activities depend upon interaction with actors with sufficient power to exploit these ambiguities. In this respect some regulatory activities (as in the case of pollution control) are particularly likely to involve this continuous interplay. Public health inspectors, pollution control officials and factory inspectors, as law enforcement agents, have to operate in situations where the 'offenders' see themselves as engaged in carrying out their legitimate business, not as polluters or producers of impure food, etc. What is being enforced by the regulator is a standard — about unreasonably high levels of pollution, etc. – that is likely to be disputed. Second, there are likely to be conflicts of interest between those who are the source of the alleged problem and those who are affected by it. On top of all this, the 'beneficiary' interest is often a latent one, because:

- either the 'victims' the regulators have a duty to protect do not know they have a problem (when, for example, pollution cannot be detected by the sense of smell, etc.);
- or they regard the problem as the lesser of two evils (when they perceive it as a choice between a polluted environment and employment – see Crenson, 1971; Blowers, 1984);
- or they are quite satisfied with a situation that others consider unsatisfactory (residents suffering from dementia in a poor-quality care home, for example).

In some cases the conflict is between a quite specific individual interest and a very general public interest. In all these situations enforcement is likely to be controversial and the enforcers may lack clear-cut forms of public support. In many systems professionals with regulatory responsibilities therefore work not with absolute rules but with principles about best practice established by expert officials and operationalised using discretionary powers (see Hill, 1983). The relationship between rules and discretion in these situations may involve 'framework laws', with officials and regulatees negotiating to fill in the details so that gradually the law becomes more codified.

What is often involved in these cases, given that officials need to work very closely with the objects of their regulatory activities, is a process of bargaining between regulator and regulatee (Peacock, 1984; Hawkins, 1984). Such bargaining will not merely deal with costs and consequences, but will also be likely to take into account past behaviour (has the compliance record of the regulatee been satisfactory?) and the likely impact of any outcome on the behaviour of others. It is in this respect that Downing (1983) and Hanf (1993) have seen what they call 'co-production' as a key characteristic of policy implementation in which the determinants of regulatory behaviour need to be seen as 'embedded in the social worlds within and outside the regulatory agency' (Hanf;109)

However, Hupe (1993) argues that this concept of co-production may also be applied to the interactions between SLBs and apparently much less powerful people such as social assistance clients, where issues about how people present their needs and circumstances and respond to questions from SLBs influence rule interpretation (see also Hasenfeld, 1992).

This can then be taken further when we bear in mind that SLBs are interacting not just with their bosses and clients but also with colleagues and the representatives of other organisations with whom they have to collaborate (see Hupe and Hill, 2007). In a short paper like this it is not appropriate to go into all the complexity of the interplay between SLBs, those with whom they interact and the interest groups who may try to intervene in the implementation process.

SLBs as active agents

My concern with the roles of SLBs as themselves active participants in the power games around the implementation of policy takes us back to the contrast I drew, amongst those who acknowledge the power of SLBs, between those who see them as typically reinforcing traditional moralities, categorising people as 'deserving' or 'undeserving', and the literature that highlights their potential responsiveness to the needs of their clients. This inevitably takes us to the questions about the extent to which street-level staff are to be categorized as professionals, and if this is the case, then the extent to which professional discretion is legitimated by either their expertise or their values (or of course both).

Obviously the answer to the first question may be that some SLB roles are appropriately seen as 'professional' while others are not. We have here two dimensions:

- Differences between occupations in the extent to which control over discretion is feasible;
- Differences in terms of the extent to which it is seen as legitimate to control the profession (an alternative way of putting this is perhaps to describe it as a professional power dimension).

But for simplicity of exposition it is perhaps possible to draw a 2 by 2 chart as in table 2.

	Control easy	Control difficult
Control seen as legitimate	Typical SLB situation (social assistance where precise rules are often drawn up to govern decision making)	Elusive SLB situation (regulatory policies and policing where elaborate control is attempted but variability of situations makes it difficult to have rules to govern everything)
Doubts about legitimacy of control	Semi-profession (Education, where structuring of activities is increasingly attempted but there is a strongly argued case for recognising the importance of a flexible interactive relationship with pupils)	Profession (Medicine, where the need to enable effective use of expertise makes control difficult and there is a strong moral argument for recognising a primary obligation to do their best for their patient)

Table 2

What we have here is a sort of fusion of the ideas about SLB discretion with the arguments about professional power and autonomy. There are debatable elements in respect of the examples given. An alternative here would be to try to draw a more complex diagram, as opposed to a 2 by 2 matrix, with dots for various groups – school teachers, university teachers, surgeons, general practitioners, nurses etc. at various points on a two dimensional scatter plot. Relevant here too is the role of scientific expertise in respect of various regulatory activities.

But even then, sitting behind this analysis, are questions about sources of power. In many respects doctors are seen as the archetypical public service professionals, and some will object to their presentation here as merely SLBs. On the other hand, while of course it is true that doctors possess expertise and that the public, in its quest for good health, values that expertise, much medical knowledge is accessible to all. What is therefore also important about the position of the medical profession today is that the state has given that profession a monopoly over many forms of care, allowed it to control its own education and socialisation process, and in many countries created a health service or health insurance system in which its decision-making prerogatives are protected (Harrison, et al., 1990; Moran and Wood, 1993).

But then this position is also subject to challenge. In respect of doctors in the UK health service Harrison and McDonald (2008, Chapter 2) have noted a variety of challenges to professionalism linked to greater public assertiveness and a decline in acceptance of the 'bio-medical model' of illness: New 'institutions of surveillance' over activities; Challenges to clinical freedom which 'formalise and codify medical knowledge' and require attention to be given to 'rules and criteria' for action; Reductions in the extent to which doctors have been able to dominate the institutions that govern their activities.

These issues may be handled in terms of issues about 'resources' in the policy process (Knoepfel et al., 2007, Chapter 4). Whilst, as suggested above, the issue that lies at the core of acceptance of the legitimacy of SLB discretion is information and/or knowledge (Ibid., p. 71-3) this needs to be seen in the context of: 'Organisation or the interactive resource' and 'Consensus or the confidence resource'.

In respect of the former, unease about the challenges to professionalism comes in concern about the extent that they involve a diminution of trust. Fox (1974), coming to the examination of this issue from a concern with industrial relations, has interestingly related rule imposition to low-trust relationships. He picks up the top-down concern with detailed prescription and shows how this creates or reinforces low-trust relations:

> *The role occupant perceives superordinates as behaving as if they believe he cannot be trusted, of his own volition, to deliver a work performance which fully accords with the goals they wish to see pursued or the values they wish to see observed. (Fox, 1974, p. 26)*

A vicious circle may be expected to ensue. The subordinate who perceives that he or she is not trusted feels little commitment to the effective performance of work. This particularly affects the way the remaining discretionary parts of the work are carried out. The superior's response is to try to tighten control and further reduce the discretionary elements. The irreducible minimum of discretion that is left leaves the subordinate with some weapons against the superior: the prescribed task is performed in a rigid unimaginative and slow way ('le cercle vicieux bureaucratique', Crozier, 1963, p. 142-161). The application of this here is to consider whether low-trust situations are particularly damaging to the quality of the work of those engaged in applying expertise in sensitive relationships with those who need their help. In this respect Ball has described developments in the UK that involve the remoulding of the 'meaning' of school teaching as an activity through political and administrative and writes of these as 'wearing away professional-ethical regimes and their value systems' (Ball, 2008, p. 149).

In respect, on the other hand, of 'consensus or confidence' on the other hand there are some interesting issues about the extent to which legitimacy stemming from democratic politics is challenged by doctrines of professional accountability. Pollitt defines this as 'accountability to the standards laid down by one's professional body' (Pollitt, 2003, p. 93). While this has (as noted above) come under attack as involving a rejection of the democratic forms of accountability, the defence to this charge involves arguing that they embody apolitical notions of direct duty of service to the public. In that sense doctors, for example, may argue that they are accountable to their patients for the service they provide and to their peers who monitor those standards of service. The public may accept this claim in terms of traditional respect for professional authority figures, but perhaps more important today is the notion that we can interact directly with professionals (indeed perhaps with most SLBs) to influence their behaviour more easily than we can influence them through political process embedded in representative democracy.

Kinds of SLBs

In the last section the introduction of the notion of different respects in which SLBs roles may be seen as professionalized highlights the fact that this concept is used to cover very different roles in policy implementation. In that respect table 2 may be seen as identifying different *kinds* of SLBs. I have elsewhere explored the problems posed in trying to embrace different kinds of policies in a unified analysis of the policy process, yet suggested that attempts to develop policy typologies have failed (Hill, 2005, chapter 7). As far as the activities of SLBs are concerned however it is perhaps important to recognise that there are at least three distinct kinds of activities: regulation (embracing within this many kinds of law enforcement), benefit provision and service delivery.

These may of course be found in combinations – people regulating and also providing services or people providing both benefits and services – so I do not want to drive the contrast too hard. Nevertheless what is entailed in confining discretion in respect of these activities may be rather different (see Mashaw, 1983; Adler, 2006)

Conclusions

The central thrust of this paper has been to provide a critique of that view of the SLB thesis that highlights nonconformity with the expectations of superiors. This offers far too simple a view of a pervasive issue in public administration, disregarding both how the characteristics of administrative tasks make discretion inevitable and how the delegation of power in this way is often a taken for granted aspect of the so-called principal- agent relationship. It is argued instead that an analysis of SLB work needs to be embedded in a view of public administration that both sees power struggles over policy content as inevitable and recognises – contrary to the simple stagist view of the policy process – that those power struggles continue throughout the life of a public policy. It also needs to recognise the complexity of the policy-programming that creates this web of 'games' around the process of translation of policy into action, as emphasised in Peter Knoepfel's work.

Then, of course, this is not to treat the normative arguments about the case for confining SLB discretion more or less as unimportant. Rather it is to argue that those arguments need to be grounded in a realistic analysis of where that discretion comes from and of what effects it has on policy outcomes.

Acknowledgement

This paper owes a great deal to my collaboration with Peter Hupe of Erasmus University, Rotterdam. I would also like to thank the Korean Association for Public Administration for giving me an opportuntiy to present a trial version of this paper at their 2008 conference, and Frédéric Varone for his insightful comments on my first draft.

References

Adler, M. (2006). Fairness in Context. *Journal of Law and Society*, 33 (4), pp. 615-38.

Ball, S.J. (2008). *The Education Debate.* Bristol: Policy Press.

Bardach, E. (1977). *The Implementation Game: What Happens after a Bill Becomes a Law.* Cambridge, Mass.: M.I.T. Press.

Barrett, S., & Hill, M. (1984). Policy, Bargaining and Structure in Implementation Theory: Towards an Integrated Perspective. *Policy and Politics*, 12 (3) pp. 219-40.

Blowers, A. (1984). *Something in the Air: Corporate Power and the Environment.* London: Harper and Row.

Bovens, M., & Zouridis, S. (2002). From street-level to system-level bureaucracies: How information and communication technology is transforming administrative discretion and constitutional control. *Public Administration Review*, 62 (2), pp. 174–84.

Crenson, M.A. (1971). *The Unpolitics of Air Pollution.* Baltimore, Md.: Johns Hopkins University Press.

Crozier, M. (1963). *Le phénomène bureaucratique.* Paris: Seuil .

Downing, P.B. (1983) Bargaining in pollution control. *Policy Studies Journal*, 11 (4), pp. 257-99.

Downing, P.B., & Hanf, K. (Eds) (1983). *International Comparisons in Implementing Pollution Laws.* Boston, Mass.: Kluwer Nijhoff.

Dworkin, R. (1977). *Taking Rights Seriously.* London: Duckworth.

Fox, A. (1974). *Beyond Contract: Work, Power and Trust Relations.* London: Faber.

Freidson, E. (1970). *Professional Dominance.* New York: Atherton.

Hanf, K. (1993). Enforcing environmental laws: The social regulation of co-production', in M. Hill, (Ed.) *New Agendas in the Study of the Policy Process.* Hemel Hempstead: Harvester Wheatsheaf.

Harrison, S., Hunter, D.J., & Pollitt, C. (1990). *The Dynamics of British Health Policy.* London: Unwin Hyman.

Harrison, S., & McDonald, R. (2008). *The Politics of Healthcare in Britain*, London: Sage.

Hasenfeld, Y. (1992). The Nature of Human Services. In Y. Hasenfeld (Ed.) *Human Services as Complex Organizations.* Newbury Park CA: Sage.

Hawkins, K. (1984. *Environment and Enforcement.* Oxford: Clarendon Press.

Hawkins, K. (Ed.) (1992). *The Uses of Discretion,* Oxford: Clarendon Press.

Hill, M. (1983). The role of the British Alkali and Clean Air Inspectorate in air pollution control. In P. Downing, & K. Hanf (Eds) *International Comparisons in Implementing Pollution Laws.* Dordrecht: Kluwer-Nijhoff.

Hill, M. (2009). *The Public Policy Process.* Harlow: Pearson Education.

Hupe, P.L. (1993a). The politics of implementation: Individual, organisational and political co-production in social services delivery. In M. Hill (Ed.) *New Agendas in the Study of the Policy Process.* Hemel Hempstead: Harvester Wheatsheaf. pp. 130–51.

Hupe, P. & Hill, M. (2007). 'Street-level bureaucracy and public accountability', Public *Administration,* 85 (2), pp. 279-300.

Jewell, C. J (2007). *Agents of the Welfare State.* New York and Basingstoke: Palgrave Macmillan, 2007.

Jowell, J. (1973). The Legal Control of Administrative, Discretion. *Public Law.* pp. 178-220.

Knoepfel, P. (1997). *Conditions pour une mise en oeuvre efficace des politiques environnementales.* Cahier de l'IDHEAP no 167. Chavannes-près-Renens: IDHEAP.

Knoepfel, P., Larrue, C., & Varone, F. (2006). *Analyse et pilotage des politiques* publiques. Zurich: Verlag Rüegger.

Knoepfel, P., Larrue, C., Varone, F., & Hill, M. (2007). *Public Policy Analysis.* Bristol: Policy Press.

Knoepfel, P., & Weidner, H. (1982). Formulation and implementation of air quality control programmes: Patterns of interest consideration. *Policy and Politics.* 10 (1), pp. 85–109.

Knoepfel, P., & Weidner, H. (1983). Implementing Air Quality Control Programmes in Europe: Some Results of a Comparative Study. In P.B. Downing &K. Hanf (Eds) *International Comparisons in Implementing Pollution Laws.* Boston, MA: Kluwer Nijhoff.

Lipsky, M. (1980). *Street-Level Bureaucracy.* New York: Russell Sage.

Marx, K. (1852). *The Eighteenth Brumaire of Louis Bonaparte.*

Mashaw, J.L. (1983). *Bureaucratic Justice.* New Haven, CO: Yale University Press.

Matland, R.E. (1995). Synthesizing the implementation literature: The ambiguity-conflict model of policy implementation. *Journal of Public Administration Research and Theory.* 5 (2), pp. 145–74.

Maynard-Moody, S., & Musheno, M. (2004). *Cops, Teachers, Counsellors,* Ann Arbor: University of Michigan Press.

Meier, K.J., Stewart, J. Jr & England, R.E. (1991). The politics of bureaucratic discretion: Educational access as an urban service. *American Journal of Political Science.* 35 (1), pp. 155–77.

Merton, R.K. (1957). *Social Theory and Social Structure.* Glencoe, IL: Free Press.

Meyers, M.K., & Vorsanger, S. (2003). Street Level Bureaucrats and the Implementation of Public Policy. In B.G. Peters & J. Pierre (Eds) *Handbook of Public Administration.* London: Sage.

Moran, M., & Wood, B. (1993). *States, Regulation and the Medical Profession.* Buckingham: Open University Press.

Murray, C. (2006). 'State Intervention and Vulnerable Children: Implementation Revisited', *Journal of Social Policy,* 35 (2), pp. 211-228.

Peacock, A. (ed.) (1984) *The Regulation Game.* Oxford: Blackwell.

Pitts, D. (2005). Diversity, representation and performance: Evidence about race and ethnicity in public organizations. *Journal of Public Administration Research and Theory.* 15 (4), pp. 615-31.

Pollitt, C. (2003). *The Essential Public Manager.* Maidenhead: Open University Press.1993.

Prottas, J.M. (1979). *People Processing: The Street-Level Bureaucrat in Public Service Bureaucracies.* Lexington, Mass.: D.C. Heath.

Weatherley, R. (1979). *Reforming Special Education: Policy Implementation from State Level to Street Level.* Cambridge, MA: MIT Press.

Whitmore, R. (1984). Modelling the policy/implementation distinction. *Policy and Politics.* 12 (3), pp. 241-68.

CHAPTER 8

Institutional Policies and Reforms of Public Administration

YVES EMERY, DAVID GIAUQUE & ADRIAN RITZ

Introduction

Currently, in Switzerland, a large number of public bodies at all levels of government (the federal administration, the cantons and the communes) have implemented major modernization programs, which place great emphasis on outputs and outcomes of public policies, and above all, institutional policies (Schedler & Proeller, 2002; Lienhard et al., 2005; Giauque & Emery, 2008). The aim of this chapter is to assess the impact of various recent institutional and managerial reforms on the Swiss administrative context. More specifically, we focus our attention on the so-called new public management modernization process that has taken place in Swiss public administration, which mainly can be characterized as an institutional policy. We address the problematic issues of the contributions developed by Peter Knoepfel, whose scientific reflections have been influential in assessing possible impacts and consequences of NPM reforms. We discuss reform impacts on both institutional and substantive policies.

Therefore, we mix a classical perspective inspired by public management theories and a political science perspective. Few publications have already adopted this hybrid theoretical framework (Gibert, 2002), except for contributions developed by Peter Knoepfel, who always tried to link public management theories and practices to institutional and substantive policy analysis.

The chapter is divided into four main sections. First, we discuss NPM and other institutional reforms in the Swiss public sector. The second section addresses the consequences of reforms such as policy formulation and implementation of NPM-like reforms from a theoretical perspective, largely based on Peter Knoepfel's publications. The third section is devoted to the presentation of results from 12 different reform evaluations in Switzerland. The perspective adopted here mainly focuses on managerial and organizational issues of NPM reforms, but also highlights the impact on substantive policies. Finally, we propose a synthesis of our main findings and suggestions for future research.

NPM and other institutional reforms in the Swiss public sector

In the reforms' context of the 1980's and 1990's, Switzerland is considered as a good student by international comparative observers (Gregory, 2007). The span and depth of the reforms in public administration can be viewed as impressive, despite the relative slowness of the decision-making process characterizing the country (Varone & Bonvin, 2004).

The main objective of this section is to briefly summarize the principal institutional and organizational transformations that have taken place since the 1970s, emphasizing the strategies of modernization developed, until recently, in Swiss federal administration. As we will see, the relative consensual way used to modernize public organizations, compared to the other strategies more frequently used in NPM-core countries (Ferlie et al., 1996), might be seen as a hypothesis which can explain the Swiss public management reforms mainly characterized by a relatively low focus on substantive policies and their outcomes.

Historical initiatives

According to R. Germann, in one of his well-known contributions (1996), the Swiss public administration reform process can be described as mainly "managerial." Initiatives have been initialized primarily to foster efficiency in the functioning of public organizations in order to look for savings. In the 1970s, confronting economic difficulties and budget and financial constraints, the first federal initiative was taken to attempt to stabilize federal public finances. Facing a deterioration of the financial situation, the Swiss Parliament adopted "la Loi fédérale instituant des mesures destinées à améliorer les finances fédérales" (RS 611.010). This text was established in order to stop the increase of public employees in federal institutions (the so-called "Personal-Stop"). This has allowed a slow expansion of the number of the public federal staff, increasing by 7.6% from 1974 to 1990. According to a Federal Council report assessing the consequences of such a "freezing strategy", it was underlined that the federal public administration suffered from a lack of resources, reducing its ability to anticipate environmental and societal changes, and thus was inclined to focus on short-term issues (Germann, 1996).

During the eighties, other modernization initiatives inspired by "value analysis" and cost-savings were launched, leading to mitigated results.

From cost-driven reforms to managerial changes

During the next decade, new reform strategies based on a more managerial approach were implemented. A first example is given by "la réforme du gouvernement et de l'administration" (RGA) based on "la loi sur l'organisation du gouvernement et de l'administration" (LOGA), which was implemented after a popular voting on the 1st of October 1997. This law was grounded in the following four main objectives:

- To increase administrative effectiveness by reducing the number of missions deployed by the federal administration or by outsourcing public services.
- To aim for profitability and public performance by reinforcing interdepartmental synergies and suppressing administrative redundancies.
- To achieve savings by modernizing financial managerial resources and cutting jobs.
- To modernize the principles and tools of public management.

Furthermore, this law (LOGA) also fostered the introduction of a new managerial system supposed to accelerate the modernization process of federal bodies. This new managerial system, "gestion par mandat de prestations et enveloppe budgétaire" (GMEB), was very much inspired by the NPM movement (Giauque & Emery, 2008), and has been deployed from 1996 in different pilot projects (Ritz, 2003). It is mainly derived from private practices and is designed to increase organizational performance through performance contracts. In order to allow administrative units more managerial freedom, political authorities define political objectives (theoretically outputs *and* outcomes), indicators, and allocate financial and human resources to enable administrative units to fulfil their operational duties.

Finally, we have to mention recent initiatives dealing with other modernization issues. In September 2005, a special delegation of the Federal Council proposed examining nine transversal projects and twenty-five departmental projects with special attention given to: identifying and eliminating duplications of roles and jobs inside the federal administration, and analysing the possibility to outsource some support services (ITC; office buildings management; etc.). This modernization stage is incorporated in a more global strategy aiming to stabilize the federal budget (Varone, 2006).

Summary and commentaries

Until recently, the main strategy used in modernization processes at the federal level can be described as managerial-driven reforms. Changes were mainly made to reach managerial performance, despite the fact that the typical Swiss way of NPM ("Wirkungsorientierte Verwaltungsführung") might have put emphasis not only on outputs, but also on outcomes (Schedler, 1995). The Swiss institutional framework, as well as the "consensual" culture characterizing Swiss political life, can probably explain this emphasis given to managerial issues rather than to more substantive transformations. Cultural and linguistic diversities, the importance accorded to "peripheral" regions, the much decentralized structure of governance, and the delicate equilibrium between political forces characterizing executive power could explain the focus of the modernization projects described above. It is very doubtful that more policy-content modernization strategies could have been successfully carried out in Switzerland. Compared to countries such as New Zealand, Canada and the UK, that have passed more heavy and substantive reforms (Pollitt & Bouckaert, 2004), the Swiss modernization program could be seen as "softer."

The "muddling-through" or incremental process (Lindblom & Woodhouse, 1994) privileged in the modernization process described above is more compatible with Swiss institutions (Varone, 1998) and to its derived characteristics than "revolutionary" reforms that have taken place in some core-NPM countries, mainly situated in Anglo-Saxon area.[1] Taking into account these institutional specificities, one can argue that managerial reforms were widely introduced to counterbalance the lack of institutional changes undertaken to this day.

Peter Knoepfel pointed out very early that the democratic deficits of such reforms underline the inconsistencies of a far too technocratic vision, considering the Swiss federal institutional characteristics, policy formulation, and implementation process. The next section of this article will deal with the last argument.

Effects of NPM-like reforms: main expectations from a theoretical perspective

NPM has been criticized not only because it was an attempt to introduce private sector methods and values into the public sector without considering the contextual features (political, cultural, organizational) of public sector organizations (Pollitt & Bouckaert, 2004), but also because NPM in its early period reduced the whole process of managing the "units" and "products" to be delivered to "customers." This managerial metaphor has of course been very useful in improving organizational structures, in some case by removing ineffective intra-organizational bureaucratic processes (Giauque & Emery, 2008), but on the other hand, it was hardly able to catch the complexity of the socio-political process, which lead to formulating and implementing substantive public policies.

When analyzing the effects of NPM reforms we can refer to the basic models of the public policy cycle according to Peter Knoepfel et al. (2006) and Knoepfel and Bussmann (1997). Theorists of NPM in Switzerland, like Schedler, pointed out the necessity of articulating two competing rationales; political and managerial. In this regard, the products at the heart of NPM must be considered not only end-products of the production process of the administration. At each step of the public-policy process, "products" can be identified and analyzed (Knoepfel, 1996). It is useful to briefly summarize the basic cycle of any public policy according to Peter Knoepfel and his colleagues (Knoepfel et al., 2001); and then to point out which added-values and problems may have been created through the implementation of NPM-like approaches in the public sector.

---

[1] However, not exclusively; the Belgian Case is typical for a "revolutionary" approach (they called it "Copernic") which has been aborted, due to a lack of political support.

Agenda setting

The first step, "agenda setting," aims at formulating a political definition of the (societal) problem to be solved. This definition should also produce a consensus about the origin of the problem (hypothesis on problem causation) and a target group of (private) actors whose behaviours should be modified in order to solve the problem to the benefit of so called "end beneficiaries". Basically, the agenda-setting process is a socio-political process by which NPM approaches generate no immediate and obvious contribution. Nevertheless, NPM puts great emphasis on the objectives pursued by administrative outputs and, in some cases, on outcomes. The figure of the citizen, renamed "customer," is also considered, but mainly in the role of "client" of administrative products and services, and less in the political role of citizen. The rhetoric of "empowering citizens," especially in the Swiss case, has to be understood as "empowering customers" of public services! Following the process described by Schedler (1995) a logical articulation should be found between outputs and outcomes. During the negotiation of the performance agreement concluded between the political level and the administrative level, the question about the political purpose should be clarified (Schedler, 1995).

Through better identification of targeted actors and a deeper knowledge about their perception of the products (customers survey), NPM should help to better customize products and therefore, improve the targeted influence on their behaviours. It is, for example, well known that people who would likely take advantage of social benefits are frequently difficult to reach, or refuse to be assisted because it's perceived to be shameful. Instead of delivering to all targeted actors the same "product" (equality of treatment), it would be more effective to customize the way civil servants communicate and interact with them.

The necessity of clearly formulated objectives should avoid ambiguous or contradictory goals, which would lead to great problems during the implementation phase. Moreover, objectives are useless if they cannot be evaluated with appropriate indicators (Knoepfel & Varone, 1999; Norman, 2007). No doubt, the focus on outputs or even outcomes, instead of inputs, should here be really useful.

Programming

The second step, programming, is about the legal framework and will be concretized through a political-administrative program (PAP), and a political-administrative arrangement (PAA). The PAP includes all of the legislative or regulatory decisions which should help implement public policy, whereas the PAA defines the responsibilities, competencies, and main resources attributed to public actors to implement the PAP. The main question is about the relevance and appropriateness of these programming tools, taking into account previous experience and comparative analyses of similar public policies.

The most expected contribution of NPM approaches (from a theoretical perspective) is the product approach; a great emphasis has to be put on their definition, their characteristics, and the work processes it is based upon. But this approach will hardly be able to catch the subtle interaction of all the other resources (Knoepfel et al., 2006) which may be used during the programming phase.

A second possibly interesting contribution of NPM is the contractualization approach between two or more actors in charge of the implementation of the public policy. In particular, the PAA may benefit from this new interaction mode which, contrary to hierarchy and its command and control mechanisms, should put the negotiation at the heart of the process and allow for more responsible and engaged behaviours on both sides.

Implementation

The third step of Peter Knoepfel's policy cycle is implementation. An institutional reform like NPM primarily focuses on reform implementation and not policy implementation. Against the background of institutional reform plans of action (strategies in a managerial conception) will lead to concrete reform outputs like new reform measures (e. g. management tools when looking at institutional policies), administrative decisions, and processes, and lastly, the products and services delivered to citizens renamed "customers." The outcome perspective should also be included, but this is hardly the case, as we will demonstrate further in this contribution.

From a classical political scientist's perspective, following the neutrality of public administration, as defined by Max Weber (Weber, 1956), administrative units are considered black boxes, acting according to the given instructions by politicians. There are now a considerable amount of publications showing that this is not the case (Selznick, 1957; Crozier, 1963); administrative units have a more or less developed freedom of action. This idea has been at the very heart of NPM approaches, with proponents insisting the "let the managers manage" axiom, as a "solution" of a paralyzed bureaucracy (Osborne & Gaebler, 1993). This entrepreneurial spirit behind NPM should decisively contribute to improving the implementation process, which means institutional policy outputs should help to improve substantive policies; no doubt, this should be the main contribution of NPM. The main expected reform outputs and impacts of NPM in this phase can be summarized as follows:

- Quality optimization: analysis and redesign of the work processes (business processes), according to quality management approaches (Emery, 2006).
- Budget and planning optimization: analysis of the costs generated by the products (direct and full costs) enhance the transparency of administrative actions and helps to better allocate resources, according to the relative importance of the products and their contribution to the strategic (political) objectives of the units.
- Managerial optimization: the leeway attributed to managers should help to reduce administrative costs, to flatten the hierarchy, and redesign the responsibility to empower staff members, leading to increased work motivation. On the other hand, the performance agreement method may lead to a fragmentation of the administrative apparatus, as pointed out by Peter

Knoepfel (2002), because each administrative unit's manager will try to optimize his business.

Evaluation

The final step within the policy cycle aims at evaluating the outcomes of institutional and substantive policies, and by answering different questions; on the one hand, we ask for direct impacts and long-term outcomes of institutional reforms in employee behaviour, immediate stakeholder reactions, long-term efficiency gains, and better-functioning public institutions. On the other hand, there are questions about substantive policies. Does the (social) problem, which has been at the origin of the public policy still exist? Clearly, NPM insists on the importance of evaluating administrative action, and processes against the backdrop of new reform measures, whereas the substantive policies are not at the heart of evaluation. The classical dimensions of this evaluation can be summarized as follows:[2]

- Quantity of the products: total amount, amount per actor or per period, geographical repartition of the products, etc.
- Quality of the products: a more subtle way to evaluate the conformity of the products according to professional technical standards, which must be clearly defined.
- Delays, timeliness of the processes: This dimension of products has been described as the most important aspect in the eyes of citizens (Kernaghan, 1999).
- Numbers and characteristics (socio-demographic) of the customers as targeted actors.
- Perception of the products by customers (so-called "satisfaction").
- Information about the (positive or negative) evolution of the social problem at the origin of the public policy: From a comprehensive view, it is necessary to evaluate the outcomes of the whole, and to be able to test the hypothesis on problem causation at both the institutional and substantive policy levels.

Effects of public management reforms

In the following sections, 12 reform evaluations are compared to the effects of the evaluated public administration reforms. Having no empirical material on the direct link between NPM implementation and outcomes of public policies, we cannot discuss the effects of NPM by following the 4 stages of the public policy cycle. It is the reason why we will then analyze the impact of NPM on the more general "policy capacity" of political authorities and the way they manage public policies.

[2] Note that a public policy analysis perspective, the first 3 points belong to the implementation phase of the whole process

The key question of this empirical portion is whether the reform elements are widespread or established in the examined administrations, and which effects have an impact on the outcome level of the political-administrative steering process.

The following global remarks on this empirical portion should be made:

- Most reforms were evaluated at the end of a trial period which lasted at least three or four years. The evaluation results were used for the decision for or against the definite implementation of the reform program.
- The reform evaluations focus on institutional policies and not substantive policies. The evaluations do not report results at the level of policy outcomes as explained in paragraph 2. Therefore, we can only speculate about the effects at the outcome level.
- The results are most positive for agency managers. For them, the expanded scope of action is worthwhile, and the newly introduced management instruments substantively improve their managerial capacity. As we will see later in this contribution, the results are more balanced for other actors, notably, members of Parliament.

Effects at the level of reform implementation

In the following section, the individual reform elements and the goals of NPM are discussed. Initially, one is interested in reform outputs, i.e., the spread and implementation of contract management, lump sum budgets, controlling, and elements for promoting customer orientation. They may lead to an improved capacity of steering substantive policies.

Contract management and lump sum budget

The new system of performance contracts has not become established on the parliamentary level. Rather, on the one hand, an individual member of parliament is receiving information on administrative services that he often cannot manage; on the other hand, the contracts are not being handled uniformly in parliament. NPM does, in fact, require a stronger connection between tasks and finances, which would however bring the parliaments excessively wide-ranging control powers within the administration. For this reason, parliament's participation in the setting of contract goals ("Approval of the Performance Contract") is controversial (econcept, 2002; Zimmerli & Lienhard, 2002). This problem can be alleviated by integrating political goals or impact goals into the lump sum budget, and by introducing the new management instruments of integrated task and financial planning at the governmental level (econcept, 2002 and 2009; Brühlmeier et al., 2001).

Crucial here are the observations that the reforms of, and the balance of powers among, the parliament, the government, and the administration are affected in as much as the members of parliament, due to their deficit NPM knowledge and a "flood of information" (see section below) can reach the agencies more quickly than the government or ministries. This shows, among other things, that agency managers were able to use these contacts advantageously when acquiring resources (Thom et al. 2001:216).

The agencies fully welcome the multi-year performance contracts and new type of lump sum budgeting (e.g. Ladner et al., 2007). This gives them the opportunity to engage in more long-term planning, and they therefore have clearer specified goals for their activities. However, the lack of an agreement between multi-year contracts and yearly budget or accounting periods is criticized.

Controlling and reporting

All of the analyzed reform institutions devote a great deal of time and money to the establishment of accounting and controlling systems. Again, it is apparent that primarily, the agencies profit from this and that the political level assesses the developments more critically (e.g. EFK, 2008). Certainly, the necessity for new instruments is not disputed; however, in most cases, there is a lack of appropriate consolidation and processing of information at the governmental level. Members of parliament bemoan the huge "flood of paper," as well as the overly detailed information. They do confirm that the overall quality of information is better than was previously the case. They lack a large number of politically relevant statements. This is related to the overall unsatisfactory formulation and measurement of targets at the impact and outcome level (see also Ritz 2007; Ritz & Sager forthcoming; Sager et al., 2009).

When establishing the control system, the heaviest demands are placed on the ministries and smaller administrative units. Here the creation of additional central controller positions in the ministries is demanded (econcept, 2000). This is the only thing that will enable the standardization and collation of the information required by the parliament.

Due to their lack of experience and knowledge, members of parliament avoid using the new instruments and prefer to rely on what is familiar. Thus, for example, the opportunity to influence the performance contract directly by using the "parliamentary mandate" was not used (Thom et al., 2001).

Elements enhancing customer orientation

Two statements can repeatedly be found in the evaluation reports. On one hand, the administration itself rates its customer orientation highly in every respect. On the other hand, customer orientation also receives high ratings from external respondents (Thom et al., 2001). It is presumed that the customer discussion that was firmly linked to the introduction of NPM has already exerted influence on the agencies and resulted in behavioural changes in the self-confidence of the "new" administrative agencies. However, if one considers the instrument level, then one notices that customer surveys are performed only in individual cases; and hardly any significant studies of the evaluators exist.

Effects at the level of reform evaluation

Here, the direct impacts of the reforms are of key importance, since long-term outcomes were not analyzed in the covered evaluation studies.

Management orientation based on the separation between strategy and operation

The fundamental NPM theory of the separation of strategy and operation (politics-administration dichotomy) between parliament and administration is dismissed in the evaluations. It would not be possible for members of parliament to ignore relevant questions in the scope of administration and not of parliament. Politically important issues are always at a "strategic" level for members of parliament, even NPM theory treats it another way. It is evident to some degree, that the performance contracts lead to a greater concentration by parliament on overriding goals and that operative intervention in matters having less political relevance can more likely be prevented (Ladner et al., 2007).

On the other hand, the aforementioned separation functions are better between the ministries and agencies. Here, there is a change in the fulfilment of roles in the sense that the ministries are able to assume a greater managerial role by examining the impact and performance goals, as well as the controlling processes, that are connected to them.

Transparency of administrative actions and cost orientation

On the parliamentary level, greater insight into administrative activities is associated with disproportionate expenses and an excess of reporting information. Nevertheless, the increased transparency is rated positively in some cases, in others, it is not (econcept, 2009; Ladner et al., 2007; Thom et al., 2001). Judged to be less positive is the linkage of services to finances. Here, in a majority of cases, the insufficient integration of policy or impact goals into the lump sum budget is apparent. An important factor influencing this connection is the parliament's handling of the performance contracts and the lump sum budget. During the pilot phases, the handling of the new instruments within special committees inside the customary parliamentary structure proved worthwhile; their level of information is very high, and they are knowledgeable on the connections between tasks and finances. A result of this was that the already existing differences in knowledge in the typical Swiss "militia parliament" were increased by the reforms. Even more important is the insight that the more detailed reporting information is, the more difficult the governance gets for a militia parliament (econcept. 2009). Thus, in Switzerland, there is currently a trend toward permanent expert committees (e.g., in the cantons of Argovia, Basel-City, Basle-Country, Lucerne, Soleure, Valais und Zurich, City of Bern), which leads to an improved integration of finances and services (NEF 2002).

On the ministerial and agency levels, controlling has contributed most to increased transparency. At the federal level, an evaluation of the so called GMEB program states that the reform agencies better deal with outputs and outcomes, and have a higher cost consciousness compared to non-reformed agencies (EFK, 2008). In individual cases, improved year-end financial statements are substantiated by the offices (econcept, 23; Rieder & Furrer, 2000), although here, other factors could have also played a role (e.g., projected savings on governmental level).

Expansion of the room for manoeuvre

Based on the evaluation results, it can be clearly confirmed that today the offices have more scope of action. This can primarily be seen in the realm of finances. Carrying forward resources from one year to the next, or opportunities for shifting resources between operating and personnel expenditures are the main reasons for this; and it promotes a more targeted use of resources. Criticism arises primarily when cross-sectional departments (financial management, central personnel management) want to have a say, and the offices are not granted genuine manoeuvrability. This is the case, for example, when new positions created on the basis of self-earned additional income remain subject to the restrictions of centrally determined staffing schedules. Other problems are related to the introduction of performance related pay practices, which are very popular in Switzerland. The effects of these systems are highly questioned in administration, as shown by newly published evaluations (Ritz & Waldner, 2009).

Employee satisfaction

If the reforms have the greatest impact on the agency managers, one can also say that employee satisfaction with NPM implementation is partially high, in the sense that employees prefer the actual situation over the former one (Ladner et al., 2007). On the other hand, new controlling tools significantly increase the workload of the employees and the pressure to perform, and lead to a so called "new bureaucracy" (Giauque & Emery, 2008).

Changes of outputs and outcomes at the level of substantive policies

With respect to many other influencing factors (Ritz, 2003), no empirical evidence can be reported concerning quantitative changes in services. Qualitatively, though, there is a trend toward increasing the service quality of the administration, which was also a partial goal of projects realized parallel to NPM (e.g., quality management). But quality measurements based on products and services have not been subjects of the analyzed evaluations. The perception of quality improvements or increased customer satisfaction by employees or customers shows a tendency toward higher quality levels (Thom et al., 2001; Ritz, 2003).

Not surprisingly, the covered evaluation studies do not analyze causal links between institutional reform and measured policy outcomes. Having empirical results at this level would lead us to a better understanding of the interaction between institutional and substantive policies. Especially research about new institutionalism shows the importance of the design of public institutions in affecting political and administrative decisions (March & Olsen, 1989).

The question is, at the level of agenda setting, programming, implementation and evaluation of public policies, do NPM reforms improve policy capacity (Painter, 2005). When analyzing the results of the effects of NPM reforms on the *parliamentary* work, then the following results are of main interest:

- Some work has been completed on the effects of NPM reforms on the actors at the parliamentary level (Ritz, 2005, Brun & Siegel, 2006; Schmidt, 2008). The aforementioned performance management systems can be summarized as having mixed results concerning policy capacity at the political level. On one hand, the new steering instruments and reform measures enhance the quality of information for parliamentarians, lead to increased transparency of administrative actions, partially increase the separation of strategic and operational decision making which leads to improvement of parliamentary supervision, especially within parliamentary (NPM-) commissions. On the other hand, MP's fear a shift of power toward the administration, report an increase of quantity of non decision making relevant information and only rare political initiatives based on administrative reports or performance information. All in all, it can be concluded that a majority of members of parliament support higher quality information and transparency about administrative actions. But this does not automatically lead to an increased policy capacity because the rational of politicians is still political and not managerial.
- Both quantity and quality of reporting information for member of parliaments have grown and lead to more transparency of administrative actions. However, reporting documents as well as planning instruments for member of parliaments are often not outcome oriented enough, which does not enhance their policy capacity (Ritz, 2009; Sager et al., 2009; Ladner et al., 2007).
- Only a few evaluations analyze the reform impact on policy outcomes by investigating the implemented performance management systems used by the members of parliament (Ladner et al., 2007; Rieder et al., 2003). When comparing these results, we can conclude that performance indicators at the outcome level are mainly neglected. Public management reforms help to establish a standardized indicator system, but policy outcomes are only in a few cases, objects of well-defined indicators. Better results show the analyzed goals at the outcome level. In comparison to the indicators, the definition of goals at the outcome level takes place, but virtually none of them are evaluated by corresponding indicators. Causal links between outputs and outcomes are based on plausibility within most NPM steering systems. This can be an adequate way for practitioner's daily work; however, it does not help much to enlighten the proposed claims of the reform efforts (Ritz, 2009; Sager et al., 2009). The reform evaluations did not investigate the use of policy evaluations, which in fact can be based on performance management systems.

As previously explained, members of the *executive*, as head of department, have played an increased role in the management of their unit. Conversely, the opportunity to strengthen the policy-steering dimension of their role has been clearly missed (Giauque & Emery, 2008), because executive members might have been slightly squeezed between MP's on one side and public managers on the other, having both more information and more power to control public policies. And also, as demonstrated in several evaluations, because the government, as collective executive body, has been rather passive toward the NPM movement, considering that NPM was all about managerial techniques, without any real influence on their political role as elected people (see for example evaluation conducted at the federal level). This situation may improve during the coming years, especially through a learning process and an appropriation of the tools implemented in NPM processes, but it will take a lot of time.

Summarizing, policy capacity can be enhanced by NPM reforms, especially when planning and controlling instruments are appropriately developed for members of parliament and government. Indicator systems respectively reporting information are linking whenever possible input, output, and outcome data. Therefore, we can reasonably assume that policy capacity as a whole has gained from NPM reforms concerning quality of information, increased transparency, and the possibility of better steering of public policies. Nevertheless, better decision making and controlling of policy outcomes based on NPM reform measures are not yet empirically confirmed.

Conclusion and research avenues

The reform initiatives that have taken place in Switzerland during the last two decades are amazing. Fortunately, a lot of scientific evaluations allow us to analyze and evaluate the effects of these reforms at the administrative level, taking a managerial perspective, as well as at the policy implementation level. At this latter level, the causality link between reforms and final outcomes is highly questionable and the data is mainly missing.

First of all, it's quite clear that these reforms have initiated profound and long-term changes in the politico-administrative system:

- Structural changes, by introducing new steering and controlling instruments, which should improve the decision making of politicians and public managers.
- Managerial changes, for example, in the way members of executive bodies interact with their public managers.
- Cultural changes, typically by developing a new and seemingly endurable "customer-orientation" among public sector employees.

A closer look at the main results of the evaluations reveal a lot of problems and limits of these reforms, especially in the link between institutional and substantive policies. The first and most operational problem is the difficulty to properly articulate all the new methods and instruments that have been implemented, without introducing a "new bureaucracy," which could negatively impact all the actors involved in the policy programming, implementation, and evaluation process. In this regard, Peter Knoepfel also copes with this kind of problem in a recent contribution (Knoepfel & Varone, 2008), taking largely into account the impacts of institutional reforms on the definition of public policies.

It is also important to optimally coordinate the information and data used at all levels of the politico-administrative system. This "technical" problem could become less important during the coming years, but it highlights a more subtle difficulty linked to the different rationales used by politicians and public managers.

The necessity to have clearly formulated objectives is not always easy to fulfil, because the description of outputs and outcomes seems to be more difficult than imagined by proponents of the NPM movement. However, because objectives are *per se* not easy to set, in some cases even not likely to be set, this may clearly limit the room for manoeuvre of elected people. As already expressed in the introduction and in the first chapter of this paper, Peter Knoepfel was aware of these issues early. In an article published in 1995, he underlined the risks constituted by indicators supposed to measure public policies' outcomes. In his contribution, he warned academics, politicians, and public managers against the danger represented by oversimplified indicators that are simply not able to capture the complexity of contemporary public policies (Knoepfel, 1995).

This in turn refers to the problematic hybridization of the managerial and the public policy approaches, two disciplines using different vocabulary and concepts. The first point on the research agenda is the conceptualization of a common-integrated framework (public management and public policies), which would be very necessary for both scientists and practitioners (Ritz, 2003). It is the *sine qua non* condition to a proper evaluation of the outputs and impacts of the reform initiatives, considered institutional policies, but also "final" outputs and outcomes of substantive policies. Data on this latter subject are largely missing, despite the modernization programs. If they were available, the knowledge about the causal link between institutional and substantive policies is still very poor (Emery & Chassot, 2009).

In this regard, the second very promising research avenue will have to deal with causal models and testing of hypothesis between institutional policies (with special focus on so-called "modernization programs") and their effects on substantive policies. The following points should be then mentioned in order to have proper research designs:

- Impacts of the same institutional policy (finance and budgeting, HR, or ICT, etc.) on different substantive policies; identification of the most "receptive" substantive policy to each of the institutional policies;
- Impacts of different institutional policies on the *same* substantive policy, implemented in different contexts (for example within the federalism);
- Design methodology which clearly determines control variables, as the causality link between institutional and substantive policies is subject to multiple influences. Control variables may be, for example, the nature of institutional systems, the level of maturity of substantive policies, or the political orientation of the government. We claim for further research on the

evaluation of institutional reforms, but more in a comparative way analyzing different types of institutions and reform contexts. One of the most prominent "founders" of the NPM, Christopher Hood, discussed NPM years ago in the light of different categories of values (Hood, 1991). He clearly showed that efficiency and effectiveness are not overall suitable goals for every public organization.

Thirdly, a future research interest lies in the similarities, distinctions, and different uses of outcome oriented control and policy evaluation. Today's administrative units are asked more and more to implement new controlling measures, even though it is not clear enough if controlling information is used for steering and if they should replace or complement policy evaluation. For example, Katia Horber shows quite clearly that MP's often follow a political logic focused on the outcome of political arbitration, rather than rational choices based on reliable indicators (Horber, 2009). The use of steering information by members of parliament, executives, and public managers, and other stakeholders taking into account the "new governance" perspective (Osborne, 2006), should then be better analyzed. This research question may be further refined by using the four stages of the policy cycle, by analyzing each stage and evaluate the impact of modernization strategies. Again, the design of such a research methodology could greatly benefit the opportunities given by a federal state, because the same substantive policies (at least in theory) have to be implemented at the regional and local levels, which may have highly different organizational (institutional policies) settings.

References

Brühlmeier, D., T. Haldemann, et al. (2001). *Politische Planung: Mittelfristige Steuerung in der wirkungsorientierten Verwaltungsführung*. Bern, Stuttgart, Wien : Paul Haupt.

Crozier, M. (1963). *Le phénomène bureaucratique*. Paris : Seuil.

econcept (2000). *Evaluation des WOV-Versuchs im Kanton Luzern: Gemeinsame Evaluation von WOV und LOS*. Schlussbericht zu Handen des Regierungsrats des Kantons Luzern. Zürich.

econcept (2000). *Evaluation WOV Kanton Aargau. Schlussbericht zu Handen des Regierungsrats des Kantons Aargau vom 21. November 2000*. Zürich.

econcept (2002). *Evaluation GRiforma. Schlussbericht zu Handen des Finanz- und Militärdepartements des Kantons Graubünden vom 30. September 2002*. Zürich.

EFK (2008). *Querschnittsprüfung über die Steuerung der FLAG-Verwaltungseinheiten durch die Departemente. Bericht der Eidgenössischen Finanzkontrolle an die Finanzdelegation der Eidgenössischen Räte*. Bern.

Emery, Y. (2006). Qualitätsmanagement in öffentlichen Organisationen. *WEKA Managementleitfaden öffentliche Verwaltung*. D. Kettiger. Zürich, WEKA. 3.5.

Emery, Y., & Chassot, F. (2009). Evolution de la politique institutionnelle de gestion des ressources humaines : quelles valeurs ajoutées pour la mise en œuvre des politiques publiques substantielles ?In P. Knoepfel. (Ed.) *Réforme de politique institutionnelle de gestion des ressources de l'action publique.* Lausanne : PPUR (to be published).

Germann, R. E. (1996). *L'administration publique en Suisse.* Berne, Stuttgart, Wien : Haupt.

Giauque, D., & Emery, Y. (2008). *Repenser la gestion publique.* Lausanne : Presses polytechniques et universitaires romandes.

Hood, C. (1991). A Public Management for all Seasons. *Public Administration* 69(1): 3-19.

Horber, K. (fortcoming). *The Power of Illusion: Evaluative Information and Policital Steering in Valais.* To be published.

Kernaghan, K. (1999). *Redécouvrir la fonction publique.* Toronto : Institut d'administration publique du Canada.

Knoepfel, P. (1995). Le "New Public Management": est-ce la panacée? *Swiss Political Science Review,* 1(1): 133-143

Knoepfel, P. (1996). Total Quality Management und Föderalismus - Betrachtungen aus der sicht des Politikanalyse. *TQM & ISO dans l'administration publique.* Y. Emery. Berne, Société suisse des sciences administratives. 34: 85-128.

Knoepfel, P. (2002). *L'éclatement de l'Etat - acht Thesen zur Abdankung der Einheitlichen, allgemeinen Staatsverwaltung.* Chavannes-près-Renens, Suisse : IDHEAP.

Knoepfel, P., Larrue, C., & Varone, F. (2001). *Analyse et pilotage des politiques publiques.* Genève : Helbing & Lichtenhahn.

Knoepfel, P., & Varone, F. (1999). Mesurer la performance publique: méfions-nous des terribles simplificateurs. *Politiques et management public* **17**(2): 123-145.

Knoepfel, P., & Varone, F. (forthcoming 2009). Politiques institutionnelles régulant les ressources de acteurs des politiques substantielles: un cadre d'analyse. *Réformes de politiques institutionnelles de gestion des ressources de l'action publique.* P. Knoepfel & F. Varone. Lausanne, Presses polytechniques et universitaires romandes. Action publique

Ladner, A., Cemerin, M. et al. (2007). *Evaluation der Parlaments- und Verwaltungsreform Neue Stadtverwaltung Bern NSB. Schlussbericht zu Händen des Stadtrats und des Gemeinderats.* Bern : KPM-Verlag.

Lienhard, A., Ritz, M. et al. (2005). *10 Jahre New Public Management in der Schweiz.* Bern, Stuttgart, Wien: Paul Haupt.

Nef, U. (2002). *Der bernische Grosse Rat im Modell NEF SOLL (Struktur, Prozesse, Dienstleistungen, Oberaufsichtstätigkeit).* Zwischenbericht der Umsetzungskommission NEF des bernischen Grossen Rats vom 23. Mai 2002. Bern.

Norman, R. (2007). Pièges de la gestion des performances et gouvernance du secteur public. In Y. Emery & D. Giauque. *Dilemmes de la GRH publique.* Lausanne, LEP.

Osborne, D., & Gaebler, T. (1993). *Reinventing Government: How the Entrepreneurial Spirit Is Transforming the Public Sector.* New York : Plume Book.

Osborne, S. (2006). The New Public Governance? *Public Administration Review* 8(3): 377-387.

Pollitt, C., & Bouckaert, G. (2004). *Public Management Reform : a comparative analysis.* Oxford : Oxford University Press.

Rieder, S., & Furrer C. (2000). Evaluation der WOV-Reform im Kanton Solothurn. Projektbericht. Luzern, Interface, Institut für Politikstudien Luzern.

Ritz, A. (2003). *Evaluation von New Public Management: Grundlagen und empirische Ergebnisse der Bewertung von Verwaltungsreformen in der Schweizerischen Bundesverwaltung.* Bern, Stuttgart, Wien : Paul Haupt.

Ritz, A. (2007). Performance Management and Output-Based Budgeting in Switzerland. Output and Outcome Data - An End in Itself or Relevant for Steering? *Conference Proceedings of European Summit of Modernising Government,* August 2006, Speyer/Germany. H. Hill. Baden-Baden, Nomos: (forthcoming).

Ritz, A., & Sager, F. (forthcoming). Great Expectations. Intentions and Reality of Outcome-oriented Public Management in the Direct Democratic Context of Switzerland. *Public Administration Review* - An International Quarterly.

Ritz, A. &. Waldner, C. (2009). *Evaluation Leistungsbeurteilung und -entlohnung in der Stadtverwaltung Nidau.* Bern : KPM-Verlag.

Sager, F., Ritz, A. et al. (2009). Utilization-Focused Performance Reporting. A Three-Step Model for the Development of Matching Goals and Indicators. *Public Money and Management - Integrating Theory and Practice in Public Management* 29(forthcoming).

Schedler, K. (1995). *Ansätze einer wirkungsorientierteen Verwaltungsführung.* Berne : Haupt.

Schedler, K., & Proeller, I. (2002). The New Public Management: a perspective from mainland Europe. In K. McLaughlin, S. P. Osborne & E. Ferlie, *New public Management. Current trends and future prospects.* London: Routledge: 163-180.

Selznick, P. (1957). *Leadership in Administration.* Illinois: Evaston.

Thom, N., Balthasar, A. et al. (2001). Evaluation FLAG: Schlussbericht der Evaluation des Projekts "Führen mit Leistungsauftrag und Globalbudget FLAG" in der schweizerischen Bundesverwaltung. Bern, Luzern.

Weber, M. (1956). *Wirtschaft und Gesellschaft.* Tübingen: Mohr.

Zimmerli, U., & Lienhard A. (2002). *Rechtsgutachten zu FLAG: Genehmigung von Leistungsaufträgen durch das Parlament.* Erstattet der Eidgenössischen Finanzverwaltung EFV.

Part III

Federalism and Multilevel Governance

CHAPTER 9

How Does European Union Law Influence Swiss Law and Policies?

ASTRID EPINEY

Introduction[1]

Switzerland as a non-member State of the European Union is not bound by European Union Law as such. Fact is, however, that European Union and especially European Community law and policies have a big impact on large areas of Swiss law and policies, which is not surprising considering the geographical, economic and political situation of the Swiss Confederation in the "middle" of Europe and the European Union. The different ways in which Swiss law and policies are influenced by EU and EC law and policies will be analysed under section 2, with a special attention to the area of environmental law. The main focus of this contribution is an analysis of selected aspects of the so called "bilateral agreements" between Switzerland and the European Community and / or the European Union and / or its Member States, these agreements being at present the most important influence of European Union law on Swiss law. A short conclusion tries to compare - from a legal point of view - some elements of the "bilateral way" to the status of a member of the European Union.

Forms of Europeanization of Swiss law: an overview

Swiss Law is influenced in various ways – whose legal effects are different – by European Community Law. One can cite mainly four different forms: "inspiration" of Swiss law by EC law ("autonomous adaptation"), international treaties, comparative law methods and a sort of indirect harmonisation by the participation of Switzerland and of the EC in multilateral agreements. These different methods of Europeanization of Swiss law are not necessarily exclusive but can overlap, so that for one legislative act two or more methods are used.

[1] I would like to thank Andrea Egbuna-Joss, MLaw, for the linguistic review of this manuscript.

Autonomous adaptation

Since Switzerland and the European Union and its Member States have a very narrow relationship, especially as far as economic relations are concerned,[2] the Swiss legislator is very often inspired by Community legislation and approximates its domestic legislation to Community law, especially to EC directives, without, however, being obliged to do so. In this sense, the decision to "copy" Community Law is an "autonomous" decision, which is the reason for this technique often being referred to as "autonomer Nachvollzug" or "autonomous adaptation".[3] The reasons for this voluntary approximation to Community Law are in most cases of an economic order: the aim is to thereby avoid economic difficulties resulting from different legislation in the European Union on the one hand and in Switzerland on the other hand. This inspiration of Swiss law by Community legislation has first been explicitly pointed out in a report of the Swiss government in 1988. The report insisted that the economic future of Switzerland depended largely on the degree to which one could assure a domestic legislation that was as "eurocompatible" as possible. A domestic legislation in conformity with European Union law was deemed necessary at least in all areas of law that were of transnational character.[4] This is the background for the fact that each "message" (a sort of preparatory document elaborated by the Swiss Government in the legislation process) contains a chapter examining the compatibility of the envisaged act with European Community Law and sometimes also with the national law of important Member States, especially the neighbouring States (Germany, France, Italy, Austria).

One can distinguish two main manners of inspiration of the Swiss legislator by European Community Law:

- First, one can more or less completely reproduce certain Community acts in Swiss law, and the aim of the legislative act is precisely the adaptation of Swiss law to certain Community acts. This very far reaching way of "autonomous adaptation" – which is the focus of this paragraph – takes place

---

[2] Cf. to this issue Rolf Weder, Swiss international economic relations: assessing a small and open economy, in: Clive H. Church (ed.), Switzerland and the European Union, 2007, 99 et seq.; Clive H. Church/Christina Severin/Bettina Hurni, Sectors, structures and suspicions: financial and other aspects of Swiss economic relations with the EU, in: Clive H. Church (ed.), Switzerland and the European Union, 2007, 126 et seq.

[3] Cf. to this technique in detail Matthias Amgwerd, Autonomer Nachvollzug von EU-Recht durch die Schweiz, unter spezieller Berücksichtigung des Kartellrechts, Basel 1998; Bruno Spinner/Daniel Maritz, EG-Kompatibilität des schweizerischen Wirtschaftsrechts : Vom autonomen zum systematischen Nachvollzug, FS Roger Zäch, 1999, 127 et seq.; Astrid Epiney/Annekathrin Meier/Robert Mosters, Die Kantone zwischen EU-Beitritt und ‚Bilateralem Weg'. Bewertung ausgewählter europapolitischer Optionen aus rechtlicher Sicht, in: Konferenz der Kantonsregierungen (ed.), Zwischen EU-Beitritt und bilateralem Weg: Überlegungen und Reformbedarf aus kantonaler Sicht. Expertenberichte im Auftrag der Arbeitsgruppe ‚Europa – Reformen der Kantone', Zurich 2006, 77 (85 et seq.).

[4] Bericht des Bundesrates über die Stellung der Schweiz im europäischen Integrationsprozess vom 24.8.1988, BBl 1988 III 249 (380).

mainly in areas in which transnational economic relations are very important. The Swiss legislation on technical barriers to trade[5] is e.g. essentially identical with the corresponding Community acts. In the field of competition law, the Swiss system is influenced to a high degree by the Community system[6] and the case-law of the Swiss competition commission very often refers to decisions of the European Commission or the European Court of Justice.[7] But also in other areas, Community acts are reproduced in Swiss law. Some directives in the field of European Private Law have, for instance, been "incorporated" de facto in Swiss law.[8] All in all, one must recognise that the "eurocompatibility" of Swiss legislation is the rule and the adoption of a legislative act which is not in conformity with European Community Law is the exception for which good reasons must be given.[9]

- Secondly, a legislative act can only be inspired in a very selective way by Community law. In this case, we are rather in the area of the application of a method of comparative law.

The question if there is a real "autonomous adaptation" or only a selective inspiration from European Community Law has to be answered by interpreting the text and the history of the legislative act in question. In the first case, difficult questions of interpretation have to be answered, so e.g. the question if the act has to be interpreted in conformity with European Community Law and the rulings of the Court of Justice, and – if the answer to this question is

[5] 'Bundesgesetz über technische Handelshemmnisse', SR 946.51. In the field of environmental law, for instance the preparatory „message" of the Swiss government to the legislative act concerning territorial planning ('Raumplanungsgesetz') refers to the Directive 96/61 respectively to the proposition of this directive, cf. BBl. 1994 III 1075.`Furthermore, in the area of legislation on genetically modified organism, the Swiss legislation refers in very large parts to the correspondent directives. Cf. to this issue Astrid Epiney/Nathalie Schneider. Zu den Implikationen des gemeinschaftlichen Umweltrechts in der Schweiz, EurUP 2004, 252 (257). An 'autonomous application' of the principle Cassis de Dijon which consists in addmitting (in principle) in Switzerland all products which can be commercialised somewhere in the European Union (cf. to this issue in detail Andreas Kellerhals/Tobias Baumgartner, Das « Cassis de Dijon »-Prinzip und die Schweiz, Schweizerische Juristenzeitung 2006, 321 et seq.), is a sort of autonomous adaptation of Swiss legislation since by doing so, European legislation (and to some extent also national legislation of Member States) becomes decisive for the question if product can be commercialised in Switzerland.

[6] 'Fusionsgesetz', SR 221.301.

[7] Cf. to this issue the yearly reports in the Annuaire Suisse de droit européen, compare the last report Patrick L. Krauskopf/Sabrina Carron, Rechtsentwicklungen im Europäischen Recht und die Schweiz: Wettbewerbsrecht 2007, Annuaire Suisse de droit européen 2007/2008, 2008, 121 et seq.

[8] Cf. to this issue Franz Werro/Thomas Probst, La jurisprudence de la CJCE en matière de droit privé et son influence sur la pratique du droit Suisse, Annuaire Suisse de droit européen 2005/2006, 2006, 453 et seq.; Franz Werro, Un reflet de l'actualité en droit privé européen, Annuaire Suisse de droit européen 2007/2008, 2008, 93 et seq.

[9] Cf. Spinner/Maritz, FS Roger Zäch (note 2), 127 (137).

in the affirmative – if also further legislative developments or further developments in case-law have to be taken into account.[10]

Over and above this, such an "autonomous adaptation" raises a lot of questions as far as the really autonomous character of this technique is concerned: in situations in which it is deemed necessary to adapt Swiss legislation on Community standards, Switzerland reproduces Community acts in whose adoption it had not been involved.[11] This situation is – from a political point of view – only defendable if this technique applies to rather technical matters and / or is restricted to a narrow field of application.[12] In this context, one can also mention that in many areas of rather technical character, Swiss legislation contains delegations which allow the government to adopt itself legislative acts which reproduce developments in Community Law.[13]

International treaties

International agreements can contain obligations for Switzerland to assure equivalent legislation in respect of a part of the *acquis communautaire.* Switzerland has up to now concluded over a hundred treaties (of more or less importance) with the European Union. The most important ones are – beside the Agreement on Free Trade from 1972 – the so-called Bilateral Agreements from 1999 and from 2004[14]. (These agreements – insofar as they reproduce parts of the *acquis communautaire* – will be discussed in further detail below.) For the purpose of our typology of the different ways European law influences Swiss law, an international agreement is – from a Swiss point of view – necessary in all situations in which the autonomous way described above does not lead to the desired results. This is the case mainly in the following situations:

---

[10] Cf. to this issue Marc Amstutz, Interpretation multiplex. Zur Europäisierung des schweizerischen Privatrechts im Spiegel von BGE 129 III 335, FS Ernst A. Kramer, 2004, 67 et seq.

[11] Cf. to this issue Karine Siegwart, Das Europa-Fenster, URP/DEP 2004, 266; Oliver Diggelmann, Der liberale Verfassungsstaat und die Internationalisierung der Politik. Veränderungen von Staat und Demokratie in der Schweiz, 2005, 114 et seq.

[12] Cf. also *infra* IV.

[13] Cf. to his issue Epiney/Schneider, EurUP 2004 (note 4), 252 (257-258).

[14] Cf. the text of these agreements in OJ 2002 L 114, 1 et seq. = BBl. 1999. 6489 et seq.; BBl. 2004, 5965 et seq. Cf. to these agreements Daniel Felder/Christine Kaddous (eds.), Accords bilatéraux Suisse – UE (Commentaires) / Bilaterale Abkommen Schweiz – EU (Erste Analysen), 2001; Christine Kaddous/Monique Jametti Greiner (eds.), Accords bilatéraux II Suisse – UE et autres Accords récents / Bilaterale Abkommen II Schweiz – EU und andere neue Abkommen, 2006; Thomas Cottier/Matthias Oesch (eds.), Die sektoriellen Abkommen Schweiz – EG, 2002; Daniel Thürer/Rolf H. Weber/Roger Zäch (eds.), Bilaterale Verträge Schweiz – EG – ein Handbuch, 2002; Daniel Thürer/Rolf H. Weber/Wolfgang Portmann/Andreas Kellerhals (eds.), Bilaterale Verträge I & II Schweiz – EU – ein Handbuch, 2007; Stephan Breitenmoser, Sectoral agreements between the EC and Switzerland: Contents and context, CMLRev 2003, 1137 et seq.; Christine Kaddous, The relations between the EU and Switzerland, in: Alan Dashwood/Marc Maresceau (eds.), Law and Practice of EU External Relations: Salient Features of a Changing Landscape, 2008, 227 (230 et seq.).

- Switzerland wishes to participate in a Community agency. The participation of Switzerland in the European Environmental Agency was e.g. only possible after the conclusion of a bilateral agreement (in 2004). The desire of Switzerland to participate in some of the Community Agencies in the area of Health Protection in the future will also have to be implemented by an agreement.
- If recognition of Swiss decisions by the European Community or its Member States is required, an international agreement is necessary to establish such an obligation of recognition. The participation at a Community system like the emission trading scheme e.g. needs to be settled in an international treaty. Otherwise the recognition of Swiss emission rights in the European Union would not be assured. But also in cases where Community Law states an obligation for Member States to introduce some sort of administrative control system, for example before a product will be admitted to the common market, only an agreement can assure that Swiss controls are recognised as equivalent to the ones in EU member states.
- Finally, if one wants to guarantee a real right to market access, an international agreement is necessary. There are such agreements e.g. in the areas of free movement of persons or of air transport.

In all these cases, a third country like Switzerland will never be allowed to participate in the decision-making process at EU-level; there are good reasons to support the opinion that such a participation would not even be compatible with the EC Treaty, even if it would only be a participation in the decision-making of an agency (at least if the agency has in some sense governmental authority).[15]

Comparative law methods

Swiss legislation and Swiss decisions are very often influenced by legal developments in other countries and in the European Union, even when there is no intention to reproduce specific legal developments. In this sense, Community law can rather be considered as a source of inspiration. The legislator examines – before adopting a legislative act – the corresponding legal developments in the European Union (and very often in some other countries, especially important Member States of the EU) and is – in one way or another – inspired by some aspects of this legislation.

But also the Federal Court ("Bundesgericht") refers sometimes to Community law in the interpretation of the European Court of Justice when interpreting Swiss law, although the Court does not reproduce Community law. This method is not only applied to find solutions in economic areas of law but more generally in cases in which the legal problems in Swiss and Community law seem to be similar. The Federal Court has for instance applied the principle

---

[15] ECJ, opinion 1/91 (EEA), 1991, I-6079; ECJ, opinion 2/92 (EEA), 1992, I-2821; cf. to this issue Astrid Epiney/Silvana Schnider, Die Europäische Umweltagentur: Eine neue „Einrichtung" der EG und ihre Bedeutung für die Schweiz, Umweltrecht in der Praxis (URP/DEP) 1995, 39 et seq.

of equal treatment between men and women as far as affirmative action is concerned in the same way as the European Court of Justice and referred explicitly to a ruling of the ECJ.[16]

As far as the courts are concerned, these references are sometimes not without problems from a methodical point of view: the Federal Court seems to apply them in a rather pragmatic way without really analyzing on what conditions and in which situations a solution applied by the European Court of Justice (or another court in the Member States) should be applied with regard to a problem in Swiss law. In our view, such a reference is only possible in cases in which it is established that the context, the systematic and the aim of the legal provision to be applied is really the "same" in Swiss and in European law. This approach implies a real analysis of the legal context in Swiss and in Community Law which one usually searches for in vain in the case-law of the Federal Court. It is definitely not sufficient to refer to a ruling of the ECJ and continue with a remark that there is no reason not to apply the same principles.

"Harmonisation" by multilateral international treaties

Finally, one has to remember that Switzerland and the European Community (and its Member States) are parties to a large number of multilateral international agreements. These treaties contain a certain number of obligations to the parties which have to be transposed in national (or supranational) law. If the European Community and Switzerland are parties to the same agreements, they therefore have the same obligations, and in this sense, international law contributes to "harmonise" Swiss law with Community Law. One can find a lot of examples of such legal developments, especially in the area of environmental protection.[17]

The "bilateral agreements"

Overview

After the rejection of the agreement on the European Economic Area (EEA) in the 1992 referendum, Switzerland has up to now concluded two "packages" of bilateral and sectoral[18] agreements with the European

---

16 ECJ, case. C-450/93 (Kalanke), 1995, I-3051 and BGE 123 I 152; ECJ, case. C-409/95 (Marschall) and BGE 125 I 21.

17 As an example, one can namely cite the Convention of Aarhus on environmental information, participation and access to justice (which Switzerland has not yet ratified) or the Convention on environmental impact assessment with its protocol of Kiev. Cf. in detail with some (more) examples and references Epiney/Schneider, EurUP 2004 (note 13), 252 (258 et seq.).

18 The notion of 'bilateral agreements' stands in contrast with the multilateral approach of these agreements. From a legal point of view, the expression is imprecise because the agreements are partially multilateral agreements (when the Member States are Parties as well). The term 'sectoral agreement' describes the legal position more precisely since it refers to the fact that each agreement treats a specific area. In this

Community and (in some cases) the European Union and the Member States. The aim of these agreements is to guarantee – since the EEA could not enter into force for Switzerland – the participation of Switzerland in some parts of the integration process taking place within the framework of the European Union. Some agreements also concern specific problems for which reciprocal obligations have been defined.

The so-called "bilateral I" agreements entered into force in 2002. They include seven agreements in the fields of public procurement, technical barriers to trade, research, road and rail transport, air transport, agriculture and free movement of persons. From a legal and political point of view, the latter agreement is of special importance.[19] The seven agreements form a "package" insofar as they are linked by a so-called "guillotine clause": They could only enter into force collectively and the non-prolongation or cancellation of each single one would result in the concomitant cancellation of all other agreements. From an institutional point of view, however, each agreement is an autonomous agreement, relating to different matters and containing its own institutional provisions. No framework agreement exists.

Contrary to the EEA, these treaties cannot be qualified as "integration agreements" since they are – from a merely formal point of view – classic international treaties which are of a static and non-dynamic character so that they do not imply a real involvement in the ongoing integration process in the framework of the European Union. They are based on the principle of equivalence of legislation and standards and from an institutional point of view, they refer to Joint Committees consisting of representatives of each contracting party deciding by unanimity. These committees shall ensure the correct application of the agreements, settle differences between the parties and modify certain parts of the treaties. In principle, no provisions of Community law are taken over. However, as already mentioned before, large parts of the politically and legally important agreements (especially the agreements on transport and on free movement of persons), refer to Community law and aim insofar at the participation in the relevant sections of the *acquis communautaire*. This contrast – the bilateral agreements as classic international agreements on the one hand with a form of "integration content"

---

contribution, we will, however, use the term 'bilateral agreements' as it has become the term most commonly used.

[19] Cf. especially to this agreement Astrid Epiney, Das Abkommen über die Personenfreizügigkeit – Überblick und ausgewählte Aspekte, Jahrbuch für Migrationsrecht / Annuaire du droit de la migration 2004/2005, 2005, 45 et seq.; Sebastian Benesch, Das Freizügigkeitsabkommen zwischen der Schweiz und der Europäischen Gemeinschaft, 2007; Walter Kälin, Das bilaterale Abkommen der Schweiz mit der EG über die Freizügigkeit von Personen, ZAR 2002, 123 et seq.; Martin Nyffenegger, Grundzüge des Freizügigkeitsabkommens unter besonderer Berücksichtigung der Übergangsbestimmungen, in: Bernhard Ehrenzeller (Hrsg.), Aktuelle Fragen des schweizerischen Ausländerrechts, 2001, 79 et seq.; Steve Peers, The EC-Switzerland Agreement on Free Movement of Persons: Overview and Analysis, European Journal of Migration and Law 2000, 127 et seq.; Edgar Imhof, Das bilaterale Abkommen über den freien Personenverkehr und die soziale Sicherheit, SZS/RSAS 2000, 22 et seq.

on the other hand – raises complex questions of interpretation which will be dealt with below.

Soon after concluding the "bilateral I" agreements, Switzerland and the European Union entered into negotiations for the "bilateral II"[20] agreements. These eight treaties deal with the "left overs" from the "bilateral I" agreements (processed agricultural products, statistics, environment, media and education, pensions and services; the latter subject has been abandoned during the negotiations) and with some new political concerns from both sides as well (taxation of savings, fight against fraud and Schengen/Dublin). The different "bilateral II" agreements are not legally connected with each other (contrary to the bilateral I); however, they are (partially) linked from a political point of view. They were signed in October 2004 and have mostly entered into force, with the notable exception of the agreement on the fight against fraud.

In our context the agreement on cooperation in the fields of justice, police, asylum and migration (Schengen/Dublin) is of major interest. It envisages – even if it is also formulated as a classic international treaty – an integration of Switzerland into the corresponding parts of the *acquis communautaire*, including in principle the obligation to adopt also its further developments.[21]

It is envisaged to conclude further bilateral agreements in the future; at present, the areas of agriculture, health, Eurojust, Galileo, emission trading, chemical regulation and electricity are of special importance.[22] As far as the content of these future agreements are concerned, one can assume that they will as far as possible integrate existing Community Law, as this is already the case in large parts of the bilateral I and II. The question of the legal interpretation and implications will therefore remain of major importance in the future.

Different forms of recurring to the acquis communautaire and their legal implications

Preliminary remarks: the interpretation of the bilateral agreements

As already mentioned earlier, the bilateral agreements reproduce, at least as far as important parts of some agreements are concerned, parts of the *acquis communautaire.* The question of the interpretation of those articles or parts of the agreements is therefore raised. The point of departure has to be that these agreements are international treaties which do not constitute special integration agreements so that the Vienna Convention on the Law of the Treaties has to be applied by analogy (since the Convention does not apply directly to treaties concluded by international organisations but large parts of the Convention, including the articles on the interpretation of international

---

[20] Text and 'Message' of the bilateral II Agreements in: BBl. 2004, 5965 et seq.

[21] To a great extent the agreement is analogous to the association agreements with Norway and Iceland. Cf. Astrid Epiney, Schengen, Dublin und die Schweiz, AJP 2002, 300 (304 et seq.).

[22] Cf. information at www.europa.admin.ch.

treaties, have attained the status of international customary law).[23] According to articles 31-33 of the Convention, an international treaty has to be interpreted in good faith in accordance with the ordinary meaning given to its terms in their context and in the light of its purpose and its objective. These principles – which cannot be analyzed in detail in this contribution – are as such rather abstract and general; in particular, the different methods referred to in art. 31 can be combined and assessed in different ways. These principles are thus somewhat flexible, and allow taking into consideration the particularities of each treaty (e.g. its contents, its objectives or its relationship with other treaties) that are decisive for its interpretation.

If an international treaty reproduces articles which are (also) incorporated in another international agreement, the Vienna Convention does not necessarily impose a parallel interpretation of the said provision. It must rather be analyzed if and to what extent such an interpretation may be coherent in application of the interpretation principles mentioned before. In this sense, the European Court of Justice has stressed that the fact that an international agreement reproduces Community law does not "automatically" lead to a parallel interpretation of the treaty with Community Law since Community Law has a special constitutional structure and contains special objectives and principles which have significant consequences for its interpretation. However, a certain parallelism can result from the application of the principles included in articles 31 et seq. of the Vienna Convention if the international agreement pursues the same objectives as Community law in the relevant area.[24]

We can therefore conlcude that in all situations in which an international treaty with a non member state reproduces parts of Community Law and in which the aim of the agreement is precisely to guarantee an equivalent situation to the one in Community law, the international agreement has in principle to be interpreted in accordance with Community law. This results not of a direct application of Community law but of an application of the Vienna Convention on the Law of Treaties.[25] With respect to the bilateral agreements,

---

[23] Cf. Walter Kälin/Astrid Epiney/Martina Caroni/Jörg Künzli, Völkerrecht. Eine Einführung, 2006, 17 et seq.

[24] ECJ, case C-312/91 (Metalsa), 1993, I-3751; ECJ, case C-469/93 (Chiquita), 1995, I-4533; ECJ, case C-465/01 (Commission/Austria), 2004, I-8291. See also ECJ, case C-467/02 (Cetinkaya), 2004, I-10895. Cf. to this issue in the doctrine e.g. Andrea Ott, Die anerkannte Rechtsfortbildung des EuGH als Teil des gemeinschaftlichen Besitzstandes (*Acquis communautaire*), EuZW 2000, 293 (294 f., 297); Astrid Epiney, Steuern, Europa und die Schweiz – Ausgewählte Aspekte der „Europakompatibilität" kantonaler Steuerregime aus rechtlicher Sicht, in: Franz Jäger (ed.), Steuerwettbewerb: Die Schweiz im Visier der EU, 2008, 75 (79 et seq.).

[25] One has, however, to admit that the rulings of the ECJ are not always coherent since the Court does sometimes admit a parallelism in interpretation, sometimes it denies such a principle in similar situations. Cf. ECJ, opinion 1/91 (EEA), 1991, I-6079; ECJ, case C-235/99 (Kondova), 2001, I-6427; ECJ, case C-63/99 (Gloszcuk), 2001, I-6369; ECJ, case C-257/99 (Barkoci und Malik), 2001, I-6557 (against a parallelism); ECJ, case C-268/99 (Jany), 2001, I-8615; ECJ, case C-162/00 (Pokrzeptowicz-Meyer), 2002, I-1049; ECJ, case C-163/90 (Legros), 1992, I-4625 (in favour of a parallelism). Cf.

one can in general conclude that – as far as they reproduce parts of Community law – they aim at an integration of Switzerland in the relevant Community law or system so that in principle a parallel interpretation is indicated.[26] There remain, however, important difficulties when applying this principle to an individual article.

Methods of reproducing Community law in bilateral agreements and their implications

a. References to existing Community law

When analyzing the different forms of reproduction of Community law in bilateral agreements, two types of references to existing Community law can be distinguished:[27]

- An agreement (or rather certain articles of an agreement) can refer directly to certain Community law provisions (e.g. certain regulations or directives) and Switzerland can be obliged to ensure an equivalent legislation and application of that legislation ("direct reference" to Community law). This technique is generally used with reference to rather technical provisions contained in secondary law, mainly in directives and regulations. Annexes II and III of the agreement on free movement of persons contain e.g. a list of legal acts that Switzerland has to apply ("equivalence of legislation"). Annex 1 of the agreement on overland transport also lists a number of Community acts containing essentially technical provisions; Switzerland has to apply provisions that are "equivalent" to these Community law provisions. The substantive law provisions in the Schengen/Dublin agreements also basically refer to the acquis communautaire by using this technique.
- Secondly, an agreement itself (or its annexes) can make an "indirect reference" to Community law by reproducing certain provisions whose content is largely or entirely based on the situation in the Community. Annex I of

---

to this case-law in detail Eckart Klein, Zur Auslegung von völkerrechtlichen Verträgen der EG mit Drittstaaten, in: Astrid Epiney/Florence Rivière (eds.), Auslegung und Anwendung von ‚Integrationsverträgen' / Interprétation et application des ‚traités d'intégration', 2006, 1 (16 et seq.).

[26] Cf. in detail the analysis of the agreement on free movement of persons in Astrid Epiney, Zur Bedeutung der Rechtsprechung des EuGH für Anwendung und Auslegung des Personnfreizügigkeitsabkommens, ZBJV 2005, 1 et seq.; Astrid Epiney/Robert Mosters, Un exemple d'interprétation des accords conclus entre la Suisse et l'Union européenne: l'accord sur la libre circulation des personnes, in: Astrid Epiney/Florence Rivière (eds.), Auslegung und Anwendung von 'Integrationsverträgen'. Zur Übernahme des gemeinschaftlichen Besitzstandes durch Drittstaaten, insbesondere die Schweiz, 2006, 57 et seq.; Edgar Imhof, Das Freizügigkeitsabkommen EG – Schweiz und seine Auslegungsmethode, ZESAR 2007, 155 et seq., 217 et seq.

[27] Cf. in detail already the analysis in Epiney/Meier/Mosters, in: Zwischen EU-Beitritt und bilateralem Weg (note 2), 77 (98 et seq.). Of course, some bilateral agreements contain also completely autonomous provisions that do not refer in any form to the *acquis communautaire*. These provisions, however, do not raise any particular question so that this category of legal provisions will not be discussed in this contribution.

the agreement on free movement of persons, for instance, adopts certain Community law provisions literally or alludes to parallel obligations that can be found in Community law. Article 1 (3) of the agreement on overland transport refers as well to the principle of non-discrimination contained in Article 12 EC Treaty. A similar solution can be found in Article 6 of the agreement on certain aspects of government procurement which contains also the non-discrimination principle.

Whenever the agreements refer directly or indirectly to the *acquis communautaire*, the complex question arises, whether and to what extent those provisions are to be interpreted in the same way as the relevant provisions of Community law. In the case of direct references to certain Community acts, a parallel interpretation is clearly indicated for two reasons: (1) there is really a reference to Community law and (2) it is obvious that the aim of this reference is precisely to guarantee a parallel legal situation in Switzerland. In cases where the reference is indirect, this question is more difficult to answer. One has to always carefully analyze if the relevant provisions really relate to Community law. This may be evident in certain cases (e.g. when reference is made to the notion of discrimination) but not in others (especially when the wording of the relevant provisions in the bilateral agreement differs in some way from the wording in Community law). Sometimes only partial reference to Community law is made. Even if one can deduce from the aim and the contents of the different bilateral agreements a general principle according to which one has to interpret the provisions of the agreement in the same way as Community law insofar as they refer to the latter, one has to analyze each provision individually in order to find out if and to what extent there is indeed a reference to Community law. Considerable uncertainties with respect to the legal meaning of the provisions of the bilateral agreements therefore remain.

Furthermore, these uncertainties need to be seen in the context of the system of legal protection which is – in the framework of the bilateral agreements (with an exception for the agreement on air transportation) – governed by the general principles applying to international treaties. Legal protection in Switzerland – where, due to a monist understanding of the relationship between national and international law, agreements are effective as such and certain provisions are self-executing[28] – is thus disconnected from the legal protection in the European Union, and Swiss courts do not have access to the ECJ within the preliminary ruling procedure. The ensuing risk of differential case-law on the interpretation of the agreements by the ECJ on the one hand (which has to interpret the agreements as an integral part of the Community legal system) and Switzerland on the other hand aggravates rather than remedies legal uncertainty. If the ECJ rules differently on a certain issue than Swiss courts, the question arises whether the latter are or will be under an obligation to modify their case-law.

[28] See e.g. Daniel Wüger, Anwendbarkeit und Justiziabilität völkerrechtlicher Normen im schweizerischen Recht, 2005, *passim*.

These issues are closely linked with the question of the pertinence of the ECJ"s case-law in cases in which bilateral agreements refer to parts of the *acquis communautaire.* Some of the agreements contain an explicit obligation to take ECJ rulings into account as far as they were rendered before the agreements where signed. According to Article 16(2) of the agreement on free movement of persons, the rulings of the ECJ (rendered prior to the date of signature of the agreement) have to be taken into account while interpreting and applying the agreement as far as the latter refers to Community law notions. Furthermore, according to the Schengen association agreement a qualified deviation from case-law may lead to the cancellation of the agreement. In other agreements, however, there is no reference to the case-law of the ECJ, even though they also frequently make use of Community law terms. But also in these cases, one has to generally refer to the case-law of the ECJ considering the aim and the subject of the agreements.[29] In any case, it is questionable which rulings are deemed relevant and how to distinguish the "old" case-law from the "new" case-law that was developed after the signature of the agreements. Furthermore, one may even ask whether and to what extent new rulings have to be taken into account when interpreting and applying the agreements. In the framework of the bilateral agreements and according to their aim and subject matter, the following general principles can be established:

- A ruling of the ECJ has in any case to be taken into account when it only repeats or applies principles which have already been developed by the ECJ.[30]
- As far as new case-law is concerned, a principle according to which also new rulings are in principle relevant when applying and interpreting bilateral agreements can be established for situations where the aim and subject-matter of the agreements indicate that an equivalent application of relevant Community law and of the corresponding provisions of the bilateral agreements is intended.[31]
- And finally, one always has to bear in mind that aim and subject matter of the agreements support the conclusion that in case of a (certain) reference to Community law notions, the relevant provisions have in principle to be interpreted in accordance with their interpretation in Community law unless there is clear evidence to the contrary in the agreements.

A consistent application of these principles could attenuate the mentioned legal uncertainties and would correspond to the aims and subject matters of

---

[29] Cf. Rolf H. Weber, Alpentransitbörse im europarechtlichen Fadenkreuz, AJP/PJA 2008, 1213 (1214-1215); Kaspar Sollberger, Konvergenzen und Divergenzen im Landverkehrsrecht der Europäischen Gemeinschaft und der Schweiz, 2003, 338-339; Astrid Epiney/Kaspar Sollberger, Zum Gestaltungsspielraum der Vertragsparteien: die rechtliche Tragweite des Art. 32 des Abkommens über den Güter- und Personenverkehr auf Schiene und Strasse, in: Daniel Felder/Christine Kaddous (eds.), Bilaterale Abkommen Schweiz – EU: Erste Analysen, 2001, 521 (528).

[30] Cf. in detail with further references and examples Epiney, ZBJV 2005 (note 33), 1 (15 et seq.).

[31] Cf. in detail Epiney, ZBJV 2005 (note 33), 1 (23 et seq.).

the agreements as well. The case-law of the Federal Court, especially its rulings rendered on the agreement on free movement of persons, is however far from clear on these issues.[32] As far as the impact of new case-law is concerned, the Court applies a very pragmatic method and very often takes over new rulings of the ECJ and simply states that there is no reason to take another view than the ECJ without, however, explaining the legal reasoning behind this approach.[33] As a result, the Court considers that it remains entirely free to renounce taking over a new ruling of the ECJ in the future without giving any special reason. Furthermore, the Federal Court is sometimes rather reserved as to the exact relevance of Community law principles and case-law of the ECJ in the Swiss jurisprudence: while in some unambiguous cases it clearly refers to the case-law of the ECJ,[34] it seems to limit references to Community law and to the (new and sometimes also the old) case-law of the ECJ in other cases. The latter is the case especially[35] when interpreting the principle of non-discrimination, a fundamental principle of Community law which has been without any doubt incorporated in several agreements, especially in the agreement on free movement of persons. The Court seems to limit the scope of application of Art. 2 of the agreement on free movement of persons, disregarding the case-law of the ECJ.[36] It sometimes does not correctly apply the notion of material discrimination,[37] and it sometimes takes

[32] Cf. in detail to the case-law of the Federal Court in the field of the agreement on free movement of persons Astrid Epiney, Zur schweizerischen Rechtsprechung zum Personenfreizügigkeitsabkommen, Jahrbuch für Migrationsrecht / Annuaire du droit de la migration 2004/2005, 2005, 141 et seq.; Astrid Epiney/Tamara Civitella, Zur schweizerischen Rechtsprechung zum Personenfreizügigkeitsabkommen, Jahrbuch für Migrationsrecht / Annuaire du droit de la migration 2007/2008, 2008, 227 et seq.

[33] Cf. for instance BG, 2A.91/2003, 4.11.2003, BGE 130 II 1. See to this ruling Hanspeter Mock/Fabrice Filliez, Libre circulation des personnes et regroupement familial: à propos de la prise en compte de la jurisprudence de la Cour de Luxembourg par le Tribunal federal, SZIER 2006, 237 et seq. See also BG, 2A.39/2006, 3.8.2006.

[34] Especially, as far as the reference to the notion of public order and security is concerned, cf. BG, 2A.39/2006, 31.5.2006; BG, 2A.315/2005, 18.10.2005. In detail to the case-law of the Federal Court on this subject Christine Kaddous/Christa Tobler, Droit européen: Suisse – Union européenne / Europarecht: Schweiz – Europäische Union, SZIER 2006, 467 (492 et seq.); Christine Kaddous/Christa Tobler, Droit européen: Suisse – Union européenne / Europarecht: Schweiz – Europäische Union, SZIER 2007, 637 (657 et seq.).

[35] See also BGE 130 II 113: With respect to the principle of free movement of workers, the Federal Court seems to defend the opinion in this ruling that the agreement takes over only a part of the fundamental freedom of the EC Treaty. It is not clear to which part the Federal Court refers to and over and above this, this interpretation seems to be in clear contradiction to the aims of the agreement expressed in the preamble and in article 1 where one can read that the fundamental freedoms of the treaty are the basis for the agreement and that the agreement should ensure a parallelism with the guarantees of the Treaty.

[36] Cf. BG, 2P.142/2003, 7.11.2003.

[37] BG, 5A_374/2008, 11.8.2008.

into account certain aspects of a new ruling of the ECJ while disregarding – without further explanation – other aspects.[38]

To sum up, the bilateral method leads inevitably to a certain number of difficulties as far as the application and interpretation of the agreements are concerned, especially when they refer to or reproduce parts of Community law. In applying a more consequent interpretation of the bilateral agreements in accordance with Community law and the rulings of the ECJ the inherent legal uncertainties could, however, be limited to a very large extent. Moreover, this approach seems also to be in accordance with aim and purpose of the agreements as far as they reproduce Community law. It is therefore very regrettable that the Federal Court"s approach is not very clear in this regard and does frequently not seem to respect the fundamental principles of interpretation according to international law. Furthermore, the Federal Court"s approach is unable to assure a minimum of legal certainty. It will often remain unclear for Swiss authorities and courts whether and to what extent Community law and the case-law of the ECJ will and should be taken into account when rendering a decision or a judgement in a particular case, which again detracts legal certainty.

b. Further legal developments

The "classic" international approach of the bilateral agreements implies that they contain – in so far unlike the EEA – in principle static obligations and that the joint committees play an important role in settling disputes and further developing the treaties. Concerning the reproduction of the *acquis communautaire*, this approach implies that one has to refer to the actual version of Community Law (including, as mentioned earlier, case-law) at the time of signature of the treaty. In other words, when Community law is modified, it is not automatically incorporated, on the basis of the bilateral agreements, in these agreements. Nevertheless, the agreements aim to ensure an equivalent legislation in Switzerland in relation to the EU, at least as far as they directly or indirectly refer to the *acquis communautaire*. However, this aim could not be achieved without taking into account the further development of Community law. Therefore, the agreements contain specific provisions for the "adoption" of new Community law. Referring to legislation, one can basically distinguish between two mechanisms of adoption[39]:

- Either the joint committee is competent to modify provisions, which is provided for several bilateral agreements. This is in general the case in respect of the annexes to the agreement where Community acts which have to be "adopted" by Switzerland are listed,

[38] So BG, 2A.275/2004, 25.5.2005 referring only partly to ECJ, case C-413/99 (Baumbast), 2002, I-7091.

[39] Cf. in detail to these techniques Epiney/Meier/Mosters, in: Zwischen EU-Beitritt und bilateralem Weg (note 2), 77 (98 et seq.). Only mechanisms that are already in the agreement itself are taken into account in this contribution. Moreover, the agreements can of course be modified at any time. A modification would, however, imply the rather ponderous international proceedings to conclude a treaty.

- or the agreements establish the obligation to adopt (in principle) the further developments of the relevant part of the acquis communautaire. Whereas the adoption takes place in accordance with domestic law, the agreement will be terminated automatically if new Community law remains unadopted. The Schengen- and Dublin association agreement includes this mechanism, and this technique will probably also be used for some of the future agreements.

In cases in which none of these mechanisms are applied, an incorporation of new legislative developments in the bilateral agreements is not possible in a simplified manner – unless a simple modification of interpretation can assure an equivalent result. The content of Annex I of the agreement on free movement of persons has e.g. in certain parts been overruled by the adoption of Directive 2004/38 on the free movement of European citizens[40]. Of course, one can always modify the agreement itself but this procedure is long and complicated. It can therefore not be expected that the Parties will want to refer to this procedure unless an exceptionally important issue is at stake.

Conclusion

The bilateral agreements aim, *inter alia*, at a participation of Switzerland in particular parts of the *acquis communautaire*, by recurring to instruments of international law. They constitute, from a formal point of view, pure instruments of international law and have no integration character in contrast to the EEA. However, when analyzing in detail the manner in which Switzerland is directly or indirectly bound to the *acquis communautaire* on the basis of bilateral agreements, one can stress the following points:

- The legal effects of the provisions contained in the bilateral agreements that refer to parts of Community law are – at least in the interpretation of the Swiss Courts – largely unclear. Especially, it is not always sure to what extent articles of bilateral agreements actually recur to Community law and have therefore to be interpreted in accordance with Community law. Moreover, the exact relevance of the ECJ"s case-law remains partly obscure. However, it is possible to remove large parts of the legal insecurity caused thereby by developing coherent guidelines in doctrine and in the case-law in order to define a "principle of parallel interpretation" and its exceptions. However, a certain uncertainty is inherent in the technique of bilateral agreements.
- Concerning legislation, Switzerland has (in fact) to apply or to "adopt" those parts of Community law referred to in the agreements. In cases in which the adoption of further developments of Community law is provided for, there will be a considerable political and economical pressure to adopt

[40] OJ 2004 L 158, 77.

the corresponding new legislation, even though Switzerland does not take part in the decision-making process in the European Union.[41]

All in all, large parts of the bilateral agreements entail a sort of "partial integration" in the legal system of the Union. The static character of the agreements does not really change this conclusion. Large parts of the bilateral agreements are in fact integration treaties, even if they have a formal character of "classic" international law treaties. This "partial integration" takes place without Switzerland contributing in the framework of the decision-making process in the European Union. Furthermore, it entails several disadvantages as far as legal security and legal protection are concerned. The question needs to be raised whether this special relationship really still makes sense or whether an accession would not be more adequate. At present, it seems that a majority of the population and the government are of the opinion that Swiss interests can be better realized by the "bilateral way" than by an accession. However, the real question to be asked in my opinion is whether Switzerland wants to accept the shift of sovereignty to the European Union that would necessarily be entailed by an accession. This question is a highly political one but the decisive factors for its answer are the following:

- First, the question arises in how many areas bilateral agreements with the obligation of reproducing important parts of Community law will be concluded in the future. The further the material scope of application of such a "partial integration without having the status of a Member" reaches, the more importance the difficulties discussed above will gain. Furthermore, the negotiations of bilateral agreements imply a huge effort for all parties involved a problem that is yet aggravated by the widening of the European Union.
- Secondly, one has to analyze in which areas Switzerland is de facto obliged to have a legislation equivalent to Community law ("autonomous adaptation").
- Thirdly, the above mentioned institutional, legal and political difficulties have to be taken into consideration.
- Finally, a decision needs to be made on whether the additional shift of sovereignty in areas which are not yet covered by bilateral agreements is the way Switzerland wants to pursue.

So, the continuation of the "bilateral way" together with other adaptations of Swiss law to the Community standard will inevitably lead to the consideration of the advantages and disadvantages of EU membership in comparison with the technique of bilateral agreements. The question of the durability of the bilateral way is also raised; even if one cannot draw a strict border line for the "acceptability" - both from a legal and a political point of view – of the bilateral way, it is clear that the more Switzerland gets

[41] In the context of the Association of Schengen, Swiss representatives will be consulted when a corresponding project is elaborated. The effect of this involvement should not be underestimated in a political context.

"europeanized" by Bilateral Agreements, the more the question of accession has to be analyzed.

CHAPTER 10

The Internationalization of National Decision-Making Processes: the Case of the Bologna Declaration in Switzerland

MARTIN BENNINGHOFF & JEAN-PHILIPPE LERESCHE

Introduction

The decision adopted by 29 European ministers of education in the Italian city of Bologna on 19 June 1999 rapidly became fertile ground for research. In the context of European studies, researchers have been able to use the Bologna Declaration to illustrate the phenomenon of Europeanization (Featherstone & Radaelli, 2003; Knill, 2005; Ravinet, 2009a) and national convergence processes.[1] In the literature on tertiary education research, this international undertaking is often analysed as a "top-down" measure that has impacted on curricula and contributed paradoxically to both the standardization and diversification of higher education in Europe (Musselin, 2006).

It is not the aim of this contribution to compare higher education policy in Switzerland with other national policies in this sector, but to interpret this political agreement from the perspective of the decision-making processes involved in a specific policy field. It will attempt to address the question as to the extent to which such an agreement expresses a change in the power relations in the current system of governance of higher education policy in Switzerland, in particular in the context of the decision-making processes that led to its (re-)definition. In other words, it will attempt to identify the extent to which and ways in which international undertakings, which are as legally unbinding as that of Bologna, contribute *a priori* to a transformation in national decision-making processes and of the levels and modes of governance of a particular policy.

This will involve reporting on the relations between the Swiss cantons and the Confederation in the context of the governance of higher education policy. To this extent, this issue echoes certain studies by Peter Knoepfel which link executive federalism and policy implementation (Kissling-Näf & Knoepfel, 1992; Knoepfel et al., 2001a). Thus, what is involved here is the location of this

[1] For a distinction between Europeanization processes and logics of convergence, cf. Palier & Surel (2007).

link within the context of the increased internationalization of national processes in the field of higher education in Switzerland.

This chapter is divided into two parts. The first part situates higher education policies within the Swiss and European contexts of the internationalization of public policies. The second part frames the analysis of the Bologna process in Switzerland in the context of the changes triggered by the process of internationalization and the resulting changes in levels within the higher education system.

The process of internationalization of higher-education policies in Switzerland and Europe

Based on the example of other sectoral policies, the decision-making policies associated with higher education in Switzerland are partly structured by political institutions, such as "federalism", "direct democracy" and the "system of concordance". These institutions influence in part the ways in which the associated actors (i.e. political parties, cantonal governments, senior civil servants, citizens etc.) can participate in political life, in general, and decision-making processes, in particular. These institutions function like "rules", based on which power is distributed, and constitute, therefore, a dimension that should be taken into account in policy analysis (Knoepfel et al., 2001b: 102-124). However, although these rules are institutionalized, that is not to say that they are set in stone. They can evolve in both spatial and temporal terms.

Following the example of other sectoral policies, higher education is an area, in which the structure of the relations between the cantons and the Confederation has evolved considerably in recent years, in particular, through an increase in intervention on the part of the federal government and its administration and the establishment of more integrated cooperative measures between the cantons[2] (Benninghoff & Leresche, 2003; Braun & Leresche, 2007).

As opposed to this and in contrast with other sectoral policies (for example, agricultural policy and environmental policy; cf. Sciarini, 1994; Knoepfel et al., 2003), the legal norms in the area of education appear to have been less

---

[2] Based on the University Support Act (Loi sur l'aide aux universités et la coopération dans le domaine des hautes écoles (LAU), i.e. Federal Act of 8 October 1999 on Support for the Universities and on Cooperation in the field of University Education), which was revised in 1999, (vertical) cooperation was strengthened in the early 2000s when the Confederation and cantons delegated a part of their responsibilities to the "new" Swiss University Conference (CUS) by giving it greater decision-making powers. As a regulatory agency based on both an intercantonal agreement (*concordat*) and a Convention between the Confederation and cantons, this new type of organizational structure would contribute to a change in Swiss federalism in a more cooperative direction (Braun & Leresche, 2007) and to the development of more delegative state action.

internationalized historically (Weber, 1994; Fischer, 2008)[3]. Thus the power relations between actors involved in the area of higher education are basically played out in the national, cantonal and academic arenas. Hence, the question arises as to how an international undertaking (i.e. the Bologna Declaration) affects the existing structure of higher-education policies and the associated decision-making procedures in Switzerland.

Various studies concerning the internationalization of certain sectoral policies in Switzerland enable the empirical clarification of this question (Klöti et al., 2005; Mach et al., 2003; Sciarini et al., 2004). According to this research, the internationalization of national decision-making processes leads to the strengthening of the power of certain actors, such as the representatives of the government and federal administration, while others, such as the federal parliament, relinquish their decision-making power, essentially becoming, in the case of the latter, a *chambre d'enregistrement* (i.e. a "voting machine" for rubberstamping the initiatives of the executive). Furthermore, at this level of public action, informal relations between actors would tend to be fostered as a result of internationalization, in particular because of the time pressure involved in the decisions to be taken. Indeed, the fact that a decision must be taken quickly makes it more difficult to involve a large number of actors in the decision-making process.

In contrast, the studies appear to disagree on the level of conflict, to which this reconfiguration of the decision-making process contributes (Fischer, 2008). It may be assumed that certain federal actors, cantonal actors (for example, the cantonal parliaments) and actors directly affected by the policy (for example, the students and teachers of the higher-education sector) would oppose the decisions taken in the context of international negotiations as they were not consulted at the time of a related decision. Thus, the question arises as to whether international agreements like the Bologna Declaration can result in greater conflict in higher-education policy given that certain key actors are not consulted and included in decision-making processes. Similarly, a question arises as to the consequences of the decisions taken in terms of the content and direction of the policies adopted as a result. In effect, the international arenas could offer certain actors a means of getting around the national decision-making structures and of imposing, through the legitimacy of a decision taken at international level, new reforms in an area of public action (cf. the theories associated with "two-level games", see Putnam, 1988).

The question of internationalization has also been explored in the area of higher education studies (Teichler, 2004; Enders, 2004) and has enabled the examination of higher education policies from new angles. An attempt was initiated in this context to theorize the development in terms of governance while dividing the different levels of decision-making power. This concept would account for a development in the way in which higher education is governed, i.e. in a less hierarchical, more coordinated, way that incorporates

[3] In contrast, based on the nationality of the personnel and students of third-level institutions, the Swiss higher education sector would appear to be particularly international (Horvath et al., 2000; Felli et al., 2007; OFS, 2008).

both state and non-state actors and takes the form of public action networks (Enders, 2004).

Of course, the objection could be made that the inclusion of an additional decision-making level does not necessarily result in the presence of more open and cooperative and less hierarchical decision-making processes as often implied by the majority of the multi-level governance approaches (Leresche, 2007). On the contrary, the decisions taken at EU level or in the context of international negotiations can translate into a very closed and far from integrative process. For example, research carried out on the Bologna Declaration (Huisman &, van der Wende, 2004) highlights the extensive latitude available to the administrations responsible for the implementation of the Bologna process, based on the vague definition of the objectives of this agreement. This would also enable certain actors to strengthen their decision-making power.

Similarly, the negotiation of the Bologna Declaration could be seen to constitute an international arena where the actors from the national systems could circumvent national actor networks and the European Commission.[4] From an initially strictly intergovernmental perspective, after the Sorbonne Conference in 1998, the concern of the states was to conserve extensive latitude *vis-à-vis* the EU bodies and retain control of "their" national higher-education policy (Croché, 2006). Thus, depending on their position in the field, the actors were able to use this type of international arena and the decisions taken there with a view to introducing new rules into the national system that benefited from "European" or "international" legitimacy but were not constrained by "European Unionization" (Muller & Ravinet, 2008). The instrumental use of the Bologna process by several countries in the conduct of their own reforms has already been documented (cf. Musselin, 2006, for the case of France). In this regard, the international level introduces not only a degree of incertitude into national decision-making processes but also, and above all, "opportunity structures" for certain actors (Knill & Lehmkuhl, 2002). It should be noted that as a non-Member State of the EU, the case of Switzerland is structurally different to that of France. "European Unionization" does not impose any direct constraints on Switzerland; however this does not mean that the measures taken by the EU do not have any affect on the Swiss political system and the policies adopted by it. This fact was confirmed by the bilateral agreements which enabled the full and complete participation of Switzerland in the Sixth Framework Programme of the European Union, thus uniting the European Research Area (ERA) from January 2004.[5]

---

[4] It should be noted that the role or influence of the European Commission increased from 2001 (Prague Conference) when it was included in the Bologna Follow-up Group along with other non-state actors such as the university umbrella organizations (European university association) and student organizations. It should also be noted that its contribution in terms of financial resources and expertise continued to increase since then (Croché, 2006).

[5] Cf. also the studies on agricultural policy, e.g. Sciarini (1994).

The Bologna Declaration: a change in the level of public action

Charles Kleiber, the Swiss State Secretary for Science and Research, signed the Bologna Declaration on 19 June 1999 together with 28 other education ministers.[6] With reference in particular to the basic principles of the *Magna Charta Universitatum* of 1988, the objectives of this declaration are located by the signatories in the "intellectual, cultural, social and scientific and technological dimensions" of a Europe whose supporters would like it to be "more complete and more ambitious". However, the economic dimension of the project is barely hinted at in the text of the Declaration based on the fact that the first university degree awarded should be "relevant to the European labour market as an appropriate level of qualification." In view of the fact that the European Commission highlighted the importance of this area for economic development in a memorandum on higher education of 1991 (Ravinet, 2009a), this quasi absence of economic valorisation of the Bologna objectives may appear surprising.[7]

In concrete terms, the Bologna Declaration proclaims several objectives which the signatory States[8] intended to pursue:

- "Adoption of a system of easily readable and comparable degrees, also through the implementation of the Diploma Supplement (...).
- Adoption of a system essentially based on two main cycles, undergraduate and graduate (...).
- Establishment of a system of credits – such as in the ECTS system – as a proper means of promoting the most widespread student mobility (...).
- Promotion of mobility by overcoming obstacles to the effective exercise of free movement (...).
- Promotion of European co-operation in quality assurance (...).
- Promotion of the necessary European dimensions in higher education, particularly with regards to curricular development, inter-institutional co-operation, mobility schemes and integrated programmes of study, training and research."

---

[6] The Swiss Confederation had already ratified the Lisbon Convention on the Recognition of Qualifications concerning Higher Education in the European Region (Council of Europe and UNESCO) of May 1997.

[7] A more retrospective and general reading after the launch of the Lisbon Strategy of March 2000, which aimed to make of Europe "the most competitive and dynamic knowledge-based economy in the world", has prompted the revisiting of the analysis of the Bologna process and the consideration of this political project as part of a broader economic process (Amaral & Magalhaes, 2004; Bruno, 2008; Longchamp & Steiner, 2008). The studies carried out by the Follow-up Group for the interministerial conferences also contributed to the revalorization of this economic dimension from the perspective of the question of employability, in particular after the bachelor's degree (Hildbrand et al., 2008). The link between the construction of the European Higher Education Area and that of research (Beerkens, 2008) was also made explicitly after the Bergen Conference of 2005.

[8] Forty-six states have signed the Bologna Declaration up to now.

The examination of these objectives reveals that, although they are relatively diverse and expressed in rather general terms, they are not necessarily insignificant.[9] In effect they relate to the duration of courses, the recognition of degrees, the mobility of students and the modes of evaluating teaching in higher education. Although the harmonization of higher education is no longer stated as an explicit objective as it was in the Sorbonne Declaration, which was adopted a year earlier,[10] the fact remains, however, that the complete realization of the objectives of the Bologna Declaration could more or less tend towards a process of harmonization of the national systems of higher education in the signatory states. And it was out of a desire to coordinate their national policies that the ministers of education signed the declaration, which is why we refer today to the "Bologna process", i.e. the coordinated implementation of the Declaration and its objectives.

Apart from the plurality of its objectives, the Bologna Declaration is characterized by its non-binding nature from the legal point of view. Like other international agreements, it could be considered as a legal measure of the "soft law" type (Abbott & Sindal, 2000), "which no external arbitrator is capable of guaranteeing and which draws [its] coercive force from the agreement of the contracting parties" (Charlier, 2005: 19). Thus, in order to attain their objectives, in addition to a bicephalous governance structure (the Bologna Follow-up Group and an office providing steering activities in the strict sense), the signatories of the Declaration created public action monitoring instruments which enable the compilation of an inventory of the measures taken and results obtained and the awarding of "scores" to the participating states (Ravinet, 2009a; Bruno et al. 2007). Therefore, a shift took place from a simple undertaking (declaration of intent) between states on the coordination of their national policies in the area of higher education (without risk of sanction, apart from "moral" sanction, if the states fail to apply the process) to the "soft" enforcement of this flexible norm, which is equipped with a tool for the evaluation and classification (stocktaking) of the progress achieved in the implementation of the stated objectives by the signatory states (pressure exerted by the "good student" syndrome, Ravinet, 2009a).[11]

At this point, the question arises as to the way in which this public action instrument, which is at once flexible and restrictive, was translated, interpreted or re-appropriated within a federalist context. And, finally, if the aftermath of Bologna gradually included the representatives of the European Commission

---

[9] The Bologna objectives would be expanded in the course of subsequent conferences, in particular through the introduction of the doctoral level (Charlier, 2006).

[10] The Sorbonne Declaration, which was signed by the ministers of education of the four biggest countries of the European Union (i.e. Germany, France, Italy, United Kingdom) in May 1998 stated its desire to harmonize "the architecture of the European higher education system" (cf. Ravinet, 2009b).

[11] If, at the risk of being anachronistic, it had been possible to establish a relationship with the Open Method of Coordination (OMC) (Amaral & Veiga, 2006) formulated in 2000 for the implementation of the Lisbon Strategy (Dehousse, 2004); given the less formal nature of Bologna, however, such a resemblance is, however, very subtle (Ravinet, 2009a).

and representatives of the universities and students from 2001, did this "opening up" of the decision-making processes to non-governmental actors also take place in Switzerland and if it did, what form did it take and what effects did it have?

The case of Switzerland is particularly interesting in view of the fact that the "national self-discipline" dimension of the Bologna monitoring tool took full effect when it was emphasized, after the Follow-up Conference in Bergen in 2005, that Switzerland would be among the pioneer states in the implementation of the Bologna reform (Etat de Vaud, 2006). Thus, what is involved here is to understand the efficacy of an original, if not novel, European instrument (albeit one that lacked legal significance) in the context of a state that is not a member of the European Union. To do this, we shall consider both the strategy adopted by the members of the Swiss delegation[12] present in Bologna for the implementation of the objectives of this declaration and the more general reforms of the higher education system devised in the late 1990s and based on a more national and "integrated" vision of the Swiss higher education system as desired by the federal government and, in particular, its State Secretary for Science and Research (Kleiber, 1999).

In this sense we interpret the Bologna Declaration here as a "window of opportunity" that presented itself for the political decision-makers, such as the Federal Council and State Secretary for Science and Research, and put to the test certain visions being formulated at the same time in the national context. In other words, this international arena constituted a political opportunity for the federal government to put new objectives on the policy agenda. The fact that the Declaration was very flexible in terms of its legal status and was located within the continuity of other international agreements and resolutions (Lisbon Convention and Sorbonne Declaration of 1998) made the opportunity all the more easy to seize.

The signature of the Bologna Declaration by Switzerland and the position of the main actors involved

The signature of the Bologna Declaration by the Swiss delegation is sometimes analysed as the solitary act of a State Secretary for Science and Research, and even as constitutionally dubious: "A declaration of intent signed by a handful of ministers and lacking any legal significance imposes a radical change of university degree courses, a new designation for academic degrees, and close and unusual coordination between the Confederation, university cantons and their universities, and all this without constitutional change, without legal backup or a popular vote. It all unfolds as though, under the influence of a magic spell, the pillars of the traditional constitutional order

---

12 The "official" Swiss delegation was composed of four people: the State Secretary for Science and Research, the Director of the former Federal Office for Education and Science (FOES), the Secretary General of the Swiss University Conference (CUS) and a representative of the Union of Students in Switzerland (VSS-UNES-USU).

separated international law from internal national law, federal law from cantonal law, and the powers of the people, parliament and the administration caved in one after the other to suddenly introduce recommendations, directives and other accreditations so as to create a new order that would appear to be the Swiss contribution to the establishment of a European Higher Education Area. Perplexed, if not terrified, the traditional university policy actors – universities, cantonal legislatures, federal and cantonal administrations, coordination bodies, students – played the game while at the same time asking themselves what had been allowed to happen to them." (Auer, 2004)

This legal opinion raises two questions, in particular, first that of consultation and the democratic legitimacy of this "declaration of intent" formulated at a European level in the broadest sense[13] and, second, that concerning the position of the main actors affected by this Declaration. The question of legitimacy had already been raised in June 2000 and June 2001 by National Councillor Hans Zbinden (Social Democratic Party of Switzerland, PS/SP) through two parliamentary interventions (i.e. a parliamentary question of 16.06.2000 and a motion of 20.06.2001 to the National Council, the main chamber of the Swiss parliament). In its response to the parliamentary question, the Federal Council (i.e. Swiss executive) refers, first, to the "open" status of the political declarations of intent like the Sorbonne and Bologna Declarations which do not involve "the parties formally". It also notes that the Rectors' Conference of the Swiss Universities (CRUS) and the CUS were consulted before Switzerland countersigned the Sorbonne Declaration and that the CUS approved it (Assemblée de la CUS of 3.9.1998).[14] The CRUS was consulted again before the signing of the Bologna Declaration. However, the Federal Council concedes that "at the time of the signing it was not possible to judge the concrete consequences that the objectives defined by these declarations would have for the different countries of Europe." Finally, the Federal Council insists on the autonomy of the universities which are deemed "first and foremost responsible for curricula and degree subjects." Furthermore, in its response to the motion one year later, the Federal Councillor adds that the new Universities Support Act (which had come into force in the meantime) provides the legal basis for the CUS to "enact framework directives in relation to university education."

In terms of the position of the main actors, the analysis carried out by Andreas Auer provides a reasonable summary of the "perplexity" that prevailed among them. While they more or less share the evaluation of the nature of the undertaking entered into by signing the Bologna Declaration (reduced political risk), the content and directions taken by the Declaration clearly gave rise to debate among them.

---

[13] It should be noted that all international treaties (which do not include the Bologna Declaration) are subject to a referendum in Switzerland and require the support of a double majority of the people and the cantons.

[14] It should be noted in passing that the consultation was carried out up to the level of the universities, for example in the EPFs (Swiss Federal Institutes of Technology), up to the level of the departments.

Thus, in a position paper of August 2000, the Union of Students in Switzerland (VSS-UNES-USU) clearly rejected the Bologna Declaration "in its entirety", in particular the introduction of a system which is divided into two cycles. It recommends to the Swiss political authorities to develop instead the specific features of the Swiss education system (duality, permeability). Although affiliated to the European Follow-up Group through the ex-ESIB (European Student Information Bureau, which became the European Students' Union, ESU in 2007), the student associations (UNES and CUAE) appeared to be clearly the most reticent when it came to the implementation of Bologna, fearing a "selling-out of knowledge" and increased selection, in particular through an increase in tuition fees. The expression of this opposition peaked with a demonstration held in front of the offices of the CUS in Berne in April 2002.[15]

It would appear that CRUS displayed some reservations prior to the signature of the Bologna Declaration, objecting in particular to the lack of time available to allow the formulation of an in-depth position by the universities, and drawing attention to the problems raised in Switzerland by the introduction of the bachelor-masters distinction as opposed to the traditional system of final diplomas: these reservations had been expressed by CRUS from late 1999, when it was commissioned by the ex-Federal Office for Education and Science for the period 2001-2003, and then by the CUS, which was given responsibility in the ensuing period for the coordination of the implementation of the Bologna process in Switzerland. Thus CRUS acknowledged the opportunity offered by Bologna for the reform of university teaching in Switzerland. However, it insisted that the bachelor's degree should not be considered as the end of a course of study but as a stage in the study process, and in doing this highlighted a divide that existed between the French-speaking third-level institutions and some of the German-speaking universities on this question.[16] The universities that were most enthusiastic about this reform (e.g. the University of St Gall) launched the first courses compatible with the Bologna principles from 2001.

As opposed to this, the business sector immediately expressed interest in the Bologna reform, which they saw as a measure that would accompany the establishment of universities of applied sciences, through *Economiesuisse* (main umbrella organization representing Swiss business). Although it acknowledged that it had not "immediately understood the true implications of Bologna", it saw in it "from the outset an opportunity for the structural and qualitative revision of university education" (Steiner, 2004). It also saw it as providing a possibility for reducing the duration of university studies, lowering the age at which young people enter the labour market and promoting the mobility of students. In clear contrast to the main university actors, the business sector obviously supported the introduction of the bachelor's degree as the first third-level degree which provides access to the labour market. Finally, in 2002, CRUS and CUS took a different direction, considering, like VSS-UNES-USU, that the degree marking the completion of third-level studies is the master. In

[15] Cf. *Le Temps*, 3 April 2002.

[16] On this divide, cf. *Le Temps*, 3 April 2002.

the debate, the view of the French-speaking universities prevailed, therefore, over the vision of certain German-speaking universities (e.g. St Gall) and the business sector.

Thus, in general, it would appear that while the flexible and relatively vague nature of the Bologna Declaration did not commit the participating states, *a priori*, in a restrictive way, the federal government was not entirely caught unawares; even if it probably did not weigh up all of the consequences, it did not sign this Declaration unexpectedly and hastily. Indeed, the Confederation had signed the Lisbon Convention in March 1998 (cf. footnote 6) in addition to counter-signed the Sorbonne Declaration in September 1998 (this signature remained little noted in the subsequent debates) and the new State Secretary, Charles Kleiber, had already formulated a catalogue of measures and objectives which he wished to implement in the coming years (Kleiber 1999). In this context, Bologna constituted an additional level that could be used to reform the system and alter its power relations. Thus, in principle the political will for the signature of this Declaration existed, even if it meant rushing both the university actors (academic authorities and student associations) and the parliamentary sectors (no prior debate) on the official grounds of the responsibility of Swiss universities in relation to the curricula offered.

It is also possible to observe in this process a direct attempt at interaction with the universities on the part of the Confederation based on a logic that involves the partial bypassing of the cantons (i.e. consultation of the CUS and the CRUS but not, it would seem, of the cantonal authorities themselves), which was likely to anticipate the role that the legislator would assign to the CUS from 2000 through the Universities Support Act and strengthen the role played by the Confederation in relation to the universities. Finally, it should be noted that the inclusion of student associations in the "official" Bologna delegation and in the subsequent Follow-up Groups (in particular at European level) did not prevent the development of a certain conflict, at least until the mid-2000s. Thus, all that remains now is to clarify how the federal government and its administration approached the task of persuading its cantonal partners and the universities to implement the Bologna Declaration.

The measures adopted for the implementation of the Bologna Declaration

The implementation of the Bologna Declaration involves a considerable number of actors. In terms of the universities, as we have seen, the CRUS was responsible for the coordination of the implementation of the Bologna process. Since 2004, it has based its activities on the Directives of the CUS "For the coordinated renewal of teaching at Swiss universities within the framework of the Bologna process" (known as the "Bologna Directives" of 4 December 2003). In the case of the universities of applied sciences and teacher education, the implementation of the Declaration is based on the Directives "For the implementation of the Bologna Declaration in the universities of applied sciences and teacher education" of 5 December 2002 issued by the Swiss Conference of Cantonal Ministers of Education (EDK/CDIP).[17] The Rector's Conference of the Swiss Universities of Applied Sciences (CSHES) and the Swiss Conference of Rectors of Universities of Teacher Education (COHEP) (CSHEP) were declared responsible for the application of these directives in the relevant universities of applied sciences and teacher education respectively.

The political (CUS, CDIP, CHES)[18] and academic (CRUS, KFH, COHEP) umbrella organizations at national level were, therefore, closely associated with the formulation of the directives for the implementation of Bologna in the three types of third-level institute in Switzerland, which made an effort to establish largely concordant directives (staggered fields of study, designation of degrees, ECTS study credits etc.) on condition that the end of the course of study at the universities of applied sciences (HES) and teacher education (HEP) could be the bachelor's degree. Despite the differences in their administrative management structures, i.e. cantonal in the case of the universities and teacher education colleges and federal in the case of the federal institutes of technology (EPF) and universities of applied sciences, these two directives are relatively restrictive in terms of objectives and coordination of the institutes involved – although the majority of them retain their autonomy[19] in relation to the introduction of the reform of the curricula in each subject or field. As we have seen, this competency on the part of the majority of the universities in relation to their curricula also explains why the cantonal legislatures were not referred to by the Bologna Declaration.

It is also why a "stage-based" and differentiated strategy was implemented not only the basis of the type of third-level institute involved but also between the different kinds of establishments. This is one of the characteristics of executive federalism which involves, in particular, differentiated temporalities in relation to implementation and varying interpretations. The first bachelor degrees were conferred in 2004 and all of the new students who registered for the winter semester of 2006-2007 at the three types of tertiary education institutions signed up for courses "compliant with the Bologna model". In addition, the Confederation provided special funding to the tune of CHF 32 million for the period 2004-2007 in association with projects organized by the

[17] These directives were issued at the suggestion of the Rectors Conference of the Swiss Universities of Applied Sciences (KFH) and the Swiss Conference of Rectors of Universities of Teacher Education (COHEP).

[18] Not to mention at the level of the Confederation, the management of the ETH Board (CEPF) for the federal institutes of technology, the Federal Office for Professional Education and Technology (OPET-OFFT) and the Federal Commission for the Universities of Applied Sciences (Commission fédérale des hautes écoles spécialisées, CFHES) for the universities of applied sciences and the State Secretariat for Education and Research (SER) for the representation of Switzerland in the Bologna follow-up bodies.

[19] Although evading the national actors who coordinated the implementation of the Bologna process, the reform of the new cantonal university laws generally gave the universities institutional autonomy which enables them to manage the reform of their curricula themselves, for example the Loi sur l'Université de Lausanne (cantonal act on the University of Lausanne) of 2004 (Etat de Vaud, 2006).

CUS for the support of the implementation of the Bologna process in the third-level institutions.

This coordination between the different bodies and types of third-level institutions for the implementation of Bologna was undoubtedly facilitated by the reform of the legal framework, on which the universities were based in the period under consideration, in particular the revision of the Universities Support Act (LAU) in 1999 and the new Federal Act on the Universities of Applied Sciences of 2005, which introduced the bachelor degree courses and the option of masters degree courses. The referendum of 21 May 2006, which provided a constitutional basis for the "Swiss educational area", should also be noted. In terms of cantonal-Confederation coordination, in the event of the failure of this coordination, article 63a, paragraph 5 of the Swiss Constitution would henceforth give the Confederation the power to legislate "on levels of studies and the transition from one level to another, on continuing education and on the recognition of institutions and qualifications". While respecting the principle of subsidiarity, this new constitutional article confers greater power on the Confederation in the area of higher education. Thus, it may be confirmed that an entire series of legal measures established after the Bologna Declaration strengthened the legitimacy of this decision *a posteriori*.

Conclusions

This analysis of the case of the Bologna process was intended to test the consequences of a declaration entered into at international level on the configuration of actors at national level, and, in particular, the governance of higher education in Switzerland. The aim was to identify the extent to which the internationalization of national decision-making processes modifies the power relations between actors in the definition and implementation of a public policy. The following elements may be mentioned in conclusion:

- First, the Bologna process illustrates an increase in the internationalization dynamic of the higher education and research policies through the standardization of degree courses and evaluation. It is a significant trend which affects a sector whose regulation standards were not very internationalized historically as they were essentially regulated at the level of cantonal laws and characterized by very strong interaction between political and academic decision-making processes.
- The increased centralization of higher education policy through the assumption of a greater role by the Confederation is also a prominent trait of the analysed processes. Its intervention and "its power of injunction" (Schwab, Surdez, 2007) in the area of higher education and research have increased constantly since the late 1960s. The reforms of the late 1990s (Baschung et al., 2009) constitute an additional step in this direction. Bologna is one example of many and emblematic of this increased centralization.[20] In effect, the Confederation entered into an international

[20] The more centralized management and rationalization of courses at the universities of applied sciences constitute another example of this.

undertaking in an area of competence that was historically the domain of the cantons. At the same time, based on a delegative logic, the cantons negotiated a partial transfer of powers through the revision of the Universities Support Act of 1999 and the cantons-Confederation Convention of 2000, which gave rise to the establishment of the new CUS. From the point of view of the actor configuration, it could be said that the signature of Bologna did nothing but accelerate or slightly anticipate a stage in a process of change that was already underway in terms of the power relations between the actors. With the establishment of new CUS and CRUS, cooperative federalism was reinforced in the management of the third level institutes.

- However a simple comparison of this process with the increased centralization of the Confederation obscures the view of a process that is more complex, in reality, and associates the double logic of the internationalization and the Europeanization of the area of higher education and research with the logics of partnership, increasing intercantonal coordination (e.g. intercantonal agreement of 1981) and greater cooperation between the universities (e.g. the "Benefri" agreement and "Lemanique triangle project" between the universities of Geneva and Lausanne and the Federal Institute of Technology Lausanne in the 1990s). These different forms of cooperation display a double change in the level of public action in the area of the universities (i.e. "bottom up" and "top down" and from institutional and functional spaces, cf. Nahrath, Varone, 2007). With the reforms of the late 1990s and Bologna, in particular, there was a shift from essentially horizontal coordination dynamics to more vertical ones (Schwab, Surdez, 2007).
- From the perspective of a revisited federalism, this process of change in the scale of public action in the university sector took original institutional forms with the creation of a delegated cantons-Confederation structure, i.e. the new CUS in 2000, a measure that would ratify a posteriori, in a way, the new constitutional article on the third level institutions (art. 63a Federal Constitution) in May 2006. This body and the body that would be able to replace it under the new law on the universities for 2012 (Universities Support Act) marks, however, a form of "decantonalization" of universities with the application of increasingly national and international or regional regulations (cooperations between third-level institutions). Thus it is clear that, in the case of disagreements or conflicts with the cantons, the Confederation will henceforth have the last say on numerous issues, in particular those relating to the recognition of institutions and university degrees. This increased power granted to the Confederation could signify the return to a more traditional executive federalism at the expense of a more authentically cooperative federalism. Apart from the fact that they signal a more incentive-based style of steering and a more delegated state action, these new action frameworks create the possibility of defining the type of cooperation and competition at national level that the public authorities would like to see being established between the different types of third level institutions and between each establishment. At the same time they enable each

establishment to define or clarify to a certain extent its "institutional profile" (types of research and teaching favoured) and its academic positioning on scales ranging from the local/cantonal to the international.

- This study also wanted to discuss the issue of conflict in the course of the internationalization of national decision-making processes based on the case of the Bologna process. The literature was divided on this question: based on the sources available, it could not be said that the signature of the Bologna Declaration and implementation of its objectives triggered the strong mobilization/opposition of the actors involved. Several reasons may be advanced to explain this low level of conflict. For the reasons indicated, the signature of such a Declaration was not debated in the traditional political arenas, such as parliament. Thus, formally, there was little possibility for expressing opposition to Bologna. Moreover, the main actors were consulted and, from one minute to the next, were convinced by such a project (CRUS, CUS). This found an echo in other projects for the reform of the system of higher education and research initiated at the level of the Confederation and contributed to the construction of a new frame of reference of this policy. Moreover, the non-binding nature of Bologna enabled its differentiated implementation based on the regional (cantons) and local (third level institutes) power relations. This is one of the characteristics of executive federalism, i.e. "secondary harmonization mechanisms" (Kissling-Näf, Knoepfel, 1992, quoted in Wälti 2001), differentiated in time and adjusted to the territorial, cultural and historical "matrices".

As is the case in other countries, the instrumental use of the Bologna reform by the public authorities and universities emerges clearly here and in this supports the conclusions of other studies on the international dimension as a political resource for the reform of the Swiss higher education and research system (Benninghoff, Goastellec & Leresche, 2009). It also shows the great diversity of dynamics and processes of "rescaling" of public action which not only occur at strictly institutional levels but can also lead to the adoption of new cognitive frames on the part of actors. Thus the question arises as to whether an institutional type change of scale (greater decision-making power of the Confederation) can rely on an instrumental and strategic perspective of the scales changes to support both a new vision of a problem and its treatment and new power relations between the actors (Leresche & Nahrath, 2007).

Due to the ensuing multi-scalar and somewhat mixed-up public action in the area of higher education, this instrumental use contributed therefore to the redefinition of the power relations between the political actors (cantons - Confederation) and between the political and academic actors (in a way, the influence of the Confederation and that of the third level institutions was strengthened through Bologna at the expense of the strictly cantonal level). The logics of political (budgetary challenges, reform of a sector, European integration etc.), academic (definition of curricula, mobility, national and international academic competition etc.), economic (labour market, competitiveness) and social (student behaviours) practices will henceforth locate the third level institutes in structures of interdependence characterized by multiple actors working on different scales.

References

Abbott, K.W., & Snidal D. (2000). Hard and soft law in international governance. *International Organization.* 54(3): 421-456.

Amaral, A., & Magalhaes A. (2004). Epidemiology and the Bologna saga. *Higher Education.* 48: 79-100.

Amaral, A., & Veiga A. (2006). The Open Method of Coordination and the Implementation of the Bologna Process. *Tertiary Education and Management.* Vol. 12, No 4, pp. 283-295.

Auer A. (2004). La déclaration de Bologne et le fédéralisme universitaire en Suisse. *Pratique juridique actuelle.* Vol. 13, N° 6, pp. 712-726.

Baschung, L., Benninghoff, M., Goastellec, G., & Perellon, J. (2009). Switzerland. Between cooperation and competition. In C. Paradeise et al., *University Governance: Western European Comparative Perspectives.* Berlin: Springer, pp. 153-176.

Beerkens, E. (2008). The emergence and institutionalisation of the European higher education and research area. *European Journal of Education.* 43(4): 407-425.

Benninghoff, M., Goastellec. G.. & Leresche. J.-Ph. (2009). L'international comme ressource cognitive et symbolique: changements dans l'instrumentation de la recherche et de l'enseignement supérieur en Suisse. In J.-Ph.,Leresche, Ph. Larédo & K. Weber (Eds) *Recherche et enseignement supérieur face à l'internationalisation. France, Suisse et Union européenne.* Lausanne : PPUR, pp. 235-255.

Benninghoff, M., & Leresche, J.-Ph. (2003). *La recherche, Affaire d'Etat. Luttes et enjeux d'une politique fédérale des sciences.* Lausanne : PPUR, (Coll. "Le savoir suisse").

Braun, D., & Leresche, J.-Ph. (2007). Research and Technology Policy in Switzerland. In U. Klöti, P. Knoepfel, H. Kriesi et al. *Handbook of Swiss Politics.* Zurich : NZZ Publishing, pp. 735-761.

Bruno, I. (2008). *A vos marques, prêts… cherchez! La stratégie européenne de Lisbonne, vers un marché de la recherche,* Ed. du Croquant.

Bruno, I., Jacquot, S., & Mandin, L. (2007). L'européanisation saisie par son instrumentation. In B. Palier, Y. Surel (Eds) *L'européanisation en action.* Paris : L'Harmattan, pp. 193-249.

Charlier, J.-E. (2005). De quelques enjeux et effets de la mondialisation. *Education et Sociétés.* N° 16, pp. 16-22.

Charlier, J.-E. (2006), ‚Qui veut encore harmoniser l'enseignement supérieur européen ? *Reflets et perspectives.* XLV, pp. 23-30.

Croché, S. (2006). Qui pilote le processus de Bologne? *Education et Sociétés.* N° 18, pp. 203-217.

Dehousse, R. (Ed.) (2004). *L'Europe sans Bruxelles ? Une analyse de la méthode ouverte de coordination.* Paris : L'Harmattan.

Enders, J. (2004). Higher education, internationalisation, and the nation-state: recent developments and challenges to governance theory. *Higher Education.* 47: 361-382.

Etat de Vaud (2006). La Déclaration de Bologne en Suisse et dans les hautes écoles vaudoises. *Les dossiers de DFJ informations.* N° 2, juillet.

Featherstone, K., & Radaelli, C. (2003). *The politics of europeanization.* Oxford : Oxford University Press.

Felli, R., Goastellec, G., & Leresche, J.-Ph. (2007). Existe-t-il un marché du travail académique franco-suisse? *Formation et Emploi.* N° 100, octobre-décembre, pp. 49-64.

Fischer, A. (2007). Internationalization of Swiss decision-making processes. In U. Klöti et al. (Eds) *Handbook of Swiss Politics.* Zürich, NZZ, pp. 547-568.

Hildbrand, Th. et al. (2008). *Die Curricula-Reform an Schweizer Hochschulen.* Bern, Zürich: CRUS/UNIZH, Heft 13.

Horvath, F., Weber, K., & Wicki, M. (2000), International research oriented of Swiss universities: self regulated or politically imposed? *Higher education.* 40, 389-408

Huisman, J. &, van der Wende, M. (2004). The EU and Bologna: are supra- and international initiatives threatening domestic agendas? *European Journal of Education.* 39(3): 349-357.

Kissling-Näf, I., & Knoepfel, P. (1992), Politikflexibilität dank zentralstaatlichem Immobilismus? Handlungspielräume kantonaler Vollzugspolitiken im schweizerischen politisch-administrativen System. In H. Abromeit, W. Pommerehne (Eds), *Staatstätigkeit in der Schweiz.* Bern: Haupt, pp. 43-69.

Kleiber, C. (1999). *Pour l'Université.* Berne : GSR.

Klöti, U., Hirschi, C., Serdült, U., & Widmer, Th. (2005). *Verkannte Aussenpolitik. Entscheidungsprozesse in der Schweiz.* Zürich,Chur: Rüegger.

Knill, C. (Ed.) (2005). Special issue "Cross-national Policy Convergence: Causes, Concepts and Empirical Findings". *Journal of European Public Policy.* 12:5, octobre.

Knill, C., & Lehmkuhl, D. (2002). The National Impact of European Union Regulatory Policy: Three Europeanization Mechanisms. *European Journal of Political Research.* 41: 255-280.

Knoepfel, P., Horber-Papazian, K., Benninghoff, M., Terribilini, S., & Wälti, S. (2001a). *Le fédéralisme d'exécution en matière de politiques publiques à incidence spatiale.* Working paper de l'IDHEAP, N° 13.

Knoepfel, P., Larrue, C., & Varone, F. (2001b). *Analyse et pilotage des politiques publiques.* Munich : Helbing & Lichtenhahn.

Knoepfel, P., Kissling-Näf, I., & Varone, F. (Eds) (2003). *Institutionelle Regime natürlicher Ressourcen in Aktion/Régimes institutionnels de ressources naturelles en action.* Genève, Bâle, Munich :, Helbing & Lichtenhahn.

Leresche, J.-Ph. (2007), Logiques de pouvoirs et gouvernance multi-niveaux. In A. Faure et al. (Eds) *Action publique et changements d'échelles: les nouvelles focales du politique.* Paris : L'Harmattan, pp. 253-257.

Leresche, J.-Ph., & Nahrath, S. (2007). Les échelles de l'action publique: question classique, objets nouveaux? In A. Faure et al. (Eds), *Action publique et changements d'échelles. Les nouvelles focales du politique.* Paris : L'Harmattan, pp. 321-331.

Longchamp, O., & Steiner, Y. (2008). Bologne, et après ? Essai d'histoire immédiate des réformes universitaires récentes. *Traverse,* N° 3, pp. 125-144.

Mach, A., Häussermann, S., & Papadopoulos, Y. (2003). Economic regulatory reforms in Switzerland: adjustment without European Integration or how rigidities become flexible. *Journal of European Public Policy.* 10(2): 302-319.

Muller. P., & Ravinet, P. (2008). Construire l'Europe en résistant à l'UE? Le cas du processus de Bologne. *Revue internationale de politique comparée.* vol. 15, N° 4, pp. 653-665.

Musselin, C. (2006). Les paradoxes de Bologne: l'enseignement supérieur français face à un double processus de normalisation et de diversification. In J.-Ph. Leresche, M. Benninghoff, F. Crettaz von Roten & M. Merz (Eds) *La fabrique des sciences. Des institutions aux pratiques.* Lausanne : PPUR, pp. 25-42.

Nahrath, S., & Varone, F. (2007). Les espaces fonctionnels comme changements d'échelles de l'action publique. In A. Faure et al. (Eds) *Action publique et changements d'échelles. Les nouvelles focales du politique.* Paris : L'Harmattan, pp. 235-249.

OFS (2008). *Personnel des hautes écoles universitaires 2007.* Neuchâtel : OFS.

Palier, B., & Surel, Y (Eds) (2007). *L'Europe en action. L'européanisation dans une perspective comparée.* Paris : L'Harmattan, 358 p.

Putnam, R. (1988). Diplomacy and domestic politics: the logic of two level games. *International organization.* 42(3): 427-460.

Ravinet, P. (2009a). Le processus de Bologne comme contournement de l'UE: les dynamiques paradoxales de construction de l'Espace européen d'enseignement supérieur. In J.-Ph. Leresche, Ph. Larédo & K. Weber (Eds) *Recherche et enseignement supérieur face à l'internationalisation. France, Suisse et Union européenne.* Lausanne : PPUR, pp. 219-235.

Ravinet, P. (2009b). Comment le processus de Bologne a-t-il commencé ? La formulation de la vision d'un Espace européen d'enseignement supérieur à la Sorbonne en 1998. *Education et Sociétés.* N° 24 (à paraître).

Schwab, B., & Surdez, M. (2007). Education and Cultural policy. In U. Klöti, P. Knoepfel, H. Kriesi et al. *Handbook of Swiss Politics.* Zurich : NZZ Verlag, pp. 787-817.

Sciarini, P. (1994). *La Suisse face à la communauté européenne et au GATT. Le cas test de la politique agricole.* Genève : Georg.

Sciarini, P., Fischer, A., Nicolet, S. et al. (2004). How Europe hits home: Evidence from the Swiss case. *Journal of European Public Policy.* 11(3): 353-378.

Steiner, A. (2004). La réforme de Bologne et l'économie. *dossierpolitique,* N° 41/2, Economiesuisse, novembre.

Teichler, U. (2004). The changing debate on internationalisation of higher education. *Higher Education.* 48: 5-26.

Wälti, S. (2001). *Le fédéralisme d'exécution sous pression.* Munich : Helbing & Lichtenhahn.

Weber, K. (1994). Higher education policy in Switzerland. In L. Goedegeburre, F. Kaiser, P. Maassen et al. (Eds) *Higher Education Policy.* pp. 265-289.

CHAPTER 11

From Centralised to Predatory Federalism: an Exploration

DIETMAR BRAUN

Introduction

For a long time, the efficiency advantages of decentralisation have been defended by public choice theory of federalism (Oates, 1972; Olson, 1969; Tiebout, 1956). Only recently, a re-assessment of the value of the role the central state plays has been undertaken that qualifies some of the overtly positive statements concerning decentralised federal orders (Oates, 1999, 2006; Rodden et al., 2003; Ehtisham & Tanzi, 2002). The more recent institutional economic approach of federalism (Figueiredo & Weingast, 2005; Weingast, 1995; Bednar et al., 2001; Filippov et al., 2004) – or the "second generation economic theory of federalism" (Iaryczower et al., 2004) – is no longer looking for the efficiency of political orders but for conditions – "self-enforcing mechanisms" – that can maintain agreed institutional contracts in federations. The approach follows Peter Knoepfel's criticism of the economic efficiency approach as its analytical perspective integrates political rationalities and takes the structuring influence of institutions for decision making into account (Knoepfel, 2002: 306).

In this view federations can be endangered by two dilemmas: overawing of the central government (CG) and free-riding by member states. Neither centralisation or decentralisation as such are condemned or promoted though it is taken as granted that a federal order can only be in equilibrium if it respects "delineated spheres of authority" of the central and regional level (Riker, 1964). A federal order that would either tilt in favour of complete decentralisation or complete centralisation would become something different, either it would fall apart as a federation in the case of complete decentralisation or, in the case of complete centralisation, it would be transformed into an order that is alike to a decentralised unitary state.

Following this approach, I am less interested in the efficiency of centralisation and decentralisation in this article than in an explanation of when centralisation goes too far so that the federation threatens to turn into a (decentralised) unitary order. I contend that this is the case when "predatory federalism" is installed, i.e. a centralised federal order in which the CG has almost unlimited powers to overawe and member states are reduced to mere "agents" of the central level. Conditions and mechanisms that can tilt centralised federations towards predatory federalism or, on the contrary, that prevent such a turn, will be analysed in this article.

In tackling this general question of under what conditions centralised federations can turn into predatory federalism, I also intend to re-focus discussions in comparative federalism on the category of "centralised federations" that until now have not been recognised and discussed as a federal group of their own. In addition, few authors have dealt with centralisation in federations (see for example Lemco, 1991). Meanwhile, we do know a lot about the pros and cons of decentralisation but much less about the characteristics and dynamics of "centralised federal orders". The analysis of favourable and unfavourable conditions of predatory federalism gives at the same time insights into the constitution and dynamics of centralised federal orders in general.

To answer the basic question, strategies of "comparative federalism" (McKay, 2000) are used: I will try to evoke the main explanatory variables by comparing three empirical examples of centralised federations – Austria, Germany, Australia – that are sufficiently distinct to allow for a search for common explanatory variables of predatory federalism. A contrasting case – Switzerland – will be used to elucidate mechanisms that help to prevent centralisation and "overshooting".

In the next section some conceptual clarifications are undertaken and the choice of centralised federations treated in this article will be explained. Follows a section on underlying structures of centralisation – types of federation and preferences of constituencies – before institutional structures of power distribution and their consequences for centralisation will be discussed.

Conceptual considerations

Each federation must decide while setting up its constitution how to distribute property rights for the various policy fields and for revenue extraction and distribution. Usually this is done by granting some exclusive powers to member states and some to the CG. The number of areas distributed to each level can vary enormously (Watts, 1996; Thorlakson, 2003) though most federations have followed some efficiency rationale of allocating powers according to the kind of public goods concerned. In addition to exclusive competences, we usually find concurrent areas, in which either both levels may act or which are left to member states as long as CG does not claim the right to legislate in these areas. Though the allocation of property rights has – with some exceptions like Canada and India – been in favour of member states in the beginning, concurrent areas and constitutional loopholes have often allowed a shift in the balance of distribution more in favour of the CG. Still, there was considerable variation in this trend and, as a consequence, the federal equilibria[1] that exist in federations can entail different degrees of centralisation or decentralisation.

Centralisation means a process in which authority in policy fields and in revenue distribution is transferred from the subgovernment level to the federal level. *Centralised federations*, as the focus in this article, are then federations in which most policy areas are in the first place decided on the federal level and where revenues are gathered by the CG and distributed by centrally administered procedures. This does not exclude veto-powers of subgovernments in the decision process but their exclusive authority to deal with policy fields in terms of law making and the right to decide above all on growth taxes are significantly limited. *Decentralised federations*, by contrast, give subgovernments an extensive number of policy area authority of their own including a certain degree of tax autonomy.

Despite a transfer of powers to the federal level, centralised federations can remain viable federations, not so much because the management of policy fields by the centre can have positive effects on social and economic development but above all because subgovernments can remain accountable to their regional constituencies. Electoral accountability is only possible if subgovernments can demonstrate their "utility" in terms of representing regional interests. Centralised federations do not exclude this: the demonstration of utility can still exist as we will discuss below in the use of implementation rights, voice or veto on the federal level, or in the defence of partisan preferences.

If electoral accountability is jeopardised in centralised federations, next to the loss of authority in policy fields and revenues, a new federal equilibrium may emerge that I will entitle "*predatory federalism*". In order to turn centralised federations into predatory federalism, it needs "predatory behaviour" of the central government, i.e. a behaviour of the "rulers" – in our context the CGs in a federal state – that devises and formalises "structures that increase their bargaining power, reduce their transaction costs, and lower their discount rates so as to better capture gains from exchanges of politics" (Levi, 1988, 16). Orders that allow predatory behaviour to unfold will be inefficient not only because the CG extracts resources at its discretion but also because actors in society have an incentive for rent-seeking. I am not interested in the effects on efficiency though but on the stability of the federal equilibrium that such behaviour may have. The more unrestrained CG behaviour is and the more it can act at its own discretion, the more member states will loose their status as genuine electoral accountable political units and as forming elements of the federation. If there are no self-enforcing mechanisms on CG, one can expect that predatory behaviour of CG will tilt the centralised federal order into a state of *administrative decentralisation*, i.e. a division of labour in defining,

---

[1] Equilibrium is a notion referring to game theory. It characterises a situation in which actors have no immediate interest to change the status quo, i.e. the existing power distribution. The status quo can entail different ways of distributing powers between actors. The notion of federal equilibria indicates that federations may be built on a different status quo.

developing and executing government tasks in which subgovernments become more or less "agents" who are in contract relationships with the "principal", the CG. The constant hollowing out of authority in legislation and revenue extraction and distribution finally leads to the undermining of democratic accountability of subgovernments and the loss of viability of their federal societies. Failing legitimacy granted by their own citizens diminishes the influence of subgovernments in interactions with the CG and motivates them to seek rent instead of representing the interests of their citizens. The federal order may still grant operational autonomy to subgovernments to develop ways and means of execution but actions of subgovernments remain strongly related to the imperatives of national decisions. In this sense then, in predatory federalism subgovernments become more administrative agencies than democratically legitimated political units with a say of their own in federal relationships. This is comparable to the status of regional units in decentralised unitary states.

In sum, if self-enforcing institutional mechanisms in centralised federal orders are lacking and predatory behaviour of the CG can unfold, this will lead gradually to a new federal equilibrium in which subgovernments are reduced to the status of agents of the CG instead of "peers". The difference with a decentralised unitary order becomes blurred at this stage.

If, therefore, predatory behaviour of the CG can tilt centralised federations towards predatory federalism, the main question becomes how to avoid predatory behaviour of the CG. In order to answer this question we will focus on three countries that according to the literature can be considered as centralised and to one example of a decentralised federation.

Centralisation has two dimensions: concentration of decision-making capacities in policy fields and concentration of revenue decisions on the central level. If the balance shifts at least on one of these two dimensions from a concentration of powers on the subgovernment level to a concentration on the federal level, this is a centralisation process. However, having said this, it is not at all easy to operationalise a concentration of decision-making rights on the central level.

One does not find any accepted systematic empirical account of groups of federal countries along the categories of "centralisation – decentralisation" and I have no intention to deliver one here. As a starting point I refer to overview in Hueglin and Fenna's authoritative book on comparative federalism. They present an "indicative" continuum of centralised and decentralised federal countries based on previous studies, without however stipulating the criteria (Hueglin and Fenna, 2006, 36). According to them India, South Africa, Germany and Australia are cases where a strong concentration process on the federal level has taken place. They exclude a federal country like Malaysia (or Austria, which they do not mention), where member states have been turned into "little more than administrative units" (ibid.). But it is exactly these kinds of federal countries which interests us most in this study as they seem to fall into the category of "predatory federalism". I will limit myself in this study to the OECD federal countries Germany, Australia, and Austria.

If one takes a quick look at the country literature on these three countries, Hueglin and Fenna's classification is confirmed:

In *Germany*, a consensus exists about the continuing process of erosion of the Länder decision-making rights as well as the increasing asymmetrical financial powers in favour of the federal government after the Second World War. A "creeping centralisation" is noticed (Elazar, 1994, 97), driven by a secular trend towards "unitarisation" of living conditions (Kilper & Lhotta, 1996; Lehmbruch, 2002; Braun, 2003 : 151).

Australia seems to "oscillate" between "greater and lesser degrees of centralisation in the exercise of powers and in fiscal management" (Elazar, 1994, 19). As in Germany, an increase of powers for the CG at the expense of States has taken place in the last century (Summers, 2002, 92), though the States have "largely retained the power to make laws in those areas of government which most directly affect people lives (...)" (ibid., 111). However, the CG is acting in almost all policy areas and it is the CG that determines to a large degree what is decided in concurrent areas in Australia (Thorlakson, 2003), above all because of its financial powers (Summers, 2002, 93). Today, Australia belongs to those federations where member states suffer the most from "vertical fiscal imbalances" (Watts, 1999; Thorlakson, 2003, 13–14). Filippov et al. summarise: "Australia (...) became one of the world's most centralized federations" (Filippov et al., 2004, 198).

Opinions about *Austrian* federalism are particularly unequivocal with regard to centralising tendencies and the dangers of predatory federalism: Austria seems to be the most extreme example among the three countries of having introduced a "system of decentralized administration rather than a federal order" (Erk, 2004, 2) despite claiming to have a federal order.[2] It stands out as a federal country in which most policy areas have been exclusively attributed to the CG (Thorlakson, 2003, 9). Most of the money of member states comes from federal taxes and transfers. Comparing the CG share in revenues and expenditures, Thorlakson finds that in the 1990s Austrian federal government had the highest share among her six federal countries. This has not changed today as a recent overview of the OECD demonstrates.[3]

While Austria seems therefore to fall into the category of predatory federalism, Germany and Australia seem not to have been subject to predatory behaviour of the CG until now. By comparing these three countries, I hope to get insights into the mechanisms that can lead federal orders to predatory

[2] "Among federations it is one of the most centralized with the Länder often serving mainly as "agents" and subordinates of the federal government..." (Watts, 1999, 30). See also (Obinger, 2005; Bußjäger, 2007)

[3] http://www.oecd.org/dataoecd/55/45/40995156.pdf. In addition, the OECD gives an overview the autonomy of local and regional governments in levying taxes, which is one indicator that could be used fairly well to point to the degree of centralisation and decentralisation in revenues. It is demonstrated that German and Austrian subgovernments rank among the countries with the lowest tax autonomy. Australian subgovernments have a somewhat better stance but they are clearly inferior to cases like Switzerland or Canada.

federalism. In addition, I will use Switzerland as a contrasting example, most of all because Switzerland is generally seen as a decentralised country that, however, has some interesting similar features with Austria and Germany in terms of the federal organisation (see the next chapter). This makes it a promising case to understand institutional obstacles to centralisation in general and to predatory federalism in particular.

The following analysis of empirical cases contains two analytical elements: first, I discuss two factors that are decisive for the kind of federal equilibrium federal countries are respecting today: one, the *type of federal organisation*, federal countries have chosen at the origins of their federation and, two, the *constituency preference distribution in the population.* Cross-tabulating these two variables gives us four likely dynamics in terms of centralisation and decentralisation. Second, the equilibrium based on the federal type and on preferences of constituencies defines power and influence in the federation. By looking into implementation rights and into co-decision rights on the federal level, it is attempted to demonstrate how (un)limited CG can be in a federation or, in other words, how well member states are protected from predatory behaviour of the CG.

Underlying structures defining the institutional equilibrium: organisational types of federal systems and preferences of constituencies

Organizational types of federal systems

Federal systems are characterised by a basic organisational set up that expresses the initial consent with regard to the distribution of powers within the federation. This consent has a lasting effect on centralisation and decentralisation. Usually, federalism literature distinguishes between two types of federal systems. I will use Börzel and Hosli's distinction of "dual" and cooperative" federalism (Börzel & Hosli, 2003, 183–4) but one could also use "intra-governmental" vs. "inter-governmental", "functional" vs. "jurisdictional" or Hueglin's and Fenna's distinction of "legislative" and "administrative" federalism (Hueglin & Fenna, 2006, 61–3). They are all quite similar. No author using these distinctions would pretend that these types exist in its pure form in reality. They are "ideal-types" that tend to catch the relevant organisational "building blocks" a federation is historically constructed upon. This makes them useful for consideration in our context. The lesson that will be drawn from this distinction is that cooperative federal countries have inherent dynamics for centralisation while dual federal countries should resist to centralisation, though in reality they often did not.

Dual federalism, best represented by the Anglo-Saxon federations (USA, Canada, Australia), is supposed to maintain a delineated sphere of competence for member states and the central state. "Independence in unity" and separation of powers between territorial units are the main principles of institution-building. Respecting the boundaries of authority drawn in the constitution should, in principle, limit each attempt of the CG (and member states) to overawe the other side.

Insufficient demarcation of authority boundaries, however, above all in concurrent areas, has contributed to a hollowing out of subgovernment competences in part by the right of the CG to legislate in areas that were also subject to member state legislation and above all by spending powers of the CG. In all three Anglo-Saxon federations revenue capacity developed in favour of the CG and this allowed intervention by giving subgovernments incentives in form of material rewards.[4] Despite these tendencies, member states kept a large number of own decision making competencies despite explicit or implicit intrusion by the central state. "Independence in unity" remains an important reference point in discourses on reforms in federalism. The organisational environment for predatory federalism is therefore unfavourable, all other things kept constant.

This is different in *cooperative federal countries* best represented by Germany, Austria, Switzerland and South Africa: cooperative federalism is built on "interdependence in unity", on a functional division of powers, in which the implementation of laws is usually taken care of by subgovernments while the bulk of laws are decided on the federal level. CG has not the administrative capacities to execute its own policies and needs the member states to do this. This organisational set up creates the interdependence. The "right to decide" and the "right to act" (Braun 2000) are often institutionalised on different territorial levels. This does not mean that subgovernments could not have their own spheres of competence with the right to decide. But usually, the areas with exclusive competence of member states are rare while concurrent areas with a predominant role of the CG are the main category of laws.

Why can this organisational form create a different dynamic compared to the separation of powers? An obvious advantage is that such "integrated" structures (Hueglin & Fenna 2006) avoid functional deficiencies like duplication, overfishing or substitution that may appear in non-coordinated dual federalism. Coordinated action between decision making authority and implementation authorities promises a better result. Efficiency can therefore be an important argument for delegation of decision-making authority to the central level, which, in due consequence, creates a better opportunity structure for the CG to use this authority in its own favour.

At first sight, therefore, cooperative federalism seems to create more favourable opportunity structures for predatory behaviour of the CG than dual federalism, as the central level becomes part of an integrated federalism where the CG is trusted with important decision making powers in a large number of domains and the role of member states is reduced because of their limited functional domain of competence, i.e. implementation. The logic of dual

---

[4] Of course, Canada has progressed in the other direction: from a more centralised federation to more decentralisation. The reasons for this are well known but will not interest us here.

federalism is to maintain the overall decision making capacities of member states, though this is limited to a defined number of policy areas.

Preference structure of constituencies

A certain autonomy in implementation and "voice" or "veto-power" at the federal level is not yet enough to understand the motivations of subgovernments in the case of cooperative federalism to delegate authority to the central level. One should introduce another explanatory variable in this context: the preferences of the population in member states.

The legitimacy of subgovernments depends on (aggregated) preferences of their constituency. The more intense preferences are linked to regional particularities and identities, the more subgovernments are forced to pursue policies trying to respect such regional bound preferences while weak regional-bound preferences allow an orientation towards national objectives.

In comparative federalism, this argument can be found in the distinction between federal systems that are based on cultural cleavages (*"cultural federalism*", (Hueglin & Fenna, 2006, 57–8); "nationality based federal units", (Kymlicka, 2005, 277)) and systems where the population respects territorial divisions out of democratic or pragmatic reasons (*"territorial federalism*"; Hueglin and Fenna, ibid.; "regional based federal units", Kymlicka, ibid.). "Cultural federalism" protects minorities by claiming a certain territory within a country. Federalism is seen as a political order that consists of *peoples* and not of *the* people (Kymlicka, 2005). Though this does not mean that there could be no supra-communal interests in such types of federalism, regional-bound preferences will usually overdetermine national priorities. As a consequence, subgovernments must search legitimacy by developing policies that take these special cultural interests into account. This motivates to opt rather for a separation of powers than for an integrated type of federalism as the recognition of "own delineated spheres" is constitutionally guaranteed. Centralisation in these countries will be looked at with distrust.

In the case of "territorial federalism" the federation is seen in the first place as a federation of the *people*. Preference distribution in one state may be comparable to another state because of similar social structures and shared (party) ideologies. It needs national parties to organise such nation-wide preferences while regional parties are more functional in the context of cultural federalism. As a consequence, conflicts between member states in territorial federalism are often identical with conflicts between party positions on the national level. The federal arena becomes in fact another arena for national party struggle. Under such conditions, demands for nation-wide equality and a harmonisation of living conditions are usually very strong, which is in turn conducive to a centralisation of decision making.

This has also consequences for the kind of legitimacy that a subgovernment in territorial federalism looks for: politicians in member states represent particular preferences dominant in a member state, i.e. the dominance of certain party ideologies, but the struggle between parties takes for the most part place at the national level. Party struggle within member states is often only a replication of the national party struggle. Regional constituencies in territorial federalism do therefore normally not expect from their elites that they develop regional specific and distinct policies from national policies but that they make a policy that is in line with the dominant party positions valid in that member state. As policies are, therefore, not defined on the regional level but on the central level, subgovernments have only low incentives to insist on a clear separation of powers or to develop their own capacities to act. If the population has nation-wide preferences, a different logic holds for subgovernments: all must be done to influence the political game on the central level and it is here that office-holding in member states becomes an important asset either to support the ideological preferences of the CG or to work against it.

It is under such a preference distribution that centralisation can become an equilibrium in the federation. This does not mean that subgovernments will be content to become administrative agents of the CG. Territorial federalism does not automatically lead to predatory federalism. One can evoke three reasons for this:

- First, there are considerations of efficiency. Above all in cooperative federalism, member states are usually but not always granted a certain degree of autonomy in executing federal laws. Subgovernments are supposed to know better how to implement such laws in the most efficient way because of their access to regional based information and preferences. As a side-effect, this creates the possibility for subgovernments to develop their own interpretation and policy priorities and distinguish themselves from other member states, at least to a certain degree.
- Second, if territorial federalism is so strongly based on nation-wide party struggle, subgovernments that are led by national opposition parties have a strong motivation to demonstrate alternatives to existing CG policies. Offices in member states become a means in national party struggle and may lead to quite distinctive policy developments though such policies are most of the time (but not always as the case of Bavaria in Germany demonstrates) limited in time and may not have lasting effects. Subgovernments led by CG parties by contrast do not have such a motivation and will prefer to be in line with national government policies.
- Third, one should be aware that the two types of preference distribution discussed here are ideal-types that represent two extremes on a continuum. It is not at all excluded that one finds member states in territorial federalism that develop a certain regional self-consciousness that is not based on cleavages but which can nevertheless lead to specific demands subgovernments should respect when developing policies. Preference distribution in these cases can be a mix of national-oriented and regional preferences.[5]

[5] In fact, one can introduce a third group of preference distribution in federations defined by territorial federalism with nation-wide parties but where one finds nevertheless some regional self-consciousness that is not based on cultural cleavages. The regional constituency in this case is subject to "multiple identities" (McKay, 2000)

All these cases demonstrate that territorial federalism as such is certainly not a one-way street towards predatory federalism. But it is also obvious that the preference distribution in territorial federalism leads to a strong orientation of regional constituencies towards the centre and that regional policies are strongly influenced by nation-wide formulated policy goals.

What can we conjecture if we combine both variables, the type of federal organisation and the preferences of constituencies, in one explanatory scheme (see table 1)

	Territorial	**Cultural**
Cooperative	Conducive to centralisation (Germany, Austria)	Centralisation trends, but countertendencies (Switzerland)
Dual	Separation of powers but centralising countertendencies (Australia; USA)	Strong tendency towards decentralisation (Canada)

Table 1 Types of federal systems and preference distribution.

One can assume that the combination of cooperative and territorial federalism is in principle very conducive to centralisation tendencies while dual and cultural federalism are unfavourable. In the "hybrid" cases one can expect that the federal system defines the opportunity structure, either in favour or in disfavour of centralisation, but that the preference structure may point into another direction. This is why it is likely that opposing dynamics with countertendencies to the dominant trend defined by the federal type play a role. Switzerland on the one hand and Australia and the USA on the other hand are examples for this. Switzerland is based on cultural federalism and is known for its decentralised setup. It experienced, however, a long period of centralisation by financial incentives since the 1960s before recently a constitutional reform stopped these tendencies. Australia, as our fourth case, has a preference distribution of the population with contradictory signals: it has a long tradition of preferences of regional constituencies directed to their region,[6] despite the lack of ethnic differences but at the same time a strong

and subgovernments have to deal with the tension between national and regional preferences. Australia is to some extent a case in point (see below).

[6] Particularities remain viable in Australia because of quite different living conditions, different historical origins, environmental conditions and particular challenges of the territory. There exists therefore a deeply rooted felt anchorage within the particular cultural traditions of a member state though this is not ethnically based (Sharman and Moon, 2003, 4-5). These distinctions are nourished by the different use and development of state institutions and cultures (Summers, 2002, 112). These historically anchored and culturally deepened differences do not only demarcate the member states against each other but there are also "longstanding feelings of vague hostility to Canberra" (ibid.).

willingness to equalise revenues in the federation. The territorial division does therefore play a role, though in a more modest way compared to cultural federalism. These differences have not given rise to local or regional parties. The party system is organised along national lines but this does not mean that the national faction dominates regional policies. On the contrary, there is federal struggle inside the parties and the regional parties have quite some influence on national policy-making. Regional factions in national parties act therefore "as a break on trends within the state" (Filippov et al., 2005: FN 8, p. 199).

In this study I compare therefore countries with a quite amenable structure for centralisation (Germany, Austria) with countries that lack each time one of the favourable conditions for centralisation (Australia and Switzerland). This should offer important insights.

Institutional constraints of centralisation

In this and the next section I intend to answer the following question: To what extent does the institutionalised distribution of powers in the four centralised federations overawe subgovernments with respect, first, to implementation rights and, second, to co-decision making on the federal level.

One of the main points in discussing types of federal systems is that dual federalism does have less reason to introduce institutional protection of member states than cooperative federalism, where interdependence is much more important. In dual federalism, member states seem to be sufficiently protected by the separation of powers. Both decision-making and implementation powers in own domains seem to be guaranteed. The institutionalisation of "joint control" on the federal level seems to be less urgent than in the case of cooperative federalism. Until today, the States in the USA for example have to lobby as all other interest groups in order to influence decisions of the Congress and the President. This situation is different in the case of cooperative federalism. Implementation powers and co-decision making rights on the federal level are the two devices that are in principle open to subgovernments in cooperative federalism to protect themselves from predatory federalism. To what extent have these powers been used in the three centralised federations? How does Switzerland differ?

Type	Country	Co-decision Making	Implementation Powers
Cooperative, territorial	Austria	Weak	Very weak
Cooperative, territorial	Germany	Strong, Veto	Relatively weak
Cooperative, cultural	Switzerland	No, but compensating mechanisms	Strong, though power of the purse
Dual, territorial	Australia	No, some compensating mechanisms	Strong, but power of the purse

Table 2 Institutional protection of subgovernments.

Implementation powers

The first interesting point to raise is that cooperative territorial federalism has not produced identical decision-making structures. Austria and Germany are similar in the very limited number of important policy areas that are at the exclusive authority of subgovernments as well as in the weak use of implementation rights compared to the two contrasting cases Switzerland and Australia. Both in Germany and Austria, member states are executing the large number of federal laws. This is the very essence of cooperative federalism.

In *Austria*, the room for manoeuvre to contest or modify federal laws within the implementation process is practically nil. The CG determines to a very large degree what is to be done and also how it is to be done (Bußjäger, 2007). Regional parliaments do not have the right to discuss these federal laws and decide on their implementation. It is therefore not astonishing that member states have become mere "administrative agencies" (Erk, 2004) of the central state, a situation which has led to internal criticism. In the attempt to reform Austrian federalism, which recently failed (Braun, 2008), propositions were made to re-equilibrate forces and to strengthen the implementation powers of member states.

The position of the *German* Länder is similar and different. In contrast to Austrian member states, German Länder were formally authorised after the Second World War to execute federal laws as "own affairs" (Art. 83 of the "Grundgesetz" (GG)). While this was meant to grant subgovernments their own domain of action, further development has demonstrated that in reality the federal government had ample means to intervene into the implementation process. This holds for all different kind of implementation processes that are distinguished in German federalism: the most far-going central powers are when subgovernments execute federal laws "under the authority of" the CG (Art. 85 GG). In this case the CG can give orders how to proceed. It is less obvious in those implementation acts where the Länder act under "legal supervision" of the CG (Art. 84 GG), which is the major part in implementation. In this case, the Länder have the right to formulate their own implementation procedures but CG can nevertheless give orders, if it feels that there are "special needs", to be conform with federal prescriptions of implementation. The Länder have influence on these decisions within the Bundesrat. Even in those areas where the Länder have kept own authority, the CG could define "framework laws" that could "considerably" pre-determine what should be done in the policy area (Laufer & Münch, 1998, 133). In the recent federal reform of 2006, however, such framework laws were abolished and the areas in question should now be completely governed by the Länder.

Overall, it is obvious that both Austrian and German member states are considerably restricted in their implementation rights but to different degrees which demonstrates the very difference between a country with centralised federalism and one with predatory federalism: the German Länder can and have used some of their implementation rights though they are constantly menaced by the "shadow of hierarchy" while such rights are not even foreseen in the case of Austria. In addition, the Länder have a collective veto in the Bundesrat which can constrain the CG in imposing implementation rules and substance. All this has not resulted in significant diverse developments on the member state level in Germany, given the strong "unitarian imperative" that is respected voluntarily by the Länder (Lauffer & Münch, 1998: 132), but it has left some room for administrative self-determination though not for parliamentary self-determination as own implementation laws are not foreseen in the Grundgesetz.[7] The recent transfer of self-determination rights in some areas (for example in higher education policy) could, moreover, add to the development of a stronger sense of self-determination.

Though *Switzerland* has applied the same principle of labour division, it has respected to a more important degree implementation powers of member states (see in general for Swiss implementation policies and institutions Knoepfel, 2002; Knoepfel et al., 2001). This is manifested in a slight difference in terms the Swiss use in comparison to Germany and Austria: They are often not speaking of "execution" ("Vollzug") but of implementation in the sense of "conversion" ("Umsetzung"). This expresses that it needs additional legal acts by the cantons – and here regional parliaments are involved – to really execute federal laws. And in the process of conversion cantons have a large room for manoeuvre to change the laws or on some occasions to not implement them at all (Linder, 1994; Braun, 2003; Vatter, 2006) though there are certain limits to this. Whether federal laws will be implemented in the sense they were formulated, depends to a large degree on the consent one can find in the

[7] The lack of rights of member state parliaments in the implementation process goes so far that there are ongoing discussions in Germany to abolish these parliaments as they lack an obvious function.

cantons and on the degree of consensus in federal parliament. This demonstrates the room for manoeuvre cantons have and the lack of powers of the CG in Switzerland.[8] In addition, very often federal laws are formulated in a very broad sense leaving exactly that room for interpretation cantons are asking for. That in the end one may find nevertheless convergence in the way cantons are dealing with federal laws depends on a process of "secondary harmonisation" (Balthasar, 2003; Knoepfel, 2002, 312), which takes place as a kind of diffusion process among cantons. By and large, one can notice, however, that Swiss cooperative federalism has granted member states considerable implementation powers.

Australia as a country with dual federalism has obviously not the same implementation structure. CG has its own administration in those domains where it is sole responsible while member states execute their own programs in their areas of responsibility. Administrations in member states do in principle not act as executing agencies of the CG. There are, however, a large number of concurrent areas, where the CG tries to influence indirectly political behaviour of member states by way of financial incentives. It is this indirect way which – as in Switzerland – opens up possibilities to overawe. Formally, however, subgovernments maintain implementation rights together with decision-making authority in a number of important policy areas.

Co-decision making rights

Powers of the second chamber in Austria and Germany could not be more different. In Austria, member states have no veto-powers but only suspensive legislative powers that can be overridden by a simple majority in the lower house. In money questions, the second chamber has not even voice (Obinger, 2005, 197). In Germany, depending on the kind of law,[9] the second chamber acts as an additional veto-player but it always has a suspensive veto in federal legislation. This makes a large difference in the status of member states: In Germany, they play an omnipresent role in federal discussions, in Austria, their influence in federal legislation is very restricted. This difference is also to be noticed in the delegation of representatives to the second chamber: Germany is the original example of the "council model" (Hueglin & Fenna, 2006, ch. 7), i.e. the nomination of representatives of the second chamber by subgovernments which are bound by an imperative mandate. In Austria, representatives are delegated by regional parliaments, which installs a somewhat stronger commitment of delegates to their regional base than it is the case in the "senate model" (ibid.), where representatives are elected by voters as in the USA and Switzerland, but it is considerably weaker than the imperative mandate that binds delegates to their regional governments.

---

[8] This is for example demonstrated by Knoepfel in the case of environmental policy (Knoepfel, 2002)

[9] One distinguishes between laws that need the consent of the Bundesrat in matters that directly concern the affairs of member states and laws that do not need this consent in all other matters. Before the reform of 2006, the number of laws with consent needed was about half of all laws, after the reform it seems to have gone down to 30–40%.

Regional parliaments do not have real binding powers and in any case, the capacity to veto federal legislation in Austria is weak.

All three types of delegation to the second chamber have not prevented regional representatives in cooperative federalism becoming above all partisan representatives and not representatives who defend regional interests (see for Austria Erk, 2004, 7, FN 27). In the case of Germany and Austria this is easily explained on the base of the preference structure of the population which is in line with partisan cleavages and not with territorial cleavages. In the Swiss case, the absence of strong territorial bindings of representatives is more astonishing. This can in part be explained by the strong anchoring of parties and politicians in their regional base which makes it difficult on the federal level to vote against cantonal interests in general as well as by the existence of compensatory mechanisms that were already mentioned: protection by the referendum and strong implementation powers.

Switzerland has in addition also informal powers of cantons on the federal level, most notably in the form of a pre-parliamentary review process. A similar procedure exists in Austria, which indicates that at least at the more informal level there is some "voice" of subgovernments. Another influence mechanism in both countries are so-called "conferences" of the member states that serve to develop a common policy stance. The federal government is often invited to participate in discussions within these conferences. This is actually the main location where Austrian states can join forces – which obviously is not easy – and put pressure on the CG both before and after legislation: if there is unanimity among subgovernments on a matter, it can become difficult for the CG to oppose this vote. On the other hand, the CG is usually well protected by party interests in this forum because member states have difficulties to develop one common point of view most of all because party cleavages often override territorial cleavages.

It is not only variety in formal veto-power that explains the differences between Austria and Germany. There are also differences in the role of the party system. Given the non-territorial preferences of the population, national parties become the main players in the federal arena and on the federal level. This means that party constellations decide whether the CG can be constrained or not. The veto power the federal system offers is only used – if one leaves aside the more seldom but nevertheless existing policy issues that polarise strongly on regional matters – if opposition parties can get hold of majorities in the second chamber. In *Germany*, this has most of the time been the case meaning that the government coalition failed to find a congruent majority of parties both in the first and second chamber. The best chances to dispose of such a congruent majority were when a grand coalition of the two major parties, the social-democrats and the christian-democrats, was formed. This happened twice, between 1966 and 1969, and more recently, since 2005. But even today, the central government cannot count on guaranteed majorities, as the party system has developed from a two-and-a-half system to a multi-partisan system with five parties, and subgovernment coalitions in the member states are often different from the grand coalition on the federal level. This means that the CG grand coalition needs additional support by an opposition party to find majorities in the Bundesrat.

In other words, member states are protected against overawing, if opposition parties are willing to restrain the CG. This, of course, is not only a matter of majorities but also of party ideology. Christian-democratic parties, for example, have in general been more inclined than social-democratic parties to respect the federal contract.

To restrain the CG in cooperative territorial federal countries depends therefore on three variables:

- the existence of formal veto powers on the federal level,
- the use of these veto-powers by a majority of opposition parties, and
- the dominance of a party ideology that is conducive to the protection of member states.

The first two conditions were often present in Germany while the third condition has played a less favourable role. The result for Germany is therefore a mixed one: Member states have voice and even veto (on many points in federal legislation) if there is a sufficient number of opposition governments on the member state level that is willing to form a majority against the CG coalition in the second chamber and if the opposition pursues a policy of member state protection. Such a protection did however often fail because of the Unitarian rationale valid in the party system and the lack of a national party that would vigorously defend a strengthening of Länder competences and revenues.

Austria lacked all three safeguards against the rise of predatory federalism. First of all, member states do not have, as discussed, veto powers on the federal level. Second, until 1999, when the first coalition between the Austrian People's Party (ÖVP) and the Liberals (FPÖ) was founded, Austria was governed by a grand coalition of social democrats (SPÖ) and the ÖVP, not only on the CG level but also in seven of the nine member states. The congruence of government coalitions has not allowed to develop the logic of partisan opposition. This has changed to some extent between 1999 and 2006, when the new coalition government of the ÖVP and the FPÖ took office but the traditional coalition of ÖVP and SPÖ was re-installed in 2006. The congruence of government coalitions has diminished and a stronger polarising element of party opposition is introduced but in most cases the former congruence of coalition governments has been reinstalled. Unlike Germany, Austria lacks therefore a strong party opposition element that could protect the Länder. To this must be added that both the ÖVP and the SPÖ have adhered to similar Unitarian objectives as German parties. Austria is therefore until today lacking any constraining elements of central government discretion. As a consequence, predatory federalism can unfold.

Both Switzerland and Australia have not introduced formal veto powers for subgovernments on the federal level. Nevertheless, this lack of formal veto powers has not resulted in Switzerland in the same centralising tendencies as in Germany and Austria. The main explanatory variables are :

- the lack of an Unitarian rationale (Braun, 2003) and the dominance of regional identity as the main reference point in the system;
- compensatory mechanisms that have been installed: most of all the double majority that is needed in a referendum and that has often protected smaller cantons but also pre-parliamentary procedures;
- the strong position of the various "conferences" that serve to organise joint opinion and action, and the strong implementation powers for cantons;
- a more fragmented and regionalised party system;
- and finally a strong representation of regional politicians in the federal parliament that give at least voice to cantonal interests.

Member states in Switzerland have therefore a number of venues at their disposition to protect themselves from overawing. This has not prevented that a "creeping centralisation" by way of conditional grants and equalisation payments has set in but the recent major reform that abolished the existing intransparent mechanisms of CG financing of cantonal activities demonstrates that the counter mechanisms against an overawing of the CG do work (Frey, 2006).

With regard to co-decision making, *Australia* has not opted to install formal veto powers for the States on the federal level which is in line with the general philosophy of dual federalism. Australia's second chamber, the Senate, was since the beginning conceived as a partisan based institution and not as a device of voice for member states. The Senate has almost the same powers as the first chamber. In this way it could, as in Germany, in principle be used as a means of the opposition to control the federal government. The situation was, however, never like this: Until 1981, the CG had congruent majorities in both chambers, which explains to a large extent – together with the favourable stance of the Constitutional Court concerning centralisation (Galligan, 1995) – the seizure of a large number of concurrent areas and the shift of revenue competences to the central level. Especially, the Labour party had a clear anti-federal stance.

Things changed since 1981 but not in favour of the large opposition parties. Instead smaller opposition parties obtained the position of a pivot in constructing majorities in the Senate, which led to considerable constraints of expanding CG powers. Also in the 1980s, the Labour party changed its attitude concerning federalism and developed a much more pragmatic stance that focused on stronger integration of member states into federal policies. Liberals and the National Party were traditionally friendlier to the maintenance of member state rights.

Both developments, the dependence of the CG on the consent of smaller opposition parties and the more supportive stance of the three major parties concerning member state rights have contributed to more constraints of CG expansion and to a policy of "collaborative federalism" (Painter, 1998, 2001; Braun, 2005), which integrated member states on the highest level in the setting of national strategies. This was to a certain extent a double-edged sword as member states had in turn to give up some of their autonomy in their exclusive policy areas, above all in competition policy, which now became co-decided by the CG. On the other hand, this gave member states "voice" in federal policies, though not veto powers. A strong majority of member states can, however, considerably co-determine federal policy strategies. Concluded agreements bind member states and oblige them to execute the agreements but agreements nevertheless leave freedom in ways how to implement them (Braun, 2005).

"Collaborative federalism" allowed moreover two other developments that reduced the financial powers of the CG - its main resource of overawing – considerably. One was the introduction of the GST, the goods and services tax, which replaced the large number of general purpose grants. This change was important because it blocked the possibility of CG to threaten member states with a reduction of money that flows into these grants. The second important development was the recent agreement on fiscal reforms,[10] which reduced the number of conditional grants – the main device for intervention of the CG – from 90 to five and made their distribution subject to joint discussion and the development of transparent criteria. This again, has reduced the discretion of the CG.

There has therefore been a substantial reduction of the overawing capacities of the CG since the 1980s.

Conclusions

When can predatory federalism unfold? This was the initial question. The analysis of three countries that are usually considered as being centralised – Germany, Austria, and Australia – and the contrasting case Switzerland has brought a number of insights concerning this question:

- Cooperative federalism has in contrast to dual federalism organisational features that lend itself to a centralisation of competences. But it is neither a necessary – as the case of Australia demonstrates – nor a sufficient condition – as the case of Switzerland suggests.
- It is the combination of cooperative federalism with a non-cultural distribution of constituency preferences (territorial federalism) that opens up large avenues for continuing centralisation. Austria and Germany are the examples. Switzerland which combines cooperative federalism with cultural federalism has by contrast maintained a decentralisation equilibrium. Territorial federalism alone is not a necessary explanatory variable conducive to centralisation. It can entail a regional self-consciousness that is different from cultural federalism but does constrain at least to some extent strong centralisation as Australia demonstrates. If such a regional self-consciousness does not exist in countries based on territorial federalism, a

[10] Intergovernmental Agreement on Federal Financial Relations, 29th November, 2008. URL: www.coag.gov.au

Unitarian rationale can set through strengthening the trend towards centralisation.

- The combination of cooperative and territorial federalism is not yet enough to explain the upraise of predatory federalism as the federal order in which CG has (almost) unlimited discretion. It needs three additional variables: formal veto-powers for member states on the federal level; incongruent majorities between first and second chamber; and federal-friendly party attitudes among CG parties and/or among opposition parties that hold office in member states. If all three conditions are lacking, which was the case in Austria, cooperative and territorial federalism easily leads to predatory federalism. Informal mechanisms of "voice" are not enough to counter these tendencies.
- Implementation rights can be an important compensating mechanism for member states if formal veto powers are lacking. If such rights are lacking and co-decision making powers are not guaranteed, predatory federalism can prevail. In Austria, both rights are practically non-existent, while member states in Germany have a somewhat larger but constrained room for manoeuvre in implementation that has recently been strengthened by granting member states sole authority in a number of policy areas.
- Germany with its strong formal veto-powers and frequent incongruities of majorities in the second and first chamber as well as minimal implementation rights, has gone a long way towards centralisation but has not been subject to predatory federalism. The danger of predatory federalism in the German system can come up if a grand coalition rules which disposes of congruent majorities in both chambers of the parliament. As the unitarian rationalc is strongly anchored in all parties, this may open up roads towards predatory federalism. Both times such a situtation occured in Germany, this has, however, not led to predatory federalism. One can therefore conclude that Germany's structure will continue to foster centralisation but that it has sufficient opposing forces to prevent predatory federalism. This is not the case in Austria.
- Switzerland has, despite cooperative federalism, not institutionalised centralised powers for the CG though there has been a period of "creeping centralisation" by means of financial incentives. A major reason – as mentioned – has been cultural federalism and the dominance of regional identity instead of rationales of unitarisation or equality. Despite the lack of formal veto powers, cantons have sufficient mechanisms to oppose the federal government, in particular implementation rights and the referendum. Recent reforms have considerably curtailed financial intervention powers of the CG. The tendency is therefore towards more decentralisation and not more centralisation.
- Australia, finally, has demonstrated that dual federalism alone is not a sufficient condition for avoidance of centralisation. The strong sense for equality in the population, congruent majorities in both chambers of parliament plus a centralisation friendly Constitutional Court, have until the

early 1980s contributed to the accumulation of competences and above all revenues on the federal level. Unfavourable structures like strong regional factions in national parties and the referendum have probably mitigated this centralisation trend but could not turn it in another direction. The change came with veto-powers of opposition parties in the Senate and a turn in party attitudes towards federalism. Collaborative federalism developed which allowed member states co-decision making rights and which led finally to a curtailing of financial powers of the CG. Traditionally, member states have more policy areas and implementation powers at their disposition than Germany and Australia. This did not change the overall centralised outlook but it introduced stronger elements of co-decision making that can protect member states. In this way, Australia has stopped short of predatory federalism in the 1980s and established a new equilibrium valid until today that maintains centralisation with protection mechanisms for member states. At the same time we can learn that predatory federalism is not necessarily only an outcome of the combination of cooperative with territorial federalism. Dual and territorial federalism can also turn into predatory federalism even if a certain regional self-consciousness exists depending to a large degree on veto powers of the second chamber.

- In sum, predatory federalism can unfold in federations with a high degree of tolerance towards centralisation
  - both in cooperative and dual federalism
  - if preferences of the population are non-territorially based
  - and if implementation powers of member states are weak or very weak
  - and, at the same time, formal veto-powers in the second chamber are missing *and* party power relations do not result in incongruent majorities between the first and second chamber *and* there are no effective parties that defend "delineated spheres of autonomy" for member states and own revenue resources.
  - Other institutional constraints, such as direct democracy, can form an obstacle but are no absolute and sufficient constraints against predatory federalism as Australia demonstrates.

References

Balthasar, A. (2003). Prämienverbilligung im Krankenversicherungsgesetz: Vollzugsföderalismus und sekundäre Harmonisierung. *Sonderheft Föderalismus der Schweizerischen Zeitschrift für Politikwissenschaft*, herausgegeben von Adrian Vatter und Sonja Wälti, 1(2003):335–354.

Bednar, J., Eskridge, W. N., J., & Ferejohn, J. (2001). A political theory of federalism. In Ferejohn, J. Riley & J. N. Rakove (Eds) *Constitutional Culture and Democratic Rule.* pages 223–267. New York: Cambridge University Press,.

Börzel, T. A., & Hosli, M. O. (2003). Brussels between Bern and Berlin: Comparative federalism meets the European Union. Governance: *An International Journal of Policy and Administratio.*, 16(2):179–202.

Braun, D. (2003). Dezentralischer und unitarischer föderalismus. Die Schweiz und Deutschland im Vergleich. *Swiss Political Science Review.* 9(1):57–89.

Braun, D. (2005). Between market-preserving federalism and intergovernmental coordination: The case of Australia. *Swiss Political Science Review.* 12(2):1–36.

Braun, D. (2008). Modernising federalism. towards convergence in the organisation of intergovernmental relations ? *Acta Politica.* 43(1):4–25.

Bußjäger, P. (2007). Das system der österreichischen Finanzverfassung und seine Reformoptionen. In R. T. Baus, T..Fischer & R. Hrbek (Eds) *Föderalismusreform II: Weichenstellungen für eine Neuordnung der Finanzbeziehungen im deutschen Bundesstaat.* pages 165–176. Baden-Baden : Nomos.

Ehtisham, A., & Tanzi, V. (2002). *Managing Fiscal Decentralization.* London: Routledge.

Elazar, D. J. (Ed) (1994). *Federal systems of the world. A handbook of federal, confederal and autonomy arrangements.* (2nd ed.). Essex: Longman.

Erk, J. (2004). Austria: A federation without federalism. *Publius.* 34(1):1–20.

Figueiredo, R.J.P., & Weingast, B. R. (2005). Self-enforcing federalism. *Journal of Law, Economics & Organization.* 21(1):103–135.

Filippov, M., Ordeshook, P. C., & Shvetsova, O. (2004). *Designing Federalism. A Theory of Self-Sustainable Federal Institutions.* Cambridge: Cambridge University Press.

Frey, R. L. (2006). La réforme du fédéralisme suisse. In R. L. Frey, G. Kreis, G.-R. Plattner & R. Rhinow (Eds) *Le fédéralisme suisse.* pages 17–44. Lausanne : Presses polytechniques et universitaires romandes.

Galligan, B. (1995). *A Federal Republic: Australia's Constitutional System of Government.* Cambridge: Cambridge University Press.

Hueglin, T. O., & Fenna, A. (2006). *Comparative Federalism. A Systematic Inquiry.* Peterborough: Broadview Press.

Iaryczower, M., Saiegh, S., & Tommasi, M. (2004). Coming together: §the industrial organization of federalism. Centro de Estudios para el Desarrollo Institutioncional, *Fundación Gobierno & Sociedad,* Universidad de San Andrès. URL: file://localhost/Users/admin/Documents/PDF-Services/
Federalism/Iaryczower%20tommasi%20federalism.pdf

Kilper, H. & Lhotta, R. (1996). *Föderalismus in der Bundesrepublik Deutschland : eine Einführung.* Volume 15 Opladen: Leske + Budrich.

Knoepfel, P. (2002). Regulative Politik in föderativen Staaten – das Beispiel der Umweltpolitik. In A. Benz & G. Lehmbruch (Eds) Föderalismus. Analysen in entwicklungsgeschichtlicher und vergleichender Perspektive. *Sonderheft der Politische Vierteljahresschrift.* 32/2001pages 306–332. Opladen: Westdeutscher Verlag.

Knoepfel, P., Kissling-Näf, I., & Varone, F. (2001). *Analyse et pilotage des politiques publiques.* Genève, Bâle, Munich: Helbing & Lichtenhahn.

Kymlicka, W. (2005). Federalism, nationalism, and multiculturalism. In D. Karmis & W. Norman (Eds) *Theories of Federalism.* A Reader, pages 269–292. New York: Palgrave Macmillan.

Laufer, H. & Münch, U. (1998). *Das föderative System der Bundesrepublik Deutschland.* Opladen: Leske + Budrich.

Lehmbruch, G. (2002). Der unitarische Bundesstaat in deutschland: Pfadabhängigkeit und Wandel. In A. Benz & G. Lehmbruch (Eds) *Sonderheft der Politische Vierteljahresschrift* 32/2001. Föderalismus. Analysen in entwicklungsgeschichtlicher und vergleichender Perspektive, pages 53–110. Westdeutscher Verlag, Wiesbaden.

Lemco, J. (1991). *Political Stability in Federal Governments.* Praeger Publishers.

Levi, M. (1988). *Of Rule and Revenue.* Berkeley u.a: University of California Press,.

Linder, W. (1994). *Swiss Democracy: Possible Solutions in Multicultural Societies.* London: Macmillan.

McKay, D. (2000). *Designing Europe. Comparative Lessons from the Federal Experience.* Oxford: Oxford University Press.

Oates, W. E. (1972). *Fiscal Federalism.* New York: Harcourt Brace Jovanovich.

Oates, W. E. (1999). Federalism and government finance. In J. Quigley & E. Smolensky (Eds) *Modern Public Finance.* pages 126–151. Cambridge: Harvard University Press.

Oates, W. E. (2006). *On the theory and practice of fiscal decentralization.* IFIR Working Paper Series No. 2006–05.

Obinger, H. (2005). Austria – strong parties in a weak federal polity. In H. Obinger, S. Leibfried & F. Castles (Eds) *Federalism and the Welfare State. New World and European Experiences.* Pages 181–221.

Olson, M. (1969). The principle of "fiscal equivalence": The division of responsibilities among different levels of government. *American Economic Review.* 59:479–487.

Painter, M. (1998). *Collaborative Federalism: Economic Reform in Australia in the 1990s.* Cambridge: Cambridge University Press.

Painter, M. (2001). Multi-level governance and the emergence of collaborative federal institutions in australia. *Policy and Politics.* 29(2):137–150.

Riker, W. H. (1964). *Federalism: Origin, Operation, Significance.* Boston: Little Brown.

Rodden, J., Eskeland, G. S., & Litvack, J. (2003). *Fiscal Decentralization and the Challenge of Hard Budget Constraints.* Cambridge MA: MIT Press.

Sharman, C., & Moon, J. (2003). Introduction. In J. Moon & C. Sharman (Eds) *Australian Politics and Government. The Commonwealth, the States and the Territories.* Pages 1–11. Cambridge, UK: Cambridge University Press.

Summers, J. (2002). Federalism and commonwealth-state relations. In J. Summers, D. Woodward & A. Parkin, A (Eds) *Government, Politics, Power and Policy in Australia.* Pages 89–118. Frenchs Forest NSW: Pearson Education Australia.

Thorlakson, L. (2003). Comparing federal institutions: Power and representation in six federations. *West European Politics.* 26(2):1–22.

Tiebout, C. M. (1956). A pure theory of local expenditures. *Journal of Political Economy.* LXIV(5):416–424.

Vatter, A., (Ed) (2006). *Föderalismusreform: Wirkungsweise und Reformansätze föderativer Institutionen in der Schweiz.* Zürich : NZZ.

Watts, R. (1996). *Comparing federal systems in the 1990s.* Kingston: Institute of intergovernmental relations,.

Watts, R. L. (1999). *The Spending Power in Federal Systems: A Comparative Study.* Kingston: Institute of Intergovernmental Relations, Queen's University.

Weingast, B. R. (1995). The economic role of political institutions: Market-preserving federalism and economic development. J*ournal of Law, Economics and Organization.* 11(1):1–31.

Part IV

Sustainable Resources Management

CHAPTER 12

Diving into Waters and Building on Houses: Insights into Resource Sustainability

NURIA FONT & JOAN SUBIRATS

Introduction

The supply and management of common-pool goods and resources is unquestionably one of the issues that have aroused the most interest among scholars in the field of political science. From the different areas within this discipline, including institutional studies, political economics, public policy analysis and more recently governance studies, attempts have been made to respond to the now-classic questions as to the sustainability of common-pool resources: Why do we need institutions to regulate the sustainability of common-pool resources? Under what conditions are these institutions created? How do they work? And finally, how does institutional change take place? The specialised literature has addressed these questions extensively and provided a number of analytical tools that have contributed to better understanding the sustainability of common-pool resources. The purpose of this chapter is not to embark on a theoretical discussion of these questions but to reflect on the most innovative contributions within this plentiful literature. Concerned with knowing the what and how of the sustainability of resources whose use is shared by a variety of users, such as water, clean air and natural habitats, Peter Knoepfel has made a decisive contribution to developing an original tool, the analytical framework of institutional regimes, which helps to break down the keys in the shift of management models of common-pool resources towards more sustainable schemes.

As an intersection between property rights theory, institutional economics and policy analysis, the analytical framework of institutional regimes enables us to grasp under what conditions the management of resources that have different rival users evolves towards more sustainable schemes. Institutional regimes result from the combination of contracts, property rights and public policies that regulate the uses of a given resource, thereby affecting an entire community of users, and their purpose is to maintain the reproductive capacity and ultimately the sustainability of the resource (Knoepfel, 2006; Knoepfel et al, 2007). One of the advantages of the analytical framework is that its point of departure is the unity of the resource as opposed to its uses or the different policies regulating it. With this, it addresses the issue of sustainability from a holistic, not fragmented, vantage point. Analysing the resource, not the sectoral policies regulating it, enables us to examine the different rivalries of use that it is subjected to and identify the situations that facilitate or hinder the sustainable renewal of the resource. The prime goal is to detect how the production of goods and services by one user interferes with the production of goods and services by another, and what leads to excesses, abuses and unregulated appropriations of this resource. For example, when an industry dumps waste into a river and thus jeopardises the use of water for human consumption, for watering crops or for fish factories downstream, there arises a rivalry between the incumbent users and excluded parties (or even victims), and in turn a critical interaction for the sustainability of the resource. From the standpoint of sustainability, therefore, a regime is coherent when the regulations of each good and service within the regime fulfil the minimum requirements to ensure the reproduction of the resource. The implicit holistic approach in the concept of institutional regimes of resources enables us to first distinguish between the sustainability of an individual use and the sustainability of a resource as a whole, and secondly add the reproductive dimension of the resource itself to the environmental, economic, social and cultural dimensions of sustainability (Knoepfel, 2006; Knoepfel et al, 2007).

The analytical framework of institutional regimes takes a long-term perspective, mainly because one of the cornerstones of the regime, namely property and use rights, are highly stable over time as the owners of these rights are highly resistant to change. These rights tend to be perpetuated and only change in the very long term, when the system regulating the rights is incapable of preventing depletion of the resource beneath minimum subsistence levels. Yet additionally, we should not lose sight of the fact that sustainability is not an absolute state, nor does it come from sudden change or specific short-term circumstances, rather it is a product of evolutionary processes. Taking a historical perspective enables us to both better grasp the cornerstones on which the regime is based and identify the moment and circumstances that lead to the collapse of these underpinnings.

The institutional regime of water is highly illustrative. A rise in the uses of water can reach critical levels at times of extreme drought if the institutional regime is internally incoherent, that is, if it has not set qualitative and quantitative limits on the use of this resource. This is when the balance between property rights and policy is the most fragile, and when the regime's institutional path is susceptible to veering off track. At this point, the elements of the policy come to the fore. Windows of opportunity open up for stakeholders who are traditionally at the periphery of the policy. Those stakeholders then mobilize resources, form coalitions, spread ideas through society, seek alliances in multi-level settings, improve their negotiating skills and ultimately manage to affect the shape of the regime. Therefore, the key to regime change lies in the web of property rights and policy.

The analytical framework of institutional regimes is particularly innovative in its approach to studying the sustainability of common-pool resources. First of all, this approach recovers the legal tradition by placing property rights at the core of the shape of institutional regimes. The heir to a long legal tradition, yet also trained in policy analysis and public administration, Peter

Knoepfel has grasped that understanding how the management regime of a given resource works necessarily entails exploring the complex system of property and use rights. When inquiring into the ownership of the rights, in water regimes for example, Peter Knoepfel's approach not only takes into account the legal regime sustaining it, often ignored by the literature on policy analysis and governance, rather he analytically rescues it and integrates it in a novel fashion into the most dynamic and contingent aspects of public policy. He understands that these aspects structure and condition the policies that regulate the uses and sustainability of water as a resource. For all of these reasons, identifying what kind of regime governs resource management in terms of both property rights – such as a regime of public, private or mixed ownership – and the uses of the resources – who has the right to use the resources and how these rules are defined – becomes crucial to understanding the regime of the resource. Therefore, we inquire as to how the property rights have been acquired and used historically, what makes it possible for them to be maintained over time and under what conditions they might be liable to change. This knowledge in the long term enables us to better understand the keys to regime change within specific temporal and spatial coordinates.

Secondly, the analytical framework of institutional regimes offers a clearly innovative approach to conducting the exercise of comparing natural and manmade resources by analytically treating them the same. In his approach, Peter Knoepfel tries to go beyond the specificity of sectoral policies and analytically compare, for example, natural habitats, clean air, housing or the cultural heritage. This comparison, which is bold from an analytical standpoint, unquestionably harbours great potential. What are the common patterns in institutional regimes for natural and manmade resources? What, for example, do the water resources or the housing stocks have to do with each other? In both cases, they are unique resources that generate different goods and services and are used by multiple users. For example, river water is used for multiple purposes that vie with each other: it is used for human consumption, it is needed to water crops, it generates hydroelectric energy, it makes industrial refrigeration possible, it is the site of fishing and free-time activities and it is simultaneously an ecological habitat and the site of navigable routes. Numerous uses also vie with each other in housing stocks: residential – providing shelter; productive – generating opportunities for investment and work; services – supplying basic services; urban planning – transport and connectivity, use of space; and social – social cohesion. The presence of multiple users vying for a single resource and threatening its reproductive capacity and economic, environmental and social cohesion is the cornerstone of Peter Knoepfel's analytical framework. Identifying common patterns of functioning in the institutional regimes of natural and artificial resources might be a risky analytical challenge, but also undoubtedly a promising one. The analytical framework of institutional regimes has been applied in numerous studies on the water regime, forest, air, landscape and housing stocks in several European countries. These studies have contributed to rendering a clearer picture of under what conditions institutional regimes are shifted towards more integrative and sustainable management models. The next two sections outline the results of two studies that have applied the analytical framework of institutional regimes in water resources and housing stocks in Spain.

Water institutional regimes

Cross-country research on institutional water regimes identifies common evolutionary patterns.[1] Generally speaking, the regimes were formed during the second half of the 19th century. As the number of different kinds of uses of water rose, the regimes, which started out simple with the uses limited to watering crops and human consumption, evolved towards more complex stages in around the mid-20th century. Swift industrialisation, rising populations and urban expansion largely explain these changes (Kuks, 2004). Starting in the 1960s, the inclusion of environmental issues on the political agenda once again increased the number and kinds of uses that vied for the resource, although the first attempts at integrating water management did not come about until the 1980s. Since then, some national water regimes have evolved towards more integrated schemes, whereas some others are still in a transitional stage. This section briefly explores the evolution of the Spanish water regime from its creation in the late 19th century until the current stage of transition towards a more integrated and cohesive regime. The section briefly identifies the major changes in both the property rights and the policy dimensions leading to new steps in the transition process.

The Spanish water regime was first institutionalised in the late 19th century. The enactment of the first and second water acts in 1866 and 1879, respectively, with later amendments contained in the provisions in the 1889 Civil Code, marked a turning point in the water regime. As in other European contexts, the regulatory framework for water was liberal and did not contain a policy dimension (Costejà *et al.*, 2004). Yet this situation was gradually altered at the turn of the century mostly due to the influential intellectual regenerationist movement, which promoted the need for the state to invest in hydraulic infrastructures as a national modernisation strategy (Costejà *et al.*, 2004). Broadly speaking, the regulatory regime as regards property rights initiated at the end of the 19th century did not change until the adoption of the 1985 Water Act. By contrast, several changes at the policy level, mostly dealing with the adoption of sectoral regulations, were introduced in the regime. In this respect, the regime created during the last few decades of the 19th century, which regulated a very limited range of goods and services, gradually gained in complexity at the turn of the century as the range of regulated goods and services increased and the coherence of the stakeholders involved in the water community was consequently eroded.

The move towards a more complex regime as regards the policy dimension was enhanced between the 1950s and the late 1970s, a period in which the water regime underwent important transformations: new water demands and

---

[1] European Water Regimes and the Notion of Sustainable Status (EUWARENESS) research Project, funded by the European Commission, 5th Framework Programme

uses – mostly related to industrial uses, the demographic boom, urban expansion and the creation of the tourism industry – heightened rivalries among uses and users. The democratisation process in the late 1970s and the institutional and policy changes derived from both Spanish membership in the European Union and the creation of decentralised political structures, the so-called State of the Autonomies, introduced new policy issues, in particular environmental protection, in the policy agenda of water regime. Parallel to these transformations, the adoption of the 1985 Water Act altered the policy regime as regards the property rights dimension and opened up an ongoing process of regime transformation over the following two decades (Costejà et al, 2004). In particular, it enhanced state intervention by means of extending the idea of the public domain and placing the emphasis on planning. Further, it promoted a more integrated approach by envisioning water as a unitary resource and introducing the concepts of sanitation, water resource, quality preservation, civil protection, environmental values and territorial planning (Costejà *et al.*, 2004). In short, the new legal framework attempted to adapt the water policy to a political, socio-economic and technological context that had been thoroughly transformed over the previous decades in terms of the increasing number of uses and users. As a result, the water regime following the mid-1980s maintained elements of deep complexity in the sense that the range of regulated goods and services had a tendency to rise, although the coherence of the stakeholders in the property rights system was scarcely reinforced.

Following the adoption of the 1985 Water Act, the Spanish water regime has undergone a process of transition towards more integrated schemes. In brief, the transition process, which is currently ongoing, can be segmented into three different stages. The first stage started in 1993, when the Socialist government presented the first of several draft versions of the National Water Plan following a mandate by the 1985 Water Act. The plan perpetuated the traditional hydraulic paradigm by which the state adopted a supply-oriented approach to regulating water, which stipulated the construction of large-scale infrastructures, namely dams and inter-basin transfers (Moral & Saurí, 2000). Yet government attempts to adopt such a planning instrument, with successive drafts released between 1993 and 1995, were unsuccessful. The projected plan was heavily contested by the donor regions, with Aragon, environmental groups and even some practitioners within the Ministry of Public Works playing a leading role. As a result, the government was compelled to withdraw the plan. Broadly speaking, the controversy emerging around the plan visualised increasing rivalries among a wide range of users and made clear that for the first time the traditional principles on which the water regime had long been grounded were considered to be openly inadequate by some segments of society.

In the second stage, covering the 1996-2004 period, the Popular Party government reformed the existing water regime in terms of both property rights and policy dimensions. More specifically, the government reformed the 1985 Water Act through the enactment of Act 46/99, which opened the door to the adoption of the National Water Plan by means of Act 10/2001. The national government strategy combined market efficiency and supply–based principles. Regarding the property rights dimension, the new framework created water banks and several public corporations, the so-called *Sociedades Estatales*. Water banks for the exchange of use rights aimed to introduce new efficiency parameters and make the water concession regimes more flexible (Font & Subirats, 2009). Water banks were conceived to be centres for the exchange of use rights for further cession to other users. In turn, *Sociedades Estatales* were public-private partnerships aiming to finance the most profitable hydraulic infrastructures, while the less profitable ones would remain in the hands of the state. Yet the creation of *Sociedades Estatales* did not imply the abandonment of water policy as an instrument of the state but meant a restructuring of funding mechanisms which would allow the state to seek private capital for profitable projects and EU funding for eligible projects (Bakker, 2002). Regarding the policy dimension, the government adopted the National Water Plan, which was passed by the Parliament. The plan promoted the construction of large-scale hydraulic infrastructures to transfer water from the surplus to the deficit river basins. The aim of the plan was to satisfy the increasing demands for water arising from the combination of cyclical climate droughts with the increase in the demand for water due to industry, tourism and urban development in the Mediterranean over the previous decade (Font & Subirats, 2009). The key project contained in the plan consisted of the transfer of 1050 hm^3 of water from the Ebro River, a central provider in the Spanish hydrological system, south along the Mediterranean coast to the Jucar, Segura and South Almería basins and north to the internal basins of Catalonia. It also included the construction of about 120 water dams and river channels on Spanish soil (Font & Subirats, 2009). Briefly, the dual national government's strategy on water policy prompted mixed reactions. On the one hand, environmentalists and the neo-liberal sectors welcomed the adoption of more flexible management instruments (Bukowski, 2007), while on the other, the National Water Plan was widely criticised by social, territorial and political stakeholders. Significantly, a broad swath of environmental and social organisations, political parties and the scientific community harnessed a wide range of political and cognitive resources to influence public opinion and exert pressure on the national government to abolish the plan. In spite of intense protests, the national government held fast to its position, as a result of which large parts of society became involved in intense informational campaigns, mobilised scientific knowledge and ideas and put increasing pressure on government.

Finally, the third stage, which was initiated in 2004, allowed the newly elected government to modify the National Water Plan and redefine the traditional supply-based approach by proposing alternative supply modes of regulation. The government modified the 2001 National Water Plan[2] by eliminating the Ebro River transfer, and shortly thereafter adopted the AGUA[3]

---

[2] RDL 2/2004 amending the National Water Plan and Act 11/2005 amending Act 10/2001 on the National Water Plan.

[3] http://www.mma.es/secciones/agua/programa/quees.htm (Retrieved: 11 January 2008).

program (2004-2008) under the leadership of the Ministry of Environment. This represented a step forward in the redefinition of the types of supply instruments, which mostly consisted of the construction of water desalinisation plants and the promotion of public water banks. Parallel to these regime developments, the implementation of the European Water Framework Directive (WFD) also contributed to redefining the national water regime. In this respect, several initiatives have been undertaken since 2005 to comply with the WFD, and many participatory experiences in various hydrographical basins have been implemented.

In conclusion, the evolution of the water regime in Spain over the past two decades responds to both transformations in the property rights regime and changes in public policy. Attempts to alter the regime during the first stage did not lead to substantive results in property rights matters, but they did leave the door open for further changes in the policy dimensions. The controversy following the release of the several versions of the National Water Plan between 1993 and 1995 reveals the extent to which the traditional planning principles are showing signs of crisis, and equally importantly the extent to which users vying for the resource were willing to mobilise resources in order to transform the institutional regime. The traditional model of water regulation, then, seemed to be ready for change. Major regime changes were undertaken. First and foremost, the public domain nature of both ground and surface water established by the 1985 Water Act was altered for the first time with the introduction of market efficiency schemes in the water regime. This change is aimed at improving the efficiency of water management in view of the growth in the number and kinds of uses from the demand side, and a context of cyclical drought from the supply side, through two kinds of instruments. On one hand, water banks decisively – albeit marginally – make a break with the tradition of public domain. The creation of centres for the exchange of use rights for further cession to other users reveals that the water regime had room for institutional innovation. The support received by both liberal economic sectors and environmentalists reveals the extent to which market efficiency parameters were claimed by stakeholders sharing a wide range of objectives. On the other hand,, state companies are incorporating market efficiency criteria in hydrological management. The openness to including market criteria in the property rights regime contrasts with the clearly interventionist nature of the water planning schemes contained in the 2001 National Water Plan. The perpetuation of a management model based on building large-scale waterworks, usually transfers and reservoirs, unleashed harsh protests and triggered profound divisions among different sectors of society.

The new government following the 2004 elections envisioned abandoning the traditional approach to water development and defining alternative supply modes of intervention, mostly consisting of the construction of desalinisation plants. At the same time, the Water Framework Directive began to be implemented in this phase by means of a complex participatory process (Font & Subirats, 2009). Nowadays, the transformations introduced in the water regimes appear to be insufficiently mature to accommodate use rivalries, make water regimes more cohesive and guarantee the reproduction of the resource. Yet, the sometimes zigzagging natures of water regime transition could reorient water management schemes towards somewhat more sustainable avenues in the long term.

Housing institutional regimes

The sustainability of the building fabric of collective housing has traditionally been related to the quality and composition of the materials used. One of Peter Knoepfel's contributions, which we alluded to above, was to expand this perspective of sustainability, seeking and including other perspectives that would give the concept of "sustainability" a more complex, richer and simultaneously more powerful dimension. Peter Knoepfel upholds the idea that the sustainability of public housing stocks should be measured by means of objective indicators of social, economic and ecological sustainability in order to make choices on urban renewal more rational and legitimate.

In accordance with his desire to combine approaches inherent in policy analysis with those that take property issues into account, he postulated that the sustainability of the building stocks, which fluctuate considerably over time and place, depends on many factors, including related public policy requirements and varying use and property rights structures. This analytical strategy was tested in a project comparing the sustainability of different public housing stocks in Switzerland, Germany and Spain (Hernandez Carr *et al*, 2007). For each stock, studies were performed to determine the degree of sustainability derived from the management strategies and to see how this had prompted changes in the institutional regimes that combine the property rights and use rights of the inhabitants and the entire set of stakeholders involved in the housing stock. The goal was to identify the components of the institutional regime that fostered or threatened the sustainability of the housing stocks so that public policy strategies that encourage this sustainability can be promoted in the future.

The social and economic transformation that Spain experienced from the beginning of the 1960s to the early 1990s led to a sharp increase in the population, while at the same time, the per capita disposable family income also multiplied in real terms. This evolution was produced in two clearly differentiated 15-year periods. The first of these, between 1960 and 1975, was clearly expansive in nature. This period witnessed over 92% of the demographic growth and 76% of the increase in family income. In the second period, 1976-1991, the rate of population increase fell, coming to a standstill over the last five years. Family incomes multiplied by 1.3, to slightly more than €6,000 per capita.

Both periods gave rise to clearly differentiated urban processes. The first of these is characterised by substantial migrations of inhabitants from the rural areas to the regions and cities with industrial infrastructures and dynamics of economic growth. Barcelona, Madrid and the other regional capitals were the main recipients of these migrants, a trend which led to a high demand for housing, intensive growth and a marked increase in population density in these cities. In the latter period, especially from 1980 onwards, there was a shift from the previous urban model, focused on the cities and their metropolitan areas, towards another model in which land development was expansive in nature. This period is characterised by a loss of population and density in the big cities in favour of a secondary metropolitan belt which constantly rose in density. Likewise, the majority of cities with more than 100,000 inhabitants expanded their urban growth into neighbouring municipalities, and the small municipalities within the sphere of influence of the big and medium-sized cities experienced growth rates that were relatively more substantial. All of this changed after the end of the last century with the massive influx of immigrants who once again raised the figures of residents in the large cities of Spain, especially in Madrid, Barcelona and along the Mediterranean coast.

The influence of this socio-economic development on the housing construction sector was very different in each period: between 1960 and 1965, it was characterised by forceful state intervention. From 1965 onwards, the state's financial resources devoted to financing and subsidising the sector were curtailed with the aim of combating inflation, and this affected both the public and private housing built under the subsidised housing system. Housing production went into recession, but this was quickly overcome by the pressure from an unmet demand that gradually became more solvent as work stabilised and income levels rose. Nonetheless, the importance of public or subsidised housing waned in favour of more free market housing being built. The 1970s saw the highest rate of activity in the sector. In 1970, it broke through the threshold of 300,000 finished homes for the first time, reaching 374,000 in 1975, the highest figure ever recorded up to that date.

Throughout the 1980s, construction experienced a major slowdown. The lower rate of housing construction was accompanied by greatly curtailed construction of public housing and a progressive rise in the selling price, far above the inflation rate and rises in family income. These circumstances triggered a housing crisis that appeared towards the end of the decade and the beginning of the 1990s. To handle this crisis, the central government issued two royal decrees aimed at tackling the housing problems. The first of these, RD 1668/1991, regarding the financing of protective measures in land matters, established a link between housing policy and land policy for the first time. The second of these decrees, RD 1932/1991, established financing and tax measures for protective actions in housing matters.

In the case of Catalonia, the Catalan government won responsibility for housing matters in 1985. The public company ADIGSA was immediately set up with the job of administering the public housing stock in Catalonia. Its actions were characterised by an increase in the investment in renovations and improvements in infrastructure, whereas the construction of new housing was substantially limited. Housing policy had been characterised by predominantly economic factors; the policy was interventionist at times of crisis, invested in public works and provided stimulation for the construction of new housing as a driving force for re-launching the economy. When these measures achieved their anti-cyclic objective, free market forces were left to meet housing needs, resulting in a sharp drop in subsidised housing.

At the present time, housing has become one of the main problems of the Spanish population. The price of land, as well as of housing, has continued to rise in recent years, while the rental housing market remains relatively unattractive – for both owners and possible tenants. In 2004, the new Socialist government created a Housing Ministry for the first time in Spain. The Ministry drew up a 2005-2008 Housing Plan, and has also approved a new Land Law that went into effect on the 1st of July 2007. One of this law's objectives is to fight the existing land speculation. In the specific case of Catalonia, problems with access to housing are also common. The three-party coalition regional government in power for the last four years has drawn up a 2004-2007 Housing Plan that was approved by the Catalan Parliament very recently. This new housing act replaces the 1991 Housing Act.

In both cases analysed in the study directed by Peter Knoepfel (Can Tusell and Can Vilardell, two public stock housing estates located in the Catalan city of Terrassa, 20 kilometres north of Barcelona), the relationship between the sustainability of a housing stock, its management by the stock owner and the role of regulations (their formal coherency, etc.) became clear. In order to further this analysis, it was crucial to examine the behaviour of the stock owner and the users-stakeholders with regard to the regulations. In the cases of both ADIGSA and the Municipal Housing Board of Terrassa (the two stock owners in this case), we were able to identify a series of specific, coherent regulations that defined the role of each stakeholder and regulated the possible rivalries between the different users-stakeholders. However, in certain aspects closely tied to the sustainability of the stock, these regulations were either not applied or not respected, or an (implicit or explicit) "agreement" had been reached between the stock owner and the users-stakeholders which in practice led to behaviours outside what is established by the regulations. There is no doubt that the consolidation of this phenomenon in the long term might have undesired effects for the management of a given housing stock, inasmuch as if the residents get accustomed to setting the rules of their own relationship with the stock owner outside the general regulatory framework (even with the latter's approval or tolerance), later it will be more difficult to change users' behaviour.

The two housing stocks analysed, Can Tussell and Can Vilardell, are a good example of this. Both stock owners, ADIGSA and the Municipal Housing Board of Terrassa (PVT), pursued an action dynamic that arose not from the stipulations in the regulations but from a series of implicit agreements, from both the past and present, which responded to the specific reality of the stock in question. Both stock owners, ADIGSA and PVT, preferred to ignore non-compliance with the regulations by other users-stakeholders in order to avoid conflicts. Over time, it was seen that this generated a dynamic that has led to an unsustainable situation, mainly from the economic standpoint, although also from the logic of the resource itself (sound condition of homes) and even from a social perspective. The issues of repairs in buildings of privately owned flats or the way cases of non-payment were handled illustrate how in some cases ADIGSA and PVT have dealt with these problems outside the regulations.

All of this highlights the importance of analysing not just the housing policy measures when tackling a study that seeks to determine the sustainability of the housing resource, but also, as Peter Knoepfel points out in his contributions to institutional regimes, whether or not specific regulations exist, and if so their extent and internal coherence. And after the experience of the analysis in Catalonia, we could also add that it is necessary to determine the degree to which these regulations are truly complied with and enforced. The sustainability of stocks cannot be examined if this other dimension of the problem is not simultaneously addressed.

Spain's public housing policy inherited a set of housing stocks left over from the Franco regime, and starting in 1980 it pursued a policy of building and repairing publicly-owned buildings that was somewhat limited and not very forward-looking when compared to the serious problems Spain was facing at the time, with a vast amount of private housing built but not sold given the economic circumstances, and an equally vast shortfall of public housing available to meet the steep demand for affordable housing. The cases analysed in Terrassa as part of the study directed by Peter Knoepfel revealed that an improvement in this policy, and especially in the sustainability of the public housing that was already built, requires greater internal coherency between sufficiently extensive regulations and an implementing policy, which has tended to be quite permissive and not very consistent with the formal provisions in place. On the other hand, it also highlighted the fact that there was no true articulation between the goods and services derived from the existence of the stock and the capacity to organise the rival uses in order to prevent abuse and conflicts.

In the theoretical perspective set forth by Peter Knoepfel, a coherent regime is one in which: 1) use rights (derived from property rights through contracts) are clearly defined; in both cases analysed, this criterion was met as the contracts clearly delineate the rights and responsibilities; 2) there are no contradictions between the public policies of a regime; in the cases analysed, this criterion is not met as there are major contradictions between public transport, education and social policies and the policies that seek the sustainability of the housing stock; and 3) there are no contradictions between public policies and contracts or property rights; in the case analysed there are also striking contradictions in this criterion given the lack of effective implementation of the clauses contained in the contracts. The presence of a conflict (and not just a rivalry) in the use of one or several goods and services has been used as an indicator of incoherencies or contradictions in the regime, and in the cases analysed in Spain, as we have mentioned above, this conflict stems from lack of coherence and consistency between the scope of the regulations and their lack of implementation, caused by pressures (demands of uses) from other policies that led to abuses in the housing stock and its subsequent deterioration. This obviously jeopardises the future sustainability of the resource. If housing stocks are to be an element of a sustainable built environment, they must not only develop themselves sustainably, but their goods and services must be able to be used sustainably by others stakeholders within the system. This means that other stakeholders, practices and policies that are often not considered part of this policy should be included in the scenario of housing policy.

Final remarks

As mentioned in our opening comments, the analytical framework of institutional regimes – viewed as the intersection between property rights theory, institutional economics and policy analysis – makes it possible to analyse the issue of sustainability while accepting and acknowledging the complexity of the stakeholders and uses surrounding the resource. Peter Knoepfel's major contribution is precisely the combination of contracts, property rights and public policies that regulate the uses of a given resource, specifically focusing on its ability to be reproduced and maintained. Starting from the resource and its necessary integrity, it addresses the complex web of policies and rivalries around it. The perspective is comprehensive and aims to identify the situations that facilitate or hinder the sustainable renewal of the resource. The cases in which this analytical perspective has been applied in Spain, namely water and public housing, demonstrate both its potential and its exigency, as it requires a systematic analysis and the inclusion of factors and stakeholders which tend to go beyond the policymakers themselves and are directly related to the resource being analysed.

It is impossible to de-link Peter Knoepfel's contributions in the field of institutional regimes linked to the sustainability of resources from his previous studies in the field of public policy analysis (Knopefel *et al*, 2001; Knoepfel, 2001). As was claimed in a recent review of John's work (2008): "The added value is the European-style policy analysis. (...) There is an assumption that policy is grounded on a particular set of socially-defined relationships (...), in sets of organisational practices and understandings". In this sense, the value of the concept of institutional regimes is that a stabilised framework of public policies, property rights and contracts ensures that use rights to goods and services remain continuous, stable and foreseeable, thus allowing these stakeholders' activities to function sustainably. In contexts of rising complexity in public policies, with constant evidence of interrelations and "contaminations", it is important to stress the significance of Peter Knoepfel's contributions, which are directly rooted in both his theoretical background and his day-to-day interactions with real policy making.

References

Bakker, K. (2002). From state to market?: Water *mercantilization* in Spain. *Environment and Planning A*. 34, 767-790.

Bukowski, J. (2007). Spanish Water Policy and the NHP: An Advocacy Coalition Approach to Policy Change. *South European Society and Politics.* 12 (1), 39-57.

Costejà, M., Font, N., & Subirats, J. (2004). The Evolution of Water Regime in Spain. In I. Kissling-Näf & S. Kuks (Eds.) *The Evolution of National Water Regimes in Europe. Transitions in Water Rights and Water Policies*, Dordrecht: Kluwer Academic Publishers, 235-263.

Font, N. & Subirats, J. (2009). Spain. Water Management in Transition: A Watered Management of the Transition? In D. Huitema & S. Meijerink (Eds), *Water policy entrepreneurs. A research companion to water transitions around the globe*, Cheltenham: Edward Elgar (forthcoming).

Hernández Carr, A., Garcia Arnaud, A. & Subirats, J. (2007). *Sostenibilitat i habitatge públic a Catalunya (1960-2005). Analisi de les dinàmiques de creació i construcció d'habitatge públic des de la perspectiva de la sostenibilitat ambiental, econòmica i social. Aplicació del concepte de regims institucionals en les polítiques públiques d'habitatge*, Barcelona : IGOP-UAB, (Unpublished).

John, P. (2008). Public Policy Analysis. In *Public Policy and Administration*, N° 23, pp.416-418.

Knoepfel, P. (2001). *Environmental Policies 1982-2000.* Bâle: Helbing & Lichtenhahn.

Knoepfel, P., Larrue, C., & Varone, F. (2001). Analyse *et pilotage des politiques publiques.* Bâle: Helbing & Lichtenhahn (series: Analyse des politiques publiques / Politikanalyse no 1).

Knoepfel, P. (2006). *Institutional Regimes for Sustainable Collective Housing Stocks, Conceptual Framework*, Lausanne: IDHEAP.

Knoepfel, P., Nahrath, S., & Varone, F. (2007). Institutional Regimes for Natural Resources. An Innovative Theoretical Framework for Sustainability. In P. Knoepfel (Ed) *Environmental Policy Analysis. Learning from the Past for the Future.* Springer, pp. 455-506

Kuks, S. (2004). The Sustainability Performance of National Resource Regime. In I. Kissling-Naef & S. Kuks (Eds) *The Evolution of National Water Regime in Europe. Transitions in Water Rights and Water Policies.* Dordrecht: Kluwer Academic Publishers. Pp.25-48.

Saurí, D., & del Moral, L. (2001). Recent developments in Spanish water policy. Alternatives and conflicts at the end of the hydraulic age. *Geoforum*, 32 (3), 351-362.

CHAPTER 13

Analysing Artificial Resources: the Added Value and Challenges of a Resource-based Approach
The Case of Housing Stocks, Landscape, Public Roads and Information

JEAN-DAVID GERBER, LEE A. NICOL, MIRTA OLGIATI & JÉRÔME SAVARY

Introduction

The study of the scope of regulations pertaining to a resource, particularly a natural resource, has traditionally been done through public policy analysis. Using an original approach, Peter Knoepfel – assisted in his reasoning over the years by his team of researchers in the *Public Policy and Sustainability* chair at IDHEAP – has developed an analytical framework that is more in-depth and closer to reality by coupling the analysis of public policies with the study of property rights. This framework, the resource institutional regime (RIR) has the advantage of providing the complete panorama of regulations applicable to a given resource and taking into account the particular uses that are made of it. Through the two analytical dimensions of extent and coherence, the framework also allows the researcher to develop concrete propositions at the end of the analysis that lead to a truly sustainable exploitation of the resource.

Always under the impetus of Peter Knoepfel, this framework – which has proven itself during the course of its frequent employment in the domain of natural resources (air, water, land, forests, etc.) – is ready to enter a new phase through its application to artificial resources (Nahrath & Csikos, 2007; Nicol & Knoepfel, 2008; Savary, 2008; Gerber, 2008; Nahrath et al., 2008).

The current contribution addresses this new development. On the basis of a presentation of theoretical elements that enable the resource and the elements that trigger the need to regulate to be identified and defined, we present four artificial resources one at a time: housing stocks, landscape, roads and information[1]. We demonstrate how these four objects of study are defined as artificial resources and in which way the RIR can be applied to them. This

[1] These four resources were selected since they correspond to doctoral research, either in progress or completed, conducted by the authors.

approach, of an exploratory nature, allows us both to study the challenges and added value of the application of this model to artificial resources and to draw some preliminary conclusion that we hope will constitute a first step for the future expansion of the framework.

The resource-based approach

This chapter illustrates the way in which the concept "resource", developed by economists, has been used favourably in political sciences to formalise the study of the rivalries that occur between actors when a scarce environmental resource does not allow for the totality of the demands placed upon it to be satisfied, leading to a political process of defining or redistributing the use rights on the resource. This section on natural resources serves as a basis on which rests our questioning of how well the concept of resource can be transposed to the human creations we call "artificial resources".

Resources as a result of a process of social construction

Etymologically, the term "resource" has always had an economic connotation. During the 16th century "resourcial" was used as a synonym of "richness" in the sense of assets of wealth and money but equally as nonmaterial reserves (skills, ingenuity, etc.). Later, the word in its plural form took on the meaning of possessed wealth. It applied to materials, humans, substances, manufactured products and energy reserves that a country or a region had at its disposal. Richness transmitted to the notion of resources the idea of power that is today associated to their possessors. In the 20th century, the term also came to represent surface and subsurface productions: we speak of agricultural, mining and oil resources that are considered "natural resources" (Oxford Dictionary).

A natural resource can be defined as "a physical or biological object, identified or hypothetical, that can satisfy human needs of a biological, technical or cultural nature" (translated from Pillet, 1993). This means that a resource is defined by its usefulness to human beings: an element of the environment becomes a resource only if it procures market or non-market goods and services for the human species since in the biophysical environment there are all types of matter and energy that, in our current technological and use states, are not likely to render service to humans.

A resource is therefore the *result of a practice*; it is the "product of a relationship", otherwise it is but "matter" (Becht & Belzun, 1975, cited in Pillet, 1993). This acknowledgement of its utility by a specific actor triggers the onset of an action that seeks to allow him or her to gain access to this element that has until then not been used: resources exist only by means of a socio-political or economic connection to "natural matter". All resources are thus economic or socio-political and are the result of a phenomenon of individual or collective appropriation (Pillet, 1993).

In consequence, a natural resource is the product of a *social construction.* A resource is perceived as such – first individually and collectively, and then politically recognised – from the moment that actors use the goods and services that contribute to the satisfaction of their direct and indirect, material or nonmaterial needs (Varone, 2001). The definition of a resource varies in time (e.g., between generations) and in space (e.g., between regions) as a function of different social expectations – that is, of the demand of certain goods and services.

Stocks, yield and reproducibility

The approach centred on resources attempts to respond primarily from an analytical point of view to the challenge presented by the (non-) renewability of resources. It is built on the notions of stock (capital), yield (fruit), and harvestable units, as well as goods and services (Figure 1).

Any given resource provides goods and/or services. Their uses vary in time and space as a function of the needs of the users. The quantity of harvestable units depends on the size of the stock and the capacity of the resource system to (re)produce ("fruit"). For example, one service provided by the resource "air" is its ability to absorb pollutants (e.g., from the combustion necessary for the functioning of engines). If, accounting for the local climate and topography, the atmospheric pollutants rejected are too great, the air quality will no longer be satisfactory thereby damaging the use of other services provided by the resource (e.g., breathable air). If the absorptive capacity of the air is exceeded in the long run, the renewability of the resource can no longer be guaranteed.

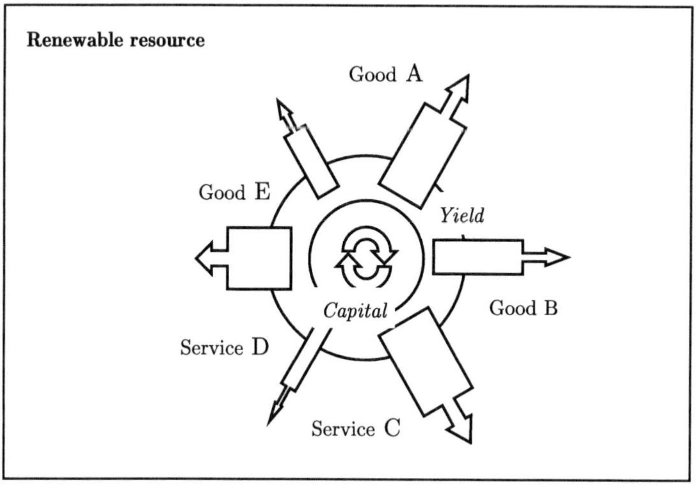

Figure 1 Renewable natural resource. The thickness of the arrows representing the goods and services provided by the resource is proportional to the intensity of their use. In a sustainable use situation, the capital (stock) of the resource (central circle) is not affected by the overall use. Source: Kissling-Näf & Varone, 2000: 38; Knoepfel et al., 2001: 18.

The reproductive capacity of a natural resource depends on the relationship between the capacity of the resource to renew its stock and its harvestable units. There exists a risk of overexploitation when the latter, either in number or in quantity, threatens the sustainability of the stock. The opposite case of underuse can also occur: all human-made habitats, such as terraced cultivation or open meadows, are at risk when they are underused. Therefore, the sustainability of a resource is a function of its potential to renew its stock and the human uses derived from it. When the stock is depleted, human action can sometimes also restore it to some extent through targeted measures (e.g. artificial ventilation of eutrophic lakes, reintroduction of juvenile fish in rivers for angling).

Rivalry and use conflicts call for regulation

Even vague attempts to exploit scarce resources often lead to use rivalries and even conflicts between the user-actors[2]. The long-term solution to these conflicts involves a political process of defining the rules of use that are deemed satisfactory by the parties involved. A state of sustainable management of resources is one in which socially and economically acceptable solutions are reached that are within the limits of what constitutes the naturally limited capacity of the stock to renew itself.

Scarcity

When the demand for a certain resource increases, the price or perceived value of the resource climbs for its users. In order to increase their profits, providers will try to sell more resource units by increasing the quantity available for sale. Such market strategies can be implemented rapidly only if scarcity is 1) not due to depleted stocks (absolute scarcity, e.g., rhino horns), 2) not cost dependent or limited technologically in terms of extraction (relative scarcity, e.g., deep-sea oil extraction), or 3) not created by social or political barriers to production or supply (socially or politically constructed scarcity). For example, A. Sen (1992) shows that famines are events whose origins are, above all, political. Correlatively, such scarcity is often limited in time and space. This mechanism encourages the withdrawal of even more resource units. If the maximisation of extraction exceeds the threshold of renewability, it can endanger the very existence of the resource (absolute scarcity). Moreover, the use maximisation of a resource increases waste generation and the destruction of other resources that perhaps had not been perceived as such previously (e.g., the absorptive and regenerative capacity of natural milieus: water, air, land). The market, therefore, creates resources that it does not govern and that evade it despite being essential to it (Pillet, 1993). Paradoxically, it is by destroying the natural world that we become cognisant

---

[2] The term "user-actor" is used in reference to actors who use a good or service of a resource. They may simply be a user of the resource or they may simultaneously be another type of actor such as owners, regulators, administrators, public authorities, etc.

of the life that characterises it and it is by increasing wastes that we become aware of their negative effects on natural resources. Thus scarcity often triggers the economic and socio-political recognition of resources.

Rivalries and conflicts

Whether it is objective, socially perceived or politically constructed, scarcity is the principal cause of conflicts that arise between user-actors of resources. These conflicts can occur on three principal levels:

- Between users (or groups of users) of a single good or service: situations of this type were the first to be studied by institutional economists given their relative simplicity and their potential to be formalised in models of self-organised local arrangements (Ostrom, 1990).
- Between users (or groups of users) of different goods or services, the use of one undermining the use of the other. The two types of uses may be exploitative (e.g., competition between users of water for irrigation or for the production of hydroelectricity) or one of the two uses may be protective (e.g., the use of water for the production of hydroelectricity *vs.* maintaining a minimum volumetric flow in rivers to ensure the survival of aquatic species).
- Between users of goods and services furnished by different resources: the farmer who eliminates a hedge to intensify production damages the landscape and the flora/fauna resource.

Insofar that conflicts cannot be regulated at the level of the resource perimeter by the user-actors themselves (resulting in what institutional economists call Common Pool Resource Institutions), the establishment of solutions to these conflicts generally necessitates a political process resulting in the creation of a legal framework that regulates the appropriation of the goods and services that generate conflicts.

Use regulation

The term "regulation" may have countless meanings but they all imply restricting or enabling (private) choice by imposing (public) rules (Eberlein, 1999). In this paper, the regulation of a resource refers to the process of rule making in connection not only with governmental activities related to the resource but also more broadly to the totality of resource governance.

The objective of the resource regimes framework developed by Peter Knoepfel and his team is to specify an analytical framework that enables the use and protection regulations that govern the actions of users of the resource to be understood. This framework has already been presented elsewhere (Knoepfel et al., 2001; Knoepfel et al., 2007; Gerber et al., 2008); therefore, we will not enter its exposition here and will leave the reader to refer to the source texts. We will, however, highlight three principal points that will guide us in the presentation of artificial resources.

1) The two sides of resource regulation: *public policy and property rights.* Property titles constitute the legal recognition of the right held by the owner a resource (or a good or service). This right would give the owner all-power on the thing possessed if it were not limited by public law whose *raison d'être* is to guarantee the predominance of the public interest. The users of resources rely on property titles (private law) and/or on norms resulting from public policy (public law) to defend their interests on the resource.[3] The regulation of resource uses, therefore, must be considered at the intersection of property rights and public policies.
2) The two dimensions of the characterisation of the resource institutional regime: *extent and coherence.* The institutional regimes framework proposes two concepts to qualify the state of regulation of a particular resource:
   - Relative extent is defined as the number of uses explicitly regulated by the regime in relation to the total number of uses that actually exist. The higher the extent, the less the uses remain free-for-all, but the more the coherence between regulations is difficult to maintain.
   - The criterion of coherence depends on the content of and the relationship between the different regulations established by the regime. It refers to the degree of coordination between the different regulations affecting the use of a resource (Kissling-Näf and Varone 2000; Knoepfel et al. 2007; Gerber et al. 2008). The internal coherence of the property rights system describes the degree of precision of the definition of the property rights system (an example of incoherence would be a situation where several actors claim landownership for a same parcel). The internal coherence of public policies describes the degree of coordination between policies governing the use and protection of natural resources (e.g. incoherencies between use and exploitation policies). External coherence describes the mode of connection between property rights and public policies. It particularly depends on the correspondence between the target groups of the policy and the holders of property rights (This correspondence is lacking when policies address target groups that do not have use rights and whose eventual changes in behaviour do not have any real effect on the actual uses of the resource). In section 4.3, we discuss a new dimension of coherence: institutional coherence. All forms of coherence are a measure of the contradictions among the regulations of an institutional regime. Thus, the more we observe a heightened resistance that is characteristic of inalienable rights held by actors, the more the coordination of rights becomes difficult and conflicts become numerous.

[3] It is evident that social norms, ways and customs, habits, but also customary law or non-written rules equally influence the room for manœuvre of the resource users. Nonetheless, we postulate that even in contexts where these norms play a larger role than in Western Europe, they always do so in relation to a framework provided by state action or inaction, the State continuing to play a structuring role, even if it is a negative or implicit one.

3) The link between the qualification of a regime and the sustainability of the resource. Based on a precise qualification of the regime using the concepts of extent and coherence, the following fundamental hypothesis can be proposed: the higher the extent and the coherence of a particular resource regime, the better the guarantee that the uses of the resources will be sustainable. Until now, this hypothesis has shown to be relevant for different resources in different contexts: thus far it has been used for the analysis of water, forests, land (Varone et al., 2002; Knoepfel et al., 2003; Nahrath, 2003), landscape (Gerber, 2006) and air (Savary, 2008).

Application of the resource-based approach to artificial resources

In this chapter, we will examine how the concept of resource, presented above in reference to natural resources, can be transposed to four artificial resources. In each of the cases, we begin by proposing a resourcial definition of the object considered, followed by describing the state of recognition of these objects in terms of resources (process of social construction). Next we mention some of the main user-actors of the resource as well as their potential rivalries and conflicts, and finally we present a few elements of regulation.

Housing stocks

The artificial resource housing stock is a secondary resource created by means of human production from the fundamental resources found in the categories of social, manufactured, natural and human capital[4]. It is defined as all collective housing buildings belonging to a single owner, regardless of whether the buildings are located in a single neighbourhood or throughout a region (Nicol & Knoepfel, 2008).[5] Since the stockowner is the key actor without whom other user-actors' regulated use rights to the goods and services of housing could not exist, this definition allows us to exhaustively address the wide variety of competing uses derived from the stock. Thus, a housing stock becomes an evolving entity that can grow, shrink and change as a function of the uses derived from it, uses that extend far beyond just shelter

[4] From the Four Capitals Model of sustainability. A "capital" refers to the sum total of resources belonging to it: social capital is everything that makes a group of human beings richer than the sum of their individual qualities; manufactured capital is composed of all resources produced by humans; natural capital is composed of all natural resources with the exception of human beings; human capital is the sheer number of human beings as well as the different qualities of each human individual. For a good definition, refer to SRD Tools.

[5] The research on housing stocks is the result of a three-year project *(Institutional regimes for sustainable collective housing)* funded by the National Research Programme 54 of the Swiss National Science Foundation in which the evolution of the institutional regime and the sustainability of various types of collective housing (cooperative, public, private) were analysed and compared in Switzerland, Germany and Spain.

to include investment, energy and water demand, urban design and demand for schools and other institutional services (Figure 2).

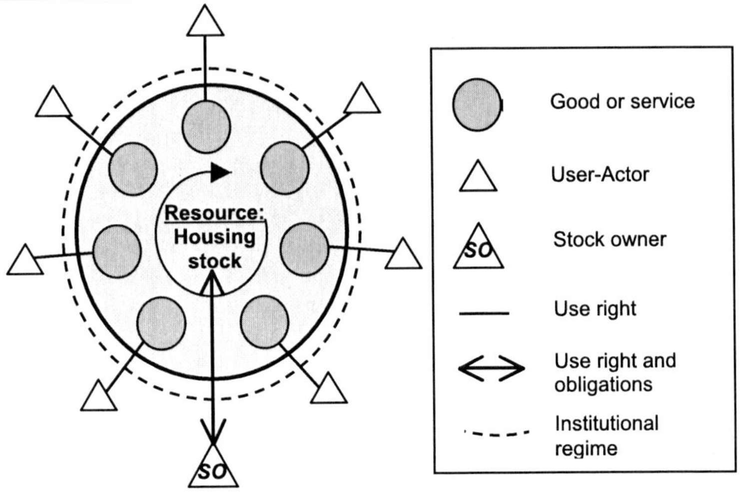

List of Housing Stock Goods and Services

RS Residential

RS 1 Living Space

RS 2 Indoor climate & technical services

NR Non-Residential

NR 1 Non-residential space

NR 2 Collective indoor space

NR 3 Functional indoor space

NR 4 Collective outdoor space

PF Production Factor

PF 1 Capital investment

PF 2 Land investment

PF 3 Labour investment

US Utility services

US 1 Energy demand

US 2 Material storage and sink

US 3 Material source

US 4 Water sink

US 5 Water source

UF Urban Function

UF 1 Design of urban space

UF 2 Demand for transit infra-structure

UF 3 Demand for institutional services

UF 3 Demand for goods and services

NM Nonmaterial

NM 1 Solving general housing needs

NM 2 Solving non-housing needs

NM 3 Shaping the landscape

NM 4 Social and cultural diversity

NM 5 Conservation & transmis-sion of values

Figure 2 The housing stock as a resource listing the different categories of goods and services to which user-actors have use rights or, in the absence of regulation, which they appropriate.

This definition based on ownership is counterintuitive. In fact, the acceptance of housing as an artificial resource of any kind – let alone one that is based on ownership and not geographical location – is still in its infancy. Ironically, although legislation does not specifically refer to housing stocks as resources, the stockowner-centred definition best reflects the state of current legislation on housing. The wide range of the housing stock's goods and services touch upon a multitude of areas such as urban planning, housing assistance, construction standards, investment and energy provision. By defining the resource housing stock in this way, we are able to apply the institutional regimes analysis to identify those regulations that influence the stockowners to manage their stock, and user-actors to use the goods and services, more or less sustainably.

Fundamental resources constitute the foundation on which housing stocks exist and are renewed. They are introduced into the system by user-actors whose principal activities depend upon the use of the goods and services of both the housing stock and the fundamental resources. These actors are not limited to the building owners and their tenants, but also comprise a broad range of stakeholders (e.g., mortgage lenders, renovators, and waste disposal service providers) who have various interests in the non-housing goods and services that housing stocks provide. Thus, the mortgage lender (the user-actor) requires capital (the fundamental resource derived from manufactured capital) to be in a position to use the housing stock's investment potential (the service); similarly, for a municipal utility service to sell water to a housing stock, i.e., use the stock's service "water sink", it requires a water source from which it can pump. Without these actors' uses of the goods and services of both fundamental resources and the housing stock, the latter could not exist or at the very least would quickly physically disintegrate.

Use conflicts can occur at the level of both the housing stock and the fundamental resources. A typical example of the former would be the conflict that can occur when the goods and services that are important for living (e.g., the living space and technical services used by tenants) are treated as secondary to the non-housing goods and services of a housing stock. For instance, when the use of a stock's investment potential by an investor with short-term profit objectives is prioritised over the use of living space by tenants (i.e., the main purpose of the stock is for investment and not for living), renovations that maintain the physical integrity of the flats may be insufficient or too infrequent. Other use-conflicts can occur at the level of fundamental resources that have direct effects on housing. For example, during and shortly after the Second World War housing construction in Switzerland slowed to a trickle due in part to cement shortages that were the result of competing uses of the raw materials (i.e., the fundamental resources derived from natural capital) which were diverted to the war effort.

The behaviours of stock owners and user-actors are constrained by an extensive set of regulations that describe the conditions under which the housing stock's goods and services can be exploited. Thus, regulations include the property rights, contracts and public policies that govern its broad range of goods and services, and therefore can range from, for instance, immigration to environmental protection to zoning. The inclusion of contracts as a separate type of regulation is particularly important to this artificial resource. In the housing institutional regime, the right for parties to draw up a contract stems from the property rights of the stockowner; without ownership of the stock, there can be no contracts. As long as they conform to the law, contracts can contain any number of stipulations and it is the effects of these stipulations on the behaviour of the different actors that are of interest in regards to guaranteeing the sustainable management of the resource.

Landscape

According to the European Landscape Convention, landscape can be defined as "an area, *as perceived by people*, whose character is the result of the action and interaction of natural and/or human factors" (Council of Europe 2001, emphasis added). Thus, due to its cultural layer and its determining relation to human aesthetic perceptions and the valuation process, which is in turn affected by cultural, social and psychological dimensions, landscape cannot simply be reduced to a natural resource (Bourassa 1991). Landscape may be understood as the sensitive and symbolic relationship of a society with space and nature (Berque, 1990; Cosgrove, 2002; Trepl & Voigt, 2005). This relationship arises when a group of observers (landscape users) assigns a special meaning to the elements of the environment that they consider important on the basis of their expectations, current fads, contemporary interests and their cultural background (Fig. 1). Thus landscape corresponds to the mental interconnection of the different resources that constitute the physical basis of landscape (referred to in this paper as: "fundamental resources", which include water, soil, fauna, buildings etc.) by a group of observers who, thanks to their shared cultural background, ascribe a specific sense to the whole (Rodewald et al., 2005).

By distinguishing landscape from its material basis (fundamental resources), the proposed definition avoids considering landscape as a "super-resource" that includes all others. This more limited definition of landscape enables the development of a framework to understand more precisely the games and strategies of actors since it distinguishes between user-actors of the landscape and those who are users of its fundamental resources but whose actions have an impact on the landscape. The distinction is important in as much as the landscape is an emerging resource: whereas certain actors believe that the landscape must be managed as a (threatened) resource, others understand it as an environmental given largely independent of human action on its milieu. Nonetheless, this process of social construction of the resource landscape has accelerated since the middle of the 1990s with the first discussions aiming to introduce in Switzerland the instrument of regional natural parks. These sanction a resourcial approach according to which the landscape must be managed by specialised and local management organisations.

Three types of actors who revolve around the resource landscape can be highlighted: (1) observers of the landscape who "consume" the resource (e.g., tourists, nature lovers and city dwellers), (2) the providers of landscape services who serve as intermediaries between the landscape and the consumers by either providing access, organising trips, creating publicity (e.g., tourist offices, hotels, tour operators and lift operators) or shaping fundamental resources to produce a particular impact on landscape (e.g. architects, landscape designers, town planners), and (3) the producers of the material basis of the landscape who upkeep the configuration of the fundamental resources that generate the landscape (e.g., farmers, developers and engineers).

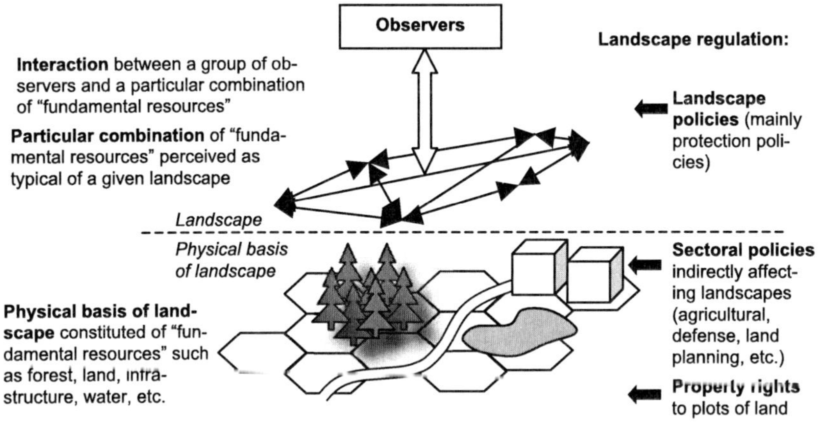

Figure 3 Breaks down graphically the definition by the European Landscape Convention, which states that landscape is "an area, as perceived by people". We introduced the term "fundamental resource" to refer to the physical resources constitutive of a given area, i.e. of the physical basis of landscape. According to this approach, a landscape is a particular spatial combination of fundamental resources to which a group of observers assigns a special meaning thanks to its shared cultural background. Through this process, it identifies this combination as a landscape service. Regulation of landscapes can be direct (landscape policies) or through their physical basis (property rights and mostly sectoral policies).

This typology of actors of the landscape allows landscape conflicts to be identified. One example of a common rivalry is that which opposes the observers and the producers of the material basis of the landscape, the latter being accused of not taking the landscape into account when acting upon its fundamental resources. Another rivalry can oppose the observers and the providers when the cost for access to the landscape is considered excessive.

Faced with these conflicts, regulation of the uses is often needed to defend the observers of the landscape who are on the whole much less protected by the law than the providers or the producers of the material basis who can assert their property titles on the fundamental resources.

Public roads domain

The domain of public roads is constituted by a decision of the legislative authority to allocate a part of the land to common use for travel. Unlike the resources housing stocks and landscape, public roads are not a secondary resource dependant on fundamental resources, but they are a substitute of the corresponding part of the resource land. The two natural resources land and air, however, are directly related to roads. These three resources influence each other. The use of their goods and services can produce rivalries and necessitate coordination (e.g., air for breathing *vs.* travelling on a road with a motorised vehicle).Whereas other goods belonging to the State, such as schools, restrict access to certain segments of the population, access to the goods and services of the public domain are free for one and all, in accordance with public policy rules (Knapp, 1991). Furthermore, in addition to resources that belong to the "natural" public domain by virtue of their general and abstract character (e.g., regions inhospitable to agriculture, such as glaciers), other groups, among them roads, are part of the artificial public domain because they are created specifically with this goal. The latter is attributed a social function by a specific juridical act. Thus, three conditions are associated to the definition of the artificial public domain, notably public roads: the public authorities must acquire the property of the resource, they must develop it, and finally they must assign to it a specific use (Moor, 1992).

The social construction of the resource is linked in its entirety to the appearance followed by the rapid expansion of cars beginning at the start of the 20th century. Roads are firstly what allowed for the disappearance of earth and stone pathways – along with their infernal dust – that had existed until then in cities. With the arrival of automobiles, roads radically transformed from a mix of functions, from trade (place of commerce), social (place of chatter), to recreation (place of play), to a mono-functional space serving uniquely the constant stream of cars. Today, the increase of road congestion and of pollution once again brings to the forefront the question of mix of functions of this part of the public domain.

The above issue refers to the user-actors of roads and to their use conflicts: 1) Motorists and those who drive motorised two-wheel vehicles are certainly in the majority and by far make the most intensive use of the resource. 2) Users of public transportation have little by little regained their status by means of roads dedicated to buses and trams or by the regulation of traffic signals but object most notably to traffic jams. 3) Cyclists are at times protected by designated cycling routes present in cities since the 1900s but are perpetually threatened by cars. 4) Pedestrians disrupt the other uses when they leave the sidewalks, common today since their invention in the 19th century, to cross the road – how careless! – to reach the other side. 5) To this list we can add, on the one hand, local inhabitants who usually take sides with public transportation, cyclists and pedestrians to decry the nuisances of motorised traffic, and on the other hand, local retailers who conversely are allied with motorists and motorised two-wheel vehicles and who justify the necessity of allowing clients to travel to come to them.

The regulation of these conflicts between actors is addressed by public policy known as the traffic code. It allows the rules of behaviour to be set to make the cohabitation of users feasible. From the perspective of use rights, the fact that the resource belongs to the public domain forbids actors from exercising the right of individual property. It is for this reason that the applicable regime is the one of "common use", allowing each and all, at all times, to use the resource. Reality, however, withstands this theory. Certain users are simply incompatible with each other. For example, during a street demonstration it is impossible to allow cars to circulate at the same time. This is why "accrued use" completes the notion of common use[6]. This criteria sets the conditions for which a request for use must be made to the authority who must then give its authorisation. We refer to "private use" in the case where the appropriation of the use is permanent (e.g., café terrace) (Moor 1992: 287).

Information

The RIR framework as applied to the other resources addressed in this article – which all have a relationship with land as a common feature – has not yet been used for information. This section, therefore, constitutes a first attempt to apply the concept of resource and institutional regime, thereby providing a line of enquiry to be further explored.

Information, as it is construed here, is defined as all created information recorded onto any type of physical medium (whether it be analogue or digital) at any stage of its life cycle (active, intermediate, final): in the sense of Carol Couture (Couture et al. 1988 : 54, Rousseau and Couture 1994 : 41-57), it is all recorded organic information.[7] This information may be produced by a public or a private body or by any other producer. It can possess a potential or known patrimonial value and, consequently, is likely to be selected for long-term preservation. Once the appropriate procedures for management and preservation are in place, information that has been selected for its archival value comes to the end of its life cycle in an establishment that has an archival function and thus becomes a constitutive part of the memory for which it was selected (Halbwachs, 1950). Once processed, analysed and understood, it transforms into knowledge, the basis of our society's functioning (Prax, 2000: 35). Information so defined is thus composed of interrelated elements and, once processed, is the source of knowledge. For this reason, it constitutes the result of a practice and possesses a strong economic connotation.

Traditionally, information thus defined is understood to be the superposition of elements that present individual characteristics (e.g., digital data, published documents or audiovisual documents). The uses that are made of them and the actors who exploit them vary in time as a function of the stage of the lifecycle of the relevant elements. Thus, regulations whose

---

6 We note that even if the flow of automobiles makes co-existence impossible in many cases, from a legal point of view it is not considered as an accrued or private use, which, in our opinion, weakens the practical scope of this triple distinction.

7 The terminology designating the object of study has yet to be established at both the practical and legislative levels, since we group together objects that are traditionally distinct and belong to the jurisdiction of different bodies (archives, libraries, document control services, etc.) and professions (archivists, librarians, records managers). Many expressions are used and a single expression may designate different objects. Thus we find terms such as "information", "documents" and "records" that are expanded to include more than their meaning.

objectives are to ensure a balance between existing rivalries and the protection of use rights is dense, very complex and gives rise to a fragmented vision of the regime.

Recently, information has begun to be considered as an artificial resource by pioneering public actors[8] : it is thus considered as a whole. This constitutes an enormous challenge, since information is multiform but – with the advent of the information and knowledge society – has nonetheless the advantage of enabling information to be viewed macroscopically as an ensemble, thereby facilitating the identification of recurrent elements. In accordance with this new perspective, we can identify two groups of users of the resource: public actors who exploit information primarily in the active and intermediate stages, i.e., as it undergoes modifications; and "everyone", who can exploit information in its final stage insofar as it is accessible. As with the resources housing stocks and landscape, information is a secondary resource created from fundamental resources: "language", which produces the capacity to dispose of codes and appropriate physical media for communicating and establishing information ; "reason", which produces the capacity to judge the archival value of a document; "space & time", which is the resource responsible for the capacity to store information; and "public space", which allows information to be made available to and valued by users. Amongst these four fundamental resources, which will not be further developed here, the most important is language (Knoepfel & Olgiati, 2007). For example, in the active stage, the capacity for information to renew and its potential for sustainability are notably linked to the capacity to produce codes that are understandable by humans or by machines; in a final stage, they are linked to the capacity to produce media able to preserve information in time. When a code (for example a computer language) or a medium is under-used, it has a tendency to disappear very quickly, which from then on prevents certain types of information from renewing in the form of stock. The disappearance of a code or a physical medium can have the effect of a use rivalry between groups of private actors (buyers) who are always on the lookout for the latest: the private market (producers of codes, systems, computer programmes, physical media, etc.) thus has an interest in limiting the lifespan of its products. This rivalry in the use of a fundamental resource, therefore, has direct effects on the resource information.

Existing rivalries and the regulations necessary for managing the exploitation of information vary not only as a function of information's lifecycle but also occur at different levels. Whereas direct regulations that originate in public policies try to follow changes in time and have a tendency to be specialised according to the domains (regulations specific to substantial public policies) and to the lifecycle stages (active, intermediary, final), the regulations concerning property rights are concrete and permanent and approach those of private law (copyright, intellectual property, protection of

---

[8] Library and Archives Canada, most notably, designates information for which it has responsibility with the term "information resources".

secrets). Amongst the indirect regulations, the most important concern the fundamental resource "language": if they are derived from property rights, they are recorded, for example, in licences; if they are derived from public policies, they are recorded in charters or in norms that are sometimes established at the international level or, again, in regulations specific to substantial public policies.

Synthesis

Although the four examples of artificial resources presented here are relatively different from one another, the juxtaposition of regulations that characterise them (Table 1) allows various interesting aspects to be highlighted.

Resources	Regulation			
	Direct (regulation pertaining to the secondary resource)		Indirect (via the fundamental resource)	
	Public policies	Property rights	Public policies	Property rights
Housing stocks	Particularly housing assistance and tenancy rights, but also urban planning, monument protection, and all others with a direct bearing on the stock.	Dictates ownership type of the stock (e.g. cooperative, foundation, real estate company), which has a direct effect on management strategies. Contracts often bridge fundamental and secondary resources, e.g., energy and water provision, mortgages.	Policies regarding environmental protection, immigration, pensions, banking, and all others with an indirect bearing on the stock.	Land property, surface rights, concessions on water, etc. Contracts often bridge fundamental and secondary resources, e.g., energy and water provision, mortgages.
Landscape	Mainly protective regulations (e.g. UNESCO Inventories, European Landscape Convention, national/regional/local landscape legislation), but also tourism	Absence, but appropriation strategies through other means: control of strategic plots of land, access regulation, intellectual property of landscape representations (labels)	Agriculture, tourism, land use planning, infrastructure, defence, etc.	Land property (incl. accession principle*), concession on water, intellectual property on the image / representation of fundamental resources
Roads	Traffic code Law on the public domain	State property. Criteria defining common, accrued and private use of the public domain. Freedom of movement	Interactions with natural resources: Air pollution Soil protection Land use planning (road planning) Noise reduction policy	Interactions with natural resources Land property
Information	Active and intermediate Information: Electronic business management (GEVER), NPM, specific regulations of substantial public policies. Final information : Policy on culture (protection of documentary patrimony) and policy on archives	Copyright; intellectual property; protection of secrets	Charters, norms, specific regulations on substantial public policies (e.g., geoinformation)	Licenses

* According to the accession principle, all immovable elements located on a plot of land (buildings, trees, etc.) belong to the landowner (unless otherwise stated in the law).

Table 1 Summary of direct and indirect regulation on four artificial resources.

In three of the four examples presented (with the exception of roads), we observe that artificial resources are the result of a superposition of fundamental and secondary resources. This signifies that an important part of their regulation is made in an indirect manner. This characteristic is a distinctive one of artificial resources in contrast to natural resources, explaining therefore their higher degree of complexity.

The comparative table shows that direct and indirect regulations by public policies – whether they apply to secondary or fundamental resources – take the form of laws, property titles or other identifiable formal regulations (mainly contracts). These are the object of a regular process of evaluation and, consequently, are modified in time in relation to the evolution of the resource.

From the perspective of secondary resource regulation by property rights, it is important to highlight the importance of property. The above examples show that, as opposed to what one might assume, artificial resources are no less affected by regulation via property titles than natural resources. As such, in addition to "classical" property in accordance to the civil code, intellectual property plays an important role (landscape, information). Thus, we observe a transposition of strategies of regulation coming from natural resources onto secondary resources: to make up for the absence of property rights on secondary resources, specific laws had to be developed. In the case of landscapes, despite an absence of property rights, users develop different indirect strategies to control it anyway in a more or less exclusive way ("privatisation" of access through cable cars or panoramic restaurants, control of strategic plots of land such as viewpoints). These regulatory mechanisms between fundamental and secondary resources are therefore surprisingly similar. Furthermore, even in the case of landscape and roads where individual property does not exist in law, we observe appropriation mechanisms adopted by actors.

From the perspective of fundamental resource regulation by property rights, the land owner plays a central role as much for housing as for landscape by virtue of the principle of accession (*cf. supra*) linked to the right of ownership of the ground. We observe that, by analogy, such a "principle of accession" exists equally in the case of other resources composed themselves of two levels of resources (fundamental and secondary). As much for landscape, housing or information, ownership of land, buildings or physical media gives broader rights on their respective secondary resources.

We note, therefore, that the actors that are best protected by law are those that use fundamental resources. This induces an increased risk of lack of coherence in the artificial resources regime that is all the more difficult to resolve since the relevant public policies are numerous and disparate. We thus repeatedly observe the necessity to develop informal management structures able to increase coherence. Even more so than for natural resources, a reflection on governance of the resource at large is necessary.

Added value and challenges of a resource-based approach applied to artificial resources

The application of the resource institutional regimes model to resources such as housing stocks, landscape, roads and information allows us to make a first assessment of the added value and challenges of the approach when it is expanded to include artificial resources. Our comments focus primarily on analytical aspects.

Analytical added value of the resource-based approach

The *raison d'être* of the RIR analytical framework is to provide a structure that enables the principal sources of regulation of a resource to be uncovered. As the examples in the previous section show, the RIR framework fulfils its role when it is applied to artificial resources. In as much as it enables different uses of the resources and different forms of their regulation to be highlighted, the application of this analytical framework would seem appropriate, all the more so since it produces interesting results for both the researcher and the practitioner by structuring diverse regulatory elements. Indeed, these disparate elements that characterise the regimes of artificial resources can originate in public policies or property rights without any apparent *a priori* relationship. The RIR framework clarifies these links by showing, for example, that tenancy rights, the price of cement and taxes on wastewater are all elements that make up the regime of housing stocks.

It is worth determining whether the advantages of the resource-based approach brought to light by natural resources (Knoepfel et al., 2001, Knoepfel et al., 2007; Gerber et al., 2008) are equally applicable to artificial resources. We can respond that at least three advantages appear as valid for artificial as they are for natural resources, although the third depends on further empirical examinations.

The first obvious added value for both natural and artificial resources consists in the ability of the approach to go beyond the limits of sectoral analyses of public policies. In this sense, the framework allows the problem to be addressed above and beyond set administrative territories and sectoral policy logic (Nahrath, 2007). Taking housing stocks for example, to be able to correctly analyse a particular situation the interaction between such disparate areas as investment and water demand must be considered. Additionally, we observe that the relevant scale of analysis for housing stocks is sometimes the neighbourhood, sometimes the agglomeration, sometimes greater, sometimes smaller, but never corresponds to the strict administrative boundaries of the commune. The RIR framework considers the whole area of the resource rather than just administrative or sectoral boundaries.

This ability to surpass sectoral and territorial approaches originates directly from the starting point of the resource-based approach, i.e., the analysis of the rivalries and use conflicts between actors who are using the resource, managing it or just concerned by its condition. To explain these conflicts, the approach goes beyond the perspectives of property rights and public policy analysis by combining the lessons of these fields of study. To pursue and defend their interests, actors mobilise either property rights on the resource or rules stemming from policies. Indeed implementation of policies either limits or upholds property rights in order to solve a particular public problem for the sake of the public interest. The RIR framework usefully describes resource users in the light of tension between property rights and public policies: both are important for understanding the origin of use conflicts and finding new ways for mitigating them.

A third added value of the approach resides in its contribution to the sustainability of resource uses. Research conducted until now on natural resources (*cf. supra*) have shown that the propensity of uses to be sustainable or not is linked to the level of extent and coherence of the regime. If there exists no indication *a priori* that call into question this hypothesis, it is clear that empirically solid studies will continue to validate it for artificial resources[9].

Analytical challenges

Despite the added values described above, the application of the RIR framework to artificial resources can present a few challenges.

The artificial resource examples described in this contribution are characterised by a large complexity. Multiple forms of regulation come into play since they exist at different levels (direct or indirect regulations in accordance with whether they apply to fundamental or secondary resources) thereby contributing to an increase in the number of elements to be analysed. As seen in the example of information, the use of the RIR underscores such complex forms of regulation that the situation remains unclear, thus creating an impetus for the development of new strategies such as the analysis of "partial regimes", choosing deliberately to exclude some fundamental resources form the analysis.

---

[9] The following projects on infrastructural resources are currently in progress:

June 2005 – March 2009: Institutional Regimes for Sustainable Collective Housing Stocks (P. Knoepfel principal investigator, co-investigators N. Kohler, Institut für Industrielle Bauproduktion, University of Karlsruhe and J. Subirats, Autonomous University of Barcelona), PNR 54, FNS Division IV.

June 2009 – December 2011: co-investigators of the research module Institutional Regimes for Resource Management in the framework of the Pro*Doc "Public Administration" (P. Knoepfel IDHEAP, F. Varone University of Geneva), financing of a doctoral thesis.

June 2009 – December 2011: direction (co-investigators : U. Weidmann (Swiss Federal Institut of Technology Zurich), G. Pflieger (Swiss Federal Institute of Technology Lausanne), F. Varone (University of Geneva)) of the project Impacts of market liberalization on the sustainability of network industries : a comparative analysis of the civil aviation and railways sectors in Switzerland, FNS Division I.

However, this feature also enables a recurring phenomenon to be identified, namely that users of secondary resources are less well legally protected than users of fundamental resources. We therefore observe an asymmetry in the degree of legal protection on which users can rely to defend their particular use of the secondary resource. As a consequence of this complex situation, the governance of artificial resources is often fragmented. This means that use rights and management responsibilities are rarely shared by the same actors and that the use of fundamental and secondary resources remains weakly coordinated. This problem is addressed in the following section, which proposes a way for the RIR framework to better integrate the issue of resource governance.

Both the definition and the uses of artificial resources change in time, occasionally very rapidly (e.g., a road can frequently change its official designated use or can be subject repeatedly to different uses). Public policies, therefore, must be adapted if they are to continue remedying the public problems for which they were originally constituted. If the change in use occurs too rapidly, informal regulatory systems can be established. In their analytical work, researchers must account for the rapid evolution of the resource by being attentive when forming the boundaries of their object of analysis, otherwise they risk analysing a reality that either does not exist or no longer exists. The resource information, for example, is composed of elements that change very quickly in time with the effect of constantly eliminating and creating new problems and challenges: in the field of communication, information shared via BlackBerry in administration offices offer possibilities other than those of traditional mail exchanges, but also present new questions. The conception of an artificial resource is also susceptible to change in space, since it is anchored in a specific territorial context. Political recognition of a resource can therefore vary in accordance with the regions considered.

We observe, therefore, that the complexity that characterises artificial resources as well as their aptitude to be modified more or less rapidly in time and in space requires a greater effort of abstraction than is perhaps required for natural resources. This effort, critical for understanding the functioning of the resource, brings with it another risk: that of distancing the researcher from the understanding that public actors have of the same resource. If, in addition to an analytical approach, the RIR framework is used for normative purposes – with the objective of proposing a more relevant way of dealing with the regulation of such and such a resource – the close cooperation of public actors is necessary to ensure reciprocal understanding.

Governance issues - new considerations for the RIR framework

The confrontation of the concepts of extent and coherence (section 2.2) with the empirical reality of artificial resources has enabled the two concepts to be developed in a way that better acknowledges the forms of governance of the resource by introducing the concept of *institutional coherence*[10]. In practice,

---

[10] This term was used for the first time in the context of a resource-based approach by Rodewald et al., 2005 without having been the object of a definition. Gerber (2005:

the above artificial resource examples illustrate the numerous attempts in progress to improve unsatisfactory situations by creating new resource management structures: regional nature parks for landscape, tenant and stock owner associations, consultation groups dealing with the management of transit (on the public domain), etc. In the language of the resource-based approach, these initiatives try to tighten the governance of resources by ideally allowing user-actors to engage in discourse over and above the political and legal institutional barriers that separate them: users of secondary resources *vs.* users of fundamental resources, owners *vs.* non-owners, residents *vs.* non-residents, authorities *vs.* "civil society", local authorities *vs.* cantonal or national authorities, etc.[11] The hypothesis that supports such initiatives is that a better coordination (vertical or horizontal) between the actors responsible for the implementation of different politico-administrative programmes but also a better knowledge of the actors amongst themselves enable modes of better coordinated use to be identified. This enhanced coordination relies on the improvement of effective opportunities of meeting each other, the bringing together of politico-administrative actors with user-actors and the possibility of actors expressing themselves on the fate of the resource for which they hold certain rights. The solutions found may be formalised in contracts or regulations, but may also remain informal. The concept of institutional coherence precisely aims to take into account this form of making uses coherent.

Whereas substantial coherence (regrouping the internal and external coherence as defined in section 2.2) measures the compatibility of rights – it being understood that these rights can originate in public policies, property titles and informal rights – institutional coherence takes into consideration the existence of mechanisms that guarantee a reciprocal coordination amongst the holders of use rights, or even compensation in the event of damages to the resource, allowing for the institutional stabilisation of the uses.

It "takes into consideration the mechanisms that enable the resolution of different rivalries than those implied by the (substantial) configuration of rights and the public policies mobilised by actors in conflict" (translated from Gerber 2005). When they take place between competing users of a natural resource, these compensation and coordination mechanisms can result in arrangements that are far more original and innovative than the measures prescribed by public policies or the system of property rights. Institutional coherence aims to take into account the fact that in the process of resolving rivalries, it is not necessarily the actors who hold the strongest rights, i.e., those of real estate, who win in the end (Gerber & Savary, in press).

122-123) refined the definition in his study on the forms of regulation on the resource landscape.

[11] As this section presents it, the concept of institutional coherence not only describes the coordination of public or semi-public actors in charge of the production of policy outputs *(political administrative arrangement)*, but also includes the users of the resource who can mobilise legally protected rights in order to defend their particular use interests.

Landscape is a good example of a resource whose complex nature makes it difficult to regulate coherently. The case of woody pasturelands, common in the Jura Mountains, illustrates this point very well: despite their agricultural character, they are legally considered forests. While forest legislation is implemented by cantons (within a strict federal framework), farming policy is strongly centralized at the federal level, which is responsible for direct payments to farmers. There is a strong incentive for the latter to clear their woody pastures in order to get more direct payments, although it is illegal under forest law. So many woody pasturelands are abandoned and transform slowly into forests. This might be acceptable if they were not so attractive to tourism and so biodiverse. How should all these interests (federal, cantonal, local and resource users) be brought together in order to preserve woody pastures despite a highly incoherent regime? Regional initiatives led, for example, by the Regional Park of Chasseral have shown that a mix of binding and voluntary agreements can be found locally after people have been given a platform to express and defend their interests (raising the awareness of concerned actors though information, enrolment of farmers in special forest plans preserving woody pastures, channelling of visitors' flow outside of biologically sensitive areas, etc.).[12]

Institutional coherence thus measures the potential developed by some public policies (e.g., parks policy, agglomeration polices, etc.) to attenuate the effects of disparity between use rights by reinforcing or upholding the social capital shared by a group of actors, whether they be users or regulators (administrators). These policies favour different actors learning the rules of the game and, consequently, improving – locally – the coherence of the regime. Seen in this light, the need for negotiation and participation that these new policies seek to satisfy appears to reflect the lack of substantial coherence of the regime (Knoepfel & Gerber, 2008). The observable attempts to locally improve the institutional coherence is therefore a clue to incoherent supra-local regulations, the symptoms of which actors – or at least those whose uses are the least well legally protected – try to fight. When satisfactory solutions for the actors are found, the permanent establishment of the new rules can be made by means of a substantial modification of the regime in effect (formalisation of informal rules).

Conclusion

The resource-based approach of Peter Knoepfel and his team has been used successfully for the analysis of natural resources. As the current research on

---

[12] While many examples can be given of an institutional regime where low substantial coherence can be compensated to some extent by high institutional coherence, the opposite situation is more difficult to find. A possible example might be a strictly regulated area, such as a national park, where conflicts have been settled through precise regulation (high substantial coherence) but where people do not collaborate with each other because they share different interests (low institutional coherence).

housing stocks, landscape, public roads and information clearly demonstrates, it is also well suited to the analysis of artificial resources. Although still open to other theoretical and empirical developments, the approach enables in a significant manner the resolution of the inability of environmental policies to guarantee the sustainability of resources. At the same time, it shines a new light on the combined problem of scarcity and the renewability of artificial resources.

The presentation of the institutional regimes analytical framework allows us to highlight the extent to which the approach, which seeks to understand the (dys-)functions of the system, finds its strength equally on the ground. Peter Knoepfel emphasises this practical use by defending values that make of him a researcher who never succumbs to the temptation of dishonest neutrality. Instead, it proposes avenues that seek to correct an unsustainable use situation, in the normative sense of the term. Peter Knoepfel has always considered the regimes framework in terms of an operational instrument that can also be used normatively, with the objective of proposing more sustainable forms of regulation to the political world (the case of the renaturation of the Thur river is a recent example).

We hypothesise that, ironically, despite the effort of abstraction that it requires, the conceptualisation in terms of natural and artificial resources presented in this chapter are favourably regarded by administrative actors partly because they have been accustomed – following administrative reforms – to thinking in terms of optimally using limited resources. In any case, the regimes framework has the principal pedagogical virtue of showing that optimal use concerns not only money, personnel, or available infrastructure, but also, and above all, the world that surrounds us. This pedagogical concern characterises the approach of Peter Knoepfel for whom researchers, far from being detached from the society in which they live, must be ready to wade into the fray to contribute to its change.

References

Berque, A. (1990). *Médiance, de milieux en paysages.* Géographiques. Montpellier: Reclus.

Bourassa, S.C. (1991). *The Aesthetics of Landscape.* London: Belhaven Press.

Cosgrove, D., (2002). Landscape and the European sense of sight – eyeing nature. In K. Anderson, M. Domosh, S. Pile & N. Thrift (Eds) *Handbook of Cultural Geography.* London: SAGE Publications, pp. 249–268.

Council of Europe, (2001). *European Landscape Convention.* Strasbourg : Council of Europe,.

Couture, C., Ducharme, J., & Rousseau J.-Y. (1988). L'archivistique a-t-elle trouvé son identité ? *Argus,* 17(2): 51-60.

Eberlein, B. (1999). L'État régulateur en Europe. *Revue française de science politique.* 49, 205-230.

Gerber, J.-D. (2005). *Structures de gestion des rivalités d'usage du paysage: une analyse comparée de trois cas alpins.* Écologie & Société. Zurich : Rüegger.

Gerber, J.-D., Knoepfel, P., Nahrath, S., & Varone, F. (2008). Institutional Resource Regimes: Toward Sustainability through combining Property Rights Theory and Policy Analysis. *Ecological Economics* 68: 798-809.

Gerber, J.-D., & Savary, J. (In press). Les ressources des acteurs des politiques publiques sont-elles appropriables? In P. Knoepfel (Ed). *Contributions à l'action publique.* N° 3.

Halbwachs, M. (1950). *La mémoire collective,* Paris : Presses universitaires de France.

Kissling-Näf, I., & Varone, F. (2000). *Historical Analysis of Institutional Regimes in Switzerland,* Working paper de l'IDHEAP, Chavannes-près-Renens

Knapp, B. (1991). *Précis de droit administratif,* Quatrième édition, Bâle: Helbing und Lichtenhahn

Knoepfel, P., Kissling-Näf, I., & Varone F. (Eds) (2001). *Institutionelle Regime für natürliche Ressourcen : Boden, Wasser und Wald im Vergleich.* Basel: Helbing & Lichtenhahn.

Knoepfel, P., Kissling-Naef, I., & Varone, F. (Eds.) avec la collaboration de K. Bisang, C. Mauch, S. Nahrath & E. Reynard (2003). *Institutionelle Ressourcenregime in Aktion / Régimes institutionnels de ressources naturelles en action.* Basel, Genf, München: Helbing & Lichtenhahn.

Knoepfel, P., & Olgiati, M. (2007). *Politique de la mémoire nationale. Etude principale I.* Rapport de l'IDHEAP, Chavannes-près-Renens.

Knoepfel, P. & Olgiati, M. (2009). *Politique de la mémoire nationale. Rapport final,* Rapport de l'IDHEAP, Chavannes-près-Renens.

Knoepfel, P., Nahrath, S., & Varone, F. (2007). Institutional Regimes for Natural Resources: An Innovative Theoretical Framework for Sustainability. In P. Knoepfel (Ed) *Environmental Policy Analyses. Learning from the Past for the Future – 25 Years of Research.* Berlin: Springer, pp.455-506.

Knoepfel, P., & Gerber, J.-D. (2008). *Institutionelle Landschaftsregime – Lösungsansatz für Landschaftskonflikte / Institutional Landscape Regimes – An Approach to the Resolution of Landscape Conflicts.* Zürich : Vdf Hochschulverlag.

Moor, P. (1992). *Droit administratif, L'organisation des activités administratives et les biens de l'Etat,* Vol. III. Berne: éd. Stämpfli et Cie

Nahrath, S. (2003). *La mise en place du régime institutionnel de l'aménagement du territoire en Suisse entre 1960 et 1990.* Thèse réalisée à l'IDHEAP. Lausanne : Université de Lausanne [http://www2.unil.ch/cyberdocuments/].

Nahrath, S. (2007). Entre transformations sectorielles et recompositions territoriales : introduction à la partie III. In A. Faure, J.-P. Leresche, P. Muller & S. Nahrath (Dirs.) *Action publique et changements d'échelles : les nouvelles focales du politique,* Paris : L'Harmattan (coll. Logiques Politiques), pp.169-175.

Nahrath, S., & Csikos, P. (2007). Les impacts des processus de libéralisation sur la durabilité des grands services urbains : propositions pour un nouvel agenda de recherché. *Urbia – Les Cahiers du développement urbain durable,* N°5, pp.115-140.

Nahrath, S., Csikos, P., Buchli, F., & Rieder, M. (2008). Les impacts de la régionalisation et de la libéralisation sur la durabilité du secteur ferroviaire en Suisse. *Flux – Cahiers scientifiques internationaux Réseaux et territories.* N°72/73, avril-septembre 2008, pp.49-64.

Ostrom, E. (1990). *Governing the commons: the evolution of institutions for collective action.* Cambridge: Cambridge University Press.

Nicol, L.A., & Knoepfel, P. (2008). Institutional regimes for sustainable collective housing. *Swiss Political Science Review.* 14(1): 157-180.

Pillet, G. (1993). *Économie écologique, introduction à l'économie de l'environnement et des ressources naturelles.* Genève : Georg.

Prax, J.-Y. (2000). *Le guide du Knowledge Management. Concepts et pratiques du management de la connaissance.* Paris : Dunod.

Rodewald, R., Knoepfel, P., Fossey, A., Gerber, J.-D., & Mauch, C. (2005). *Institutionelle Regime für nachhaltige Landschaftsentwicklung.* Ökologie & Gesellschaft. Zürich : Verlag Rüegger.

Rousseau, J.-Y., Couture, C. et al. (1994). *Les fondements de la discipline archivistique,* Sante-Foy : Presses de l'Université de Québec.

Savary, J. (2008). *Politiques publiques et mobilité urbaine. Analyse de processus conflictuels dans quatre villes suisses,* Zürich : Ruegger Verlag

Sen, A. (1992). *Poverty and famines : an essay on entitlement and deprivation,* Oxford : Clarendon Press

Schellenberg, Th. R. (1956). The appraisal of modern public records. *Bulletins of National Archives,* 8,133-278.

SRD Tools. Methods and tools for evaluating the impact of cohesion policies on sustainable regional development. Glossary. http://www.srdtools.info/glossary.htm

Trepl L., & Voigt A. (2005). Landschaft als Organismus. Zwischen Naturwissenschaft und Ästhetik. *Politische Ökologie.* 96: 28-30.

Varone, F. (2001). Comparaison des régimes institutionnels du sol, de l'eau et de la forêt. In P. Knoepfel, I. Kissling-Näf & F. Varone (Eds) *Institutionelle Regime für natürliche Ressourcen: Boden, Wasser und Wald im Vergleich.* Basel, Genf : Helbing & Lichtenhahn.

Varone, F., Reynard, E., Kissling-Naef, I., & Mauch, C. (2002). Institutional Resource Regimes: The Case of Water Management in Switzerland, *Integrated Assessement. An International Journal,* 3 (1):78-94.

CHAPTER 14

Indicators of Sustainable Development in Switzerland: Between Techno-scientific and Politico-normative Logics

CHRISTOPHE CLIVAZ

Introduction[1]

The question concerning the selection of long-term policy tools has been dealt with in a marginal fashion by the policy analysis specialists. The latter are more interested in the power relations between actors, the role of ideas and representations and those of institutions and organizations than in the issues associated with the choice of policy tools. This relative disinterest in the choice of tools can be explained *inter alia* by the fact that political scientists have concentrated on policy implementation and evaluation in their studies rather than on policy formulation, i.e. the phase in the policy process, during which the selection of instruments usually takes place.

In this paper, we position ourselves within the theoretical current of policy design and discuss the question concerning the development of systems of sustainability indicators (SSI) which are considered as tools for the quantification of the sustainability of public authorities. Switzerland provides the empirical terrain for the contextualization of our study which focuses specifically on the following two questions:

- How does a SSI influence the power relations between actors?
- Why and how does such a system become an instrument that is normative in scope?

In attempting to provide answers to these questions, we refer in particular to the work carried out by Peter Knoepfel. In addition to developing a model for the analysis of public policies (Knoepfel et al. 2006a), which we will refer to below, he also expressed an interest in several of his studies in the topic of local Agendas 21 and/or the evaluation of sustainability (Knoepfel et al., 2006b; Knoepfel, 2005a and 2005b; Knoepfel & Münster; 2004; DuPasquier et al., 2003).

[1] We would like to express our sincere thanks to the two editors of this volume, Stéphane Nahrath and Frédéric Varone, whose comments and suggestions helped us to improve significantly on the quality of this contribution.

The theoretical context: policy design and policy tools[2]

The focus of the policy-tools approach

The policy design approach is interested in the way in which policies are developed. Varone (1998) reveals that what is distinctive about this approach is the particular emphasis it places on the choice of policy tools, a question that constitutes a major factor in all State intervention. According to this author, the focus on the choice of tools has three major implications for policy analysis:

- the definition of a new unit of analysis: given that it is more clearly defined than the concept of a policy or action programme, the concept of a tool enables the clear identification of the dependent variable;
- the reversal of the (dependent) variable to be explained: the models based on policy implementation and evaluation consider the policy tools as an independent variable while the policy design approach sees it as a dependent variable;
- the scope limitation and clarification of the empirical observation unit which facilitates the comparative analysis of the choice of tools and, moreover, policies.

Thus, the use of tools as an access point enhances the reflexive field of policy analysis. In particular, it highlights the importance of not considering the choice of tools as a purely rational and technical process. Varone stresses that even if the tools are interchangeable from a technical point of view in terms of fulfilling one and the same policy objective, this does not apply from the political perspective as "each tool generates its own political economy: it involves a system of action that is determined and constituted by institutional structures, actors, resources and particular procedures" (Varone, 1998:71). Similarly, Lascoumes and Le Galès (2004a: 12-13) reveal that "the notion of an instrument of public action [i.e. policy tool] makes it possible to go beyond the functionalist approaches, which are primarily interested in the policy objectives, to consider public action from the perspective of the tools that structure its programmes. (...) The tool-based approach makes it possible to access dimensions of public action that are otherwise less visible. (...) Policy tools are not axiologically neutral tools and equally available. On the contrary, they carry values, and are endowed with an interpretation of the social and precise conceptions of the proposed mode of regulation."

Before discussing the political character of these tools in more detail, it makes sense here to focus for a moment on the actual definition of a policy tool.

Policy tools: definition and typologies

According to Schneider and Ingram (1990: 527) and Howlett (1991: 2), policy tools comprise all of the techniques at the disposal of governments for

---

[2] This presentation of the theoretical context is based mainly on the studies by Varone (1998) and Lascoumes & Le Galès (2004a).

the implementation of their policies. They "constitute the logical link between the social problem being dealt with and the objectives targeted by a policy" (Varone, 1998: 25). In their publication "*Gouverner par les instruments*" ("Governing through Tools"), Lascoumes & Le Galès (2004a : 13) present a more detailed definition that highlights the fact that the tools are institutions in the sociological sense of the term which structure public policies: "A policy tool constitutes a tool with which is at once technical and social and organizes specific social relations between the public authorities and their target groups based on the representations and meanings which it is endowed." Furthermore, the same authors refer to the policy tool as a "technical general-purpose tool endowed with a concrete conception of the relation between politics and society and supported by a regulative concept" (Lascoumes & Le Galès 2004a: 14). Thus, a tool is a generic instrument that may be mobilized by different sectoral policies.

Conversely, a policy or action programme generally uses several types of instruments. Since the groundbreaking study by Hood (1983) on the "Tools of government", several authors have presented typologies of policy instruments (cf. Varone, 1998: 33-36; Knoepfel et al., 2006a: 173-174). It is not our intention here to discuss the relevance of these different typologies,[3] but to present a recent one with the aim of rendering the above-presented definition of policy tools more concrete. The following table refers to the typology proposed by Lascoumes & Le Galès, who were inspired, in turn, by that defined by Hood (1983).

This typology differentiates between policy tools on the basis of the role devolved to the State and the type of legitimacy mobilized. The first two types of policy tools (legislative and regulative, economic and fiscal) correspond to the "classical" tools of State intervention while the three last ones (conventional and incentive-based, informative and communicative, norms and standards) emerged more recently as a result of the evolution of the State towards a less restrictive role and one based more on communication and negotiation. Historically, this increase in the instruments used would mark the shift from a regulative State to a propulsive State (Morand, 1991), an inciting State (Bütschi & Cattacin, 1993) or an animator State (Donzelot & Estèbe, 1994).

As we shall show in greater detail in section 4, we consider the SSI as both informative and communicative tools and as norms, standards and "best practice" tools. As informative and communicative instruments, the SSI are intended in particular to raise the awareness of all actors (elected representatives, administration, companies, NGOs, associations, population) in relation to the topic of sustainable development. By disseminating information about the level of sustainability of a public authority, they should contribute to the awareness of these actors of the challenges and problems that the latter

[3] Varone (1998: 35-36) stresses that no typology has emerged as dominant among the scientific community and presents the limitations of the different existing typologies, in particular their difficulty in facilitating the operationalization of the concept of a tool.

must face. However, the SSI also constitute norms and standards. We would like to refer here to a quotation from Lascoumes and Le Galès (2004b: 363) which, in our view, is perfectly applicable to these systems of indicators. "They [i.e. the norms and standards] are based on a mixed legitimacy which combines a scientific and technical rationale, which contributes to the neutralization of their political signification, with a democratic rationale based on their negotiated development and the cooperative processes they trigger." This link between the technical and political legitimacy of SSI is at the core of our inquiry, the nature of which will now be clarified.

Type of Instrument	Type of Political Relations	Type of Legitimacy
Legislative and Regulatory	Social Guardian State	Imposition of a General Interest by Mandated Elected Representatives
Economic and Fiscal	Wealth Producer State, and Redistributive State	Seeks Benefit to the Community Social and Economic Efficiency
Agreement-Based and Incentives-Based	Mobilizing State	Seeks Direct Involvement
Information-Based and Communication-Based	Audience democracy	Explanation of Decisions and Accountability of Actors
De Facto and De Jure Standards Best Practices	Adjustments within Civil Society Competitive Mechanisms	Mixed: Scientific/Technical, Democratically Negotiated and/or Competition, Pressure of Market Mechanisms

Source: Lascoumes & Le Galès (2007: 12)

Table 1 Typology of policy instrument.

The political nature of policy tools

As has already been stated, these tools are anything but neutral instruments without political implications. The challenges involved in the selection and "life" of the tools are multiple in nature and, without making any claim of being exhaustive, we formulate two of them in the form of two general questions which are illustrated on the basis of SSI.

How do the SSI influence the power relations between actors? There is no doubt that the choice of one tool or another does not remain without consequences for the power relations between the opposing actors. Thus Lascoumes and Le Galès (2004a: 16) reveal that the tools "determine in part the way in which the actors behave, creating uncertainties in relation to the effects of the power relations, leading to the favouring of certain actors and interests and the dismissal of others, restricting the actors and offering them resources, and acting as a vehicle for the representation of problems. Thus the social and political actors have very different capacities for intervention based on the selected tools. Once established, the latter provide political entrepreneurs with new perspectives for use and interpretation, which are unpredicted and difficult to control and thus feed into a dynamic of institutionalization (Stone et al., 2001). They determine in part the resources that may be used and by whom."

For example, local Agenda 21 processes often mobilize tools such as consultation and participation which enable "lay" actors, who do not necessarily have specific technical skills or political legitimacy, to assert themselves as new actors in the decision-making process while, previously, they were excluded from this process. In the case of the SSI it will be attempted to establish whether or not the process of development of these systems includes "lay" actors, and, if it does, whether this inclusion operates in a different way depending on the institutional level involved (i.e. municipality, canton, Confederation). We shall also ask about the way in which the SSI alter the relations between the administrative services and about the expertise profiles mobilized to accompany the development and implementation of these systems (i.e. specialist vs. generalist).

Why and how are the SSI endowed politically? Policy tools are frequently presented as the outcome of a technical choice aimed at ensuring the resolution of the social problem addressed by the public policy. It is true that in the context of "good" governance and the repositioning the latter involves for public and private actors in the decision-making process, the researchers sometimes tended to place the emphasis on "techniques" enabling the provision of the best possible response to the problem to be resolved and to ignore the questions of power and legitimacy. This phenomenon is particularly prominent in the case of New Public Management, which tends to "technologize" and, therefore, "depoliticize" public action, by increasing the use of indicators, norms and standards. More fundamentally, Lascoumes and Le Galès (2004a: 25-26) ask whether the proliferation of tools does not constitute an attempt to eliminate the political questions while focusing on the means rather than the objectives. It would appear, in effect, easier to find a consensus between the actors regarding the means (tools) to be used as opposed to the finalities of the public action. These authors go even further by presenting the hypothesis that "the debate surrounding the tools may provide a useful smokescreen for the governmental elites to dissimulate less worthy objectives, depoliticize the fundamental political questions and create a minimum consensus on reform while relying on the apparent neutrality of tools which are presented as modern and whose effects will make themselves felt in the long term" (Lascoumes & Le Galès, 2004a: 26-27).

Thus, it would appear important to express an interest in the political scope of tools beyond their technical legitimacy. The SSI are often considered by their flatterers as eminently scientific constructions which enable the "objectivization" of the situation of a public authority in relation to sustainability. In this section, we will question this so-called "scientific quality": What role does "normativity" play in the SSI? How and why are these systems politically endowed to become tools with a normative aim? This line of enquiry will be extended through the analysis of the SSI on the basis of the concept of the "political-administrative programme" (PAP) developed by Knoepfel et al. (2006a: 166-189), i.e. by addressing the question as to the extent to which the SSI constitute not only tools ("operational elements" in the language of Knoepfel et al.) but also evaluative elements and even policy objectives.

The SSI as policy tools

In the context of a sustainability evaluation, the objective may be to evaluate the sustainability of a public authority or to evaluate the effects of a project, a programme or policy (OCE, 2004: 12-13). In this paper, we are solely interested in the former possibility, i.e. the development of SSI whose aim is to measure the situation of a public authority in relation to sustainable development. In concrete terms these systems should provide information about the main economic, environmental and social characteristics of an institutional territory, their current "level" of sustainability and their evolution over time. Thus, what is involved here is not evaluation tools which aim to analyse the effects of a project or policy and to obtain a "profile" of their strong points and weaknesses with a view to optimizing them.[4]

Since the objective of the SSI which we are examining is not the analysis of policy effects, the question arises as to whether these systems actually constitute policy tools, in other words whether they really have any effect on certain actors with a view to resolving a problem. In answering this question, we base ourselves on the policy analysis model developed by Knoepfel et al. (2006a). According to this analytical framework, the implementation of a policy tool should modify the actions of target groups whose behaviour is considered as responsible for the collective problem in question with a view to resolving or at least attenuating this problem and, as a result, improving the situation of the end beneficiaries (the groups subjected to the negative effects of the problem). Thus, in the case of the SSI, we need to pinpoint the collective problem to be resolved, the target groups and end beneficiaries involved.

In a way, what is involved here is "finding" the policies that use the SSI as intervention tools. In our view, public authority's sustainable development or Agenda 21 processes constitute such policies. More precisely, these processes may be considered as "meta" policies, the objective of which is to coordinate the different sectoral policies so as to ensure that the public authorities develop

---

[4] For a general overview of these tools for the evaluation of sustainability, cf. Knoepfel and Münster (2004).

in a way as sustainable as possible.[5] The social problem to be resolved is, therefore, the "unsustainable" economic, environmental and social development of these public authorities. In the framework of these policies of a rather particular nature, the SSI make it possible to identify the fields (e.g. air quality) in which the (evolution of) the situation is not "sustainable" and, as a result, to identify the target groups (e.g. drivers) and the end beneficiaries (e.g. asthmatics) indirectly through the policies relating to other fields (e.g. transport policy). Thus, in our view, the SSI may be considered as policy tools.

Before discussing the political nature of these SSI, we need to explain the reasons behind their emergence and briefly explore the initiatives that exist in Switzerland in this regard.

The reasons behind the emergence of indicators of sustainable development

As stressed by Meadows (1998: 1), we use indicators intuitively for tracking complex systems, which are of interest to us and which we need to control. Moreover, we have a rich vocabulary for designating the concept of an indicator: e.g. sign, signal, symptom, omen, index, measure etc. Indicators are a necessary element of the flood of information which we use to understand the world. As stated by Bossel (1999: 9), they link us to the world by condensing the complexity of the latter into a set of relevant information that can be mastered, in a number of observations that provide a basis for our decisions and guide our actions.

On the level of public action, according to Knoepfel (2005b: 115ff) the emergence of the indicators for sustainable development is rooted in a more general trend for the recourse to indicators, a trend he explains in terms of the conjunction of the following three factors:

- the desire or obligation to evaluate the efficiency, effectivity and effectiveness of policies;
- the emergence of the issue of sustainable development which raised the question of the quantification and evaluation of the sustainability of State actions;
- the administrative reforms associated with New Public Management which are accompanied by the establishment of controlling systems.

Historically, the indicators for sustainable development emerged with the aim of challenging GDP (gross domestic product) which was previously considered as the sole indicator of the well-being of a nation. From the 1950s, voices were raised against this interpretation of GDP and, in 1987, the World Commission on Environment and Development (later known as the Brundtland Commission) demanded that new methods be developed that would go beyond the simple consideration of economic aspects and would also incorporate social and ecological factors. This appeal was taken up again in

[5] Taking the federal level in Switzerland as an example the document "Sustainable Development Strategy" (CF, 2008) may be considered as the text, on which the Swiss Confederation's sustainability policy is based and which enables the latter to fulfil its constitutional mandate in this regard (Articles 2, 54 and 73 of the Federal Swiss Constitution).

Agenda 21 which was adopted at the Earth Summit in Rio de Janeiro during the United Nations Conference on Environment and Development in 1992. The final chapter of this Agenda[6] stresses in particular that indicators of sustainable development should be developed to provide solid bases for decision-making at all levels. Numerous efforts have been made in the intervening fifteen years by public authorities, NGOs and scientists to establish and test such indicators at the global, national, regional and local levels.[7] Indeed, some commentators refer to a veritable "indicator industry" (Fromm et al., 2000: 1).

In the minds of their promoters, the indicators should enable the public authorities to establish whether or not they are on the path to sustainable development. These indicators are necessary to evaluate at different territorial levels how "sustainability" evolved in the past and thus enable the prediction of its future. Measures to improve or maintain sustainability can only be implemented on the basis of such indicators (Schuber, 1998: 410). The indicators also facilitate the comparison of different public authorities as long as the indicators used are identical. Based on such a comparison, the latter then have at their disposal indications in relation to the degree of progress they have made in the direction of sustainable development. However, we can observe today that the data available to political-administrative actors are frequently insufficient and/or inadequate and that the latter often have to take decisions without having the appropriate information at their disposal. In this context, the indicators contribute to the identification of the potential weaknesses of public action and in signalling the areas in which it is necessary to make changes. "The indicator decodes a multitude of information for the purpose of guiding political decision-making and consultation. Its ultimate purpose is to transmit information or a signal (often originating from the expertise) so as to become an aid to political decision-making (identification of problematical issues, the formulation of priorities, formulation and implementation of the decision, follow-up and evaluation of the impacts of decisions)." (Blanchet & November, 1998: 17)

The SSI in Switzerland

The topic of sustainable development has become well established at all institutional levels of Swiss federalism. The Confederation, cantons and municipalities have all had to position themselves in relation to this topic – albeit to different degrees. Thus, the Confederation developed a sustainable development strategy (CF, 1997) in 1997 which has since been updated twice (CF, 2002, 2008). According to the Federal Office for Spatial Development (ARE), 15 cantons (out of 26) and 165 municipalities (out of 2636) have

---

[6] http://www.un.org/esa/sustdev/documents/agenda21/english/agenda 21chapter 40.htm

[7] The website of the International Institute for Sustainable Development (http://www.iisd.org/measure/compendium) contains a "Compendium of Sustainable development Indicators Initiatives"). The following studies, which present a series of approaches and experience in this area, are also worth consulting: Clivaz et al. (2002); Fromm et al. (2000); Blanchet & November (1998); Hardy & Barg (1997).

initiated a sustainable development process, generally under the heading of local Agenda 21.[8] The more heavily populated municipalities in particular have initiated this process, which explains why the 6.3 % of the municipalities that have adopted a sustainable development strategy account for 30 % of the Swiss population.

With respect to the indicators of sustainable development, as already mentioned above, we are only interested here in the systems of indicators whose aim is to measure the "sustainability" of a public authority at a given moment in time. The Swiss Confederation developed its own system in the context of the MONET project *("MOnitoring der Nachhaltigen EnTwicklung"*, i.e. "Monitoring of Sustainable Development"). This system, which comprises 130 indicators, should enable political-administrative decision makers to know where Switzerland is positioned in relation to sustainable development (OFS, 2003).[9] On the website of the Federal Office for Spatial Development, the Confederation states that "Indicator systems should:

- Initiate debate between stakeholders in society about the goals and the direction of sustainable development;
- Measure the current status of sustainability, indicate trends over time and identify areas for action;
- Inform the public and political decision-makers about the status of sustainable development and thus enable potential problem areas to be identified at an early stage;
- Enable comparisons (benchmarking) and, as a result of the ensuing competition, motivate people to step up their efforts to achieve the goals."[10]

The "multiple-objective" dimension of a SSI is clearly highlighted here. It is not merely a question of measuring sustainability so as to improve public action but equally to increase the awareness of all of the actors involved and to enable the comparison of the various public authorities.

The Swiss Confederation also initiated the project "*Indicateurs centraux pour les villes et les cantons*" ("Key indicators for the towns/cities and cantons") which, based on the experience gained by certain cities like Winterthur (Klooz & Schneider, 2000) and Zurich (Schultz et al., 2001) in particular, resulted in the definition of a limited number of indicators for the areas of the environment, the economy and society (around twelve indicators per area). The purpose of the indicators was to make it possible to evaluate at strategic level whether a canton or town/city is on the path towards sustainable development and, in particular, to facilitate the comparison of the situation in different towns/cities and cantons (Ernst Basler + Partner AG & Novatlantis, 2003; ARE, 2005).[11] Finally, certain municipalities and cantons developed their own

[8] http://www.are.admin.ch/themen/nachhaltig/agenda21/index.html?lang=en
[9] http://www.monet.admin.ch
[10] http://www.are.admin.ch/themen/nachhaltig/00268/index.html?lang=en
[11] http://www.are.admin.ch/themen/nachhaltig/00268/00552/index.html?lang=fr

SSI, notably by adding to the list of indicators defined by the project "Key indicators for the towns/cities and cantons".[12]

On the political nature of SSI

We shall return below to the two questions highlighted at the beginning of this article (cf. chapter 2.3) and answer them on the basis of the experience gained in Switzerland in relation to the development and implementation of SSI.

More power-sharing with civil society actors

Having adopted new tasks over the course of time, the Confederation, cantons and municipalities created new specialized administrative services to assume responsibility for these tasks. The result was a proliferation of services which functioned on the basis of an essentially sectoral logic. In this context, the development of a SSI challenged these sectoral logics and pushed for the decompartmentalization of the services. Thus, in the context of a research project which we carried out a few years ago,[13] we observed that certain services had data that would be of interest to other services but that the information did not circulate, particularly because the managers wanted to protect their services from external scrutiny and thus retain a greater level of power. It could also be hypothesized that the development of SSI tends to consolidate the power of the service responsible for this system in the medium and long term, in particular if the latter is a service specifically dedicated to sustainable development as opposed to a sectoral service to which this task has been assigned (i.e. spatial planning, urbanism, environment, statistics etc.). This hypothesis, the verification of which is rendered difficult at present due to the recent nature of the available experience, considers that for a new "sustainable development" administrative unit created ex-nihilo, the development and management of a SSI constitutes an opportunity to establish its power through the central position conferred on it in terms of the concentration of information flows.

The processes for the development of SSI also stress the fact that the indicator must be included in the more general framework of the formal procedures that govern the functioning of the administration. Sustainable development is the potential bearer of a new political "culture" which challenges the traditional decision-making procedures. In the system of double

[12] For an account and overview of Agenda 21 processes in Switzerland and the significance accorded to the question of indicators of sustainable development, see Knoepfel (2005a: 330-337).

[13] Project "Indicateurs de durabilité au niveau local – Elaboration et mise en œuvre d'un système d'indicateurs du développement durable adapté aux besoins des communes suisses" ("Indicators of sustainability at local level – Development and implementation of a system of sustainability indicators adapted to the needs of the Swiss municipalities"), 2002-2004, financed by the Strategic Fund of the University of Applied Sciences Western Switzerland (HES-SO).

delegation, which remains dominant and involves the delegation by the citizen of his decision-making power to both elected representatives and the technicians (Callon et al., 2001), "dialogue-based" procedures are increasingly common that relativize the powers and competences usually conferred on the latter and share them with civil society actors (NGOs, associations, companies, residents etc.).

Moreover, the fact that the Swiss Confederation initiated the project "Key indicators for the towns/cities and cantons" may be interpreted as a desire at federal level to retain control over the development of indicators at the cantonal and municipal levels so as to ensure the comparability of the indicators necessary for benchmarking. It may be confirmed, however, that while the definition of a standard set of indicators applicable to all public bodies of a similar size certainly enables the comparison of these bodies between themselves, it scarcely takes into account their specific territorial and institutional features. As stressed by Both et al. (2003: 222), "the proposals in relation to indicators should also be associated with the requests and practices of the territorial actors". Moreover, over the course of time, it has been possible to observe the emergence of general trend in several projects aimed at developing indicators of sustainable development (Pastille Consortium, 2002: 6; Clivaz & Babey, 2003), which consists in a shift from "top-down" approaches, whereby the indicators are defined by researchers and experts, to "bottom-up" approaches, whereby the indicators are (also) defined through participative processes that include local actors.

Hence, the process of definition of indicators of sustainable development may enable certain actors, in particular those originating from the world of associations and private sector, to access decision-making arenas – or rather the periphery of these circles – to the extent that their influence is generally limited to the choice of indicators and not to the actual decision-making which the quantification of the latter should give rise to. In reality, this phenomenon of emergence of new actors arises above all at the local level where it is easier for civil society actors to be included in the development of SSI. As opposed to this, the Confederation's MONET system, the system associated with the project "Key indicators for the towns/cities and cantons" and the system used in the canton of Vaud (UDD, 2006) were developed within the administration with the help of private external consultancies and are only rarely open to other types of actors. Hence, it may be confirmed that the development of a SSI has different effects on the power relations between actors depending on the institutional level at which it operates. At federal and cantonal levels, it only causes marginal changes to these relations while the effect is more significant at municipal level.

Finally, we shall end this analysis of power relations by highlighting the return of "generalists" at the expense of "specialists" in the management of the SSI. If it is true that the generalist/specialist distinction is somewhat artificial (and where does the boundary between them lie?), the need to adopt a global and transverse approach to the sustainability of a territory or policy requires the skills of generalists who are capable of understanding the economic, social and environmental dimensions of a public authority. While the skills of specialists may still be required to feed the databases necessary to the functioning of systems of indicators, when it comes to the development of these systems and the interpretation of their results, they make way for those of the generalists.

A "technical" tool with a strong political dimension

The experience gained in Switzerland shows that the development of a SSI often enables the fundamental examination of the main challenges that face the public authorities involved. For example, in the context of the aforementioned research project, we observed that the debate in the town of Le Locle rapidly became focused around the topic of housing due to the demographic situation that faced it (Babey & Clivaz, 2005). Several approaches for resolving this problem of vacant housing and housing that was unsuited to the needs of the population were discussed. The debates also focused on the question as to which actors should be associated with the resolution of this problem, and highlighted the need to expand the circle of actors traditionally included in the decision-making process and to promote public-private partnership. In Morges, another municipality that participated in this research project, it was questions surrounding the environment and transport that emerged as the focus of the debates as the town has significant problems in this area that need to be resolved.

Thus, we confirm that, as far as the administrative and political actors are concerned, there is little sense in talking about indicators of sustainable development without referring to concrete problems directly connected with local concerns. The question about the indicators would largely appear to act as a mere pretext that enables the local actors to discuss concrete problems within their public authority and to increase their awareness of the concept of sustainable development. In this sense, the question concerning indicators of sustainable development does not eliminate politics and the aims of the public action. On the contrary, it puts them at the centre of the debate. And, contrary to what we were able to observe in relation to power relations, it would not appear that this statement differs according to the institutional level involved. Thus, at federal level, the definition of the MONET system of indicators involved the definition of theories of sustainable development which triggered numerous and lengthy discussions on the nature of sustainable development.

The question that arises here, therefore, is if the indicator does not constitute a technical instrument but incorporates a strong political dimension, what is its normative scope? Knoepfel (2005b) defends the thesis that "the indicator becomes the norm" and develops it, in particular, by analysing the case of SSI. Thus, he emphasizes that these indicators have a clear normative orientation because they should make it possible to quantify whether or not the development is going in the right direction, even if the targets to be aimed at are not precisely known (Knoepfel, 2005b: 125). According to Peter Knoepfel, "all processes that define absolute targets based on the methods currently used for processes known as 'benchmarking' are problematic because they conceal their normativity residing precisely in the choice of the basic sample (in addition to that of the choice of the indicator itself)" (Knoepfel, 2005b: 127).

Thus, he proposes not that the development of all systems of indicators should be abandoned but that absolute targets should not be set and that the indicator should be calculated periodically to see whether the public authority is progressing in the desired direction or not.

Similarly, Meadows (1998: 9-10) notes that all of the indicators incorporate an element of subjectivity. The choice of an indicator is based in effect on certain norms and certain values that define what is important to quantify. And defining what is important is a fundamentally subjective act. Moreover, there is a reciprocal influence between values and indicators: if the indicators result from values (we measure what concerns us) they also contribute to the shaping of the values (what concerns us is what we measure). On the other hand, the selection of the elements that should be measured causes the elements that are not included to be shifted automatically to the secondary level, in particular all of the processual and relational aspects which are difficult to quantify while being primordial in terms of the concretization of the principles of sustainable development at the level of a public authority (Deschenaux, 2003 : 240).

In this context, it is easier to understand why the development of a SSI is an eminently political process which often triggers considerable reticence on the part of elected representatives and local administrative managers. The choice of an indicator is not innocuous in effect and is far from being a merely "technical" matter: the performance of a given service or fulfilment of a given political objective will be evaluated based on this measure. The political-administrative actors are particularly sensitive to the political dimension of the indicator. Thus, several municipalities refused to take part in the aforementioned research project and explained their refusal in part by the fear of having "to provide an account" on the basis of indicators that would not necessarily show the town in its best light. Another phenomenon that attests to the political nature of SSI was the way in which the ranking of Swiss towns, which is published each year by a weekly Francophone newspaper and based on set of economic, environmental and social indicators, was discontinued following the exertion of pressure by the *Union des villes suisses* (Association of Swiss Towns and Cities) on the institute in charge of compiling this ranking. The towns/cities with a "poor" ranking did not appreciate seeing themselves publicly designated as under-performers in relation to the quality of life they offer. Similarly, the cantons of Geneva and Vaud and the city of Lausanne refused to feature in the ranking produced in the context of the project "Key indicators for towns/cities and cantons".[14] In these examples what is at stake is the definition, through the indicators, of norms and standards based on which the public authorities are evaluated and made to compete with each other.

---

[14] Although it is not possible to go into this in further detail here, it should be added that the implementation of this type of ranking in which all of the economic, social and environmental information associated with a public authority are summarized in a single composite indicator, raises serious conceptual and methodological reservations.

The political scope of a SSI also manifests itself through the fact that it is located at several levels of the political-administrative programme of a public policy. We have already seen that it may be considered as a policy tool even if its relation with target groups is more indirect in nature. It also constitutes in a rather obvious way an evaluative element as it enables the evaluation of the degree of sustainability of a public authority and the evolution of the latter over time. And, finally, it also participates in part in the definition of the sustainable development policy of a public authority by defining, often implicitly (e.g. through the comparison of the results obtained by other public authorities), the "ideal" values to be attained. As Knoepfel et al. (2009: 476) stress in relation to nature conservation and landscape protection inventories, it may be noted in a somewhat similar way in the case of the SSI that these tools link the different components of the political-administrative programme in a transverse way.

Finally, the fact that a SSI is found at almost all of the phases of the policy cycle should be noted. In effect such a system:

- participates in the (re)definition of the problem (the "sustainability) by "objectivizing" reality (or more precisely a part of the reality, the one measured by the indicators);
- is a central element during the development of the political-administrative programme (tools, evaluative elements and objectives as we have just seen);
- constitutes in a way an "implementation act" (realization of the system of indicators) for which we have seen that the "impact" (modification of the behaviour of the target groups) and the "outcome" (contribution to the resolution of the problem) are difficult to demonstrate;
- enables the evaluation of the degree of sustainability of a public authority and in a more or less direct way the fulfilment of the objectives of its Agenda 21 or sustainable development policy.

Based on this we can understand better the political investment, to which a SSI is subjected on the part of the different policy actors.

Conclusion: the paradoxes of SSI

Far from confining itself to a purely technical problem, the development of SSI proves to be a fundamentally political operation that can have significant repercussions both on the level of political debates and administrative procedures. In this sense, a public authority that seeks to establish a SSI should not fail to examine the fundamental challenges that concern it and the role it expects to assign to the different political and administrative actors and to civil society actors. Our analysis has shown that the challenges associated with the development of a SSI are different depending on the institutional level involved. This observation applies, in particular, to the question as to who participates in the choice of indicators with the municipal level being more suitable for the integration of citizens and associations than the cantonal and federal levels where the choice of sustainable development indicators remains largely the prerogative of experts from the administration and private consultancies.

Thus, one may question what appears to be a paradox here: do participative processes only contribute to reinforcing the political power of the established political-administrative actors? Lascoumes and Le Galès (2004b: 318) note, in effect, that "certain tools such as indicators, benchmarking and best practices, which are often presented as being essentially aimed at the collection and comparison of information, may emerge in certain cases as powerful instruments of restraint controlled by the State." The development of systems of indicators, the comparison with other public authorities and diffusion of best practices often constitute central aspects of sustainable development processes be they at local, cantonal or national level. Therefore, if we adopt Lascoumes and Le Galès's hypothesis, these processes, which are supposed to lend greater weight to civil society actors through the establishment of participative procedures, merely strengthen the power of the elected representatives and civil servants. Although the experience in Switzerland is too recent to allow us to draw definitive conclusions in this regard, in our view it tends to show that the political-administrative actors have succeeded for the most part in retaining control over the processes of development of SSI even if civil society actors were integrated into these processes.

Unlike regulatory, economic or contractual tools, the informative and standardization (normalization) tools are not very restrictive in legal terms. The restriction is there, however, but exercised in a different manner: it involves more the social pressure exercised by the definition of standards, the comparison with other public authorities and increase in the level of information available to the actors involved. Thus once an indictor has been adopted, it tends to become the norm through which the "performance" of public action is evaluated. It is in such a context that Peter Knoepfel (2005b: 128) stresses the risk that the increasing recourse to indicators may pose. Having acted himself as an expert providing support the to Confederation and public authorities in the implementation of systems of indicators, he admits to having underestimated the risks associated with the spread of this type of tool in the context of public action. Using a watchword, which we ourselves adopt and which constitutes another paradox of the SSI, he appeals to "give the unquantifiable the place it deserves".

References

ARE – Office du développement territorial (éd.) (2005). *Indicateurs centraux pour le développement durable des villes et cantons.* Rapport du Cercle Indicateurs, Berne.

Babey, N., & Clivaz, C. (2005). *La définition d'indicateurs du développement durable: d'un problème 'technique' à une remise en cause des logiques politico-administratives – Le cas de la Ville du Locle (Suisse).* Paper presented at the conference "Développement urbain durable Gestion des ressources Gouvernance", Lausanne, 21-23 September 2005, 10 p.

Blanchet, C., & November, A. (1998). *Indicateurs de développement durable appliqués à l'aménagement du territoire.* Genève: Conseil économique et social (CES) / Centre universitaire d'écologie humaine et des sciences de l'environnement (CUEH) / Institut universitaire d'études du développement (IUED).

Bossel, H. (1999). *Indicators of sustainable development: Theory, Method, Applications.* Winnipeg: International Institute for Sustainable Development (IISD).

Both, J.-F., Da Cunha, A., & Mager, C. (2003). Evaluation du territoire, développement durable et indicateurs : un pragmatisme raisonné. In A. Da Cunha & J. Ruegg (Dir.) *Développement durable et aménagement du territoire.* Lausanne : PPUR. pp. 221-238.

Bütschi, D., & Cattacin, S. (1993). L'Etat incitateur : nouvelles pratiques de la subsidiarité dans le système du bien-être suisse. *Annuaire suisse de science politique.* 33: 143-162.

Callon, M., Lascoumes, P., & Barthe, Y. (2001). *Agir dans un monde incertain. Essai sur la démocratie technique.* Paris : Seuil.

CF – Conseil fédéral suisse (2008). *Sustainable Development Strategy : Guidelines and Action Plan 2008-2011.* Berne.

CF – Conseil fédéral suisse (2002). *Stratégie 2002 pour le développement durable.* Berne.

CF – Conseil federal (1997). *Le développement durable en Suisse. Stratégie.* Berne.

Clivaz, C., & Babey N. (2003). Les indicateurs du développement durable comme instrument de pilotage des communes suisses. *Revue économique et sociale* 61(4) : 195-202.

Clivaz, C., Babey, N., Bigler J.-M., & Perini, D. (2002). *Elaboration d'un système provisoire d'indicateurs du développement durable au niveau local.* Sierre: Centre de compétences HES-SO Puma.

Deschenaux, C. (2003). Indicateurs et développement durable: le cas d'Air-Valais en tant qu'agenda 21 local. In A. Da Cunha & J. Ruegg (Dir.) *Développement durable et aménagement du territoire.* Lausanne : PPUR, , pp. 239-245.

Donzelot, J., & Estèbe, P. (1994). *L'Etat animateur : essai sur la politique de la ville.* Paris : Esprit.

DuPasquier, A., Knoepfel, P., & Münster, M. (2003). *Etat des lieux des démarches de développement durable dans les communes.* Berne : ARE/IDHEAP.

Ernst Basler + Partner AG, Novatlantis (2003). *Indicateurs centraux pour le développement durable des villes et des cantons.* Zollikon.

Fromm, E., Kratochvil, R., Lindenthal, T., Milestad, R.., & Brunner, P.H. (2000). *Nachhaltigkeit erkennbar und planbar machen.* Wien: SUSTAIN (Verein zur Koordination von Forschung über Nachhaltigkeit).

Hardi, P., & Barg, S. (1997). *Measuring sustainable development : review of current practice.* Ottawa: Industry Canada, Occasional Paper Number 17.

Hardi, P., & Zdan, T. (Eds.) (1997). *Assessing Sustainable Development: Principles in Practice.* Winnipeg: International Institute for Sustainable Development (IISD).

Hood, C.C. (1983). *The tools of government.* London: MacMillan.

Howlett, M. (1991). Policy instruments, policy styles, and policy implementation. National approaches to theories of instrument choice. *Policy Studies Journal* 19(2): 1-21.

Klooz, D., & Schneider, T. (2000). *The Sustainable Development Barometer and the Key-Indicator-Set: Two Tools and their Application in the City of Winterthur.* Proceedings of the Symposium Making Sustainable Regional Development Visible. Evaluation Methods and Indicators in the Regional Context, Schloss Seggau, Leibnitz, November 13-15, 2000, pp. 37-48.

Knoepfel, P. (2005a). Régimes institutionnels de ressources naturelles et démarches de développement durable au niveau local (Agenda 21). In A. Da Cunha, P. Knoepfel, P. Leresche. & S. Nahrath (Dir.) *Enjeux du développement urbain durable. Transformations urbaines, gestion des ressources et gouvernance.* Lausanne : PPUR, pp. 329-352.

Knoepfel, P. (2005b). Quand les indicateurs deviennent la norme – trois variations sur un thème avec finale sine brio. In B. Bovay & S. Nguyen Minh (Eds) *Mélanges Pierre Moor.* Berne: Staempfli, pp. 115-128.

Knoepfel, P., Nahrath, S., Savary, J., & Varone, F. (2009). Analyse des politiques de l'environnement. Zürich, Coire : Rüegger (à paraître).

Knoepfel, P., Larrue, C., & Varone, F. (2006a). *Analyse et pilotage des politiques publiques.* Zürich, Chur : Rüegger.

Knoepfel, P., Münster, M., & Corbière-Nicollier, T. en coll. avec P. Lehmann, (2006b). *WinWin22 – un outil de planification et d'évaluation de projets d'Agenda 21.* Chavannes-près-Renens: IDHEAP, Working paper de l'IDHEAP 9/2006.

Knoepfel, P., & Münster, M. (2004). *Guide des outils d'évaluation de projets selon le développement durable.* Berne : ARE.

Lascoumes, P. & Le Galès, P. (2007). "Introduction: Understanding Public Policy through Its Instruments – From the Nature of Instruments to the Sociology of Public Policy Instrumentation", Governance: An International Journal of Policy, Administration and Institutions 20(1): 1-21.

Lascoumes, P., & Le Galès, P. (2004a). L'action publique saisie par les instruments. In P. Lascoumes & P. Le Galès (Dir.) (2004) *Gouverner par les instruments.* Paris : Presses de la Fondation nationale des Sciences politiques, pp. 11-44.

Lascoumes, P., & Le Galès, P. (2004a). De l'innovation instrumentale à la recomposition de l'Etat. In P. Lascoumes. & P. Le Galès. (Dir.) (2004) *Gouverner par les instruments.* Paris: Presses de la Fondation nationale des Sciences politiques, pp. 357-370.

Meadows, D. (1998). *Indicators and Information Systems for Sustainable Development.* Winnipeg: International Institute for Sustainable Development (IISD).

Morand, C.A. (Dir.) (1991). *L'Etat propulsif. Contribution à l'étude des instruments d'action de l'Etat.* Paris : Publisud.
OCE – Office de coordination pour la protection de l'environnement du canton de Berne (2004). *Développement durable dans le canton de Berne / Evaluation de la durabilité, Introduction et guide.* Berne.
OFS – Office fédéral de la statistique (2003). *Le développement durable en Suisse. Indicateurs et commentaries.* Neuchâtel.
Pastille Consortium (2002). *Indicators into action.* A practitioners' guide for improving their use at the local level.
Schneider, A., & Ingram, H. (1990). Behavioral assumptions of policy tools. *Journal of Politics.* 52(2): 510-529.
Schuber, R. (1998). Indikatoren für Nachhaltigkeit. *Schweizerische Zeitschrift für Volkswirtschaft und Statistik.* 134(3): 391-414.
Schultz, B., Keiner, M., & Schmid, W.A. (2001). *Nachhaltigeitsindikatoren für die Stadt Zürich. Schlussbericht.* Zürich : ORL-Institut.
Stone Sweet, A., Sandholtz, W., & Fligstein, N. (Eds) (2001). *The Institutionalisation of Europe.* Oxford: Oxford University Press.
Varone, F. (1998). *Le choix des instruments des politiques publiques.* Berne : Haupt.

Part V

Epistemology and Methodology of Comparative Policy Analysis

CHAPTER 15

A Methodology for the Comparison and Evaluation of Public Policies

CORINNE LARRUE & KATIA HORBER-PAPAZIAN

Introduction

The comparative approach to policy analysis developed by Peter Knoepfel belongs to the studies carried out from the 1970s by political scientists interested in questions surrounding the implementation of public policies in different political-administrative contexts. This trend, which unfolded initially in America (see in particular Pressman & Wildavsky, 1973; Bardach, 1984), subsequently spread to Europe (Ashford, 1978; Lundquist, 1980; Maintz, 1980; Vogel, 1983). The application of this type of analysis concerns "emerging" policies or policies that are "under construction", such as, for example, environmental protection policy, health promotion policy and unemployment policy, and necessitates analyses of a qualitative nature.

The comparative analysis of public policies therefore positioned itself in contrast to the approaches previously developed in "comparative politics", which focused on entire political systems. The latter were published in the journal "Comparative Politics" (under the editorship of LaPalombara), in particular.

The comparative policy approaches are based on case studies involving a more or less significant number of cases (see, in particular, Asford, 1978; Vogel & Kun, 1983) and/or statistical analyses relating to an extended period of time and large number of countries (in particular Castles, 1998). Furthermore, quali-quantitative analyses that systematically combine these two types of methodological approach have emerged since the late 1980s (Ragin, 1987, *Revue Internationale de politique comparée*, 1994).

One of the publications that is most typical of the thinking in this regard is Ashford's book: "Comparing Public Policies: New Concepts and Methods" (1978). The main questions raised here concern the capacity to produce a "comparative theory of states" based on the observed permanence of the structural elements associated with the policies adopted by different governments. However, this objective has scarcely been attained.

These approaches quickly prompted questions in relation to the relevance of a comparative approach, which were rapidly followed by questions relating to its feasibility. In effect, the question of the comparison of policies implemented on one and the same topic in different countries refers back to that of the relevance of a comparison, considering the number of variables to be taken into account ("*many variables, small number of cases" cf. Lijphart, 1975*). However, from the early 1980s, the *Revue internationale de politique comparée* would constitute for the Francophone world a forum for debate on the comparison of public policies. The journal published accounts of the different methodological approaches applied to specific policy fields such as health, social policy and environmental policy. Finally, in more recent times, both the study by Lallement and Spurk (2003) and issue 2004/3 of the *Revue internationale de politique comparée* presented an assessment of the approaches developed in this regard.

What emerges from these various assessments is, first, that the development of comparative policy analysis may be observed at different levels: i.e. on the level of researchers but also on that of decision-makers and the media (Hassenteufel, 2005). The latter two levels favour the use of the comparative approach to identify the best policy "models". This development contributed, on the one hand, to providing inputs for reform strategies in different countries (this is particularly applicable to the work of the OECD on New Public Management) and also, in the case of the researchers, to the formulation of comparative strategies and methods (Lima, Steffen, 2004).

More generally, several contributions associated with these comparative policy processes may also be reported (Lallement & Spurk, 2003; Lima & Steffen, 2004): a distanced view of the researcher's own country enabling the advance identification of the non-identified variables; the capacity to test (and, therefore, revitalize) hypotheses on the causality of the phenomena observed in the different countries; and, finally, the clarification of comparative intersectoral, national and international strategies and analytical methods.

Peter Knoepfel's work constitutes a particular methodological contribution in this context. The comparative analytical framework developed by this author stands out on the basis of the level of detail of the analyses carried out and the cross-referencing of the variables used. To be more precise: first, this analytical framework relates not only to the development of public policies but also to the process of policy implementation and therefore always leads to the creation of a specific analytical grid; and, second, the variables used in the analysis are threefold: the emphasis is placed on the actors and their configurations, the institutional rules and the resources mobilized.

We shall return to these different dimensions. We will revisit the analytical grids produced in this way while systematically questioning their operationalization, their contributions and their limits. In doing this, we will present the new paths opened up by these studies for the construction and stabilization of analytical methods in the area of comparative policy analysis and policy evaluation. Thus we will explore: (a) the production of normative frameworks; (b) policy implementation; and, finally, (c) evaluation.

A method for the comparative study of policy programming

"To enable the comparison of the data collected in different countries, all comparative research that would like to go beyond a simple juxtaposition of national Reports should determine accurately the dependent variables to be explained and use a necessarily limited number of explanatory variables." (Knoepfel, Larrue 1985, p. 54).

The comparative approach to policy analysis as developed by Peter Knoepfel is based, therefore, on the identification and construction of dependent and explanatory variables which are defined *a priori* as a basis for the collection of empirical data. Applied to the development of public action programmes, this analytical framework enables us to understand the processes behind the production of these programmes and to link them to their respective content. The proposed methodological framework seeks, therefore, to define the analytical variables in a rigorous way and to produce reliable hypotheses which the analysis will attempt to test empirically.

The analytical frameworks used in comparative policy research generally aim "to compare the characteristics of a national system with those of other systems and, in this way, to refer to the established universals and differences" (Sartori, G., 1994). To do this, according to Giraud (2004), "*the comparative analysis of public action has numerous and diversified theoretical frameworks at its disposal today. The institution-based approaches, the cognitive approaches, the analytical frameworks based on policy regulation, the socio-historical approaches based on policy tools or, again, focused on the observation of practices*" (Giraud, 2004, p. 149).

For its part, the approach proposed by Peter Knoepfel emphasizes the *substantial content* of action programmes and the game played by the actors that leads to their definition. The prism of the proposed analysis remains, nonetheless, that of institutions which are understood in terms of the rules, constraints and opportunities they offer to actors who mobilize different action resources in this context (Chapter 1, Knoepfel, Larrue & Varone, 2000).

However, Peter Knoepfel's approach is specific in that it considers the normative framework and its production as a simple stage in the development of a policy, for which it merely constitutes one product among others. Thus, it does not constitute an intermediary product or a final product whose referents must be understood as proposed, for example, by the cognitive approach to policy analysis.

According to the "Knoepfelian" approach, a policy programme is constituted, therefore, of all of the legislative and regulatory decisions of both the central state and the local authorities necessary for the implementation of public policies.

The prism of implementation orients the comparative analysis of public policy programmes. It is the capacity to frame implementation that is central in the analysis of public policy programmes and therefore implicitly constitutes the comparative structure. The public policy programmes and their production process are not compared in themselves but in relation to what they tell us about the capacity to frame the implementation processes.

The constitutive elements of a public action programme as identified by Peter Knoepfel and Helmut Weidner from 1982 (Knoepfel, Weidner, 1982) are, therefore, keys to the comparison of this framework capacity.

Five constitutive elements were identified by the two authors. First and foremost of these are the **policy objectives**. They "*define the status to be attained by the adopted solution that would be considered as satisfactory. They describe the desired social status in a field of action once the public problem is resolved*" (Knoepfel, Larrue & Varone, 2000 p 154). In terms of the framing of the implementation of a policy, the definition of concrete options is therefore supposed to generate stronger framework capacity: "*The more concretely the values are formulated, the easier it is to establish whether they have been effectively realised (or not). This increases the opportunities open to a policy's end beneficiaries to demand the best solutions to the problems affecting them, through either political or legal means*" (Knoepfel, Larrue & Varone, 2000, p. 155).

However, the concept of an objective remains difficult to tackle. The discussion of the objectives refers back to the finality of the action undertaken and the logic of the action to be taken. The pluralist nature of the processes of formulation and legitimation of policy programmes creates space for numerous divergences between the actors or for contradictions in relation to the definition of objectives. This is even truer if the process takes place within different geographical, political and institutional frameworks. Therefore the identification and comparison of objectives between different programmes can prove a very difficult exercise.

However, with respect to environmental policies, to which the analytical framework was applied in particular, this kind of identification was not only possible but actually productive in the majority of cases. Thus, for example, the analysis of clean-air polices carried out by Peter Knoepfel and Helmut Weidner in the 1980s resulted in the demonstration of the fact that these very concrete objectives were defined in all countries in terms of SO2 per m3 of air (immission limit value). While these objectives were clearly established in the German legislation on air quality, for example, in the case of the French regulations, they were based on highly opaque technical calculations. Thus, it was the research of this "constitutive element" of the policy programme which, although it does not correspond to a formal decision-making category in France,[1] made it possible to demonstrate the – *de facto* if not legal – existence of this element within the public policy programme. Furthermore, this type of analysis enables the consolidation of the concept of an objective as an analytical category.

[1] The lack of definition of objectives in terms of a enforceable air quality standard was even presented at the time as doctrine by the Minister of the Environment, who argued the fact that the definition of air quality objectives could be interpreted as granting the right to pollute in areas in which pollution lay below the envisaged threshold values.

It should be noted, however, that one of the main consequences of European integration was the harmonization and, above all, institutionalization, of the definition of the objectives to be attained by the policies of the EU Member States. The case of the Water Framework Directive (WFD: Directive 2000/60/EC of 23 October 2000) is particularly illustrative in this regard. The promulgation of the WFD gave rise to a formalized, concerted and negotiated process in all of the Member States of the European Union for the definition of water policy objectives at national level and at water-basin level. It would be very interesting to carry out a comparative analysis of these processes, similar to that carried out by Bouleau on France (Bouleau, 2007). In effect, analyzing to the processes of definition of these objectives also enables a return to the construction of the "sense" of the action to be carried out and its capacity to channel the implementation processes.

The second element identified in the analytical framework is the **evaluative elements**. According to Peter Knoepfel and Helmut Weidner's analytical grid, what is involved here is "*data to be collected so as to facilitate the ascertainment of the extent to which the defined objectives have been fulfilled*" (p. 155). This constitutive element is, again, particularly suited to technical policies such as policies for the prevention of pollution. In fact, *ex ante* evaluation exercises, which are formalized to a greater or lesser extent, increasingly result in the identification of indicators and other numerical elements to be quantified for the evaluation of the policy implementation programmes. The use of this analytical category makes it possible to demonstrate, for example, the extent of the influence of the European Union on the definition of these elements in each Member State. Indeed, the very consideration of the existence of such a category prompts the research and presentation of the debates surrounding policy evaluation in each country. However, in many countries these debates and evaluation processes are carried out *ex post*, i.e. after the implementation of the policy. In these cases, the data to be collected for the evaluation of the policy effects are also defined on an *ex post* basis. The analytical category "evaluative elements" emerges, therefore, as inoperative or artificial: depending on the countries or policies involved, the concept of evaluative elements is not constitutive of a normative framework or of the process of development of a public policy programme. Its use as an analytical category may prompt the analyst to over-estimate its role in the framing of the policy implementation process.

The **operational elements** are the third constitutive element of a public policy programme. What is involved here are measures planned with a view to fulfilling the policy objectives. The operational elements reflect the dominant intervention hypothesis, i.e. the hypothesis formulated in relation to the levers that make it possible to alter the behaviour of the target groups. These operational elements define specifically the target social groups of the public action. The approach in terms of policy tools is relatively traditional in public policy analysis, including in the comparative approaches. It has prompted numerous analyses, in particular to highlight the links between the dominant conception of the problems to be resolved and the instruments selected to overcome them. Thus, for the supporters of policy analysis based on instruments, a policy instrument constitutes "a both technical and social tool that organizes the specific social relations between state authority and its target group based on the representations and meanings associated with it" (L. Boussaguet et al., 2006, p. 269).

The four modes of action presented as operational elements by Peter Knoepfel et al. refer to mechanisms which are well identified today: regulatory mode, incentive mode, persuasive mode and the direct provision of goods and services. Of course what is designated as a tool here refers, in reality, to generally mixed mechanisms and, strictly speaking, constitutes very general categories which are subdivided into multiple sub-categories. Nevertheless, the comparison of these combinations of operational elements between different action programmes enables the identification of "policy styles" (Morand, 1991, Richardson, 1982), and, above all, the comprehension of the contingencies behind the choices made in each country. Furthermore, the identification of these modes of action makes it possible to anticipate the different resources necessary for their implementation (cf. Chapter 3, Knoepfel, Larrue & Varone, 2000).

Thus, while incentive mode requires resources of a more monetary nature, regulatory mode generally requires resources of a legal, human and interactive nature and, above all, the resource "confidence" for its implementation. Similarly, persuasive mode requires cognitive type resources or "confidence" and it would appear that the direct provision of goods and services requires property assets and/or monetary resources. The capacity to structure the implementation process will depend, therefore, on the level of the different resources that can be mobilized by the actors responsible for the application of the policy in question. The comparative analysis of policy tools enables, therefore, the identification of the configurations best or worst suited to the implementation processes.

Finally, recent policy analyses demonstrate an evolution in the conception and production of the frameworks for public action: i.e. the emergence of the public as a new policy operator. This new figure, the implications of whose emergence in terms of the procedural elements will be seen later, is linked with what is known as "empowerment", that is "the process whereby an individual or group acquires the means of strengthening its capacity for action and emancipating itself" (Bacque, 2005). These developments have led to the emergence of policies of a *constitutive* nature aimed at giving the actors the capacity to mobilize consultation bodies, which are institutionalized to a greater or lesser extent, so as to anticipate and/or manage conflicts. They have also resulted in the adaptation of the modalities of public action and in their being based on the capacity of the target groups to appropriate the required behaviours and even propose new types of public action (for example in the context of participative budgets). Here too, it is the mobilization of the analytical category of operational elements that enables the comparison of modalities of public action and the highlighting of their similarity and differences.

The fourth constitutive element identified in the analytical framework of public policy programmes is the **political-administrative arrangement.** This concept of an arrangement or configuration of actors echoes that of the public action network largely developed by other authors (e.g. Le Gales & Thatcher, 1995). In this regard, the comparison between the *potential* implementation arrangements instituted in the framework of national public action programmes constitutes an original analytical element. It is not so much the network of actors effectively involved in the implementation of the policy that is identified here but that identified *a priori* during the formulation of the policy. As in the case of policy tools, the comparison of these actor configurations between countries or between different policies makes it possible to anticipate the framing of the implementation processes.

Lastly, the fifth constitutive element of a programme is the **procedural elements.** Identifying the specific forms of interaction between political-administrative actors and between the target groups and beneficiary groups makes it possible to apprehend the allocation of different resources at the disposal of the parties involved in the implementation of a policy. These procedural rules, which underlie the interactions between actors during policy implementation, vary in nature: i.e. constitutional principles, administrative law and modes of legal recourse. They do not prevent the development of more informal modes of interaction throughout the implementation process but have the capacity to structure these processes (hence the procedures constitute a mandatory framework for the production of formal and information interaction). It is possible to observe, moreover, an ever-increasing profusion of these procedural elements which are supposed to impose more significant restrictions on the implementation processes. This kind of development results therefore in the establishment of processes of co-construction of public action as is the case, for example, with the planning contracts between the state and regions in France (*contrat de plan Etat Région*) and the agreements between the Federation and Provinces in Canada.

By way of summary, it may be said that this analytical grid of policy programmes enables the demonstration of the *scope* of a policy programme. In identifying the five constitutive elements and in attempting to identify their content for each country, the analytical framework makes it possible not only to identify the missing elements but also to understand why they are missing by comparing the processes that led to their definition. Moreover, the application of this grid to numerous policies of different types has enabled the confirmation of its robustness.

The grid produced in this way enables the framing of the analysis of the process of policy formulation. This "pro forma" approach to the identification of programmes makes it possible to take the challenges and tensions at the heart of the processes involved in policy development into account in greater detail. The interactions between the different actors are therefore associated with each of the constitutive elements and lead to the identification of the coherencies and incoherencies between them and, above all, the configurations of actors at the centre of these "detours".

However, this type of analysis is based on a relatively cumbersome investigation process involving the detailed analysis of the different products (documents, discourses, media etc.) generated in the course of policy development. Thus, to apply such a grid in an effective way, it is necessary to mobilize analysts specialized in the area of policy in question in each country under examination. This enables the combined use of a shared grid and the detailed analysis of the processes involved.

On the other hand, as a result of its sometimes excessive simplification, the application of this analytical grid may result in the cognitive dimension of the country's policies being missed out on and to an extent, therefore, in the falsification of the results of the analysis. For example, the use of incentive instruments in the context of environmental policy in France can be explained more by the structural weakness of the Ministry of the Environment than by an *a priori* reflection on the efficacy of this type of instrument. The comparative analysis of the public policy programmes on the basis of the proposed analytical grid does not always enable the consideration of this type of factor.

A method for the comparative analysis of processes of implementation

As we have seen, the main interest of the comparative policy analysis method is its focus on the implementation processes. Overall, it is the combination of case studies in different regions and localities of different countries, carried out on the basis of a common protocol, which constitutes the main contribution of the methodological framework proposed by Peter Knoepfel. In effect, this framework makes it possible to demonstrate the variations that exist not between countries but between the different regions and localities within these countries. The comparison of several implementation configurations enables, therefore, the identification of common factors between these processes and, in this way, the relativization of the impact of the normative framework on these implementation processes.

More precisely, the focus of interest of the comparative analysis of implementation processes as proposed by Peter Knoepfel derives from both the analytical dimensions used and the conclusions it sanctions in terms of the building of local public action.

With regard to the analytical dimensions, the proposed framework rests on the identification of the interaction between the political-administrative arrangement established for the implementation of the policy, the target groups and beneficiary groups, which Peter Knoepfel et al. identify as the triangle of actors of a public policy. This kind of focus makes it possible to reach a detailed understanding of the definition of the problem to be resolved for each of these actors and the processes of opposition or collaboration that exist between them. This kind of analysis also facilitates the combining of the contributions of the sociology of organizations with the more legal conceptions of policy implementation processes as, in effect, the attention is focused not only on the production of outputs arising from the administrative activity but also on the power relationship related to this production and their effects. Moreover, the proposed approach claims also to incorporate an explanatory or demonstrative aim. However, to apply this, the analyst faces a dilemma between the detailed and precise reproduction of the cases involved and generalization through a consistent of number of cases. Furthermore, the question also arises as to the comparability of actors in a political-administrative world that is becoming more homogeneous in formal terms: for example, although regional parks are found in many European countries, even if they play similar roles, they do not correspond to the same political-administrative reality. Finally, the categories of social actors used in this analytical grid remain reasonably fluid and merit a more precise definition.

With regards to the construction of local public action, the proposed approach enables to demonstrate of the importance of the development of implementation strategies which are formalized to a greater or lesser extent. It is the research and identification of "action plans", the existence of which is often anything but transparent, that makes it possible to apprehend these strategies. Thus, such analyses enable the demonstration of the adoption of managerial type approaches to policy implementation processes – even if such an approach often remains an imponderable in relation to public policies (at implementation level in any case). Furthermore, they make it possible to attain a more detailed understanding of the bilateral relations established and the processes of exchange between the administration and target groups. Such analyses facilitate the disclosure of the different relations between the administration and civil society, in the different regions and countries, and the place of the stakeholders in the policy process.

From a comparative point of view such analyses enable the definition of the specific features of the implementation processes in each research area and the demonstration of the relevant invariants. In this way, it has been possible to clarify the relations between governments and the governed in the area of environmental policy, the emergence of para-structures, the importance and role of decentralized actors etc. with the help of studies carried out in different fields of the environment by analysts using this analytical grid.

However, particular attention may be paid to the conduct of this type of research. In order to apprehend concretely the policy implementation processes in several locations and/or regions of several countries, it is necessary to mobilize national teams to carry out case studies on their individual countries and/or regions and to involve them in the interpretation and comparison of the case studies.

In effect, the strength and subtlety of this type of analysis rests on the establishment of a network of researchers who have been working together for several years: the process requires a long period of learning process in collaborative research which enables the development of a comparative framework based on mutual knowledge of the thematic (in this instance environmental protection) and national contexts.

This linking of collective and individual practices makes it possible to avoid the pitfall of inadequate knowledge of national and local contexts, on the one hand, and the juxtaposition of local and/or national situations, on the other.

This type of process also rests on the choice of concrete cases for specific analysis. This raises important questions in relation to the methodology of the selection of case studies and their representativity.

To illustrate this work and the questions that arise in connection with it, we would like to return to the research protocol created and used in the context of the analysis of the implementation of nature conservation policies which we coordinated in the framework of a European project (Larrue & Knoepfel, 1998).

As part of this project, it was planned to select two case studies in each of the four countries studied: Spain, France, Italy and Switzerland.

- first, cases involving an environmental protection policy that resulted in the imposition of a significant economic and land-related restriction at local level and a more diffuse environmental benefit for the entire community; a case involving the protection of a wetland was selected.
- second, cases involving a spatial planning policy that triggered significant environmental pressure at local level and a more diffuse economic benefit for the entire community; cases involving the construction of transport infrastructure were selected in each of the countries under examination.

Two types of cases were studied for each of these policies: i.e. cases involving the local and/or regional promotion of nature conservation (four cases) and cases involving the centralized promotion of nature conservation (four cases). The protection of natural areas had to be established in each case study selected. This voluntary selection of "success" stories enabled us to study the conditions behind effective nature conservation under fundamentally different institutional configurations.

Finally, during the comparison of the selected cases we prioritized the demonstration of the permanence of certain conditions of policy implementation that were similar in contexts that differed *a priori* in terms of the allocation of powers[2] and decentralization.[3]

This type of process requires the surveying of the entire national territory in the quest for cases that satisfy the defined criteria. A necessarily rapid survey of this kind may result, therefore, in the identification of cases that will not defy detailed analysis, on the one hand and in missing out on more representative cases of the national policy implementation conditions, on the other.

---

[2] The criteria for the selection of the cases made it possible to attain a variance in terms of the environmental protection and spatial planning competencies (central vs decentralized).

[3] In effect, the selected countries represent a diverse spectrum with regard to this criterion: France (predominantly centralized), Italy (in the process of regionalization), Spain (mixed), and Switzerland (federal).

The protocol then concerned the **analytical method** and comprised five phases:

- Phase 1: analysis of the national policy context
- Phase 2: reconstruction of the chronology
- Phase 3: analysis of the actors involved
- Phase 4: reconstruction and analysis of processes of interaction between the actors
- Phase 5: interpretation of the results: identification of conditions for the implementation of the analysed policy

These five phases were carried out simultaneously in the five countries studied and in the two cases selected for each country. Each phase gave rise to the production of intermediary documents: analytical reports of national environmental policy over a period of around 20 years in each country; presentation of the different phases of the decision-making processes analysed; monograph of each (main) actor identified; report presenting the interaction between the actors in the course of the process.

Coordination between the teams through joint seminars for the presentation of these elements enabled the progressive appropriation of each case by all of the researchers from the national teams. This appropriation was a prerequisite of the interpretation of the case studies to be produced jointly at the end of the analysis of the different national situations.

Finally, the **comparison** was also the subject of a specific protocol. Based on the collective interpretation of the cases, a number of comparative hypotheses were formulated which were then worked on and reported by each team. These hypotheses related for the most part to:

- the types of protection provided based on the cases in question (reactive protection vs. proactive protection, decentralized protection vs. central initiative);
- the actors and their modes of cooperation (centre/periphery relation);
- the resources mobilized by the different actors and the challenges of the process;
- the impact of national and European environmental protection policy;
- the institutional contexts (centralized vs. decentralized).

The product of the comparison should lead to the identification of common conditions for success found in the different cases.

This experience illustrates the difficulty involved in such a comparison: the *outputs* to be analysed are generally numerous as are the actors to be interviewed. The historical context of each case must be apprehended in detail to enable the researchers to reach a good understanding of the interaction between administrations and target groups or beneficiary groups. Thus, the application of a protocol for the conduct of case studies enables the demonstration of the multiplicity of the modes of public action and their effects and the comparison of the actor configurations at work.

However, the application of this approach to local configurations may be too rigid and may lead to the neglect of more subtle role of social regulations (outside of the political-administrative sphere), which are ignored in the analysis framework but remain, nonetheless, a significant factor of understanding.

Nonetheless this type of process which is enriched gradually by its applications enables the comparative analysis of complex implementation processes and the apprehension of the effects.

Finally, the comparative analysis of implementation processes facilitated by the analytical framework developed by Peter Knoepfel et al. has led to the identification of differentiated implementation strategies for one and the same policy both between countries and between different implementation localities in one and the same country. These analyses have also paved the way for the highlighting of factors that explain the differences or similarities identified and, among these, the role played by the regulatory system of each country (rights to the ownership and use of land and natural resources, in particular).

A method that can be used for policy evaluation

It is not possible to evaluate public policies, programmes or action plans without analysing and contextualizing them. Therefore the third section of this chapter is devoted to the contribution made by the model developed by Peter Knoepfel in the area of policy evaluation.

For specialists in policy evaluation, *evaluating a policy, programme*[4] *or action plan means passing judgement on one piece of data in reference to another (Rangeon, 1993) while applying research procedures originating from the social sciences (Rossi, Freeman, Lipsey, 2004) so as to collect information for specific users in a systematic way with the aim of reducing uncertainty, improving effectiveness and supporting decision-making (Patton,1997).*[5]

Thus the question arises as to whether the evaluator can base his or her activity on the analytical model proposed by Peter Knoepfel. This analytical model is, in effect, very effective for all evaluative processes as it enables the examination of a policy, programme or action plan from the phase of their agenda-setting to the point at which they trigger their effects. Therefore, this model could also become a reference for policy evaluators who may be led to compare the observed reality with the model in the course of their work.

The effectiveness of the grid for the analysis of public policies lies in the fact that, like the actor configurations, each element of the public action programme may constitute an explanatory variable in an evaluation model.

---

[4] A programme operates one or more policy objectives which justify the policy from which they arise. It is demarcated in terms of schedule and budget.

[5] This definition was developed for the policy evaluation course given by Katia Horber-Papazian at the IDHEAP.

Moreover it is interesting to note that each policy phase predetermines the next to a certain extent. Thus, the application of the model makes it possible to understand the consequences that an erroneous hypothesis regarding the causes of a public problem may have for the hypothesis regarding the state intervention and, hence also, its capacity to resolve the problem. The same applies to the lack of action resources at the disposal of the actors which will have a direct impact on the quality of the outputs and effects triggered by the policy. Therefore, this model has a predictive value for the evaluator who will examine it based on the example of Figure 1 below.

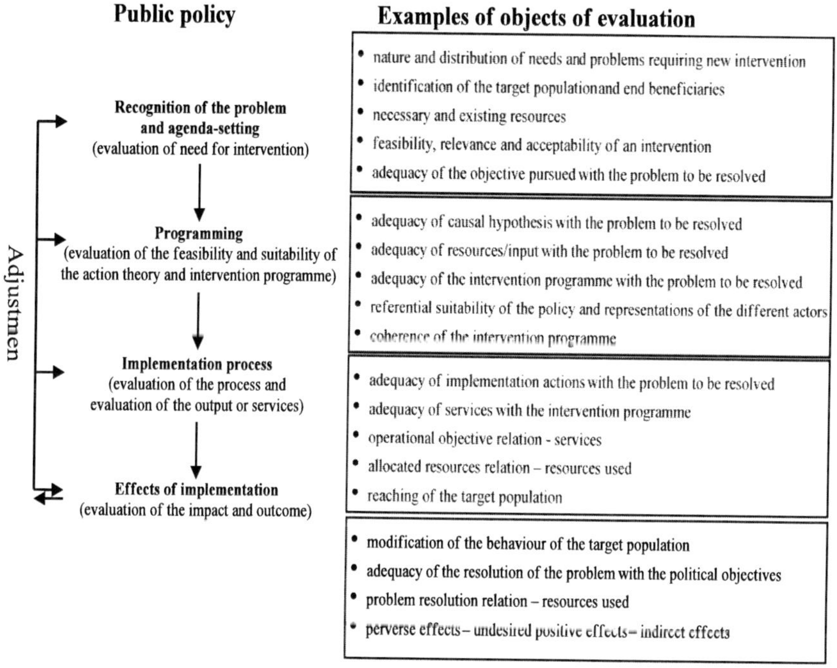

Figure 1 Policy evaluation objects[6].

Thus, what is of interest in this model for all evaluators is that it enables them to take inspiration from a very rich range of explanatory variables which give them access to the mysteries of public policies and to what has been considered as their "black box", i.e. the political and administrative processes that shape them. Every causality model constructed as part of the evaluation of a policy, programme or a specific measure may, therefore, take inspiration from the analytical model developed by Peter Knoepfel by adding other explanatory variables defined on the basis of the questions posed by the evaluation and the implementation context. This model is also very robust when it comes to proposing adjustment measures.

---

[6] This table was developed for the policy evaluation course given by Katia Horber-Papazian at the IDHEAP.

However, the application of the analytical model is not exempt from issues and uncertainties for evaluators who attempt to use it.

The Swiss political system is characterized by executive federalism. In this context, the formulation and implementation of a policy involves the intervention of federal actors who define a political framework in most cases. This policy is then concretized by the cantonal actors in the cantonal implementation laws. The cantonal spatial planning policies, for example, enable the cantons to appropriate the objectives defined in the context of the substantial federal policy, often re-interpret and complete them, prior to delegating a part of the implementation to the municipalities, on the basis of the cantonal-municipal division of tasks. The latter, in turn, pass regulations while re-appropriating the objectives of the superior level. In this federative case in point, the application to the letter of the analysis based on the triangle of actors proposed by Peter Knoepfel may perturb evaluators. As rightly stressed (Sager/Rüefli 2005) in this context, the model should be adapted to multi-level governance; in the case of spatial planning, for example, land owners constitute the target groups or actors, whose behaviour needs to be changed to resolve the problem or respond to a social need from the point of view of the political-administrative actors. However, it may be considered that the cantons also constitute a target group for the Confederation as the federal legislation enjoins them to define crop rotation areas or cantonal master plans which are accepted or rejected by the Federal Council in the same way as the cantons pass measures aimed at obliging the municipalities to change their behaviour in the management of their development zones to ensure appropriate land use. Therefore, in this case, the political-administrative actors are also a target group of the Confederation just as the municipalities are a target group for the cantons.

The application of the model not only surprises the evaluator in the case of a multi-level approach but also in the context of the evaluation of social policies, for example professional integration policy where the unemployed person may be both the target group and beneficiary of the measures implemented. Like every other model, the model proposed by Peter Knoepfel needs to be adapted by evaluators so as to take the multifunctional roles of the actors into account. Furthermore, rather than allow himself / herself to be disturbed by the problems in applying the model, the evaluator may draw highly instructive conclusions from this multi-functionality for the analysis, which this model allows to emerge.The place of evaluation in Peter Knoepfel's model is open to discussion. He presents evaluation in his analytical model as the fourth stage in the policy cycle and as the sixth policy product, which is referred to as "scientific evaluative statement". "*The scientific evaluative statements on the effects of the public policy aim to demonstrate the (eventual) changes in the behaviour of target groups (impacts) and the effects triggered among the end beneficiaries (outcomes) and to evaluate scientifically and/or politically the relevance, effectiveness, efficacy and efficiency of the policy which has been applied to a greater or lesser degree."*[7]

The aim of this definition is to demonstrate that the scientific evaluative statement may be the circumstance of a multitude of actors and rest on different foundations, including an evaluative process carried out on the basis of a rigorously scientific approach. This implicitly raises the question as to the utility and use of evaluations carried by experts in decision-making processes as has frequently been demonstrated by past experience (in particular Weiss, 1998; Widmer, 2004; Fornerod, 2001) and reminds us that the results of evaluations may influence decisions but are rarely their only determining element.

On the contrary, the positioning of evaluation as the fourth stage in a sequential model poses a particular problem for evaluators who specialise in policy evaluation. In effect, as illustrated by the diagram shown below, evaluation may take place throughout the policy cycle (*ex ante, concomitant, ex post*) through the posing of questions adapted to the given moment of intervention.

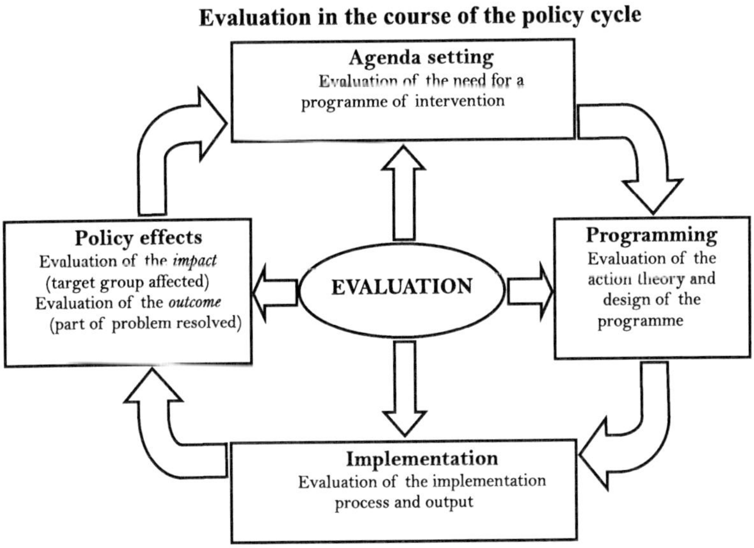

Figure 2 Evaluation in the course of the policy cycle[8].

The importance of the role of evaluation in the processes of formulation and implementation of public policies as we understand them are neither analysed nor adequately recognized in the analytical model proposed by Peter Knoepfel, for whom evaluation only makes sense if it enables the

---

[7] Knoepfel Peter, Larrue Corinne, Varone Frédéric (2006), *Analyse et pilotage des politiques publiques* (2e édition), Volume 2, Verlag Rüegger. p. 126.

[8] This diagram was developed for the policy evaluation course given by Katia Horber-Papazian at the IDHEAP.

demonstration of the effects of the measures based, in particular, on evaluative elements defined in the administrative programme. This limited understanding of the role of evaluation does not enable the apprehension of the increasingly significant role assumed by the latter in political-administrative reality throughout the policy cycle, the objects of which are demonstrated in Table 1 above and the objectives of which are to act as an information and, above all, readjustment tool.

As opposed to this, by insisting on the importance of evaluative elements since his early writings,[9] Peter Knoepfel has done pioneering work within the political-administrative world, in particular in Switzerland, and paved the way for the current debate on the place and role of indicators in the decision-making processes, their use by decision-makers and the difficulty in defining targets.

The enormous contribution made by Peter Knoepfel's work resides, finally, in the fact that he succeeded in enabling his analytical model to evolve over the course of his research, consultancy and teaching activities. While it is clear that his model may be applied in the analysis of a policy, it must also be noted that evaluators who analyse policies in their entirety, e.g. health policy or environmental protection policy, are rare. As opposed to this, there are numerous evaluators who are called on to evaluate one among the programmes that constitute public policies (programme to prevent tobacco addiction, AIDS etc.). However, the concept of the "programme" has not yet been introduced into the Knoepfelian model. We wager that, like the recognition of the role of evaluation throughout the policy cycle, this concept will be introduced in a subsequent edition of the book "Public Policy Analysis".

Conclusion

The contributions of the analytical model for the understanding of the modes of agenda setting, formulation, implementation and evaluation of public policies in different countries are undeniable. Both the design and application approaches developed on the basis of this model have made it possible to apprehend the conduct of these policies and provided a reference for their evaluation. The teaching of this model in Switzerland, France and Belgium has prompted students, some of whom have subsequently become policy actors themselves, to integrate all or part of the concepts and ideas used and has enabled evaluators to reconstruct the logic of evaluated policies. Of course, the use of this model cannot result in the production of policies whose content conforms completely to the analytical "model" or provides a normative framework for evaluations, however it aims to throw a critical light on public policy and the associated interaction with an aim to improving their management.

---

[9] P. Knoepfel, C. Larrue, 1984.

Thus it may be confirmed that the strength of the analytical framework proposed by Peter Knoepfel lies in the concepts established and shared, for the most part, by the policy analysis community and, increasingly, by policy evaluators. Its effectiveness or efficacy depends, however, on the long-term involvement of a network of researchers. In the case in point, this network expanded over the course of time and enabled the evolution of the concepts produced.

However, in focusing on the comparison of the modes of production of public policies, this type of approach does not enable the apprehension of phenomena that evade comparison. The analytical framework is based on the idea of a comparability of the processes studied and places the emphasis on this comparison. In this sense, the proposed framework makes it difficult to apprehend specific local or national institutional factors associated with the process being studied. It identifies them without, however, explaining them. Therefore, generally speaking, a return to what is not comparable could benefit the proposed approach. This would necessitate the challenging and re-examination of the comparative studies carried out up to now.

References

Ashford, D. (1978). Comparing Public Policies : New Concepts and Methods. Sage Publication. 254 p.

Bacque, M.H. (2005). *L'intraduisible notion d'empowerment vue au fil des politiques urbaines américaines. Territoires,* N° 460 pp. 32-35.

Bardach, E. (1984) *The implementation Game: What Happens After a Bill Becomes a Law,* Cambridge: The MIT Press. 322 p.

Bouleau, G. (2007), *La gestion française des rivières et ses indicateurs à l'épreuve de la directive cadre,* thèse ENGREF.

Boussaguet, L. et al. (2006). *Dictionnaire des politiques publiques.* Presse de Sciences po.

Castles, F.G. (1998). *Comparative Public Policy.* E. Elgar.

Fornerod, S. (2001). *A quoi et à qui servent les évaluations? Une recherche sur la place des évaluations dans les processus de décision et d'apprentissage dans l'administration fédérale.* Mémoire de MPA, IDHEAP.

Giraud, O. (2004). La comparaison comme opération de réduction de la complexité. Le cas de la formation professionnelle. *Revue internationale de Politique Comparée,* Vol. 11, N° 3, pp. 349-368.

Hassenteufel, P. (2005). De la comparaison internationale à la comparaison transnationale. Les déplacements de la construction d'objets comparatifs en matière de politiques publiques, *Revue Française de Science Politique,* vol. 56, N° 1, pp. 113-132.

Knoepfel, P., & Larrue, C. (1984). *Les politiques de mise en oeuvre dans le domaine de la lutte contre la pollution atmosphérique : évaluation comparée de l'action de trois directions interdépartementales de l'industrie en France,* Cahier de l'IDHEAP N° 18.

Knoepfel, P. & Larrue, C. (1985). "Les politiques publiques comparées : tourisme intelligent ou vrai progrès? le cas des politiques comparées de l'environnement", *Politiques et Management public,* 1984, vol. 2, n°3, pp. 45-63.

Knoepfel, P., & Weidner, H. (1982). Formulation and Implementation of Air Quality Control Programmes: Patterns of Interest Consideration. *Policy and Politics,* Vol 10 N°1, pp. 85-109.

Knoepfel, P., Larrue, C., Varone, F., & Hill, M. (2007). *Public Policy Analysis,* Bristol: The Policy Press.

Lallement, M., & Spurk, J. (Dir) (2003). *Stratégie de la comparaison internationale.* Paris : Editions du CNRS.

Larrue, C., & Knoepfel, P. (1998). *Environmental Protection, Subsidiarity Principle and Spatial Related Policies,* Final report contract N° ENV4-CT96-0238, 205 University of Tours, mai 1998.

Le Gales, P., & Thatcher, M. (1995). *Les réseaux de politique publique.* L'Harmattan.

Lima, L. & Steffen, M. (2004). Comparaisons internationales en politiques publiques: stratégies de recherche, méthodes et interpretation. *Revue internationale de politique compare.* Vol. 11 N° 3, pp. 339-348.

Lundquist, L. (1980). *The Hare and the Tortoise: Clean Air Policies in the United States and Sweden.* The University of Michigan Press. 248 p.

Maintz, R. (Ed). (1980). *Implementation Politischer Programme. Empirische Forschungsberichte.* Konigsstein,TS: Athenauer.

Morand, C.A. (Ed) (1991). *L'Etat propulsi.,* Paris : Publisud.

Patton, M.Q. (1997). *Utilization-focused evaluation: the new century text.* 3rd edition, Thousand Oaks: Sage.

Pressman, J.L., & Wildavsky, A. (1973). *Implementation.* Berkeley: University of California Press, 290 p.

Ragin, C. (1987). *The comparative Method.* Berkeley: University of California Press.

Rangeon. F. et al. (1993). *L'évaluation dans l'administration.* Centre universitaire de recherches administratives et politiques de Picardie (C.U.R.A.P.P.), PUF.

Revue internationale de politique comparée N° 1, 1994.

Richardson, J. (1982) (Ed) *Policy Style in Western Europe.* London: Allen and Unwin.

Rossi, P.H., Freeman, H.E., & Lipsey, M.W. (2004). *Evaluation. A Systemic Approach.* 7th Edition, Thousand Oaks: Sage.

Sartori, G. (1994). Bien comparer, Mal comparer. *Revue internationale de politique comparée,* N° 1, 1994, pp. 19-36.

Vogel, D. (1987). The comparative study of Environmental policy: a review of literature. In Dirkes et al., (1987) *Comparative Policy research Learning from Experience.* London: Gower.

Weiss, C.H. (1998). Have we learned anything new about the use of evaluation? *American Journal of Evaluation.* Vol. 19, N° 1, pp. 21-33.

Widmer & Neuenschwander (2004). Embedding Evaluation in the Swiss Federal Administration. Purpose, Institutional Design and Utilization. In *Evaluation*, Vol. 10(4), 391-41.

CHAPTER 16

A Pragmatic Constructivism

PHILIPPE WARIN

Introduction

Pragmatic constructivism is characterized in a particular epistemology based on the quest for parametric objectivity. In Peter Knoepfel's public policy analysis, this theoretical perspective relates to the study of the construction of marks of objectivity (that is, the measures contained in or inferred by a policy: problems, criteria, procedures, mechanisms, norms) which, according to him, make up the substance of policies. The place granted to the concepts of "actors", "resources" and "institutional rules" in the proposed analytical framework is a clear illustration of this (Knoepfel, Larrue & Varone, 2006) [1] However, this quest is unlikely to be successful if there is no empirical endeavour to explain the interactions between the three concepts. This is why Peter Knoepfel has constantly formulated the equation between actors, resources and rules, in operational terms – in both his research work carried out in close proximity to public action (through various mandates) and in his teaching in Switzerland and abroad.[2] The policy analysis defended by him is constantly shaped by a pragmatic perspective. The aim is to gain insight into concrete (observable) practices, through which actors produce a shared normative signification, particularly in terms of an hypothesis on problem causation (who or what is "guilty" or "objectively responsible" for the collective problem to be resolved?) and an hypothesis on state intervention (how can the collective problem be alleviated or resolved?). This pragmatism is located in a constant effort at methodological realization, which is systematically aimed at exploring the explanation for this trilogy (actors, resources, rules) and its interactions as a pragmatic concept. Peter Knoepfel always expects the explanation of a policy to cite factors that are *important.* For him the idea of importance (as for the pragmatists, Hilary Putnam (1990) in particular) is always dependent on the reason for asking the question *why?* In this instance, why such-and-such an actor, rule or resource?

The constructivist pragmatism which, in my opinion, characterizes Peter Knoepfel's approach to policy analysis can be explained. This is my objective here. To that end, I will (1) indicate the systemic and non-positivistic nature of

[1] This reference work is the main theme of this chapter.

[2] As I was able to witness by accompanying him for several years at a seminar in the Institut d'Etudes Politiques de Grenoble.

his approach; (2) highlight his adhesion to the methodological principle of the contingency of analysis; and (3) demonstrate the axiomatic neutrality of the approach. This will reveal the utility of his analytical framework in finding answers to a fundamental question: i.e. *how are public policies made?*

A systemic and non-positivistic approach to policy

The pragmatic constructivism characterizing the framework for policy analysis proposed by Knoepfel can be explained, first, in terms of its simultaneously systemic and non-positivistic conception of policy. He sees policies as a cascade of decisions and activities, the interactions of which produce observable results. This is what makes the system. The idea of *system* implies the consideration of both decisions and activities as perpetual combinations which aim to establish equilibriums between actors – i.e. from deciders to stakeholders – and through them between different social interests. These equilibriums are necessarily partial and provisional at each step of the policy cycle. In this regard, Peter Knoepfel postulates a renewal of them. In a sense it is summed up in the reproduction of one of his works (Peter Knoepfel is also an artist) found on the cover of *Analyse et pilotage des politiques publiques*, which brings to mind "Tinguely's Machine".

At the same time, Knoepfel's approach is also non-positivistic. It starts with observed facts which give policies their substance and avoids referring to them as an ideal type (Coenen-Huther, 2003). However unlike *scientific positivism* (as defined by Auguste Comte) it does not give up asking the question *why?* Consequently, for Knoepfel, policies are inevitably an *act* that is visible and can, therefore, be grasped by the analyst. For this reason, the proposed approach seeks to develop a scientific analysis of public policy, based on the study of variables to be explained (the "*products*" of a policy) by means of explanatory factors (the actors, resources and institutional rules). The idea is to consider these six products[3] from two points of view: i.e. substantial ("*How to solve the public problem?*") and institutional ("*Which actors are going to contribute to the next step in solving the problem, based on which rules and using which resources?*"). The kaleidoscope of explanatory variables changes for each product examined, however the questions remain the same: why such-and-such an actor, rule or resource?

By reasoning in terms of dependent and independent variables, the production of any proposal pertaining to the explanation of a phenomenon ("*Why this definition of this public problem? Why this politico-administrative programme?*" etc.) is subject to the control of its statements. The analyst is urged to follow a logical reasoning inspired by the Popperian principles of *The*

[3] The products are: 'the political definition of the public problem', 'the politico-administrative programme', 'the politico-administrative arrangement', 'the action plans', 'the implementation outputs', 'the evaluative statements on the effects of a public policy'.

Logic of Scientific Discovery (Popper, 1959[4]) for this purpose. To be valid, the approach must respect the "golden rules". For example, Knoepfel always recommends the question "*Why is there not such-and-such an actor, resource, or rule?*". Thus an analysis of policies, whose statements can be falsified, is produced. According to Knoepfel, "*the proposed analytical model can be applied in various scientific perspectives, that is, to describe, interpret, explain or even anticipate the content of a policy*" (Knoepfel, Larrue & Varone, 2006: 276). If it is to be more than an impressionistic account, under no circumstances may the analysis exclude the study of observed facts. Its relevance lies in the reconstruction of the overall logic of a system of decisions and activities taken as a whole. To that end, it is necessary to highlight observed facts and to note their compositional effects. The analysis thus requires a depersonalization and complexification of the logical reasoning ("*Why these variables and not others?*") by integrating multiple feedback loops. In this way, linear reasoning loses its plausibility and relevance. Two aspects are particularly important here: first, the fact of highlighting the validity of each observed fact, insofar as it is possible to find the "right reasons" for their presence or absence by reconstructing explanatory variables; second, and above all, the fact of highlighting the simultaneity of explanatory variables, from which it is possible to specify the dynamics of policies on the basis of parts of their content.

To explain the logical reasoning at work, consider for a moment what Peter Knoepfel and his co-authors call the "*Product n° 1*" of a policy, "*the political definition of the public problem*". The initial idea is that there are no policies without decisions or activities (legislative, regulatory, administrative, etc.) designed to implement them. The problems addressed by policies are highly specific however: they are problems that are politically defined as public.

If a social problem is the subject of a political controversy it becomes a political problem. From this point of view there is nothing original about the proposed approach. It fits into the *agenda-building* perspective, which shows that the emergence of a problem is accompanied by a process of problem-framing, during which the actors propose their definition of the situation based on their own perception of the problem (Cobb & Elder, 1972). But it is also part of the constructivist approach to public problems, now dominant in North American research,[5] which, under the impetus of John Kitsuse's and Malcolm Spector's group at the Society for the Study of Social Problems, strongly emphasizes the social construction of the meaning of things and events (Gusfield, 1981, 1984; Spector & Kitsuse, 1987). It also embodies the cognitivist conception of "*agenda-setting* as a *"continuous operation of construction and symbolic reconstruction"*" (Padioleau, 1982: 26). The importance of ideas in the political definition of the public problem is not overlooked. The authors point out that "*the assessment of problems depends not only on the objective conditions of the situation deemed to be problematical, but also on its evaluation and*

[4] First English translation.

[5] For an overview of precursory debates, see: Schneider, 1985; Holstein & Miller, 1993.

subjective weighting (that is, the political definition) by the actors concerned" (Knoepfel, Larrue & Varone, 2006: 145). Knoepfel nevertheless approaches the issue of agenda-setting (like everything else) from a pragmatic perspective. Like the North Americans, he advises the analyst to strive, above all, to account for the stakeholders' representations of the nature of the problem. To that end, and somewhat akin to researchers in ethnomethodology, the interactionists (Blumer, 1971) or sociologists of science (Latour & Woolgar, 1979), he proposes the same dimensions of operational analysis ("*intensity, perimeter, novelty, urgency of the problem*") as those, around which the actors struggle concretely to reach a political definition of the public problem. It is in this struggle, and not only for pre-established reasons linked to statuses or institutional context, or for existing cognitive schemes (or *framing*), that the "*political entrepreneurs*" so dear to Cobb and Edler *effectively* appear as actors. The analyst then has the possibility of recognizing them if he or she is prepared to undertake an empirical inquiry. For that purpose, it is necessary to examine these dimensions (and others, Knoepfel recommends) as precisely as possible, to show that a situation becomes a public problem not because of its intrinsic characteristics, but because of the way in which the actors construe these dimensions to ensure that the situation appears on the political agenda.

The contingency of policy analysis

This systemic and non-positivistic approach means *ipso facto* that it is necessary to try to inter-relate decisions and activities; it is naturally situated in the here-and-now of interactions between the two. The epistemological foundation of this approach to public policy analysis is the contingency of the analysis. As Erhard Friedberg, who defends the pragmatic value of the scientific analysis of organizations, says, it is based "*on the implementation of an intuitive and progressive choice of the outlines and central points or sensitive areas whose study allows for the best progress to be made in the understanding of the whole*" (Friedberg, 1993: 244). Hence, policy analysis and its results are historically situated. It is an empirical explication of a construct that the historically and spatially situated actors ("*public actors*", "*target groups*" and "*beneficiary groups*", in Knoepfel's terminology) have instituted to produce the processes of exchange and power that interweave the interactions between decisions and activities. Clearly, an explanation such as this is also historically situated and its demonstration, as both Knoepfel and Friedberg say, cannot claim to exhaust reality or to propose a general model. The validity of the analysis lasts no longer than the policy itself; it loses its relevance as soon as the policy changes. The course of public policies is by no means automatic. It is subject to the uncertainties of the interactions between decisions or activities. Moreover, their duration is subject to the possibility of challenging the "*hypotheses on the causes*" of the problems to solve and the *"hypotheses on the state solutions"* to provide, on which they are based at some point.

The contingency of the analysis does not mean that one should disregard the diachrony and study of change in the definition of the problem causation and state intervention hypotheses, as is so often believed (Friedberg, 1993: 244). Public policies are not eventless; they really happen. Moreover, they have a historicity in so far as – produced by historically and spatially situated actors – they are only meaningful for a limited period. Peter Knoepfel situates himself, therefore, in a synchronic perspective and warns us that the systemic and non-positivistic approach to public policy, which he defends, must recognize the temporal contingency of the analysis thus produced. In his opinion, there is nothing stable or timeless about a policy. On the contrary, it is a dynamic process of interaction. Hence, the empirical knowledge of the structural mechanisms – especially the general and specific "institutional rules" influencing the actors' games and stabilizing interactions between decisions and activities – is what enables the analyst to describe and understand policy transformation (or abandonment) processes. The highly instructive example of the public problem of "poisoned water" enables him to get this theoretical message across. From the witches of yesteryear burned at the stake to today's farmers forced to change their production techniques, Peter Knoepfel uses allegory to talk about the historicity of the definition and treatment of a public problem. Moreover, the historicity of public policies is a principal component in this approach in that this dimension accommodates enduring and international comparisons as precisely explained in this book.

The (Hegelian) conception of the historicity of the problem causation and state intervention hypotheses underlying the choice and way of acting explains Peter Knoepfel's interest in "*causal stories*" or, in other words, in public policy discourses which define the problems and legitimize the meaning of the action to be undertaken. His approach to public policies draws explicitly on the assets of cognitive perspectives which, in public policy analysis, serve to indicate the structuring importance of the "*causal stories*" (Stone, 1989) and, more recently, the "*normative frameworks*" or "*scalar narratives*" (Mahon & Johnson, 2006) that point out the "right" key known for the definition of public problems and legitimate policies and the appropriate means of dealing with them. With Peter Knoepfel (unlike Erhard Friedberg and Michel Crozier) the contingency of the analysis does not lead to a refusal of the importance of ideas in the policy production process for fear of a conception postulated in political terms, like "*totalism*", i.e. as a producer of a general meaning whose effective scope cannot be demonstrated empirically (Leca & Jobert, 1980: 1149-1153). Knoepfel believes that the analyst's work consists in identifying competing causal stories so as to understand how a dominant "problem *causation hypothesis*" emerges in a conflictual debate. We are very close here to "the approach by reference frameworks" developed in France on the basis of Bruno Jobert's and Pierre Muller's work (Jobert & Muller, 1987; Faure, Pollet & Warin, 1995). Yet with Knoepfel, as with Friedberg (Warin, 1997), the existence of a community of rules, a collective project, founding agreements and higher principles – all explanatory variables taken into account in the cognitivist approaches to policy – structures the field of action less explicitly than it does the capacity of the actors – who are placed in necessarily unequal negotiating positions in relation to the portfolio of resources at their disposal[6] – to impose a definition of the causal hypothesis and the intervention hypothesis.

The pragmatism of the approach is measured, therefore, in terms of the deliberately *a minima* treatment reserved for the actors' personal variables (interests, motivations, intentions, beliefs). These exist and influence the actors' behaviours but they are excluded from the analysis because they are not independent of the actors. Pragmatism here resembles a form of *realism.* The analyst retains only those statements which enable him or her to relate any consideration of the actors and their rationale empirically to the reciprocal conditioning between context (set of resources and rules) and action (interactions between decision and activities). In other words, apart from the observation of this mutual conditioning, nothing can be said about the actors' action from the scientific point of view. The proposed approach thus excludes the personal variables that reduce the predictive capacity of the analysis. From a theoretical point of view, we can see that it is carefully kept apart from propositions designed to surpass the rustic utilitarianism of the neoclassical theory of *homo economicus* (Etzioni, 1988, and before him an entire series of heterodox economists: Leibenstein, 1976; Akerlof, 1984). It is however based on a *logical positivism,* which to some extent brings to mind the ethnomethodologists' position when they contend that, apart from analyzing the processes through which the actors construct the situations they are simultaneously living and producing, the analyst has nothing but "*stories for the telling*" (Garfinkel, 1985).

In this type of approach the actors' power is concentrated in this capacity to control the resources and to mobilize them in a context of institutional rules so that they can impose both their opinions and demands on others. From this point of view, Peter Knoepfel does not problematize the political aspects of relations between actors much. He confines himself to an *a minima* conception of the political, amounting to the exchange of resources between the types of actor that he proposes to study: "*public authorities*", the "*target groups*", whose behaviours have to be changed to solve the public problem, and the "*beneficiary groups*" of the policy that is made and implemented. The power is incorporated into the political interaction that guides the definition of the problem causation and state intervention hypotheses, through the mobilization of resources within the framework of pre-established rules. The pragmatic constructivism characterizing this approach to policy is then locked in by the granting of (systemic and non-positivistic) methodological priority to the endogenous explication of explanatory variables. This complicates the connection with the substantive approaches to politics in the production of policies. Starting with this comment, we can now try to discuss this consequence of constructivist pragmatism in public policy analysis, to characterize its specificity with even more precision.

---

[6] The main resources studied are: '*force* (violence resource); *law* (legal resource); *staff* (human resource); *money* (monetary resource); *information* (cognitive resource); *organization* (interactive resource); *consensus* (trust resource); *time* (temporal resource); *infrastructure* (patrimonial resource); *political support* (majority resource)'.

An axiomatic neutrality

From the perspective of pragmatic constructivism, policies mobilize configurations of actors, resources and rules with the aim of directly producing or coordinating the responses required to meet the collective needs recognized as falling within the province of the state or other public authorities. From this point of view they are "*instituted policies*". In this respect the policy approach concerns the actual realization of outputs that are supposed to influence the behaviour of the groups or individuals believed to be at the root of the public problem to be resolved. It studies the performance of these configurations, sometimes following explicit engineering goals, as in the case, in particular, of the evaluation of policies or action programmes. The complex configurations of actors, in particular at the level of the "*politico-administrative arrangement*" of a policy, representing the structured whole of public and para-public actors responsible for its implementation, produces what we now call policy governance. Many research studies are devoted to it, both in France and abroad. They analyze how the logics of reconstruction of public action are structured by the forms of mobilization of the social actors, especially by the shifting of traditional boundaries between legitimate (or incumbent) actors and challengers. Analytical tools have been developed for examining these interdependencies – such as the notions of "*networks*" for linking up actors (Thatcher, 2004) and "*forums*" for the channels of influence on public action (Boussaguet, 2004) – and identifying the importance of the qualification of the objects of action in the processes of actors' interference, especially around the notion of a "*public problem*" (Sheppard, 2004).

This presentation of policies is not, however, the first one selected to explain the role of politics in policy-making. Another approach consists in considering policies as "*instituting policies*", in so far as the process and political implications of their production lie in the very definition of the problems to be resolved (Giraud & Warin, 2008). Within this approach, policies effectively mobilize institutional configurations. However these are studied less for the outputs of the policies that they decide on and implement (resource allocation, setting legal or administrative rules, decisions on equipment programmes, etc.), than for the relations of domination that they institute in order to structure the political field of action. In this instance, policies are processes involving the social definition of reality, and are analyzed as such.

The policies are "*instituting*" in so far as they develop a representation of the action to be undertaken, which integrates a dual hypothesis on the causes of the problem to be dealt with and the solutions to be provided. The construction of what is then called a *"normative frame"* is at the very heart of the policy production process (Jobert, 1999). This is of particular interest to policy analysts in France. One of the pioneers in this respect, Robert Axelrod, demonstrated it in his own way in terms of the cognitive maps of political elites which are mobilized in public decision-making (Axelrod, 1976). This construction is an eminently political moment, which determines which actor wins or loses. Contradictory interests are expressed and sometimes open up crisis zones which politics has to manage. The return to stability then consists in drawing on a repertory – representative of the political culture – of symbolic and cognitive elements that serve to guarantee the maximum possible compliance on the part of the actors.

The approach to public policies as "instituting policies" is presented as a structural approach to politics. It highlights the political regulation of the social order or, in other words, the need to contain the centrifugal forces stemming from contradictory interests, which would otherwise make it impossible to produce any policies at all. The public policy approach to politics raises specific questions with original theoretical foundations. In particular, the importance granted to contradictory interests explicitly takes into account the Habermassian analysis of the fragility of social cohesion and, more implicitly, the analysis of the state proposed by Nobert Elias.[7] Social cohesion is threatened by both the disparities between the different ensembles that structure society and the non-adhesion of subjects, capable of analysis and judgement, with values and symbols that justify the permanence of a social order. The politicians' specific task is to maintain the political community by safeguarding its structured components and the integration of individuals. To analyze it as such, this alternative approach to public policies asks two questions: How do the main components hold together as a whole? And, how do the different individuals, situated in relation to these structural components, adhere to the political community? This conception of the politicians' work refers to a set of actions and functions conceived of as a whole. Politics is, therefore, more a dynamic, a process that tends to include actors and institutions, than a passively occupied space.

The mastery of this fundamental function of politics spurs the ambitions of actors who understand that by dominating the representation of the social reality on which it is necessary to act, they occupy a key position *de facto*. The regulation of these ambitions is needed to ensure social order. It functions in the very production of policies, and determines their form and content. This regulation of ambitions is directly political; it is the business of whosoever accepts the pre-eminence and continuity of stabilized symbolic and cognitive elements. The fact of mastering discourse on the values, norms and rules that have to be complied with for problems to be addressed, puts him or her at the heart of the configuration of actors. We find an anthropological conception of politicians (and politics) here, insofar as this power is that of the *pacifier* whose means are limited to speech (Clastres, 1974: 175-176) and whose hegemony (or monopolization) constitutes the state as a function of arbitration (Elias, 1975), as per the conception of the state theorized by Hobbes ([1642] 1982). This political regulation is nevertheless a result of a mobilization of legitimate constraint (Jobert, 1998). Public action cannot do without arguments for ranking and making more or less compatible the use of political resources. The study of this regulation or the practice of political power is, therefore, crucial here. It concerns above all the clashes between representations of social reality, which necessarily highlight the divergence of interests. This point of view

[7] For Elias, both the problem and *raison d'être* of social order is to render the interdependence of individuals (*individuals need one another*) and their conflicts (*but their interests oppose them*) compatible, to ensure the conditions of *living together* (Elias, 1975).

also corresponds to recent analyses. In the late 1990s Renate Mayntz concluded a dialogue with Niklas Luhmann, who pointed out the inanity of politics faced with the irrepressible reinforcement of interests contradictions and with auto-referentiality of ensembles that structure society, by redefining politics as the *"management of interdependencies"* (Mayntz, 2001). The function of politics, thus defined by the famous German political scientist, is compatible with Luhmann's diagnosis: i.e. to avoid the shocks and contradictions resulting from the pursuit of the process of differentiation. This conflict management, central in policy-making, reveals the underlying ambiguity of politics. In a democratic context, politics does not amount to avoiding the shocks of differentiation. It must also find ways of reconciling political equality with social inequalities, as the latter also depend on the ways in which social interests are structured. This debate, which first emerged between Niklas Luhmann and Fritz Scharpf (Luhmann, 1990 ; Scharpf 1990), has had an enduring influence on Peter Knoepfel, who participated directly in the founding research programme directed by Scharpf and Mayntz in the 1980s (Knoepfel, Weidmer, 1982). Indeed, the approach to policies as "instituting policies" is clearly apparent in Knoepfel's approach around the question of the potentially conflictual relations between target groups and end beneficiaries and other actors, who are also affected by the effects of a policy. While the politics in the theoretical model may be rather subtle (and in Knoepfel's teaching), this main dimension is never entirely lacking. The demonstration of its existence is not, however, the ultimate goal in Knoepfel's policy approach.

The understanding of policy in the approach to instituted policies outlined under the pragmatic constructivism perspective implies an understanding of the processes through which this shared signification of problems and solutions is not only produced, but also produces effects of meaning throughout the course of a policy. That is why it seeks to consider each product of a policy from both a substantial and institutional point of view. Peter Knoepfel equips us with useful tools for identifying the variables to be explained and the explanatory variables, and for understanding the substance of the outcome of the interactions between decisions and activities. He is, however, more vague when it comes to the question of the semantic productivity of problem causation hypotheses and state intervention (ideas and social representations) – that is, when the subject is not totally avoided. Policy analysis does not stop when it has defined the play of hypotheses characterizing the *raison d'être* and orientation of a policy. It could even be said that it starts when one wonders which effects of meaning this shared normative signification is going to produce next, particularly during the shift from the "product" of one public policy to another.

This remark prompts, therefore, the question as to whether the "Knoepfelian approach" to policy contains a theory of "*shared cooperative action*", at least if the pragmatic hypothesis is applied (Bratman, 1992; Coleman, 2001), according to which the semantic productivity of the definition of problems and solutions could be judiciously analyzed in terms of cooperative action. The approach developed by Peter Knoepfel seems somewhat allusive on this point. It appears to have little concern for integrating reflection on the "social system" when the actors interact. Yet it also seems to show that the definition and implementation of a policy cannot be summed up in the achievement of objectives that are intentional or attributed to one or more actors; they also stem from the renewal or transformation of shared beliefs. In other words, the pragmatic constructivism proposed by Peter Knoepfel takes policy analysis to the extreme, insofar as the explanation of a policy is based on a combination of independent observable variables (actors, resources and rules). The advantage of this epistemological position is to ensure that policy analysis does not go astray – at the other extreme – in the study of the meaning attributed *to* and produced *by* public action, but remains apprehendable from the outside. It is probably correct to point this out at a time when cognitivist approaches are conquering much of the field of policy studies (for France, see: RFSP, 2000). The risk that is run here would be to lose sight of the (supposed) realism needed by the scientific approach, and to focus exclusively on the knowledge, ideas, representations and beliefs of the actors involved. The reason is that they make it possible to describe what politics really resembles, at the observable level of the reciprocal conditioning between context (a set of resources and rules) and action (interactions between decisions and activities).

The proposed approach does not aim, therefore, to show that policies are the result of conflicts between groups of actors who mobilize to guarantee the satisfaction of "*causes*" stemming from shared beliefs and norms (Sabatier & Jenkins-Smith, 1993). This possibility is not, however, denied. It is just that Knoepfel does not consider that the aim of policy analysis is to say that the actors share the same "worldview", no more than it is to show that they act out of self-interest. Peter Knoepfel's analysis is noteworthy in so far as it does not impose a cardinal theory of the actors as explanatory factors in the birth and implementation of policies. His pragmatism is characterized – as I have said – by a deliberately *a minima* treatment of the actors' personal variables (interests, motivations, intentions, beliefs). He sees beliefs and interests as inputs that are potentially relevant within the explanatory variables as a whole. If they exist, the analyst will have to account for them by induction. This approach is resolutely oriented towards a methodology for policy analysis. It is based, therefore, on axiomatic neutrality so as to avoid theoretical debates and standpoints which are sterile for the analyst whose analysis helps to steer policy.

For all of these reasons, the constructivist pragmatism underpinning Peter Knoepfel's approach is clearly distinguished from policy analysis as "*pragmatic of democracy*", as it appears from the cognitivist perspective (Giraud & Warin, 2008). By proposing to approach policies as essentially intellectual constructions, *loci* of debate, and places of transformation of social representations of the reality to be dealt with this other perspective chooses explanatory variables which are substantially different (actors' logics and interests; social representations; institutional rules that strongly frame – or not – political interaction; possibility – or not – of rigorous and transparent procedures; scenes of debate, controversy or communication; alliances and power struggles etc.). At the same time, and above all, the variables that are to be explained change. They are "*products*" not of policies, as with Knoepfel, but of the permanent production of the social order through the political work of reconciliation of contradictory interests, which policies support. Policies are characterized here by the necessary adjustment of social representations which change sooner or later. In this case they are studied because, through the possibility of viewing problems and solutions differently, they can call for changes in institutional configurations and sometimes even in aspects of the political culture. As a field for political expression, public policies appear to be a democratic affair; they help to maintain the social order by making its renewal possible. In other words, these two perspectives do not have the same scientific goal. In the one, policy analysis serves reflection on politics and democracy. In the other, it aims to understand how policies are made – and that is the underlying intention of the approach developed by and around Peter Knoepfel.

* * *

In the final analysis, the constructivist pragmatism which I see as characterizing the public policy analysis proposed by Peter Knoepfel can probably be explained by his idea of his profession as a university lecturer, researcher, expert and, at the heart of all that, teacher and adviser. The axiomatic neutrality characterizing his approach corresponds to his main objective of equipping analysts, scientists and practitioners with a framework for understanding situations. His scientific contribution lies in the fact of making possible an *ethnography of public policies.* By being wary of the analyst who has only *"stories to tell"*, Peter Knoepfel reminds us in a way of an international figure in anthropology, Claude Levi-Strauss, who started his famous popularized book *Tristes tropiques* ([1955] 1985) with the following incipit: "*I hate journeys and explorers*". Let us therefore dare to compare pragmatic constructivism at the service of a logical reasoning in policy analysis to Lévi-Strauss's break with the travel novel genre, with the aim of establishing an intellectual experience of another kind, that of structural logic.

The axiomatic neutrality that is the framework of the pragmatic constructivism of this approach nevertheless raises a fundamental question that I will leave open: the question of whether it reduces policy analysis to a technique. The history of the social sciences shows how axiomatic neutrality has served as a requisite for intellectual strategies for promoting reformist formulae that do not challenge the socio-economic order (Guilhot, 2004). I certainly do not believe that Peter Knoepfel's scientific contributions serve this type of goal. Along with other European academic institutions (e.g. the International Management Institute, and the Environmental Research Institute of Berlin), the *Institut des Hautes Etudes en Administration Publique,* where Peter Knoepfel worked for a long time and of which he was also Director, is one of the main places in Europe where the interaction between research and application have contributed to the complete renewal of training in public management, and to the development of the *"policy sciences"* on the basis of a critical view of "*public administration theory*" (Thoenig, 1985: 2). In the context of this international perspective, his approach to policy analysis contributes deliberately to a questioning of the policy dimensions that defy the mode of analysis so dear to this theory. Like Dror and others, who strove to introduce organizational or institutional factors, conflicts, ideologies, and even the social value of time – outrageously neglected by institutions such as the Rand Corporation in their biased analysis of government action (Dror, 1968 and 1970) –, Peter Knoepfel endeavours to explain the importance of a methodical approach to the explanatory variables of public policies, which denaturalizes categories and gives depth to the analysis of government decisions and activities. His aim is to provide the means of producing complete scientific statements on which the debate on public policy can be based. From this point of view, his approach helps to make policy analysis a real government science as it shows – mainly through the study of resources – the diversity of approaches (and sciences), from which government authorities can act.

References

Akerlof, G.A. (1984). *An Economic Theorist's Book of Tales.* Cambridge, MA: Cambridge University Press.

Axelrod, R. (Ed.) (1976). *Structure of Decision: the Cognitive Maps of Political Elites.* Princeton: Princeton University Press.

Blumer, H. (1971). Collected Behavior. In A.M. Lee (Ed.) *New Outline of the Principles of Sociology.* New York: Barnes and Noble: 167-222.

Boussaguet, L. (2004). Forums. In L. Boussaguet, S. Jacquot & P. Ravinet (Dir.) *Dictionnaire des politiques publiques.* Paris : Presses de Science Po: 226-232.

Bratman, M. (1992). Shared Cooperation Activity. *Philosophical Review:* 327-341.

Clastres, P. (1974). *La société contre l'État.* Paris: Les Éditions de minuit.

Cobb, R., & Edler, C. (1972). *Participation in American Politics: the dynamics of Agenda-Building.* Baltimore: John Hopkins University Press.

Coenen-Huther, J. (2003). Le type idéal comme instrument de la recherche sociologique. *Revue française de sociologie.* 2003, 3(44): 531-547.

Coleman, J. (2001). *The Practice of Principle: In Defence of a Pragmatist Approach to Legal Theory.* Oxford: Oxford University Press.

Dror, Y. (1968). *Public Policy Making Reexamined.* San Francisco: Chandler.

Dror ,Y. (1970). Prolegomena to Policy Sciences. *Policy Sciences.* 1: 135-150.

Elias, N. (1975). *La dynamique de l'Occident.* Paris : Calmann-Levy.

Etzioni, A. (1988). *The Moral Dimension.* New York: The Free Press.

Faure, A., Pollet, G., & Warin, P. (Dir.) (1995). *La construction du sens dans les politiques publiques. Débats autour de la notion de référentiel.* Paris : L'Harmattan.

Friedberg, E. (1993). *Le pouvoir et la règle. Dynamique de l'action organisée.* Paris : Seuil.

Garfinkel, H. (1985). Sur le problème des correctives. *Pratiques de formation (analyses), Ethnométhodologies.* 11-12, vol. 2, Paris, EHESS.

Giraud, O. & Warin, P. (Dir.) (2008). *Politiques publiques et démocratie.* Paris : La Découverte.

Guilhot, N. (2004). Une vocation philanthropique. Georges Soros, les sciences sociales et la régulation du marché mondial. *Actes de la recherche en sciences sociales.* 151-152: 36-48.

Gusfield, J.R. (1981). The *Culture of Public Problems: Drinking-Driving and the Symbolic Order.* Chicago: Chicago University Press.

Gusfield, J.R. (1984). On the Side: Practical Action and Social Constructivism in Social Problems Theory. In J. Schneider & J. Kitsuse (Eds) *Studies in the sociology of social Problems.* Norwood, NJ: Ablex Publishing Corporation: 31-51.

Hobbes, T. ([1642] 1982). *Le Citoyen ou les fondements de la politique.* Paris : Garnier- Flammarion.

Holstein, J., & Miller, G. (eds.) (1993). *Reconsidering Social Constructionism: Debates in Social Problems Theory.* Hawthorne, NY: Adline de Gruyter.

Jobert, B., & Muller, P. (1987). *L'Etat en action. Politiques publiques et corporatismes.* Paris : Presses Universitaires de France.

Jobert, B. (1998). La régulation politique : le point de vue d'un politiste. In J. Commaille & B. Jobert (Dir.) *Les métamorphoses de la régulation politique.* Paris . LGDJ: 119-144

Jobert, B. (1999). Des Etats en interactions. *L'Année de la regulation.* vol. 3 : 77-95.

Knoepfel, P., & Weidner, H. (1982). Formulation and Implementation of Air Quality Control Programmes: Patterns of Interest Consideration. *Policy and Politics.* 1 (10): 85-109.

Knoepfel, P., Larrue C., & Varone, F. (2006). *Analyse et pilotage des politiques publiques.* Zurich : Verlag Rüegger.

Latour B., & Wollgar S. (1979). *La vie de laboratoire. Production des faits scientifiques.* Paris : La Découverte.

Leca, J., & Jobert, B. (1980). Le dépérissement de l'Etat. A propos de "l'Acteur et le système" de Michel Crozier et Ehrard Friedberg. *Revue française de science politique.* 6 (30): 1125-1170.

Leibenstein, H. (1976). *Beyond Economic Man: A New foundation for Microeconomics.* Cambridge, MA: Harvard University Press.

Lévy Strauss, C. (1985). *Tristes Tropiques.* Paris : Plon (Terres humaines).

Luhmann, N. (1990). Politische Steuerung: Ein Diskussionsbeitrag. *Politische Vierteljahresschrift.* (PVS), 3 (30): 4-9.

Mahon, R., & Johnson, R. (2006). NAFTA, the Redesign and Rescaling of Canada's Welfare State. *Speakers' Corner.* Carleton University, School of Public Policy and Administration: http://www.carleton.ca/spa /Publication/ NAFTA% 20Johnson %20and%20Mahonrevised.pdf

Mayntz, R. (2001). Zur Selektivität der steuerungstheoretischen Perspektive. In H.P. Burth & A. Görlitz (Dir.) *Politische Steuerung in Theorie und Praxis.* Baden-Baden: Nomos: 17-27.

Padioleau, J.G. (1982). *L'Etat au concret.* Paris : Presses Universitaires de France.

Popper, K.R. (1984). *La logique de la découverte scientifique.* Paris : Payot.

Putnam, H. (1990). *Représentation et réalité.* Paris : Gallimard.

RFSP (2000). Les approches cognitives des politiques publiques. *Revue Française de Science Politique* 2 (50).

Sabatier, P., & Jenkins-Smith, H. (Eds.) (1993). *Policy change and Learning: An Advocacy Coalition Approach.* Boulder, CO: Westview Press.

Scharpf, F.W. (1990). Politische Steuerung und Politische Institutionen. *Politische Vierteljahresschrift.* (PVS), 3 (30): 10-15.

Schneider, J.W. (1985). Social Problems Theory: The constructivist View. *American Review of Sociology.* 11: 209-229.

Sheppard, E. (2004). Problème public. In L. Boussaguet, S. Jacquot & P. Ravinet (Dir.) *Dictionnaire des politiques publiques.* Paris: Presses de Science Po : 347-354.

Spector, M., & Kitsuse, J.I. (1987). *Constructing Social Problems.* Hawthorne, NY: Aldine de Gruyter.

Stone, D.A. (1989). Causal stories and the formation of policy agendas. *Political Science Quartely.* 2 (104): 281-300.

Thatcher, M. (2004). Réseau (policy network). In L. Boussaguet, S. Jacquot & P. Ravinet (Dir.) *Dictionnaire des politiques publiques.* Paris: Presses de Science Po: 384-390.

Thoenig, J.C. (1985). L'analyse des politiques publiques. In M. Grawitz & J. Leca (Dir.) *Traité de science politiques,* vol. 4 : *Les politiques publiques,* Paris : Presses Universitaires de France : 1-60.

Warin, P. (1997). La contingence des acteurs : apports et limites pour une analyse de la négociation. In J.P. Gaudin & G. Novarina (Dir.) *Politiques publiques et négociation. Multipolarités, flexibilité, hiérarchies,* Paris : CNRS Editions : 107-123.

Biographies of the editors

NAHRATH, Stéphane (1966) is professor of political science at the University Institute Kurt Bösch (IUKB) in Sion. His teaching, research and publications lie in the domains of tourism policy, environmental policy, land use planning, urban governance, institutional regimes for sustainable resource management, as well as market liberalisation of network industries.

E-mail: stephane.nahrath@iukb.ch

VARONE, Frédéric (1966) is professor of political science at the University of Geneva. His current research interests include comparative public policy (sustainable management of natural resources, regulation of biotechnologies), program evaluation and public sector reforms (e.g. New Public Management, liberalization and privatization of public services).

E-mail: frederic.varone@unige.ch

Biographies of the authors

BENNINGHOFF, Martin (1966) is senior researcher at the Observatory Science, Policy and Society (OSPS) of the University of Lausanne. His research domains are research policy studies, comparative public policy and social studies of science. Among his publications are *La recherche, affaire d'Etat* (with J.-Ph. Leresche, PPUR, 2002), *La fabrique des sciences* (with J.-Ph. Leresche, F. Crettaz von Roten, M. Merz, PPUR, 2006)

E-mail: martin.benninghoff@unil.ch

BRAUN, Dietmar (1952) is professor of comparative political science at the University of Lausanne. His research interests focus on comparative federalism and science and technology policies. He studied political science in Amsterdam (NL) where he also obtained his PhD degree. He has been researcher at the Max-Planck-Institut for the Study of Societies in Cologne, Germany and assistant professor at the Institut for Political Science at the University of Heidelberg.

E-mail: dietmar.braun@unil.ch

BRESSERS, Hans (1953) is professor of policy studies and environmental policy at CSTM, the centre for studies in governance and sustainable development of the University of Twente in the Netherlands. He published recently a/o. Achieving Sustainable Development: The Challenge of Governance Across Social Scales (2003, with Walter Rosenbaum), Integrated Governance and Water Basin Management (2004, with Stefan Kuks) and Governance of Complexity in Water Management: Creating Cooperation by Boundary Spanning Strategies (2009, with Kris Lulofs).
E-mail: j.t.a.bressers@utwente.nl

DENTE, Bruno (1946), is professor of Public Policy Analysis at Politecnico di Milano, where he is the president of the Scientific Council of The Centre for Administration and Public Policies (CAPP). He is also scientific director of the Istituto per la Ricerca Sociale, Milano. His current research interests include administrative reform, public policy evaluation and metropolitan governance.
E-mail: bdente@irsonline.it

CLIVAZ, Christophe (1969) is assistant professor of comparative tourism policies at the University Institute Kurt Bösch (IUKB) in Sion. He obtained a PhD in Public Administration at the Swiss Graduate School of Public Administration (IDHEAP). His research fields and teaching activities concern the governance of tourism resorts and the comparative analysis of (local, regional, national and international) tourism policies.
E-mail: christophe.clivaz@iukb.ch

EMERY, Yves (1960), Ph.D. from the University of Geneva, is professor at the Swiss Graduate School of Public Administration in Lausanne (IDHEAP), in charge of the unit «Public Management and Human Resource Management». He is Research Director and Consultant in public organizations at national and international level. His main areas of interest and publication are: work motivation, competency management and employability, rewards systems and training strategies in public organizations. Among his most recent publications: Giauque D. & Emery Y. (2008). Repenser la gestion publique, PPUR, in "Le savoir Suisse", Lausanne.
E-mail : yves.emery@idheap.unil.ch

EPINEY, Astrid (1965) is professor in European and Public International Law at the University of Fribourg (Switzerland) and director at the Institute of European Law. Her teaching, research and publications lie mainly in the areas of European Environmental Law, Fundamental liberties, European Constitutional Law, Transport law, European migration law as well as the relationship between Switzerland and the European Union.
E-mail: astrid.epiney@unifr.ch

FLÜCKIGER, Alexandre (1967) is professor at the Faculty of law of the University of Geneva. He is director of the Centre for Legislative Studies, Techniques and Evaluation (CETEL) and of the Department of Constitutional Law. His current research fields include public, constitutional, administrative and environmental law, affective sciences and law, legislative drafting (legistic), electronic legal research and data protection law.
E-mail: alexandre.flueckiger@unige.ch

FONT, Nuria (1964) is professor of political science at the Universitat Autònoma de Barcelona. Her current teaching and research interests include new modes of governance, with a particular focus on environmental governance, Europeanization of environmental and cohesion policies, and EU institutions and policy-making.
E-mail: nuria.font@uab.cat

GERBER, Jean-David (1975) is a postdoctoral fellow in the Department of Environmental Science, Policy, and Management at UC Berkeley. He obtained his PhD in Public Administration at the Swiss Graduate School of Public Administration (IDHEAP). His current research interests include political ecology issues such as conflicts over the access to natural and cultural resources, governance of resources, property rights to resources and land use regulations.
E-mail: jean-david.gerber@nature.berkeley.edu

GIAUQUE, David (1971) is assistant professor in sociology of organizations and public administrations at the Institut d'Etudes Politiques et Internationales (IEPI) of the University of Lausanne (Switzerland). His teaching, research and publications lie in the domains of sociology of public administrations, administrative reforms, as well as human resources management in public organizations. Among his recent publications are *La bureaucratie libérale* (Paris, L'Harmattan, 2003) and together with Yves Emery *Paradoxes de la gestion publique* (Paris, L'Harmattan, 2005).
E-mail: david.giauque@unil.ch

HILL, Michael (1937) is Emeritus Professor of Social Policy at Newcastle University. However, he remains active as a Visiting Professor in the Department of Politics at Queen Mary College, University of London and at the School of Applied Social Science, University of Brighton. He is the author of many books including three that have been published in recent revised editions: *The Public Policy Process, Implementing Public Policy* (with Peter Hupe) and *Understanding Social Policy* (with Zoë Irving). His research includes studies of social security policy, social care policy and environmental policy.
E-mail: michael_j_hill@msn.com

HORBER-PAPAZIAN, Katia (1957) has been professor of Local Politics and Policy Evaluation at the Swiss Graduate School of Public Administration (IDHEAP) in Lausanne since 1990. She carries out research and commissions in the areas of territorial reform, the allocation of tasks to the cantons and municipalities, intervention modalities and decision-making processes at local level, public action steering and institutionalization of policy evaluation as well as national policy evaluations.
E-mail: katia.horber-papazian@idheap.unil.ch

KRIESI, Hanspeter (1949) is professor for comparative politics at the University of Zürich. He directs the National competence centre for research 'Challenges to democracy in the 21st century'. Together with David Snow und Sarah Soule he edited the *Blackwell's Companion to Social Movements* (2004). Among his more recent publication there is also *Direct Democratic choice* (Lanham Md, Lexington Press, 2005).
E-mail: hanspeter.kriesi@pwi.unizh.ch

LARRUE Corinne (1957) is Full Professor at the University of Tours. She is currently Director of the CNRS research Center CITERES (Cité Territoire Environnement Société) at the University of Tours. Her major field of research and teaching has been policy analysis with emphasis on environmental and regional policies.
E mail: corinne.larrue@univ-tours.fr

LINDER, Wolf (1944) is professor of Political Science and Director at the Institute of Political Science at the University of Bern. His main fields in research and teaching are the Swiss Political System, Direct Democracy, Policy Evaluation and the process of democratisation in developing countries. Among his publications are *Swiss Democracy – Possible Solutions to Conflict in Multicultural Societies* (London/New York, Macmillan 1994) and *Schweizerische Demokratie – Institutionen, Prozesse, Perspektiven* (Bern, Haupt 2005)
E-mail: wolf.linder@ipw.unibe.ch

LERESCHE, Jean-Philippe (1959) is professor at the Institut d'Etudes Politiques et Internationales (IEPI) and director of the Observatoire Science, Politique et Société (OSPS) of the University of Lausanne (Switzerland).. His main researches deal with research and higher education policies in Switzerland. Among his recent publications are *Recherche et enseignement supérieur face à l'internationalisation. France, Suisse et Union européenne* (with Ph. Larédo and K. Weber, Lausanne, Presses polytechniques et universitaires romandes, 2009).
E-mail: jean-philippe.leresche@unil.ch

NICOL, Lee Ann (1971) holds a PhD in public administration from the Swiss Graduate School of Public Administration (IDHEAP). She has a Masters of Science in Community and Regional Planning from the University of British Columbia and Bachelor of Engineering from McGill University, Canada. Her primary research interests are in planning and housing issues and sustainable development.
E-mail: leeann.nicol@idheap.unil.ch

OLGIATI, Mirta (1975) is PhD Student at the Swiss Graduate School of Public Administration (IDHEAP). Graduated in French literature, Philosophy and History of arts and holding a Master in Public Administration from the same Institute, she is specialising on recordkeeping and archiving policies, as well as information and heritage policies in general.
E-mail: mirta.olgiati@idheap.unil.ch

RITZ, Adrian (1970) is assistant professor at the Centre of Competence for Public Management at the University of Bern. He is also managing director of the Executive Master of Public Administration (MPA) at the University of Bern. His primary interests in research and teaching are public management, public sector reforms, public human resources management and performance management in public sector organizations
E-mail: adrian.ritz@kpm.unibe.ch

SAVARY, Jérôme (1977) is Director of Mobilidee, a company specialized in mobility analysis and management for the public and private sector. He obtained a PhD in Public Administration at the Swiss Graduate School of Public Administration (IDHEAP). His research fields concern the sustainability of natural and artificial resources, the comparative analysis of environmental policies, the institutional rules and the evaluation programs.
E-mail: savary@mobilidee.ch

SUBIRATS, Joan (1951) is professor of Political Science and Director of the Institute of Government and Public Policy at the Autonomous University of Barcelona. He has a PhD in Economics. His research fields include Policy Analysis, Democratic Innovation, Public Participation and local and regional government. He has been a visiting scholar at different universities and Prince of Asturias Distinguished Visiting Professor at Georgetown University (2002-2003.)
E-mail: joan.subirats@uab.cat

WARIN, Philippe (1958) is CNRS senior research fellow at the Institut d'Etudes Politiques of Grenoble, and director of the Observatoire des non-recours aux droits et services (ODENORE) created by the ministère de l'Enseignement supérieur et de la Recherche (France). His main researches deal with the question of the limits of social integration through policies. Among his more recent publication there is *Politiques publiques et démocratie* (Paris, La Découverte, 2008), edited with Olivier Giraud.
E-mail: philippe.warin@ipe-grenoble.fr

WEIDNER, Helmut (1948), is a political scientist. He is also Senior researcher at the Social Science Research Center (WZB) and private lecturer (Privat-Dozent) at the Free University Berlin. He has had an extended cooperation with Peter Knoepfel over many years. His major topics of research are: Cross-national analysis of environmental policy and capacity building; climate policy and equity. He acted as (co-)director of several major cross-national studies on these issues. Among his numerous publications are: inter alia, *Alternative Dispute Resolution. Experiences in 12 Countries*, 1998; *Capacity Building in National Environmental Policy. A Comparative Study of 17 Countries*, 2002 (co-edited with Martin Jänicke), *Climate Change Policy and Equity*, 2005.

E-mail: weidner@wzb.eu